POWERSHOP 3

New Retail Design

Frame Publishers
Amsterdam

CONTENTS

ACCESS

004

SORIES

005

&ROLLS

by ITO MASARU DESIGN PROJECT/SEI

1

WHERE Tokyo, Japan WHEN April 2009
CLIENT Tachiya Company DESIGNER Ito Masaru Design Project/SEI (p.680)
TOTAL FLOOR AREA 41 m² SHOP CONSTRUCTOR Hearts
PHOTOGRAPHER Kozo Takayama

The popular shopping district Daikanyama in central Tokyo has gained another worthwhile destination for shoppers. Between the designer boutiques and upscale bakeries, the Tachiya Company – a well-established Japanese distributer focusing on belts – opened an accessories shop called &Rolls. Ito Masaru was asked to come up with a design that would underline the concept of 'the real thing'. The idea behind this was that in a time of worldwide economical crisis, only real and glamorous can survive, and everything fake gets discarded. This idea was translated into making visible the use of different materials. Instead of using the colour black to create a space that exhales mystery and luxury – a concept successfully applied by Masaru in other shops – he decided to shift the focus to the textures of materials, showing their richness and

contrasting them with a bright colour red. The interior has the ability to adapt to changing times through its simplistic design, called 'Neo Minimalism' by Masaru. This aspect also ensures that the shop looks very clean and organised. The atmosphere is one of comfort with a hint of nostalgia, achieved through the use of antique pieces of furniture in the space combined with age-old materials such as plaster, mortar, tin, steel and glass. The contemporary factor is created through the use of modern design pieces, including the central Dear Ingo pendant lamp designed by Ron Gilad for Moooi.

1 The simplistic interior focuses on the long-established craft of belt-making.
2 A mix of old and new was applied, combining antique furniture with contemporary design pieces.

3

The design had to underline the
concept of 'the real thing'

4

3 In the back, a product space in red differs
   completely from the main retail area; a
   design choice made to surprise customers.
4 Custom-made hooks, based on an antique
   model design, are fixed to a glass wall.
5 The top of the tin wall panel curves into the
   ceiling and hides the air conditioner piping.

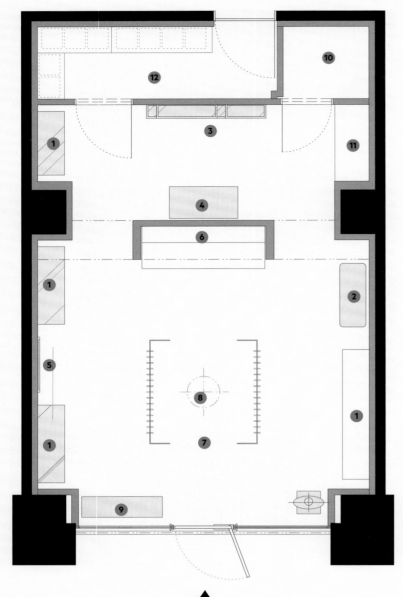

The atmosphere is one of comfort with a hint of nostalgia

1 Shelves
2 Cinema seating
3 Shelf wall
4 Antique cabinet
5 Mirror
6 Post office shelving system
7 Glass walls/display
8 Pendant light
9 Showcase
10 Fitting room
11 Cash desk
12 Storage

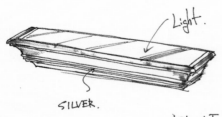

Light.

SILVER.

<SHELF>.

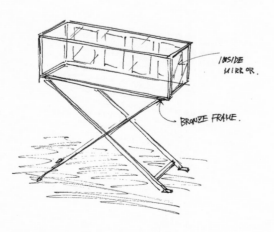

INSIDE MIRROR.

BRONZE FRAME.

& ROLLS

An old candy showcase was converted into an accessories display.

The tin-panelled wall contrasts starkly with the red area in the back.

The walls outside the shop are painted in the same colour scheme to visually extend the space and attract attention from passers-by.

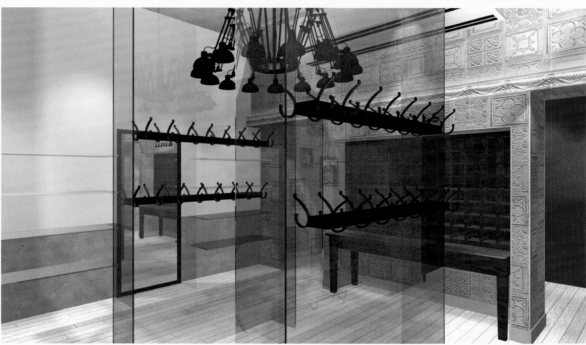

Rendering showing the hooks for the belts. Once the belts were all in place they visually represented a 'waterfall of belts'.

The product area in the back has a lower ceiling and combined with the red walls this constitutes a more intimate atmosphere.

4°C

by TONERICO

2

WHERE Tokyo, Japan WHEN September 2011
CLIENT F.D.C. Products DESIGNER Tonerico (p.686)
TOTAL FLOOR AREA 324 m² SHOP CONSTRUCTOR Sogo Design
PHOTOGRAPHER Satoshi Asakawa

The label 4°C is a well-established Japanese bridal and fashion jewellery brand. In addition, 4°C is the temperature of the water underneath a layer of ice, when a lake or pond has frozen over. Fish can still survive at this temperature but often have to do so at a slower pace. The water below the insulating ice layer thus becomes a space of calmness. This natural phenomena has been taken as a source of inspiration for a new 4°C shop in Tokyo, designed by Tonerico. Near the entrance, metallic laser-cut letters and numbers – which have been linked into each other – form strings that are suspended in a row from the ceiling, giving the impression of water bubbles rising upwards. Translucency within the shop is achieved by installing glass shelves and display cases and objects made of steel rods. Apart from aligning the interior to an underwater world, this approach also emphasises the delicateness of the products on display. Large mirrors on the walls and ceilings make the space to appear endless and also create a slight level of disorientation. White is the dominating colour and is combined with white-finished oak flooring, wall and ceiling panelling. Customer consultation areas on the first floor are fitted out with comfortable white leather seats, sofas, pouffes and benches and also white translucent curtains cordon off the door to the storage area. The entire space breathes an air of silence and serenity.

1 The simplicity of the logo and the shop front design vividly contrast with the cluttered streets of Shinjuku, pointing out a place of calmness.
2 All decorations are narratives of an expression of water.

3

4

5

3 Beneath the staircase, a built-in, framed consultation area with a fake-leather sofa creates a picturesque scene.
4 The first floor, with its white ceiling, has an atmosphere similar to that of a bridal salon.
5 The staircase is clad in white-finished oak panels, with one strip of mirrors that visually enlarge the space and gives a slight feeling of disorientation, as one would experience in an underwater world.
6 Metallic laser-cut letters and numbers, spelling out the brand name, are made into an installation resembling water bubbles.

6

4°C is the temperature of the water
underneath a layer of ice

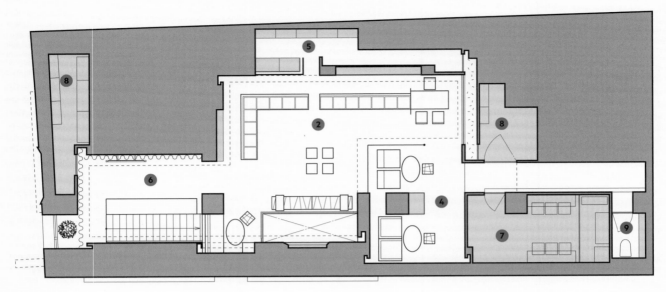

First floor

```
0    1 m
```

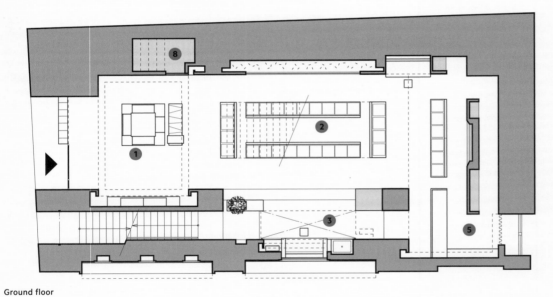

Ground floor

1 Display
2 Retail area
3 Consultation area
4 Consultation room
5 Cash desk
6 Gallery
7 Staff room
8 Storage
9 Lavatory

Rendering of the proposed design of the storefront.

The built-in consultation area is intended for couples shopping for wedding rings.

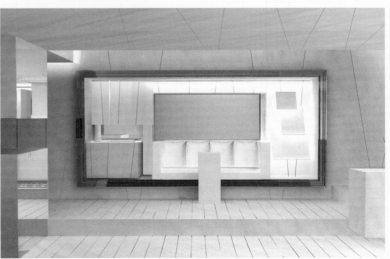

Rendering of the steel rod display element which greets customers at the entrance of the store. This walk-in tower reaches up into the first floor where it can be viewed from the gallery.

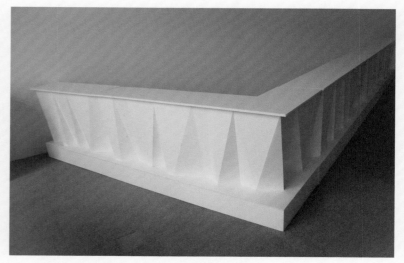

Model of the central display element on the ground floor.

Strings suspended from the ceiling give the impression of water bubbles

STEEL ROD DISPLAY ELEMENT

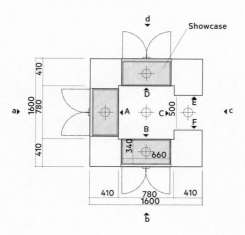

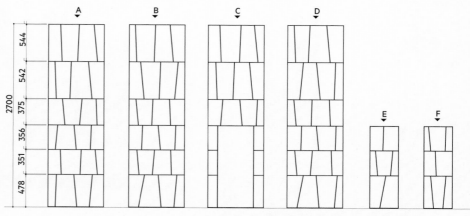

Showcase

Steel rod welding melamine printing finish (white)

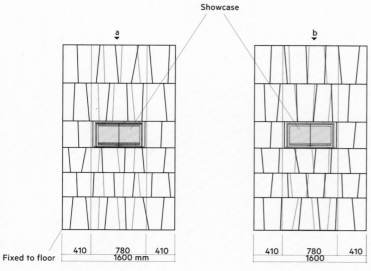

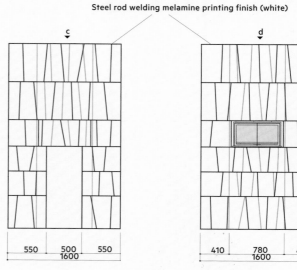

Fixed to floor

410	780	410
	1600 mm	

410	780	410
	1600	

550	500	550
	1600	

410	780	410
	1600	

ANDRÉ OPTICAS

by SOUSASANTOS

2

WHERE Lisbon, Portugal WHEN June 2010
CLIENT André Opticas DESIGNER SousaSantos (p.685)
TOTAL FLOOR AREA 515 m² SHOP CONSTRUCTOR Artefacto
PHOTOGRAPHER FG+SG

Since its foundation in 1981, the eyewear brand André Opticas has been selling glasses of leading fashion brands and designers and also of its own collection, with the ability to tailor glasses to customers' requirements thus creating personalised and unique pieces. It has opened shops at five different locations in the Lisbon district over the years, its latest addition being designed by SousaSantos. For the new shop, one of the requirements was that the product presentation would span the entire space. As the products themselves are very small and the space fairly big, the design team came up with a display that extended onto the complete wall surface. This display element forms a net of vertical and horizontal backlit slits covered by Plexiglas in a steel and MDF frame. The horizontal slits provide a platform on which the eyewear can be placed and classical nosepiece-holds are fixed to the vertical slits for further display possibilities. The ceiling features similar constructions but here the slits function as lamps. This notion of continuity and movement has been carried through in the design of the entire space. Dark wood covers all the floors of the multi-level space. Cabinets, counters and private consulting desks are all custom-made from white-lacquered MDF and seem to hover a few centimetres above the floor. The abundance of white gives the space a clean and somewhat medical atmosphere. Black Chesterfield sofas, plush carpets and modern design chairs, such as Hannes Wettstein's 367 Hola chair, create a sense of luxury.

1   The store spreads over two floors with the retail and consultation area downstairs and the laboratory and offices upstairs.
2   At the back of the store there is an outside area that has been furnished in style with Philippe Starck's Ghost Chairs.

3 Suspended from the double-height ceiling, a black, ornamental chandelier adds to the luxurious atmosphere.
4 A black plush rug on the Sucupira hardwood floor and Chesterfield sofas make the waiting area a comfortable space to spend some time.
5 Three desks at the back of the store are dedicated to individual client consultations.

3

4

An abundance of white gives the space a clean and somewhat medical atmosphere

SOUSASANTOS

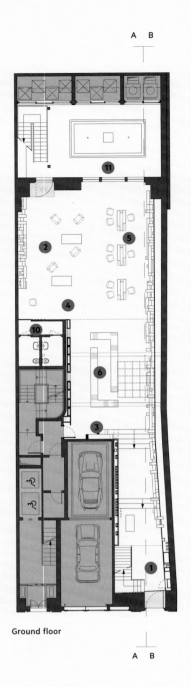

Ground floor

First floor

1 Hall
2 Retail area
3 Coffee area
4 Waiting area
5 Consultation area
6 Main counter
7 Laboratory
8 Office waiting room
9 Office
10 Lavatories
11 Backyard

WALL DISPLAY

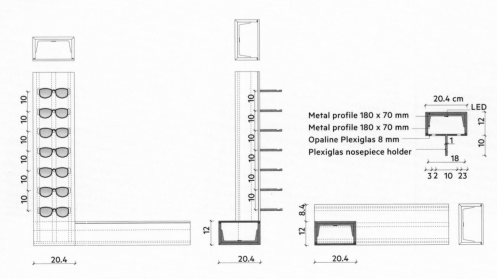

Metal profile 180 x 70 mm
Metal profile 180 x 70 mm
Opaline Plexiglas 8 mm
Plexiglas nosepiece holder

20.4 cm
LED

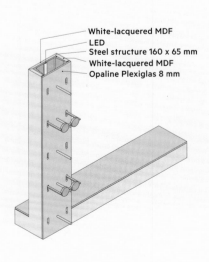

White-lacquered MDF
LED
Steel structure 160 x 65 mm
White-lacquered MDF
Opaline Plexiglas 8 mm

The notion of continuity and movement has been carried through in the design of the entire space

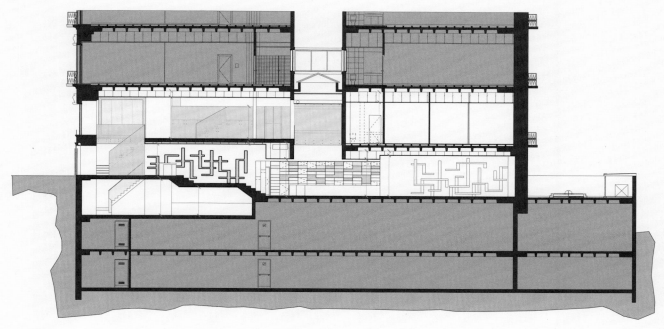

Section AA

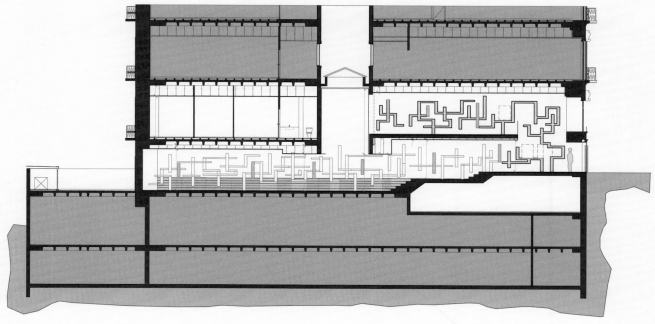

Section BB

BELFRY TASHKENT

by IPPOLITO FLEITZ GROUP

2

WHERE Tashkent, Uzbekistan WHEN September 2009
CLIENT Republic of Uzbekistan DESIGNER Ippolito Fleitz Group (p.679)
TOTAL FLOOR AREA 340 m² SHOP CONSTRUCTOR Riedl Messe-/Laden- & Objektbau
PHOTOGRAPHER Zooey Braun

In September 2009, Uzbekistan celebrated the 2200th anniversary of the founding of its capital city Tashkent. This festive occasion also marked the ceremonial opening of the Palace of International Forums, a government building located on the central Amir Timur Square. The interior of the palace was designed by Ippolito Fleitz Group. The interior of Belfry Tashkent, an exclusive jewellery shop housed in one of two historic bell towers, was also designed as part of the project. Here, the design firm combined old and new, the historic exterior and contemporary interior, creating a fascinating synthesis. Entering the space is like stepping inside an ornate jewellery box. Dark walls are overlaid with laser-cut decorative ornamentation, made from highly-polished stainless steel panels, creating a second skin. An ornate tinted mirror that covers the entire back wall, concealing the back door, reflects the interior, optically-elongating the space. A plush beige carpet further enhances the feel of luxury. Glass-topped display cases, also clad in tinted mirrors, showcase the pieces of jewellery. Each display case is fitted out with spotlights that precisely illuminate the precious merchandise. The lighting was in the hands of Pfarré Lighting Design, the team of which also designed the lighting element that swirls across the ceiling.

1 The walls are completely overlaid with laser-cut decorative ornamentation, made from highly-polished stainless steel panels that are set apart from the wall surface and enter the space itself.
2 Precisely illuminated jewellery display cases are in part equipped with monitors.

Entering the space is like stepping inside an ornate jewellery box

3 The length of the room is optically elongated by means of ornamental, tinted mirrors on the end walls and a dynamic lighting element which crosses the ceiling.

4 Only a few selected openings, such as windows and display cases, break through the steel wall panels.

4

Belfry Tashkent is located in a historic bell tower next to the Palace of International Forums.

The combination of old and new creates a fascinating synthesis

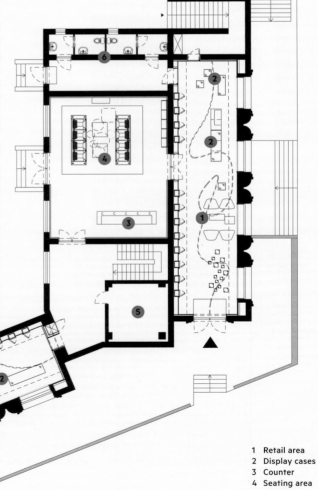

1 Retail area
2 Display cases
3 Counter
4 Seating area
5 Staff area
6 Lavatories

TWO CONNECTED ORNAMENTAL PANELS

Connection point

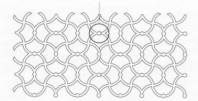

Detail of closed
connection point

Detail of open
connection point

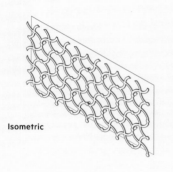

Isometric

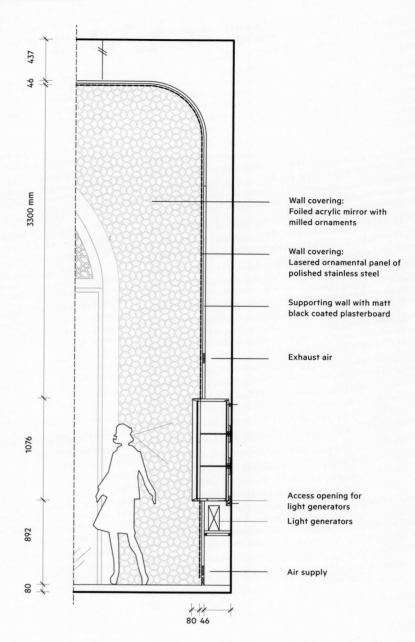

Wall covering:
Foiled acrylic mirror with
milled ornaments

Wall covering:
Lasered ornamental panel of
polished stainless steel

Supporting wall with matt
black coated plasterboard

Exhaust air

Access opening for
light generators

Light generators

Air supply

437
46
3300 mm
1076
892
80

80 46

DETAIL OF PANEL ATTACHMENT TO WALL

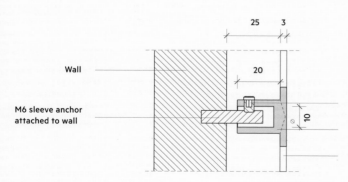

25   3

Wall

20

M6 sleeve anchor
attached to wall

10

M5 grub screw

Sleeve nut welded onto
ornamental panel

Ornamental panel
(polished stainless steel)

BERANI JEWELLERY

by PROTOTYPE DESIGN LAB

1

WHERE Toronto, Canada WHEN March 2011
CLIENT Berani Jewellery DESIGNER Prototype Design Lab (p.684)
TOTAL FLOOR AREA 300 m² SHOP CONSTRUCTOR Prototype Design Lab
PHOTOGRAPHER A-Frame (Ben Rahn)

Located in Toronto's Bayview Village shopping mall is Berani Jewellery, retailer of high-end jewellery brands. The main inspirations of its collection are elegance, eternity and quality. Prototype Design Lab created the interior of the shop. Aiming for a harmonious balance between cosiness and sophisticated function, the design team incorporated luxurious materials and custom upholstery, and combined them with contemporary details. Almost every element in the store is custom designed. The focal point is a series of black displays appearing to sprout from the ground in the centre of the main retail area. Their design was inspired by the *Nymphaea*, a genus of flowered aquatic plants. Sparkling pieces of jewellery displayed on them are like dew drops on lily pads while the high-gloss flooring of French vanilla marble resembles the smooth surface of a pond. Crystal pendants are suspended from the ceiling above the display cases to place extra emphasis on this area of the space and add to the glitter and glamour. Customised canopy chairs placed in a row provide clients with comfort and a sense of privacy during one-on-one meetings with sales associates. Further in the back is the Swarovski shop-in-shop where all of the walls are lined with Brazilian Santos Rosewood cabinets that run from floor to ceiling and feature illuminated display niches.

1 The initials of the brand name are also incorporated in the shop. They make an appearance in the intricately-cut woodwork of the doors and the door handles.
2 Jewellery displays inspired by aquatic plants appear to sprout from the glossy flooring in the main retail area.
3 Santos Rosewood wall cladding that is used throughout the entire store continues in the Swarovski shop-in-shop.
4 Dark oak shop window displays also feature the brand name initials.

2

High-gloss marble resembles the smooth surface of a pond

4

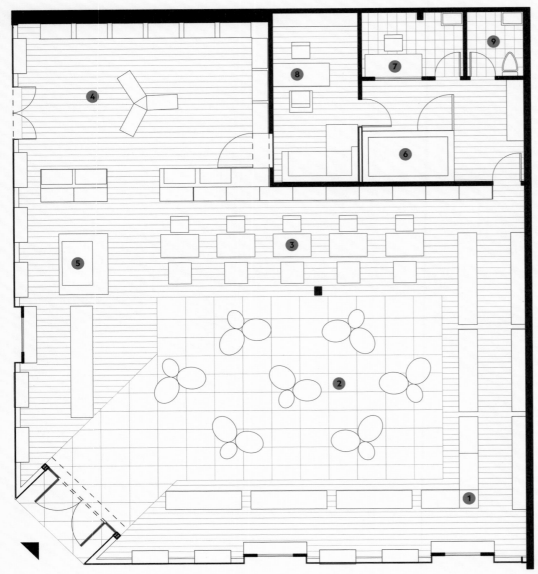

1 Brand counter
2 Jewellery display area
3 Private client table
4 Swarovski shop-in-shop
5 Cash desk
6 Vault
7 Goldsmith workshop
8 Office
9 Lavatory

Sparkling pieces of jewellery on the displays are like dew drops on lily pads

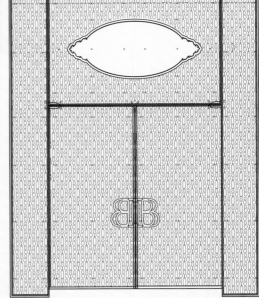

Drawing and fabrication photos of the wooden entrance door, made utilising CNC (computer numerical controlled) technology.

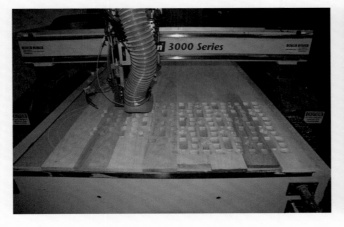

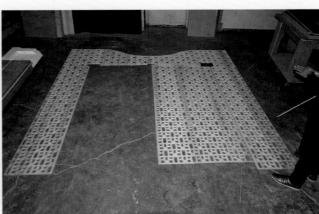

Sketches of the Nymphae displays show how they
resemble the aquatic plant of the same name.

NYMPHAE DISPLAY

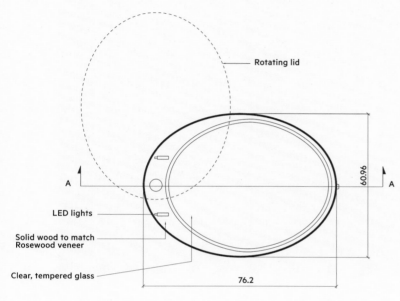

Rotating lid

LED lights

Solid wood to match
Rosewood veneer

Clear, tempered glass

60.96

A — A

76.2

Top view

The Nymphae displays are fabricated from blackened steel.

Clear, tempered glass

76.2 cm

Solid wood to match
Rosewood veneer

Pivot device for rotating lid

LED light

15.56

16.83

Locking device for lid

Blackened steel body with
clear powdercoat finish

Wire for LED lights

93.35

Base plate bolted to floor and
covered with stone flooring

1.27

29.2

Section

CA4LA FACTORY

by LINE-INC

1

WHERE Nishinomiya, Japan WHEN September 2010
CLIENT Weave Toshi DESIGNER Line-Inc (p.681)
TOTAL FLOOR AREA 360 m² SHOP CONSTRUCTOR D. Brain
PHOTOGRAPHER Kozo Takayama

The Japanese fashion brand CA4LA makes quality hats for a clientele that consists of both men and women. With 18 shops in Japan, the brand mainly focuses on the local market, although the company also has a shop in London. There are many designers working for the company who each have a very unique take on hat designing. Line-Inc was approached to design a new factory and showroom for CA4LA where the work of these creatives would be produced and exhibited. The brief to Line-Inc also outlined that the hat designers would also visit this space and use it as a laboratory. The building that was chosen for this purpose was located in Nishinomiya, a city between Kobe and Osaka, and was a former warehouse. The design team of Line-Inc based its approach on the brand's ideology – 'Made in Japan' – which comes about due to the fact that 70% of the company's products are produced locally. The building was renovated and the space filled with over a thousand wooden hat forms that have been used by traditional hat makers. To underline the factory aspect, all new details were designed as if they have existed for a long time, having been well-used over the years. This also kept the existing charm of the building intact. The crystal chandeliers, Chesterfield sofas and floral-motif carpets fit right in.

1 The showroom on the first floor has oak wood bookshelves that showcase the hats, complemented with oak wood tables with aluminium legs and vinyl leather chairs.
2 A former warehouse was transformed into a factory and showroom for the brand.
3 Full-height glass doors emphasise the warehouse character of the space.
4 On the ground floor, rows of shelving racks hold over a thousand old wooden hat forms.
5 Next page: A glass wall separates the showroom from the workshop area.

2

3

4

Designers
would visit
this space and
use it as a
laboratory

CONRADT OPTIK

by IPPOLITO FLEITZ GROUP

2

WHERE Mosbach, Germany WHEN February 2009
CLIENT Conradt Optik DESIGNER Ippolito Fleitz Group (p.679)
TOTAL FLOOR AREA 210 m² SHOP CONSTRUCTOR Riedl Messe-/Laden- & Objektbau
PHOTOGRAPHER Zooey Braun

The refurbishment of Conradt Optik coincided with the business being handed over to the next generation of owners, who wish to shift the businesses focus to a select segment of brands and individual customer care. Ippolito Fleitz Group renewed the entire building facade as part of the renovations, thereby making the shop's new profile immediately evident from the outside. Long windows stretch down to the ground, giving maximum insight into the representative interior, which in itself became the window display. Two entrances lead to the service counter, which is the shop's centre piece. A curved rear wall masks the workshop areas and divides the shop into various product zones. Three recessed horizontal bays, spanning almost the entire length of the wall, feature a large part of the eyewear collection while drawers in the wall provide storage. Parallel to the windows on the longitudinal side are three floating displays. These are set at a slight angle and are reserved for the optician's range of sunglasses. Free-standing display cases provide space for special presentations. The recessed ceiling is decorated with a pattern of fine lines in blue, brown and mauve, meant to evoke associations with an iris, and differentiates the customer service area from the shop floor.

1 Glasses are displayed in three recessed horizontal bays, which span almost the entire length of the rear wall.
2 Customer service takes place at two 'conference islands'.

3 A deep-pile, anthracite-coloured carpet is laid through the entire shop. This ensures good acoustics while enhancing the soft and flowing character of the interior.
4 The store has two entrances which both lead directly to the central counter.
5 The visual that is used on the ceiling has also been integrated in the company's branding and is used on paper bags, amongst other things.

3

4

5

The pattern of fine lines evokes associations with an iris

DANIELLA LEHAVI

by K1P3 ARCHITECTS

1

WHERE Tel Aviv, Israel WHEN January 2010
CLIENT Daniella Lehavi DESIGNER k1p3 architects (p.680)
TOTAL FLOOR AREA 90 m² SHOP CONSTRUCTOR Golan Constructions
PHOTOGRAPHER Daniel Sheriff

Daniella Lehavi is an Israeli designer of premium leather goods. The brand's flagship store is located in central Tel Aviv, in a building that dates from the 1920s. The team of k1p3 architects was in charge of the design of the retail space with a priority to reveal and recreate the original eclectic design features of the building, emphasising them within the shell of the space and then contrasting them with clean white furnishings on which to display the designer goods. The original features were highlighted by exposing the existing high ceilings, incorporating an art-deco geometry in frosted glass on the large back windows and laying a vintage-patterned wooden parquet floor. Custom-made cast concrete display counters are imbued with an ornamental imprint around their perimeters which also corresponds to the historical features of the building. Matt-lacquered white carpentry is utilised as a flowing composition throughout the three rooms of the boutique. Conceived as one continuous entity, the carpentry starts next to the entrance on the front wall as simple wall panelling, supporting on it individual shelves and emphasising the geometry of the three arched windows above. It then unfolds into a series of wall-mounted large boxes which are connected by a single horizontal shelf. The next room sees the carpentry covering the entire space – walls and ceiling – with in-built display cabinets and discrete storage aspects. In the third room, the white element continues under the large windows and acts both a display surface and additional storage.

1 A modern translation to classic wooden wall panelling was applied to the decor, making its way throughout the entire store, only interrupted by cabinets on to certain walls.
2 The concrete cast display tables were custom made.
3 Frosted glass back windows with an art-deco geometry refer to the building's 1920s origin.
4 Steel vitrines reinforce the arched windows.

2

3

4

DICOKICK

by JAMO ASSOCIATES

1

WHERE Tokyo, Japan WHEN April 2009
CLIENT Good Smile Company DESIGNER Jamo associates (p.680)
TOTAL FLOOR AREA 61 m² SHOP CONSTRUCTOR Loop Planning Studio
PHOTOGRAPHER Kozo Takayama

Cat Street in the Harajuku district of Tokyo is a popular gathering place for young locals with a strong and individual sense of style. The street is filled with restaurants, cafes and boutiques, and has now also become the location of Dicokick's first flagship store. The Japanese accessory brand had been selling its unique and often limited edition jewellery successfully though the internet. For the brand's shop, design firm Jamo associates had a goal to create a strong design that would make the store stand out from the other boutiques in the street and entice people to step inside. As the available floor area was only 60 m², Jamo had to furnish the space in such a way to maximise the number of customers the store could accommodate. The designers chose to create an impact with those elements that do not take up much

space – such as floor, walls, ceiling and windows – as opposed to achieving such an effect with big furniture pieces. The playfulness of the colourful accessories on display is reflected in the interior as well. Dots became the main visual element and decorate the cupboard that lines the back wall, the display cubes that are scattered throughout the space and the light-emitting panels on the ceiling. Even the pendant lights match this shape. One wall at the back is covered in bright red wallpaper to attract attention and serves as the background for a handwritten beginning of a story about a little boy in Paris, an abstract from the French film *The Red Balloon*.

1 The shop Dicokick is located on the busy Cat Street in the Harajuku district of Tokyo.
2 The backlit ceiling panels curve onto the walls and feature the same playful dots as the counter.
3 Herringbone patterned oak wood is used to cover the floor.
4 A few cubes are the only furniture elements that aren't placed alongside the wall but in the centre of the space. However, these can be moved easily to create more room.

3

2

The designers had to maximise the number of customers the store could accommodate

4

FIELL

by DASTRO RETAILCONCEPTS

2

WHERE Apeldoorn, the Netherlands WHEN November 2009
CLIENT Fiell DESIGNER Dastro Retailconcepts (p.676)
TOTAL FLOOR AREA 70 m² SHOP CONSTRUCTOR Ideko Interiors
PHOTOGRAPHER Wim van Gelderen

Fiell, the jewellery brand of wholesaler Kennai, opened its first store in the Dutch city of Apeldoorn in order to cater to the consumer directly. Dastro was briefed to design the interior. Targeting fashion-oriented young men and women, some keywords from the brief were: black, white, glossy and innovative. The corner shop has a lot of window space which the designers decided to take advantage of. Black smoked glass panels line the shop windows giving passers-by a glimpse of the collection. Also, the black and white presentation walls inside the shop are visible from the outside. As the walls consist of panels placed in a 45-degree angle, the logo printed on them seems to move as the viewer walks by, looking at it from different angles. Magnetic hooks can be placed anywhere on the walls to display the major part of the collection. The remaining pieces are presented in four glass display cases, mounted on top of a chrome base with serrated edges that also contains a set of drawers. The linear design of the display cases also appears in the pattern of the carpet. All features in the interior have the same black and white chrome or gloss finish. The only splash of colour in the shop comes from two illuminated columns with continuously changing imagery. This retail concept is planned to be rolled out in more shop locations within the Netherlands.

1 Black smoked glass panels line the shop windows.
2 The client's logo – a feather – is printed on the wall and seems to move as the viewer walks by.

DASTRO RETAILCONCEPTS

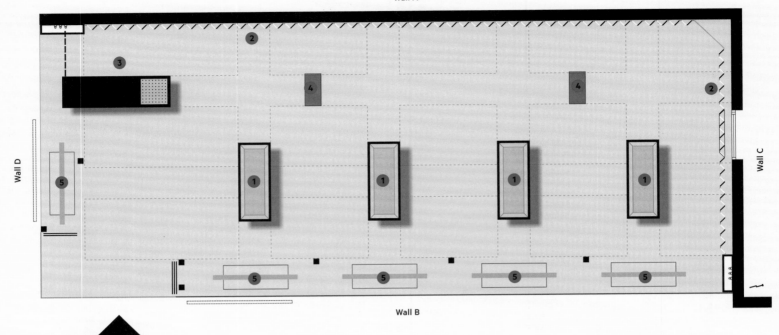

Wall A

Wall D

Wall C

Wall B

1 Display cabinets
2 Wall presentation
3 Cash desk
4 Columns with graphics
5 Displays

ANGULAR WALL DRAWING

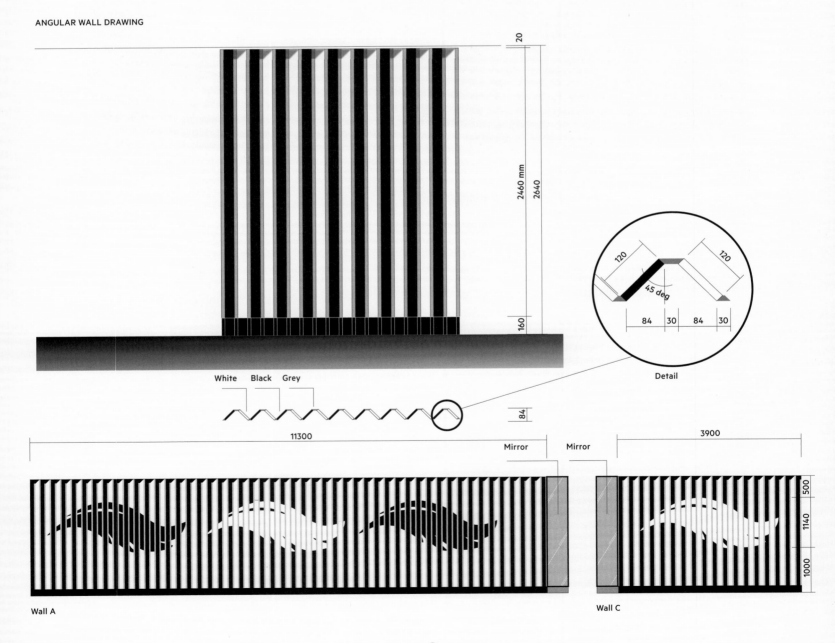

20

2460 mm
2640

160

White   Black   Grey

120   120

45 deg

84   30   84   30

Detail

84

11300

Mirror   Mirror

3900

500

1140

1000

Wall A

Wall C

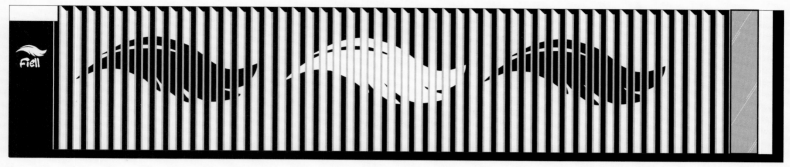

Wall A

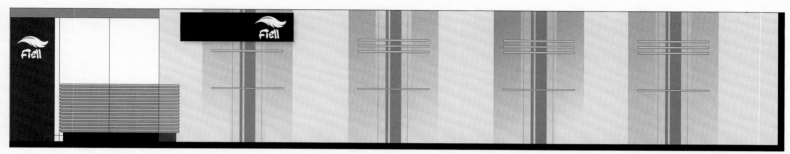

Wall B

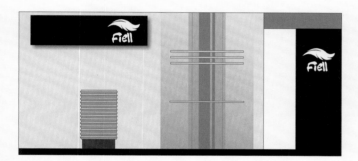

Wall D

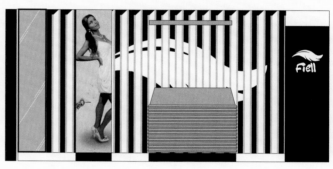

Wall C

As the viewer walks by, the logo on the wall seems to move

FREITAG REFERENCE EDITORIAL SPACE

by FREITAG

1

WHERE Zurich, Switzerland WHEN September 2010
CLIENT Freitag DESIGNER Freitag (p.678)
TOTAL FLOOR AREA 70 m² SHOP CONSTRUCTOR Nijo Architects
PHOTOGRAPHER Nici Jost

With their history of manufacturing bags inspired by messengers on wheels, the Freitag brothers looked to those messengers who write on paper when it came to designing a temporary space for the launch of their new product line. The company studio in the centre of Zurich was transformed into an editorial space and printing facility, as well as a shop selling the new Reference range of unicoloured tarpaulin products. The personal 'reference' within these new products goes to the messengers – reporters and journalists – who are independent, critical, investigative and sometimes daring. In line with this, throughout September 2010, a *Freitag Reference* daily newspaper was produced as a unique piece of editorial, with the same recycled philosophy as the original Freitag concept, i.e. produced from bits and pieces of various other 'real' new and current newspapers, with each issue having an eye-catching headline. An authentic newsroom atmosphere was given to the temporary shop by the use of vintage furniture pieces, the pivotal focus being the 200-year-old printing press. The products were displayed in a shelving system that contrasted against the original stone slabs on the floor and the walls and ceiling with exposed cracks in the plasterwork. The entire space and concept breathed new life into old material, aptly linking with the company's new product range and the next chapter in the Freitag story.

1 International newspapers line the side window. The laptops on the desk provide visitors with internet access for inspiration and exchange.
2 The basket of the bicycle in front of the temporary shop is filled with newspapers ready to be delivered.
3 Every morning at 8.00 am for one month, there was an editorial meeting for the daily issues, which were compiled leading to the publication of the one-edition newspaper *The Reference.*

The pivotal
focus was the
200-year-old
printing press

2

3

FREUDENHAUS OPTIK

by TOOLS OFF.ARCHITECTURE

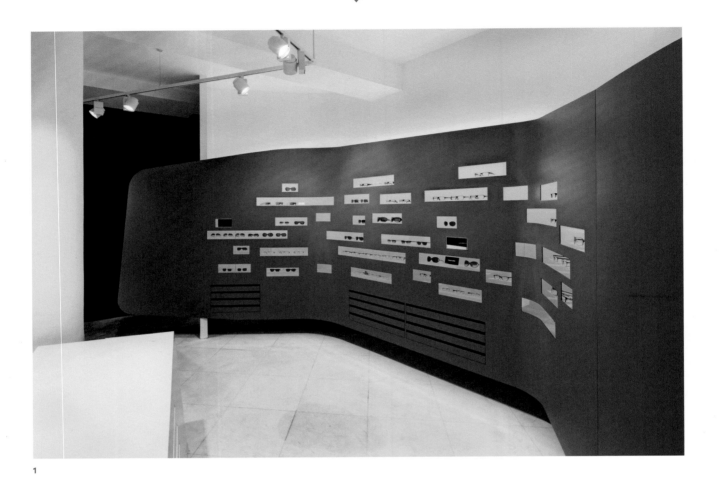

1

WHERE Munich, Germany WHEN April 2010
CLIENT FreudenHaus Optik DESIGNER tools off.architecture (p.686)
TOTAL FLOOR AREA 50 m² SHOP CONSTRUCTOR tools off.architecture
PHOTOGRAPHER Lothar Reichel

The German eyewear retailer FreudenHaus Optik has a number of stores in its hometown of Munich and worldwide. The brand considers glasses not to be just a technical instrument, but they are also an important personal expression, as well as a fashion statement. Each glasses wearer is unique, as too is each FreudenHaus Optik shop. The newest store in Munich was designed by tools off.architecture and is located on one of the city's most exclusive shopping streets. A spatial concept was conceived for the interior theme with the application of a levitating second skin. The design has a futuristic white decor and comprises an angular wall which wraps around the right-hand side of the small space. It actually divides the showroom into two areas: the exterior and interior display. From inside the store, the only outside aspect that can be seen is through the glass entranceway; the rest of the shop window is sectioned off behind the display wall. The glasses are displayed on the wall in elongated niches of different lengths. These are illuminated with differently coloured lighting, which can be changed and developed seasonally according to the merchandising concepts for the brand. The thematic wall creates a visual display system that has a curved smooth surface and discrete storage in the form of hidden drawers. At first, these look like grooves in the wood, which resemble the decoration on the Corian display furnishings positioned on the opposite side of the shop, where a long mirror hung is also positioned on the wall to enhance the spatial perception of the store.

1 The lighting of the shop was done by Erco.
2 The left wall is completely clad in mirrors. The black wall at the far end of the shop conceals five storage cabinet doors.
3 A sculptural wall, made of Corian, acts as a second skin within the space, containing both display niches and storage drawers.

2

A spatial concept was conceived with the application of a levitating second skin

3

GOODS

by ANTONIO GARDONI

1

WHERE Brescia, Italy WHEN February 2010
CLIENT ASCOM DESIGNER Antonio Gardoni (p.673)
TOTAL FLOOR AREA 120 m² SHOP CONSTRUCTOR Ipotesi Spazio Cavalli
PHOTOGRAPHER Ottavio Tomasini

Shopkeepers association ASCOM asked Antonio Gardoni to give shape to a large empty space in the Franciacorta Outlet Village which was to house different temporary shops. As this meant that the products for sale could be anything ranging from guitars and books to clothes and accessories, a main requirement for the interior design was that it could easily be adapted. As the characteristics of the products and brands were unknown, Gardoni opted for a neutral grey as the dominating colour. The existing industrial concrete floor is complemented by grey-lacquered plywood that covers the walls. Handles and tiny slits on the grey walls hint at the surprise this space has in store. When pulling out, sliding aside or rolling up the plywood panels, a bright yellow interior pops out, revealing a wealth of functions including changing rooms, a cash counter, mirrors and display elements, such as drawers, hanging rails, niches and shelves. A series of trolleys can be used to occupy the central space to display more products and, when not in use, can be stored in the small back stockroom. Part of the in-store communication plan, fluorescent tubes on one of the walls can be individually switched on or off in order to have them display text. Repositionable letters on a large light box above the entrance inform passers-by about the temporary commercial activity inside, while a countdown board in the shop window emphasises its temporary nature.

1 Gardoni chose grey as the dominating colour in order to provide a neutral backdrop for the broad and continuously-changing product variety that is sold here.
2 Plywood panels positioned 65 cm in front of three existing walls conceal many product displays that can be pulled out as needed.
3 The flexible space is complemented with specially-designed trolleys.

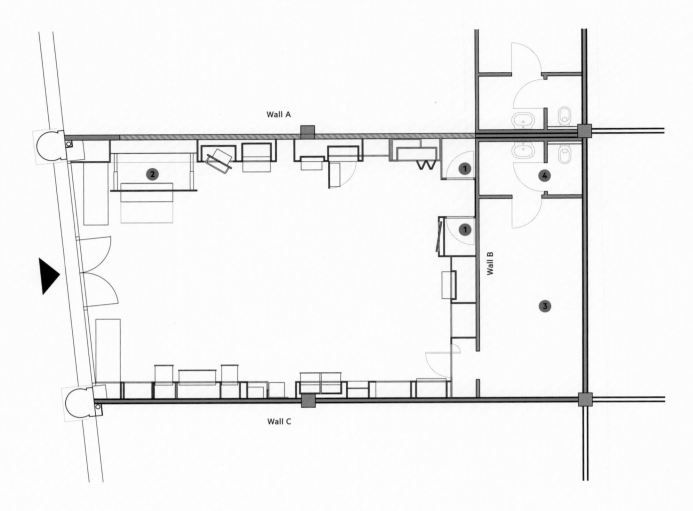

Wall A

Wall B

Wall C

1 Fitting room
2 Cash desk
3 Storage
4 Lavatory

Products for sale could range from guitars to accessories

Initial design sketch.

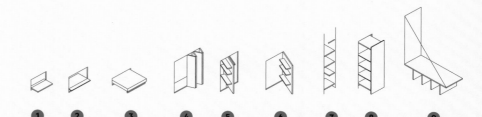

Wall A

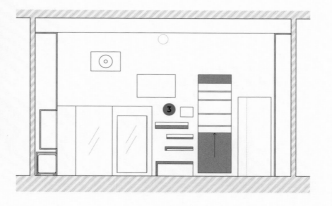

Wall B

Wall C

Drawings of the wall panelling illustrate the countless configurations that are possible for the product display.

HOFSTEDE OPTIEK

by NOWOTNY ARCHITECTEN

2

WHERE The Hague, the Netherlands **WHEN** February 2010
CLIENT Hofstede Optiek **DESIGNER** Nowotny Architecten (p.682)
TOTAL FLOOR AREA 240 m² **SHOP CONSTRUCTOR** Van der Plas
PHOTOGRAPHER Raoul Suermondt

The optician Hofstede has been a family-run business for over 100 years. In 1966, the optician opened a shop in The Hague and today it still occupies the same address. Alexander Nowotny was commissioned to redesign the shop's interior in order to cater to the market of young new customers while also maintaining the existing, more conservative clientele. Therefore, the space had to be entertaining and seductive without being loud or vulgar. Also it had to embody the opposite of the often-seen monotonous, overfilled shop windows and endless display racks of this genre of store. By designing the space as a walk-in sculpture, Nowotny Architecten turned shopping into an artistic experience. When moving through the shop, the composition of curved, slanting, rising and falling lines changes continuously, as the clients'

perspective changes. Mirrors further enhance the impact. The dominant element of the shop design is the combination of white-plastered surfaces and strongly-grained wooden surfaces. In the entrance area, the white plaster has also been combined with metallic materials, such as steel and chrome, as well as Perspex. This is where the open sunglasses display is positioned, to encourage impulse buying. The mid-shop area with the consultation counters has a lower ceiling. Its wood panelling continues on the wall that is also partly covered in dark violet-coloured velvet. Combined with purple leather upholstery, warm colour-changing LED lighting and relaxing music, this whole area has an intimate atmosphere. In the rear, a staircase features projected images and leads to the mezzanine.

1 A combination of frosted and clear glass,
   and the Perspex cubes behind this, create
   a visually exciting view into the shop.
2 The facade consists of glossy black granite
   with the 'Hofstede' lettering milled out and
   highlighted with LED light.

5

The space had to be exciting and seductive without being loud or vulgar

6

3 The composition of slanting, rising and falling lines changes continuously.

4 Each consulting desk in the mid-shop lounge area is equipped with a small flat screen on a pedestal to provide digital assistance in advisory talks.

5 The entrance area, with its high ceiling, is designed in such a way so as to encourage impulsive buying.

6 Only selected products are presented in showcases. The remaining collection is shown on request.

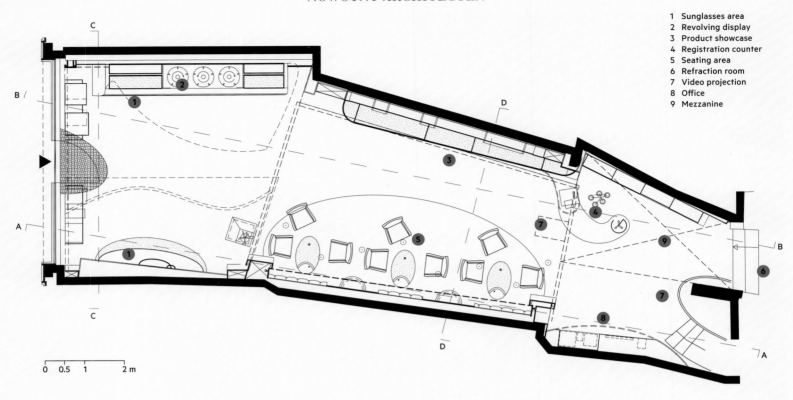

1 Sunglasses area
2 Revolving display
3 Product showcase
4 Registration counter
5 Seating area
6 Refraction room
7 Video projection
8 Office
9 Mezzanine

0   0.5   1   2 m

By designing the space as a walk-in sculpture, shopping was turned into an artistic experience

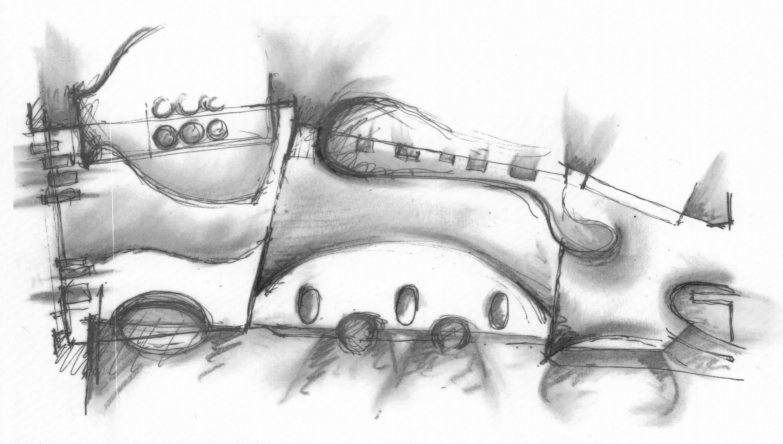

Initial design sketch showing the flowing shapes created by the layout of the natural stone flooring and sculptural wall panels.

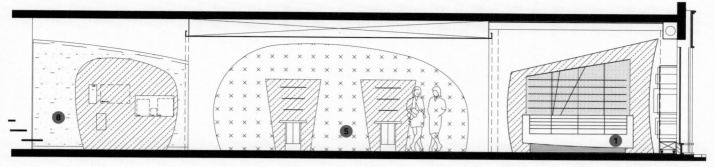

Section AA

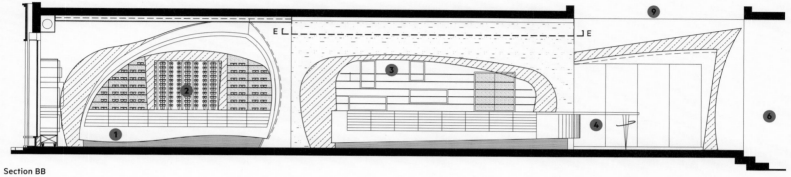

Section BB

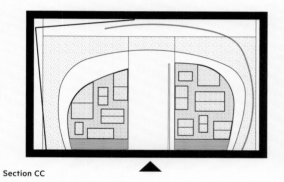

Section CC

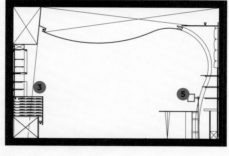

Section DD

Concealed LED light fixture, edge with titanium finish

Curved luminous ceiling

Acrylate bent into shape and back-lit
Back panel of frosted acrylate

Glass showcase with shelves and doors

Glazed top drawer
Drawers with curved fronts and veneer finish

Embedded drawer rails

Concealed LED lights

Stainless steel cover panel

Section EE

HUNKEMÖLLER

by CRENEAU INTERNATIONAL

1

WHERE Rotterdam, the Netherlands WHEN November 2010
CLIENT Hunkemöller DESIGNER Creneau International (p.676)
TOTAL FLOOR AREA 250 m² SHOP CONSTRUCTOR Beerens
PHOTOGRAPHER Iwein Maassen

The international lingerie chain Hunkemöller recently underwent a complete brand facelift and Rotterdam was chosen as the location of a new flagship store. The brief called for evolution, not a revolution, and so Creneau International took the image of the brand and stepped it up a notch. The team drew inspiration from a first class hotel, with an aim to create an environment that gives customers a warm, friendly and service-oriented feeling, with all the comforts of home but a little more mischievous. The store has a white, pink and black colour palette and an entrance reminiscent of a hotel lobby, with its high ceiling, banisters and reception counter. The 'just-in' new-product arrivals are displayed on a 6-m-high wall of stacked, open suitcases. A recurring cross-pattern metal meshwork is used in the stair handrails and display tables as a yet a subtle reference to the brand's early years, which started as a corsetry shop in 1886. Venturing into the store, the atmosphere gets more intimate and darker colours predominate. The fitting room area, in matt black, is reminiscent of a hotel corridor where each door has a peephole and various 'Do not disturb' and 'I need assistance' doorknob signs. There is even room service; ring a bell in the fitting room and the shop attendant appears with a trolley full of lingerie. The design is feminine but not too sweet, charming but not too precious. It has a self-assured air, just like the Hunkemöller lady, and fragments from her imaginary diary can be found in handwritten notes which together form a quirky chandelier overhead.

1 Products are presented as a buffet of cakes and sweets.
2 Handwritten notes, which can be found hanging near the entrance, are an interesting read for customers.
3 The dressing table in the fitting room presents a room service menu.
4 The store is designed like an open and light hotel lobby.

2

3

There is even room service

4

KIRK ORIGINALS

by CAMPAIGN

1

WHERE London, United Kingdom WHEN January 2011
CLIENT Kirk Originals DESIGNER Campaign (p.675)
TOTAL FLOOR AREA 65 m² SHOP CONSTRUCTOR Crane Interiors
PHOTOGRAPHER Hufton + Crow

Eyewear brand Kirk Originals asked Campaign to design its new flagship store in London. A shop was called for that looked unlike any other optical store and was more reminiscent of a fashion shop. It had to trigger instant brand recognition and provide a unique experience. The client wanted to reinvent the eyewear store with the budget of a pop-up shop and within a 5-week time frame; Campaign's design reflects this challenge. The team created a stark contrast to the conventional, clinical white box of traditional opticians by using a restricted palette of monochromatic colours and modest materials. Along the blue–grey painted walls are 187 white powder-coated steel sculptural heads, affectionately referred to as 'winkies'. Each one adorns a unique pair of glasses and can be tilted or repositioned to create clusters of craning heads,

illuminated by spotlights as if works of art. Winking eyes make an appearance in the store in various guises. A series of larger-than-life lenticular printed eyes are suspended in the front window, simultaneously winking and catching customers' attention as they approach and enter the store. Integral to the shopping experience, the Kirk Originals identity is interwoven throughout the space: a succinct account of the brand's origins has been rendered in graphic text over two walls at the entrance, while a black-and-white projection on the back wall playfully re-works the Kirk Originals logo through a continual kaleidoscopic loop. Side-stepping the expected, Campaign has transformed the 65-m² interior space to create a memorable destination for eyewear aficionados.

2

Steel sculptural heads are affectionately referred to as 'winkies'

3

1 A clear view into the store shows a black-and-white projection on the back wall that re-works the client's logo through a continual kaleidoscopic loop.
2 The interior reflects the irreverence that Kirk Originals demonstrates in the design of its frames, which ignore convention.
3 A cluster of 'winkies' display the glasses.

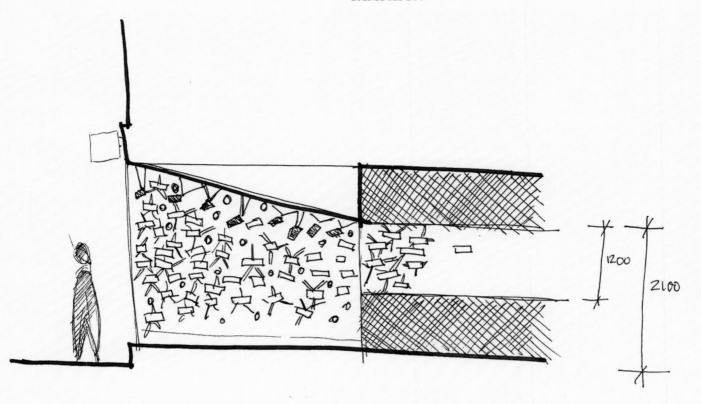

The interior was reinvented with a pop-up shop budget and a 5-week time frame

Sketches showing the positioning of the eyewear displays and the view from the entrance into the back of the store.

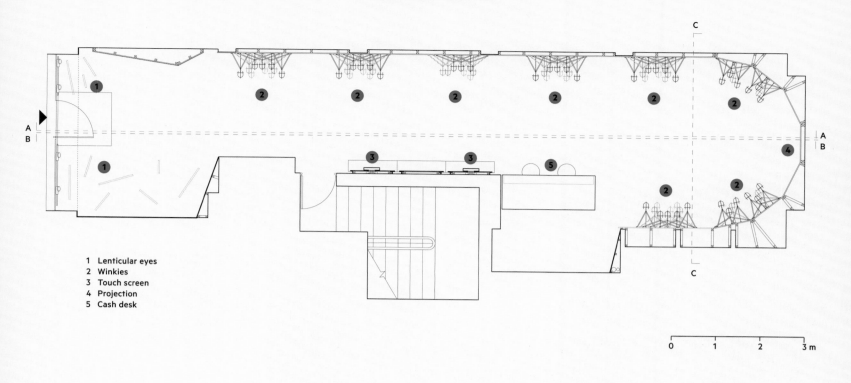

1 Lenticular eyes
2 Winkies
3 Touch screen
4 Projection
5 Cash desk

0   1   2   3 m

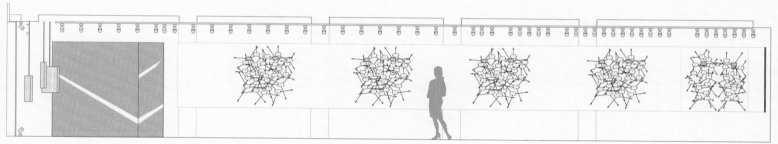

Section AA

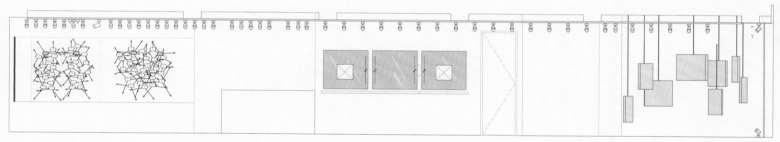

Section BB

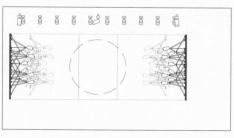

Section CC

KOMPLEMENTAIR

by AEKAE

2

WHERE Zurich, Switzerland **WHEN** April 2010
CLIENT Komplementair Accessoires **DESIGNER** Aekae (p.673)
TOTAL FLOOR AREA 140 m² **SHOP CONSTRUCTORS** Gregoryclan and Aekae
PHOTOGRAPHER Nico Schaerer

Komplementair is a shop that sells accessories by various designers. Its name refers to the accessories complementing an outfit. When Aekae was brought aboard, the designers decided to also use this reference for the interior design of the Zurich boutique. Staying true to the location, an old railroad viaduct, the original stonework was made part of the concept and left intact. Instead of the products being organised into categories, such as jewellery, sunglasses, shawls and weekend bags, they are arranged in assorted groups of different items. The items are displayed on various product islands scattered over both floors of the two-storey space. Each island consists of second-hand furniture pieces, compiled to form a bigger structure with various platforms and niches. After the search for all the furniture pieces, a lot of on-site work was required, experimenting with different layouts. The most eye-catching aspect of the shop is the installation that incorporates a Steinway grand piano, which gets played on special occasions. To create a neutral backdrop for the accessories, each platform was fitted out with a lacquered mdf surface in either black or white. The pendant lighting system creates additional display elements above the furniture; simply by wrapping their cables around brass rods, a geometric feature is created – that can be adjusted in height accordingly – from which products can be suspended.

1 A focal point of the shop is a composition of furniture pieces including an original Steinway grand piano.
2 Nothing was allowed to be fixed to the original stonework of the old viaduct, therefore the display elements either suspend from the ceiling or just lean against the walls.

3

4

3 The lighting system combines brass rods for hanging items, with the height of the lampshades adjustable by simply wrapping their wires around the rods.
4 The cash desk is a simple black-lacquered structure that contrasts with the white poured-concrete flooring and the rough stone walls.
5 All display platforms were created out of second-hand furniture.
6 On the first floor, various reclaimed parquet panels form a flooring patchwork that complements the black furniture structures.

5

The original stonework of an old railroad viaduct was made part of the concept

LEO PIZZO

by DIEGO BORTOLATO ARCHITETTO AND GIANLUCA RE ARCHITETTO

1

WHERE Milan, Italy WHEN November 2009
CLIENT Leo Pizzo DESIGNERS Diego Bortolato Architetto (p.677) and Gianluca Re Architetto (p.678)
TOTAL FLOOR AREA 50 m² SHOP CONSTRUCTOR Barth Innenausbau
PHOTOGRAPHER Jürgen Eheim

Italian jewellery brand Leo Pizzo has been around for three decades and has stores at prime locations all over Italy. Its new store in Milan was opened in 2009 in the historical and well-known Galleria Vittorio Emanuele II, just opposite of the Duomo. Cooperating on the project, Diego Bortolato Architetto and Gianluca Re Architetto designed the interior for the luxury boutique. The aim for this store was to promote and raise awareness of the production philosophy of Mr Leo Pizzo: hand-made jewels which are characterised by high quality and traditional details, with top-class gems. An automatic 4.6-m-high door welcomes customers into a double-height entrance area which is designed as a museum space, exhibiting jewels in different kinds of showcases. The application of various materials – natural walnut, bronze, painted glass and natural lime-stone flooring – was inspired by the Milanese museum Villa Necchi Campiglio. The central counter was handcrafted by a carpenter and features special hinges and many intricate details. Natural lime-finished boiseries are placed throughout the store in glass display cases, showing off the sparkling gems. A quiet area in the back, fitted out with a proper desk, leather chairs and accessories, provides a more intimate space for meetings with customers.

1 The central counter is made from walnut and back-painted glass.
2 The main retail area has an impressively high ceiling. The back of the shop features a private consultation area which has a lower ceiling providing more intimacy.

LOOK OPTIEK

by BENSCHOP THE RETAIL FACTORY

1

WHERE Leiden, the Netherlands WHEN December 2010
CLIENT Look Optiek (Hans and Helene van Schie) DESIGNER Benschop The Retail Factory (p.674)
TOTAL FLOOR AREA 155 m² SHOP CONSTRUCTOR Benschop The Retail Factory
PHOTOGRAPHER Unit 300 (Silvain Wiersma)

Having refurbished the former shop of opticians Hans and Helene van Schie in 2002, Benschop was once again approached by the couple in 2010. This time the brief was to design the interior of their new and much bigger Look Optiek shop in the centre of the Dutch city, Leiden. Working with the architectural column in the centre of the space, instead of around it, Benschop decided to make it the focal point of the shop. A construction of steel tables of different heights and with glass and leather tops in alternating colours seems to fan out of the column. The structure serves as a display element for the glasses as well as a seating and consultation area. The majority of the glasses are housed within the integrated drawer system along the right-side wall of the space. Above the drawers are glass shelves that run the length of the wall and along the shop windows, presenting selected items from the collection. On the left side of the shop, the floor seamlessly curves into the wall and ceiling, partly enveloping the space and serving as a backdrop for another product presentation element. A semi-transparent, wooden slat wall separates the shop area from the atelier and refraction rooms in the back, creating some privacy. Completing the shop's new look, Benschop also designed a new logo that emphasises the client's personal approach towards its customers.

1 A construction of tables fanning out around a central column is a consultation, seating and display area.
2 Integrated drawers in the right wall hold the majority of glasses.
3 The floor curves into the product wall and ceiling, enveloping the space.

2

The floor
seamlessly curves
into the wall,
partly enveloping
the space

MYKITA

by MYKITA

1

WHERE Monterrey, Mexico WHEN May 2010
CLIENT Mykita DESIGNER Mykita (p.682)
TOTAL FLOOR AREA 70 m² SHOP CONSTRUCTOR Mykita
PHOTOGRAPHER Vicente Maroquin

Glasses of the German eyewear brand Mykita can be found in many stores all over the globe. The brand also has six stores that are completely dedicated to its own product range, which are designed by Mykita's team of designers according to its philosophy of having all phases of production to marketing under one roof. The shop in Monterrey is housed in the same building as the popular design hotel Habita. This landmark building, designed by Agustin Landa, has a curved exterior and comprises exposed concrete and glass, with white and wood-coloured facade elements. Mykita decided to let the shop interior completely blend in with the architecture. The store is split into three sections: the bright sales area at the front, the kitchen, and the separate workshop and refraction room in the back. Its interior design was kept to a minimum in order to retain the full effect of the wedge-shaped space with its exposed concrete walls and concrete coffered ceiling. The dominant design element is the backlit presentation wall which can accommodate over 500 pairs of glasses. It extends 12 m along the full extent of the interior and is angled towards the back of the shop. Directly facing it, is a sales counter of slightly shorter length but also with a slight angle at the far end. The mini-kitchen is separated from the front by a wall that is two-thirds full height. Large mirrors running behind the sales counter increase the room's apparent size and, in addition, enable customers to view themselves from virtually any angle.

1 The point where the presentation wall and the sales counter meet marks the end of the retail area; behind it are the kitchen and refraction rooms.
2 Large mirrors above the sales counter increase the store's apparent size.
3 Perforated steel angle beads – usually used to support heavy-duty shelving – form the presentation wall.

1

The store was created to be a sensual experience that customers would remember

OCTIUM

by HAYON STUDIO

◆

2

WHERE Kuwait City, Kuwait WHEN October 2009
CLIENT Octium Jewelry (Alanood Al Sabah and Fahad Al Hajiri) DESIGNER Hayon Studio (p.679)
TOTAL FLOOR AREA 200 m² SHOP CONSTRUCTOR Chateau Royale
PHOTOGRAPHER Nienke Klunder

Octium is a high-end jewellery boutique, located in the 360 shopping mall in Kuwait's capital. Its owners search the world for the most exclusive pieces by various artists and designers and needed a shop that would do justice to their precious finds. Besides having an impressive space to showcase their sparkling goods, they wanted to make sure that shopping for jewellery would become a sensual experience that customers would remember. Creating an interior that is anything but standard, Jaime Hayon custom-designed almost every single element. Brass doors in the masculine black marble exterior facade of St Laurent open up into a contrasting feminine world of soft, organic shapes – there is no single corner to be found in the entire store. Hayon applied a broad array of ways to showcase the jewellery, with the various areas all featuring different elements. Theatrical large-scale furniture, suspended lamps that 'fall' all the way into the glass displays below and a 7-m-long natural walnut display elements with brass crutch-like supports all offer the jewellery to the clients in a more stimulating way. The central area features complex multi-legged tables with integrated display cases springing from them. A light installation above the circular purple table consists of white cylinders of differing diameters, suspending from the ceiling like stalactites. By using contrasting finishes, like glossy lacquered woods, natural walnut, shiny ceramics and luxurious fabrics, Hayon created a balance between tradition and technology.

1 The name Octium is derived from *octo* (Latin for 'eight') and its logo, an octagon, has eight sides. Eight stands for infinity and in this case links to the process of increasing passion and knowledge. Eight is also the number of 'stalagmites' of the light installation in the centre of the store.
2 Adding to the feel of magic, ceramic lamps suspend from the ceiling, 'falling' inside the glass display cases.

3

3 Ceramic lights from Hayon's Copa Cabana collection for Metalarte illuminate the display cabinet.

4 Every element in the store was either custom-designed for Octium or previously designed by Hayon for other labels, such as the Tudor chairs in the private consultation area from the Established & Sons collection.

5 The soft and feminine design was inspired by the traditional Mediterranean custom of using lime as a finish to give interiors an organic feel with rounded corners.

Fantasy and imagination meet function and quality

5

View from the entrance into the store.

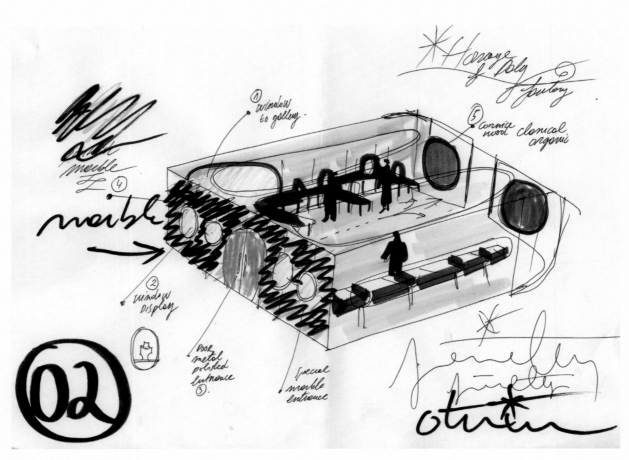

Sketch indicating the layout of the entrance
and main retail area.

The long chestnut display cabinet was inspired by and designed as a tribute to Salvador Dali.

The soft organic shapes were inspired by traditional Mediterranean construction methods

Sketches of various jewellery display possibilities; each 'microworld' presents the selection of one specific jewellery designer.

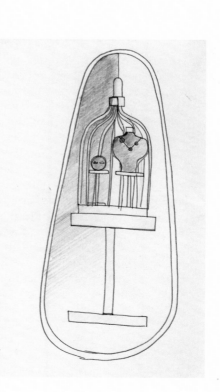

PODIUM

by ART BUREAU 1/1

1

WHERE Paris, France WHEN October 2009
CLIENT Podium DESIGNER Art Bureau 1/1 (p.673)
TOTAL FLOOR AREA 50 m² SHOP CONSTRUCTOR Art Bureau 1/1
PHOTOGRAPHERS Alexander Izar and Charles Delcourt

Opposite the well-known store Colette on the Fabour St Honore street in Paris, a new boutique has opened its doors. The fashion company Podium decided it was time for a jewellery store and approached the Russian design firm Art Bureau 1/1 to make the most out of the available 50 m² of retail space. As the jewellery collection is very unique – Podium focuses on handcrafted pieces of famous jewellery brands that are made by using ancient or rare techniques – the interior design had to reflect this too but without drawing attention away from the jewellery. However small the floor area may be, the interior leaves a big impression on visitors and passers-by. The designers applied a dark, gothic theme to the interior that matches the Podium logo and many of the collectors' items that are on display.

Large ferrous metal chests of drawers with glass showcases have been custom-designed for the store. The black-lined cabinets, some of which are fitted out with animal skulls that serve as display elements, are crisply lit with modular spotlights from within, as well as by vintage lamps positioned at random angles, as if they are stretching and bending to peer at the gems. Aged and etched metal is utilised throughout the store against the dark stained wood with the chairs in the client consultation area richly upholstered in red velvet and black leather. The mirror-clad back wall makes the store look larger than it actually is and gives customers plenty of opportunity to admire the jewellery when adorning the exclusive pieces.

1 The logo reflects the shop's gothic interior.
2 The central showcase with a glass dome is made from manually-aged metal. Jieldé lamps which are attached to it illuminate the merchandise.
3 A mirror on the back wall makes the shop space look larger.
4 The carved cabinet was custom designed for the store and made from solid oak.

2

Podium sells jewellery pieces that are made using ancient or rare techniques

3

4

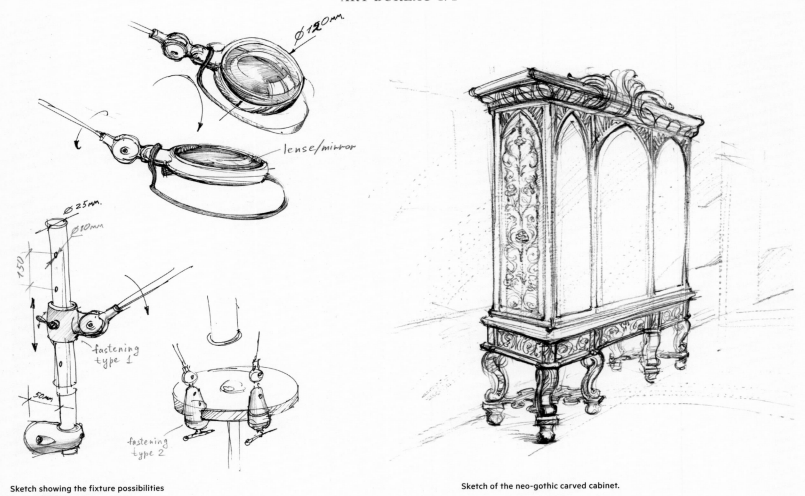

Sketch showing the fixture possibilities
for the Jieldé lamps.

Sketch of the neo-gothic carved cabinet.

Most of the furniture pieces have been custom-designed for the store

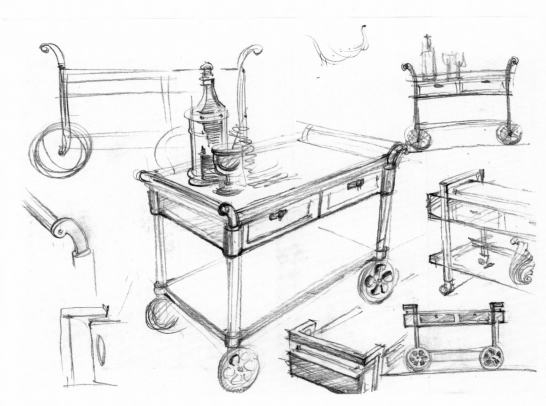

The display table is based on the design of an
old liquor trolley.

WALL SHOWCASE

Front view

Side view

750 mm

30   30

750

690
684

NANO III LED 24 V DC

484

A   A

85   137

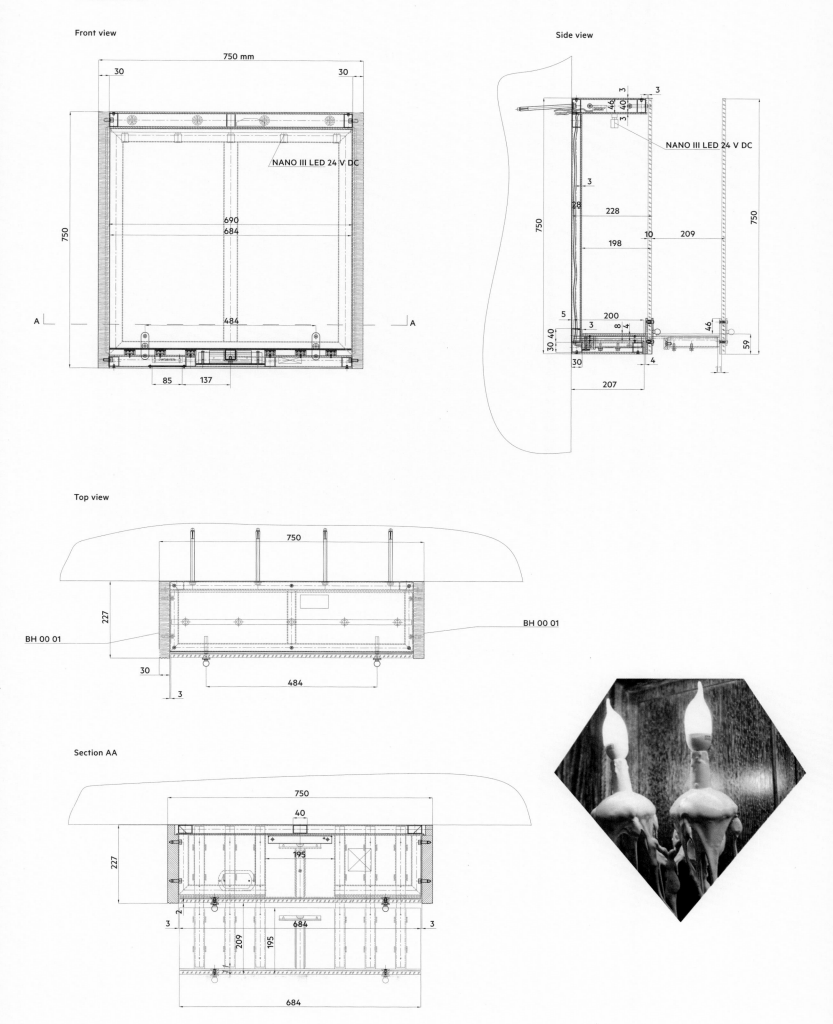

3   3

46
40
3

NANO III LED 24 V DC

750

3

28   228

198   10   209   750

5   200

30 40   3   8   4   46

30   4   59

207

Top view

750

227

BH 00 01   BH 00 01

30

484

3

Section AA

750

40

227

195

3   2   3

684

209   195

684

PRINCESSE TAM TAM

by UXUS

1

WHERE Paris, France **WHEN** March 2011
CLIENT Princesse Tam Tam **DESIGNER** Uxus (p.686)
TOTAL FLOOR AREA 59 m² **SHOP CONSTRUCTORS** Visplay and Vizona
PHOTOGRAPHER Dim Balsem

Design agency Uxus was invited to create a new retail platform for the French lingerie brand Princesse Tam Tam. Elevating the customers' perception of the brand at retail level, as well as becoming the starting point for a global roll-out, were the main objectives. The majority of the store elements had to be instantly recognisable and were thus custom designed to create a signature style for the chain of stores. A bespoke white oak display system was developed to layer garment displays, featuring softly rounded corners and a series of modules that create a calm, effortless rhythm throughout the store. Echoing the floor's white painted planks, a series of randomly stacked drawer units complete the atelier look and provide extra storage space where needed. In the lingerie collections, vibrant colours and contemporary patterns are used but the design team opted for the opposite in the interior: an elegant colour scheme of neutral taupe with soft whites, punctuated by the brand's signature violet. The fitting rooms, cash desk and the shop window are lined with laser-cut felt and together with the suspended Lolita lights, designed by Nica Zupanc for Moooi, give the store a chic feminine touch. To also give the shop a contemporary edge, interactive touch-screens and dramatically-lit showcases were installed in the fitting rooms while the shop window features monitors displaying fashion shows.

1 The latest lingerie collections are featured in one of the storefront windows, positioned in cut-outs of the laser-cut felt panels.
2 Fagerhult spotlights are positioned in the slats of the white oak beamed ceiling.
3 The fitting rooms are decorated with taupe felt drapes and violet Balsan wool carpet.
4 The white decor in the shop is a crisp backdrop for the merchandise.

2

3

Suspended Lolita lights give the store a chic feminine touch

4

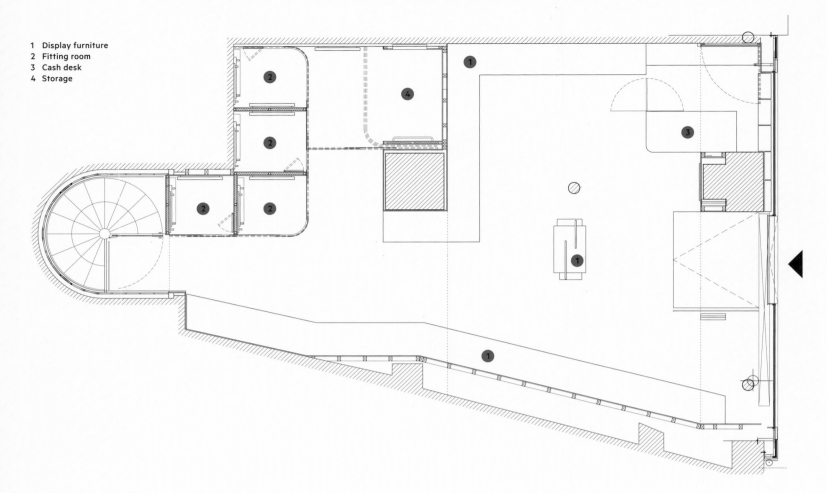

1 Display furniture
2 Fitting room
3 Cash desk
4 Storage

The display module design instils a calm and effortless rhythm in the store

On the right hand side of the entrance, the felt strip panels have 'windows' cut-out where products or video monitors can be positioned.

FELT PANELS

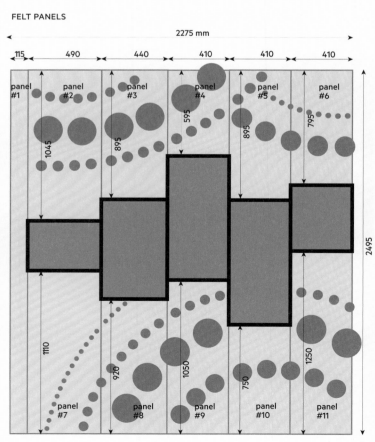

Renderings illustrating views of the product display systems in-store.

FACADE

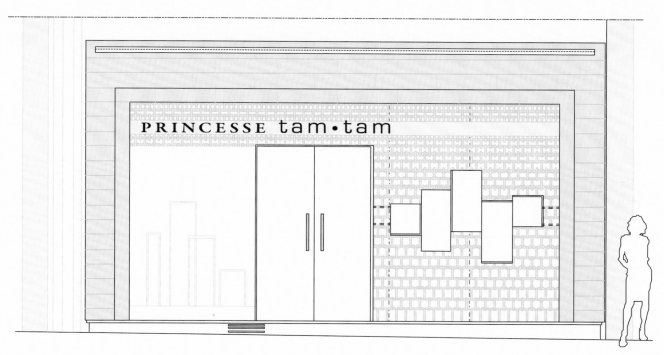

View from front

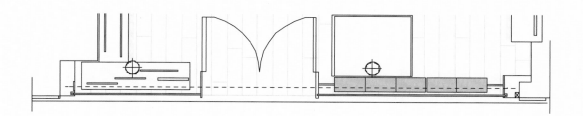

View from above

PROPERTY OF...

by PROPERTY OF...

1

WHERE Amsterdam, the Netherlands WHEN May 2010
CLIENT Property Of... DESIGNER Property Of... (p.683)
TOTAL FLOOR AREA 45 m² SHOP CONSTRUCTOR Jamaka Services
PHOTOGRAPHER Joris Bruring

When the Property Of... brand owners were exploring Amsterdam during a trip in 2010, they were not looking to buy a shop – but when they discovered a vacant corner lot in the canal district, they realised they had stumbled across the ideal location for their new European flagship store. The brief for the in-house design team was to create a space where customers were put at ease by incorporating a blend of design elements that were visually and emotionally familiar. Building on the owners' origins, the Amsterdam space identity incorporated a cafe function, a dynamic aspect is given to the space that might otherwise feel very static. The primary design challenge was working with the limitation of a small space whilst trying to rationally integrate elements of a working café alongside a clear retail display. The interior is decorated with a mix of tungsten pendant lamps, various custom timber pieces and reclaimed ceramic tiles, with the black and white chequerboard effect on the floor adding to the old-style bistro-type atmosphere. Products are displayed on every surface, from branded hooks and atop vintage furniture. A unique environment has been created where customers can browse through the latest collection on display whilst grabbing a freshly brewed cappuccino; the daily changing cast of characters, activities and 'life' that unfold within this inviting space is a constant source of inspiration.

1　Property Of... sells classic men's bags and a full range of accessories.
2　The brand name 'Property Of...' was crafted to refer to the identity of the product owner rather than to a designer. A 'menu board' of product names, all being men's names, on the mirrored wall behind the counter highlights this concept.

S.OLIVER ACCESSORIES

by DFROST

2

WHERE Frankfurt, Germany WHEN November 2010
CLIENT s.Oliver DESIGNER dfrost (p.677)
TOTAL FLOOR AREA 90 m² SHOP CONSTRUCTOR Schreinerei Furch
PHOTOGRAPHER David Franck

Fashion brand s.Oliver briefed dfrost to design its first boutique dedicated to accessories only. It had to be a completely new retail concept that would adequately handle the high product density of accessories while incorporating all functional requirements of the existing s.Oliver stores. The essence of the dfrost concept consists of atmospheric and emotional spaces, deepening the ordinary understanding of retail design. Referring to the local fauna, illustrations of magpies, badgers, robins and squirrels are displayed on the walls and furniture of the sales area, like drawings in a storybook. Vintage-style furniture pieces and charming objects, such as bird cages, bell jars, moss-overgrown tree logs, piles of leather-covered books and old black-and-white postcards, invoke a feel-good atmosphere and invite the

customers to discover new details on every visit. In order to facilitate the ever-changing collections, the design is completely modular. From the angular furniture, made of white stained spruce wood, to the filigree metal frames and the graphics, everything can be adjusted, changing the look of the store every season. Ensuring a harmonious ensemble of product presentation and interior design, the designers incorporated elements such as the elegant leather bench with hat rack that serves as a product display.

1 The shop decor creates a warm, feel-good atmosphere which attracts passers-by to enter the store.
2 Key products and charming objects were incorporated in the interior design, creating a harmonious ensemble.

3

Everything can be adjusted ensuring a harmonious ensemble of product presentation

3 Charming objects play a dominant role in the interior, including bird cages used as product displays.
4 In-store, artwork consists of wall and furniture tattoos that are changed and updated seasonally.
5 Fun elements pop up in every corner, surprising the customers.
6 The store was designed as a woman's boudoir and therefore gives room to many everyday objects one would expect to find there.

4

6

5

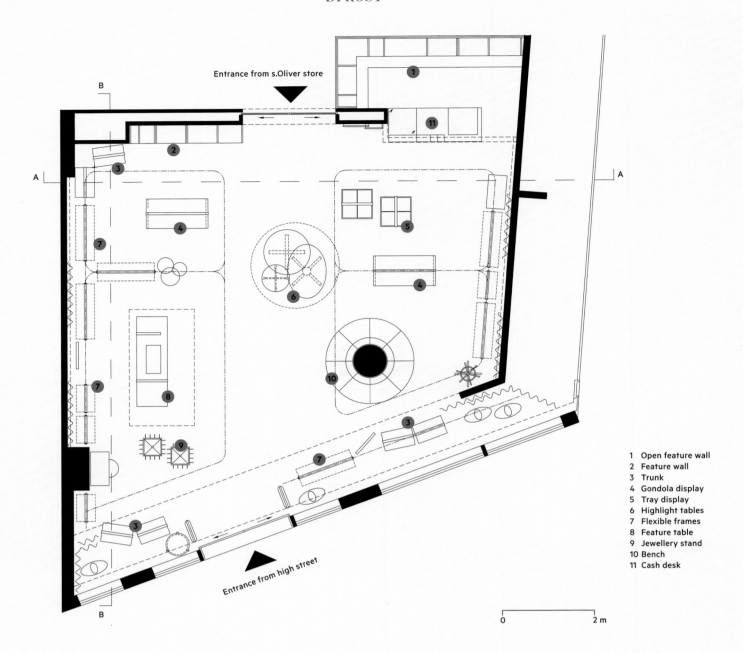

Entrance from s.Oliver store

Entrance from high street

1 Open feature wall
2 Feature wall
3 Trunk
4 Gondola display
5 Tray display
6 Highlight tables
7 Flexible frames
8 Feature table
9 Jewellery stand
10 Bench
11 Cash desk

0   2 m

The look of the store can be changed every season

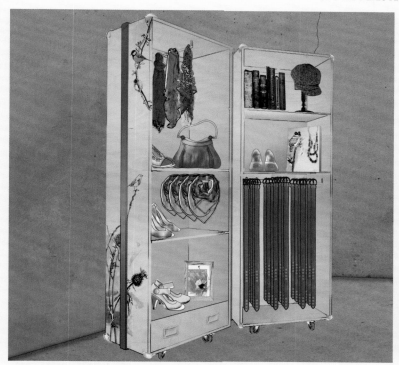

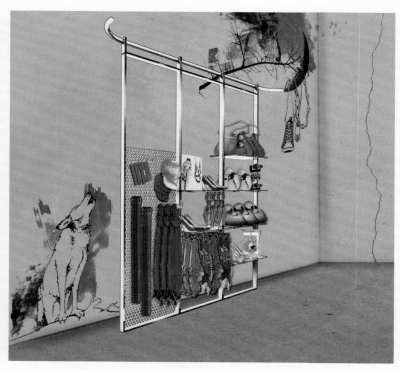

The display cabinet was designed as a suitcase.

The modular, metal display system can be fitted out with shelves, hooks and rails as the collection requires.

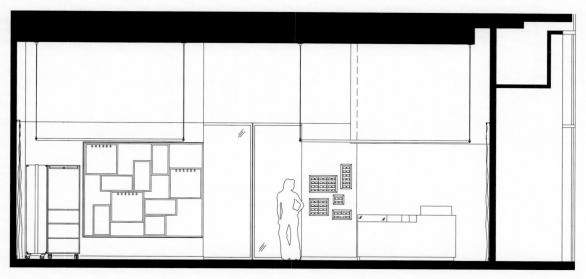

Section AA

Section BB

THE COUNTER

by RAËD ABILLAMA ARCHITECTS

1

WHERE Beirut, Lebanon **WHEN** December 2009
CLIENT Cherine Magrabi **DESIGNER** Raëd Abillama Architects (p.684)
TOTAL FLOOR AREA 78 m² **SHOP CONSTRUCTOR** MAC
PHOTOGRAPHER Joe Kesrouani

Raëd Abillama Architects was asked to design the interior for The Counter, a new eyewear store that opened in Beirut in 2009. It needed a concept that could be applied to a wide variety of shop locations of different sizes. The architects came up with a building block concept that consists of four elements that can be combined in different ways to create fitting solutions for future shops: a central counter, a vertical display shelving system, a multifunctional wall and a VIP area. Conceptualising the shop's name, the counter became the main priority of the interior design and was placed in the centre of the store. It is a focal point and a key structural element that fulfils the needs for an attractive display, personal space for the customer and storage possibilities. By displaying eyewear in the same way that jewellery shops often display their precious objects – encased behind glass – the aesthetic value of the frames is enhanced. The frames are set at an angle and back-lit in order to enhance their design and colours. The lower part of the counter consists of drawers that contain additional frames and cases for packaging. This configuration provides some privacy for the customers as they can look at all the designs without having to ask the shoppersonnel, opening drawers and using the counter top in front of them as their personal space. More privacy is offered by the enclosed VIP area at the back of the shop.

1 The display shelving system is enhanced by a back-lit curtain that covers the entire wall.
2 Overview of the shop from the entrance.
3 An enclosed VIP area is located in the back of the shop.

2

Displayed as
precious objects
encased behind
glass, the aesthetic
value of the frames
is enhanced

MULTIFUNCTIONAL WALL

Top view

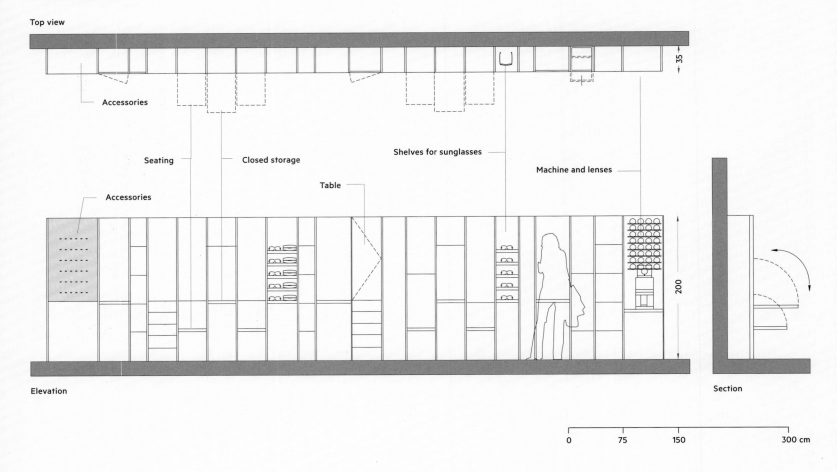

Accessories

Seating   Closed storage   Shelves for sunglasses

Table   Machine and lenses

Accessories

35

200

Elevation   Section

| 0 | 75 | 150 | 300 cm |

Four elements make up the concept and can be applied to future shops

Section of the counter.

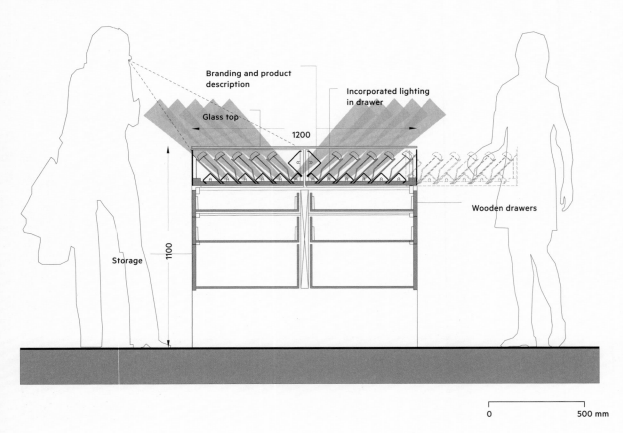

Branding and product description

Incorporated lighting in drawer

Glass top

1200

Wooden drawers

1100

Storage

| 0 | 500 mm |

Multifunctional wall axonometric.

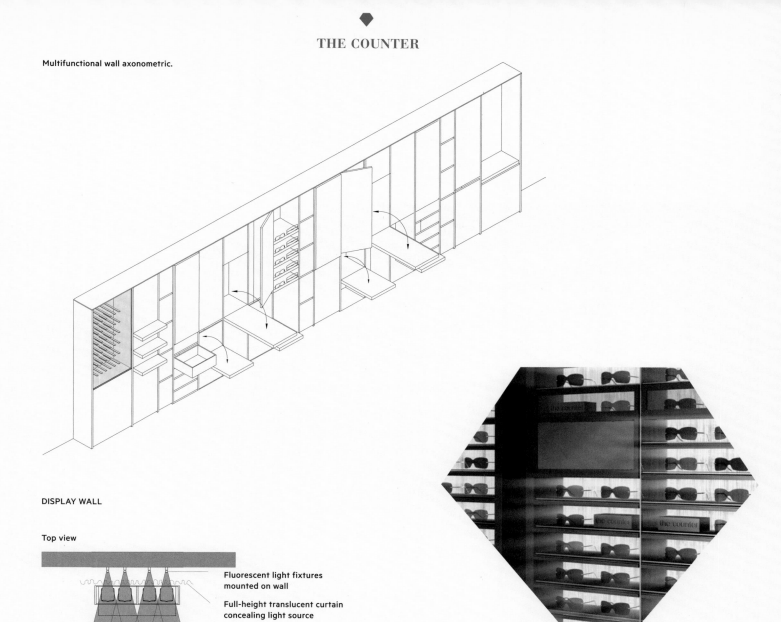

DISPLAY WALL

Top view

Fluorescent light fixtures mounted on wall

Full-height translucent curtain concealing light source

Elevation

Section

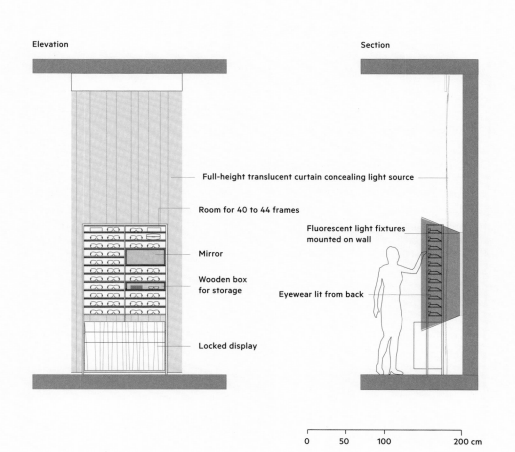

Full-height translucent curtain concealing light source

Room for 40 to 44 frames

Fluorescent light fixtures mounted on wall

Mirror

Wooden box for storage

Eyewear lit from back

Locked display

```
0        50        100              200 cm
```

VILLA OPTICA

by BLEEKER CONCEPTS

1

WHERE Apeldoorn, the Netherlands **WHEN** September 2010
CLIENT Villa Optica (Gerben Sinke and Willemijn Stam) **DESIGNER** Bleeker Concepts (p.674)
TOTAL FLOOR AREA 120 m² **SHOP CONSTRUCTOR** Timmerhuusken
PHOTOGRAPHER Bleeker Concepts

The design brief given to Bleeker Concepts for Villa Optica's new shop was 'to create a modern, warm but exquisite environment where our ambitions in the field of eye care come to full advantage and where our customers, both young and old, feel at home'. The ambitions of the optometrists are versatile and all aspects of high quality eye care – technical, medical and fashion – had to be integrated into the concept. The shop also had to appear large and spacious. As the two-storey building is quite narrow, the biggest challenge the designers faced was to create a clear and accessible routing through the shop. Two examination rooms, a laboratory, consultation area and cash desk were created on the ground floor, while the first floor houses the office, kitchen, an additional examination room and another laboratory. Product displays and lounge areas are on both floors. To make the first floor easily accessible, the staircase was given a prominent place in the store. Floating wooden treads were integrated into the feature wall which is made of light oak strips, mutually arranged to create a relief. The wood gives the store, which is predominantly white, a warm and friendly atmosphere. Colour accents were introduced by yellow, pink and red display boxes that highlight special glasses from the collection, and large blown-up photographs of models wearing the glasses.

1 Illuminated shelves behind the staircase display part of the glasses collection. The sunglasses are displayed on the other side of the stairs, closer to the entrance.
2 A long consultation table emphasises the depth of the store. Above, the Hollywood chandelier by Brand van Egmond suspends from the double-height ceiling, connecting the two levels.
3 As eye-catching aspects, coloured boxes are used in the display niches in the store for presenting featured products.

2

Both young and old customers had to feel at home in this store

3

BODY
HEALT

108

AND
HCARE
109

AESOP

by SCHEMATA ARCHITECTURE OFFICE

1

WHERE Tokyo, Japan WHEN December 2010
CLIENT Aesop DESIGNER Schemata Architecture Office (p.684)
TOTAL FLOOR AREA 75 m² SHOP CONSTRUCTOR Sekiguchi Constructor
PHOTOGRAPHER Alessio G. Guarino

Aesop is a skincare brand with 42 international concept stores worldwide. For its first signature store in Tokyo, an old vegetable shop was refurbished to create a functional yet poetic retail space. The essence of the store came from a soon-to-be-demolished house, which architect Jo Nagasaka stumbled across when seeking inspiration in the early stages of the project. Immediately he recognised the possibilities for reusing the wooden boards and beams and, working closely with Aesop, a design was conceived that would salvage the materials and give them a rejuvenated lease of life within the new shop. The concept saw the space stripped down to the bare essentials and reconditioned with a raw, simple and warm aesthetic. Reused timber, handles and furniture found in the abandoned house were integrated into the design amidst the skeleton of what once was the vegetable shop, subtly and sympathetically paying homage to Japan's well-established tradition of fusing the traditional with the modern. Features such as pipes and drain covers, as well as the ceiling, floor and walls, were left uncovered and highlighted by coating in epoxy resin. The understated design highlights an appreciation of raw everyday materials and echoes Aesop's minimalist packaging, rows of which can be seen at first glance on entering the store, stacked high on the product wall.

1 The counter tops of the cash desk and the display tables were made of epoxy resin.
2 Most of the woodwork was carried out by the company Zest.
3 Two sinks, between the shelves of the product wall, are installed so that customers can wash their hands between testing different products.

2

The understated
design echoes
Aesop's minimalist
packaging

3

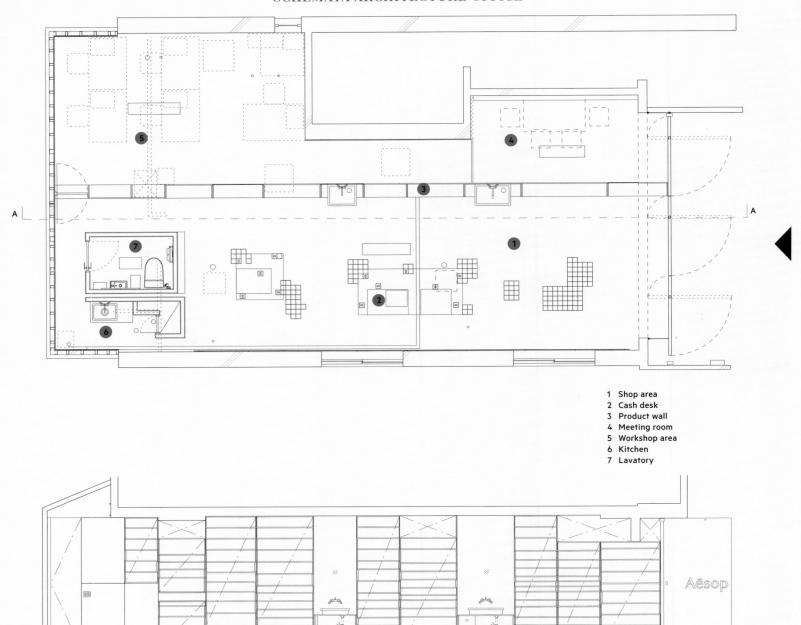

1 Shop area
2 Cash desk
3 Product wall
4 Meeting room
5 Workshop area
6 Kitchen
7 Lavatory

Section AA

Used window sills, planks and cabinets were given a new lease of life in the Aesop shop.

Most materials used in the shop came from this residential house that was scheduled for demolition.

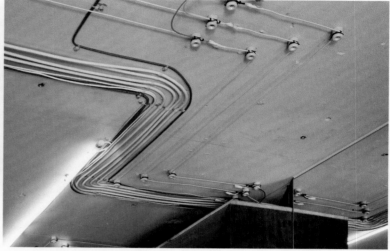

An old-style Japanese electric wiring system that is often used in wooden houses was installed.

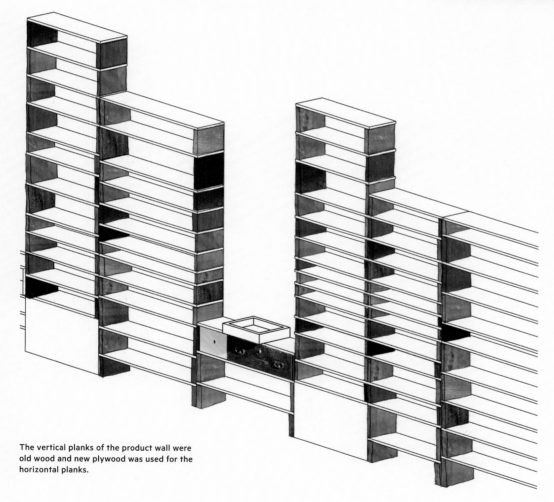

The vertical planks of the product wall were old wood and new plywood was used for the horizontal planks.

An old medicine cabinet was transformed into a tester box.

Reused timber from an abandoned house was integrated into the skeleton of the store

AUDIONOVA

by ZEST DESIGN + ARCHITECTURE

1

WHERE Aalst, Belgium WHEN August 2009
CLIENT Schoonenberg DESIGNER Zest Design + Architecture (p.687)
TOTAL FLOOR AREA 180 m² SHOP CONSTRUCTOR Zest Design + Architecture
PHOTOGRAPHER Reporters

AudioNova provides products for progressive hearing comfort and has over 30 hearing centres across Belgium. A new store in Aalst was designed by Zest Design + Architecture according to the brief which called for a re-interpretation of the AudioNova store concept which aims to avoid treating customers as patients but still communicate hygiene and professionalism. Thus, the team veered away from a design that was too clinical and instead – linking in with the brand's forward-thinking attitude – focused on highlighting state-of-the-art technologies. The objective was to have an atmosphere adapted to the function of the different areas. Soft materials and curved shapes were used to reinforce the fluidity of this concept and to reach a balance between the welcoming reception area and the hygienic 'hearing environment'.

Open, accessible and fluid are the design aesthetics that customers first experience on entering, and these aspects flow right throughout the space, from the waiting area to the consultation rooms and laboratory. Fresh green accents of the corporate palette are seen in the furnishings and sculpted furniture. A charcoal grey wall in the waiting area adds an austere air of professionalism, with an elongated, illuminated display counter exhibiting the very latest high-tech products. A corridor that connects all aspects of the space is lined with an with an eye-catching installation. The 'waves wall' – constructed from gloss-white lengths of laser-cut wood – is reminiscent of oscillating sound waves travelling down the auditory canal.

1 The reception desk is made from fibreglass over a wood and metal structure.
2 The sculptural wall element reflects in the blue-tinted glass door of one of the onsultation rooms.
3 View of the waiting area. The colours were chosen in order to make clients feel less like patients while still communicating that it is a hygienic and professional environment.

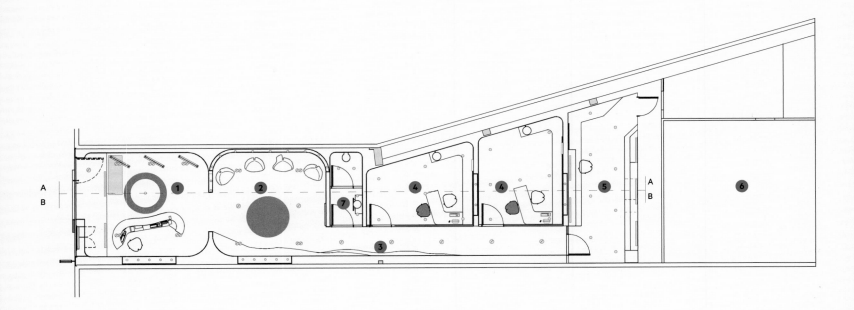

1 Reception
2 Waiting area
3 Waves wall
4 Consultation room
5 Laboratory
6 Storage
7 Lavatory

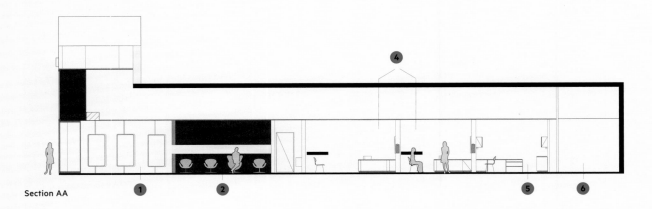

Section AA

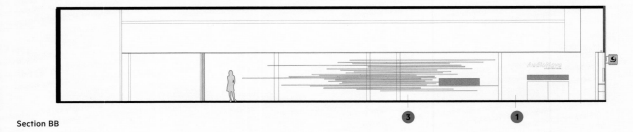

Section BB

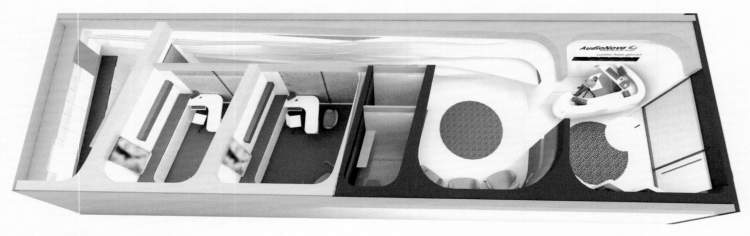

The three-dimensional floor plan shows that fluid
lines have been carried out in every detail: from
room division to furniture.

Waves wall

Side view of wood planks

Top view of wood planks

The concept communicates hygiene and professionalism without being too clinical

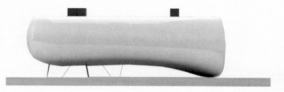

Featuring a reception side and an administrative side, the cash desk has a double function. The reception position is standing, the administrative one is sitting.

CRÈME DE LA CRÈME

by PLAZMA ARCHITECTURE STUDIO

1

WHERE Vilnius, Lithuania WHEN November 2008
CLIENT Alteus DESIGNER Plazma Architecture Studio (p.683)
TOTAL FLOOR AREA 100 m² SHOP CONSTRUCTOR Solid Supply
PHOTOGRAPHER Raimondas Urbakavicius

Fragrance and beauty care boutique Crème de la Crème needed a simple yet exceptional interior for its flagship store in Vilnius. Plazma Architecture Studio answered the brief, the main premise of which stated that a non-standard approach to solutions and functionality was required. The biggest challenge was to reconcile the requirements of a multibrand exposition within the design aesthetics of the project. The concept devised by the team was one of clean lines and calming tones, with a blend of simple shapes and structures which would imbue an organic ambience in the shop. There is a delicate balance between simple architectural forms and elegant designer furniture. The shop is reminiscent of an inviting gallery with the products exhibited against a backdrop of natural materials and a neutral colour

palette. High-gloss black table tops and shelving units on the walls create a stark contrast against the blond wood fixtures. The shipping-crate display island in the centre of the store adds an essence of industrial chic to the sophisticated boutique. Illumination is an important aspect in the design with an array of lighting utilised to highlight the merchandise, including the cluster of designer pendant lampshades at the back of the store, the strip lighting discretely hidden in the display units and the overhead spotlights around the circumference which create interesting shadows, sometimes making it appear as if the shelves are floating.

1 Enhancing the industrial chic look of the store are the cast concrete flooring and custom-designed crate display.
2 A cluster of Tom Dixon's Felt Shades hovers above the product display tables.
3 Three-legged Shell Chairs and a coffee table, all designed by Hans J. Wegner, are placed in the centre of the shop.

DOUGLAS

by SCHWITZKE & PARTNER

1

WHERE Berlin, Germany **WHEN** September 2010
CLIENT Douglas **DESIGNER** Schwitzke & Partner (p.684)
TOTAL FLOOR AREA 730 m² **SHOP CONSTRUCTOR** Koster Ladenbau
PHOTOGRAPHER Oliver Tjaden

Douglas is a global retailer of multibrand fragrances, cosmetics and skin care. The design for its department store on the Tauentzienstrasse in Berlin was the vision of Schwitzke & Partner. The concept was to create a beauty Mecca for people of all ages at this prestigious location, reflecting the vibrant lifestyle of the German capital city within the shop walls. As soon as customers enter the store, they are introduced to the young world of glamour and vitality amid the decorative cosmetics displays, with an air of the city's club and nightlife resonating within the space. A dynamic sea of light and colour welcomes them, with moving LED lights wrapping around from one side wall, up and over the ceiling, and down the other side. The illuminations of the LED belt are reflected in the expanse of mirrored surfaces,

thus connecting the entire cosmetics department with the chromatic flow as well as the solid blocks of bright red and glossy black colours that adorn the walls and floors. Located towards the rear of the ground floor below the red escalator, so as not to obstruct customer flow, is the checkout area with its angular mirror-clad counter, bar stools and neon signage which add further to the nightclub atmosphere. The first floor reflects the calmer side of the city and is decorated with more subdued shades including cool blues and pale yellows. Between the modern product presentations, classic upholstery and antique cabinets are interspersed. The angular counter design is repeated upstairs with either mirrored or neutral panelling applied depending on the individual locations.

1 Cheeky Jeeves & Wooster pendant lights
illuminate the mirror-clad cash desk. In the
background are Tom Dixon's Mirror balls.
2 The bright red colour of the escalator was
chosen as a reference to women's products.
3 Customers can test out the products in the
make-up zone, where LED lights on the walls
and ceiling are arbitrary programmable.

2

A dynamic sea of light and colour reflects the vibrant lifestyle of Berlin

3

EAU DE PARFUM

by INGIBJORG AGNES JONSDOTTIR

1

WHERE Reykjavik, Iceland WHEN July 2010
CLIENT Andrea Maack Parfums DESIGNER Ingibjorg Agnes Jonsdottir (p.679)
TOTAL FLOOR AREA 70 m² SHOP CONSTRUCTOR Gísli Þór Sverrisson
PHOTOGRAPHERS Torfi Agnarsson and Ingvar Högni Ragnarsson

Andrea Maack Parfums is an Icelandic fragrance house that was founded in 2009 by visual artist Andrea Maack, whose visual projects blur the boundaries between art, fashion and consumerism and act as the inspiration for her scents. In the summer of 2010, a temporary retail space popped up in downtown Reykjavik to launch three new fragrances inspired by Maack's pencil drawings and created through collaboration with French perfumery APF. Bridging the layers of creativity, Ingibjorg Agnes Jonsdottir designed the space – as well as the perfume bottles and packaging – according to the client's brief which required a purity of focus linking between art and consumerism. What Jonsdottir wanted was for people to experience a journey when walking around and between the walls in the shop; the challenge was to make customers feel like they were purchasing wearable and affordable art in an exclusive haute couture environment. Three centrally-positioned presentation walls each had openings of different dimensions, allowing customers to get a glimpse of the next display wall, until they reached the third and last one where the scents could be tested. Wrapping around the space were the white exterior walls which had decorative classical mouldings, mirroring the designs on the perfume boxes. The simple yet sculptural walls gave a sense of the clean space of an art gallery, where people were allowed breathing space to make up their mind about the perfumes.

1 Three presentation walls showed the perfume bottles and boxes.
2 Confetti covered the floor, obtained from an old print company that still punches holes manually. The confetti had to be changed every week to maintain a fresh, clean look.
3 Scents could be tested at the third and last presentation wall which had a niche containing paper blotters.
4 The three different scents all had the same embossed packaging.

ANDREA MAACK

2

Customers should feel like they were buying wearable and affordable art

3

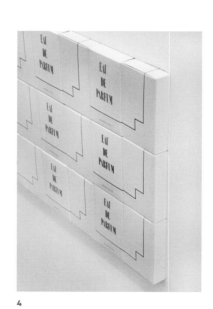

4

ESCENTIALS

by ASYLUM

1

WHERE Singapore, Singapore **WHEN** October 2010
CLIENT Luxasia **DESIGNER** Asylum (p.674)
TOTAL FLOOR AREA 232 m² **SHOP CONSTRUCTOR** DHdeco
PHOTOGRAPHER Lumina Photography (Edwin Tan)

Escentials is a 'cosmeceutical' store which houses niche brands that cater to a new generation of informed and spontaneous customer, demanding something different to fulfil their beauty and wellness needs. With outlets throughout Asia, the new retail store in Singapore required a qualitative and selective style. The concept for the shop created by Asylum was one akin to walking into a stylish Parisian apartment, characterised by elegance and tinged with chic-ness. With a classic black and white colour scheme, the design was executed in such a way to emphasise the need for experiential shopping. With unique atmospheres created for the different sections of the store, customers can enter the consultation area and have a feeling of walking into someone's living room with its luxurious furniture to relax upon. There is a patio-like area with whimsical stands highlighting new product arrivals, a library that acts as a make-up room, a dining room for delectable skincare products and even a greenhouse where the fragrant range of fragrances are displayed. Different textures – such as white-washed wood, mosaic tiles and wallpaper with monochromatic designs – are juxtaposed together to create distinct characters for each of the spaces. Carefully-selected furniture serves as a distinctive platform for the display of products. The white woodwork cabinets in different shapes and patterns create a clean backdrop for the products, with their different hues adding a splash colour to the space.

1 In the store's entrance area, a black-and-white mosaic mimics a carpet underneath the customised table that displays new product arrivals.
2 Fragrances are displayed in the shop's greenhouse area.
3 Marcel Wander's Zeppelin lamp is suspended from the ceiling of the living room where customers can discover the full range of cosmetics.

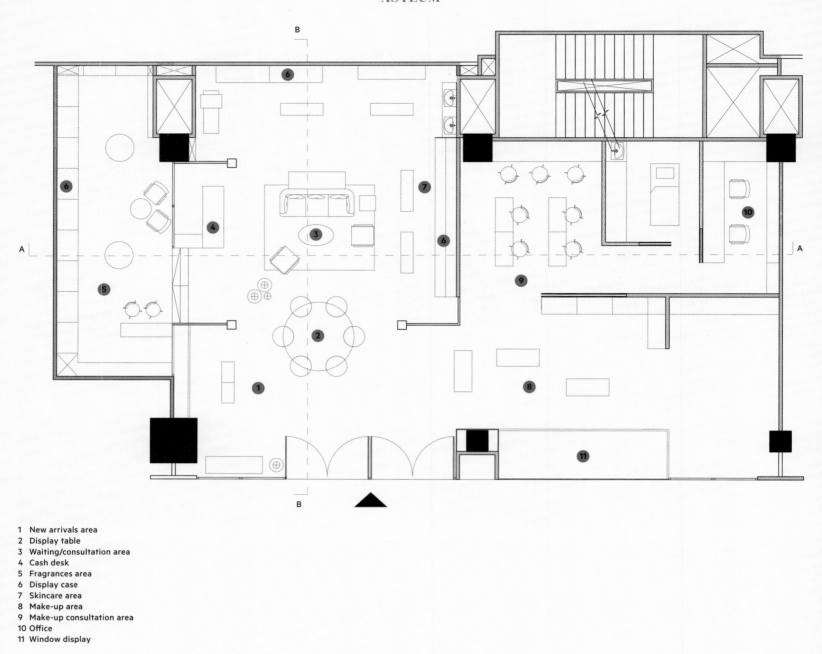

B

A ——————— A

B

1 New arrivals area
2 Display table
3 Waiting/consultation area
4 Cash desk
5 Fragrances area
6 Display case
7 Skincare area
8 Make-up area
9 Make-up consultation area
10 Office
11 Window display

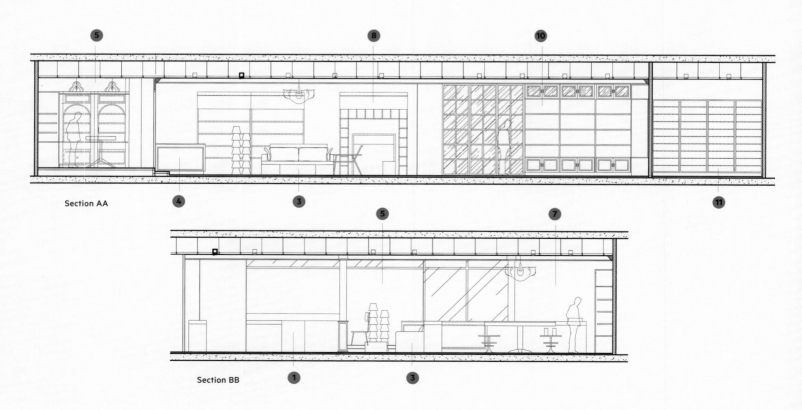

Section AA

Section BB

The three-dimensional floor plan clearly shows the apartment concept of the store which facilitates experiential shopping.

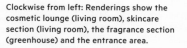

The concept was a stylish Parisian apartment characterised by chic elegance

Clockwise from left: Renderings show the cosmetic lounge (living room), skincare section (living room), the fragrance section (greenhouse) and the entrance area.

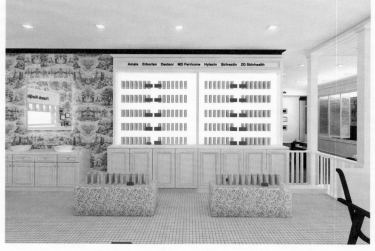

LOGONA & FRIENDS

by ITO MASARU DESIGN PROJECT/SEI

1

WHERE Tokyo, Japan **WHEN** November 2009
CLIENT Logona Japan **DESIGNER** Ito Masura Design Project/SEI (p.680)
TOTAL FLOOR AREA 132 m² **SHOP CONSTRUCTOR** Hearts
PHOTOGRAPHER Kozo Takayama

The German cosmetic brand Logona has natural and organic products at the core of its global business. When the brand's first shop was opened in Tokyo, Ito Masaru and his team were responsible for the interior design. The location of the shop was to be in Omotesando, in the centre of the fashion district. Even though this is an 'architectural showcase' area of Tokyo, featuring a multitude of fashion flagship stores within a short distance of each other, the Logona store is on a pedestrian side street with few tall buildings and lots of green space and sunlight. The design team wanted the relaxed atmosphere of the neighbourhood to flow right into the heart of the store also. The concept for the shop is natural and organic, mirroring the brand aesthetic of Logona. Great importance was put on simplicity

and quality in the design, using distinct textures that customers would never get tired of. An earthy colour palette of dark moss green and slate grey was used, along with natural materials such as iron and stone, marble tabletops, waxed wood floorboards and exposed concrete walls and ceiling. The space is divided up with merchandise displayed at the front of the shop, with feature displays in the centre and around the edge, walls lined with glass-encased cabinets. At the back is a seating area and consultation space, with the basement treatment rooms accessed from a side entrance.

1 The existing exterior is left untouched;
   the designers simply used a canopy as a
   name-board, which simultaneously offers
   protection from afternoon sunlight.
2 The brand's philosophy is carried through in
   the interior design by using natural
   materials such as wood, concrete and steels
   as much as possible.
3 View of the kitchen and consultation area in
   the back of the shop. This space is also used
   for seminars about macrobiotics.

2

3

The relaxed
atmosphere of the
neighbourhood
flows right into the
heart of the store

Basement

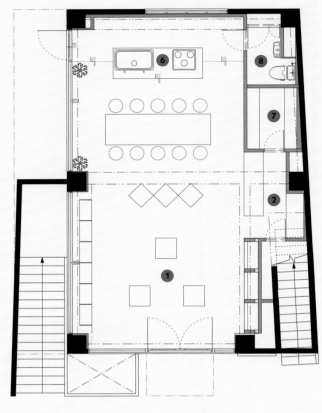

Ground floor

1 Retail area
2 Cash desk
3 Reception
4 Treatment room
5 Staff room
6 Kitchen
7 Storage
8 Lavatory

Sketch of the shop front showing the stairs
leading to the treatment rooms at the
basement level.

Renderings of the retail area on the ground floor. The wooden herringbone floor was chosen to give the space a warm atmosphere.

The concept is natural and organic, mirroring the brand aesthetic

Sketch of the reception area in the basement which gives access to four treatment rooms.

LUNASOL

by TONERICO

▲

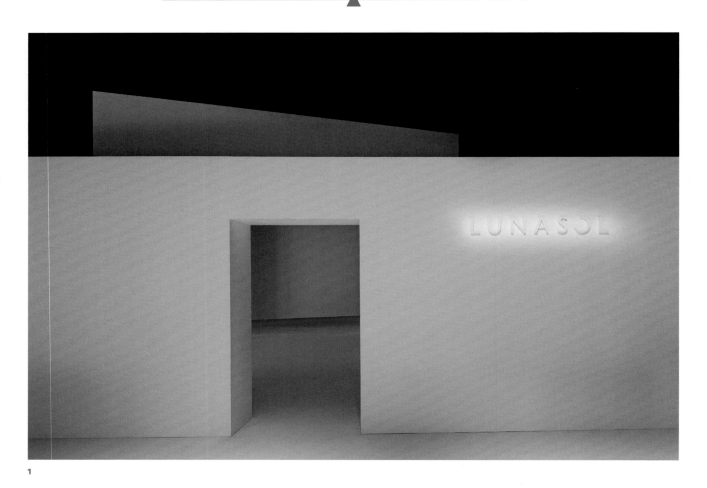

1

WHERE Tokyo, Japan WHEN November 2010
CLIENT Kanebo Cosmetics DESIGNER Tonerico (p.686)
TOTAL FLOOR AREA 290 m² SHOP CONSTRUCTOR D-9
PHOTOGRAPHER Kazutaka Fujimoto

When Japanese beauty brand Kanebo wanted a temporary retail space for the launch of its 2011 Lunasol cosmetics collection, Tonerico was commissioned to realise this transitory venture, which was *in situ* for a fleeting 24 hours. The Lunasol brand concept is linked to the sun and the moon, both of which have an effect on tidal flow and it is the splendour of the transitioning ocean that inspired the design team. Aiming for an ephemeral and formless mood in the space, a serene and surreal atmosphere was summoned. A key aspect was to visualise and emphasise the beauty of light shining through water. In a gesture of great clarity and magical moodiness, Tonerico used a minimum of materials to eschew narrative and enhance brand focus, creating a luminous environment decorated with white needle-punched carpeting and walls clad in paper-based fabric. Central to the design is a floating abstract cube, bathed in shifting shades of blue light that changed throughout the day. With its suspended white walls, it is as if its structure weightlessly floats deep in the ocean in the waves of light. A solitary, sleek display counter positioned within one wall enticed customers towards their first interaction with the products and, further on, they were encouraged to learn about and try the products at round tables in the 'touch-up space'. The softly-lit architecture allowed a minimum of products to be displayed in a sparse presentation, bringing each item into focus by doing away with the clutter common to department-store cosmetics counters.

1 Simplicity and serenity was the essence of the silent space.
2 The architecture of the showroom had an air of weightlessness. Central to the design was a floating abstract, archetypal form of a house, intended to give visitors a feeling of surprise and delight.
3 Products were displayed on a narrow ledge.

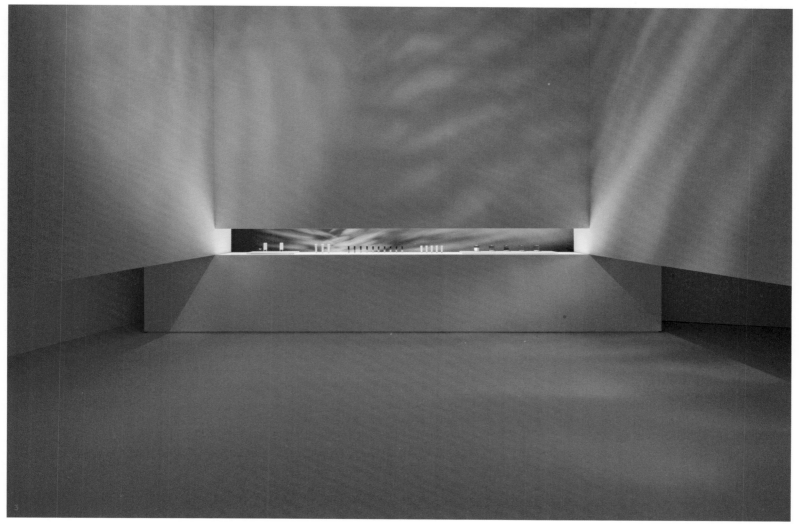

4

A key aspect was to visualise and emphas
the beauty of light shining through wate

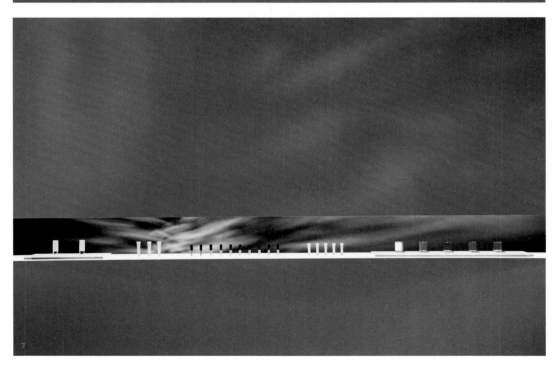

4 View from the presentation area to the
   touch-up area where customers were invited
   to try Lunasol products at round tables in a
   spacious white environment.
5 Entrance to the product exhibition space.
6 All the surfaces were bathed in shades of
   blue light that changed during the day. This
   particular colour of blue is called *mizu-iro* in
   Japanese, meaning 'the colour of water'.
7 The products were showcased at a lower
   point of view. By illuminating them from
   behind, the designers created a strong
   visual impact. The lighting design was done
   by Yuko Yamashita of Y2 Lighting.

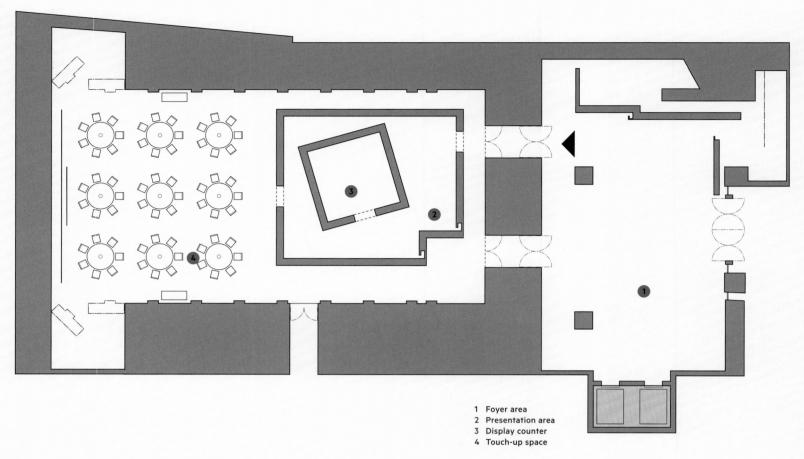

1 Foyer area
2 Presentation area
3 Display counter
4 Touch-up space

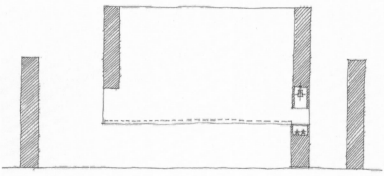

Sketch of the floating cube in the presentation
area indicating the position of the products.

The Lunasol brand concept links to the sun and the moon

Rendering showing the view from the presentation
area into the cube with the product display.

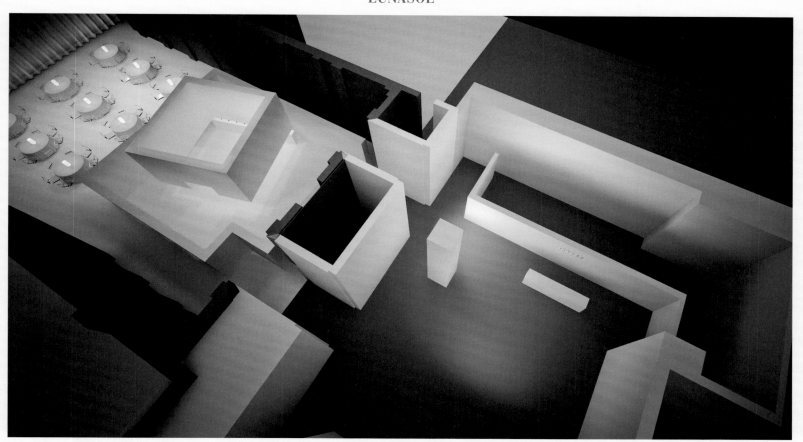

Three-dimensional floor plan.

Renderings proposing the lighting effects for the presentation area. The dappled light gave visitors a sense of sun-kissed ripples of water.

MINATO PHARMACY

by KEISUKE FUJIWARA

1

WHERE Tokyo, Japan WHEN August 2010
CLIENT Minato Yakuhin DESIGNER Keisuke Fujiwara (p.680)
TOTAL FLOOR AREA 37.5 m² SHOP CONSTRUCTOR YS Kobo
PHOTOGRAPHER Satoshi Asakawa

Five years after its flagship store was established in Tokyo, the pharmacy chain Minato looked to renew its brand presence with a second store in the Japanese capital. The design of the shop was executed by Keisuke Fujiwara and his team utilising one primary decorative material – Japanese ash – which interweaves a natural essence into the interior space. The entire length of one side wall is decorated with a complex myriad of stacked wooden boxes which are fused together, morphing into a floating seating element towards the rear of the store. This bespoke shelving system introduces a three-dimensional spatial quality into the shop design and allows diverse product display options. Some shelves are fitted with lighting panels to highlight the geometrical patterns and others are fitted with steel back panels to be used as magnetic information boards. In stark contrast to the angular elements of the display wall is the organically-shaped counter which includes a sweeping circular surface at one end. The ceiling is covered with ash-effect wallpaper apart from one white recessed aspect which is illuminated with indirect lighting to give an impression of a higher and bigger space. Incorporating an essence of the brand into the shop, porcelain tiles in corporate hues have been fitted in a randomised pattern behind the cash desk. The design team chose this contemporary eye-catching aspect for the internal elevation in order to accommodate the client's requirement of introducing a subtle brand identity into each shop so that such design aspects could be easily translated in other stores.

1 The round-shaped counter contrasts with the angular shelves.
2 Shape and depth variety of the boxes allow the pharmacy staff to display the products in a flexible way.
3 The box-shaped shelves provide a strong three-dimensional impression in the space.

2

Japanese ash interweaves a natural essence into the space

3

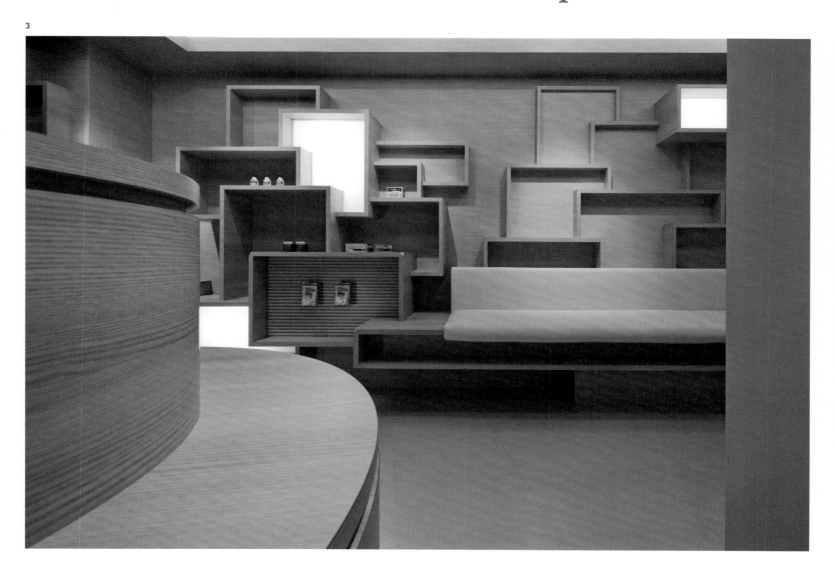

OKINAHA

by COAST AND AS BUILT ARCHITECTS

▲

2

WHERE Waterloo, Belgium WHEN December 2009
CLIENT Jean Rousseau DESIGNERS Coast (p.676) and As Built Architects (p.673)
TOTAL FLOOR AREA 150 m² SHOP CONSTRUCTOR As Built Architects
PHOTOGRAPHER Serge Anton

The sale of anti-ageing products is a lucrative global business. When a new commercial territory in this field was recently established in Belgium, Coast was commissioned to establish the new anti-ageing brand and retail space. The brief from the client was simple: create an environment of wellness. The store name Okinaha originated from a concept based on the vision of longevity and purity with a strong influence coming from Okinawa, the Japanese island where individuals live longer than anywhere in the world. From the brand identity to the realisation of the first concept store, the Coast team was inspired by luxurious purity and oriental simplicity, creating for the customer a relaxed atmosphere for their health-related shopping experience. The interior was designed in collaboration with As Built Architects to have three distinct zones: a central spatial aspect for special retail presentations, the library of books displayed in a cosy wood-lined niche at the back of store and the awe-inspiring forest of trees. The space is almost entirely white apart from the sleek black counters and the products lining the walls adding a splash of colour. The minimalist approach to the design ensures the impact of its nod to nature. Positioning the five imposing tree trunks at the front of the store in the double-height ceiling space creates a memorable aspect not only within the store but also from the street through the glass-fronted facade.

1 Coast's creative model includes brand elements such as the 'rising sun' as a graphic logo.
2 The forest area is clearly visible from the outside. Five large tree trunks are placed in the store, representing longevity.

3

The minimalist approach to the design ensures the impact of its nod to nature

4

3 One wall in the store is completely dedicated to nutriments with integrated shelves, cabinets and a fridge.
4 The central 'chimney' area acts as a focal point and is where special retail actions take place.
5 In the back of the store is the library, clad in wood and with black flooring it is visually separated from the rest of the space.

YOU

by KONCEPT STOCKHOLM

1

WHERE Stockholm, Sweden WHEN August 2010
CLIENT Concept You DESIGNER Koncept Stockholm (p.680)
TOTAL FLOOR AREA 180 m² SHOP CONSTRUCTOR –
PHOTOGRAPHER Jörgen Ahlström

When hair stylist Steve Terry was looking to open a new salon in central Stockhom, Koncept was commissioned to answer the brief. What was required was a highly professional design that was sure to put a smile on the customers' faces. The resulting outcome is a salon, named You, which is luxurious whilst at the same time has a fun, rock-and-roll feel. The customer is the focus of the concept, with personal messages adorning the walls, floors and fixtures making it clear that, 'This is about you'. The interior has rough concrete walls which are in stark contrast to the polished dark-wood furnishings which proliferate the front part of the shop. Towards the back, white wood panelling and high-gloss tiles are utilised to distinguish the distinct areas of the salon. To maximise the space available, the ceiling heights have been raised and skylights added to ensure daylight floods the shop. Classic shelving elements are incorporated to ensure product displays are immediately evident to customers as they enter, with light-hearted aspects coming from the slogans which are graphically positioned around the space. These phrases – which all incorporate the word 'you' – are included in different type-faces on the floors, packaging, walls and even on flight cases which are quirkily used as storage spaces.

1 When entering the hair studio, visitors first encounter the retail area.
2 Bringing a smile to people's faces are quirky details such as plastic ice cream cones and a vintage typewriter.
3 The wooden floor from Kährs is partly decorated with stencilled graphics.
4 Flight cases are used as cabinets in the store when they are not taken on a journey or used at an event.

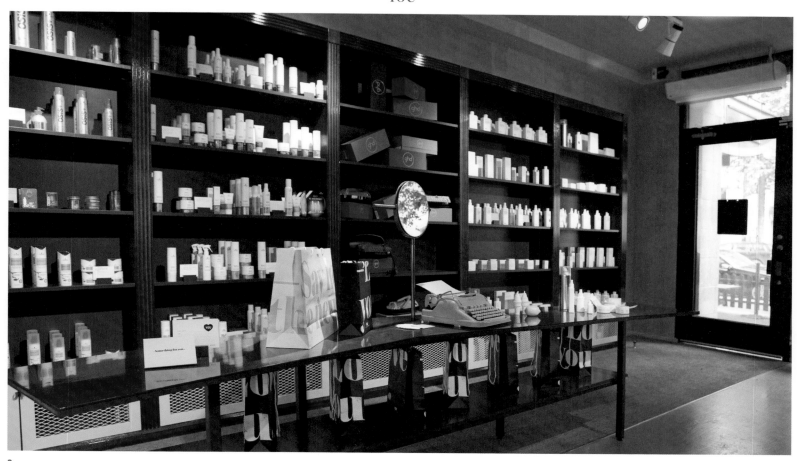

2

The design makes it clear that 'This is about you'

3

4

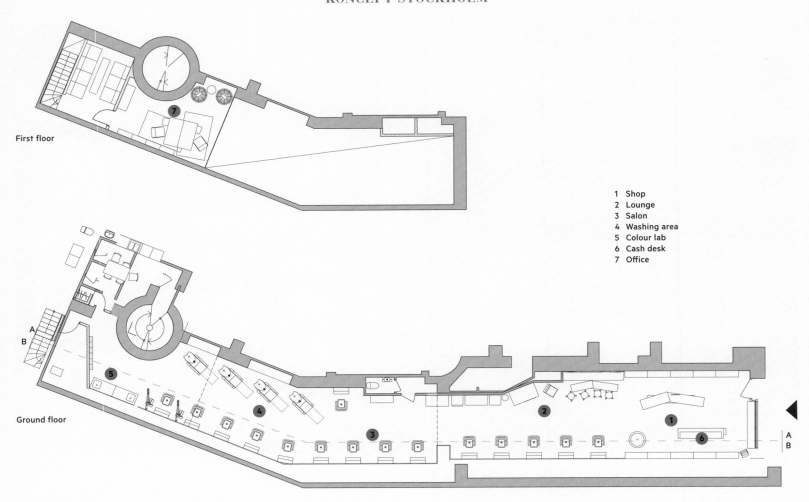

First floor

Ground floor

1 Shop
2 Lounge
3 Salon
4 Washing area
5 Colour lab
6 Cash desk
7 Office

'It's all about you' is the retail concept. Notes and other objects communicating this message are found all over the store.

A large quote that reads 'Everybody loves you' was drawn on a fully-tiled wall.

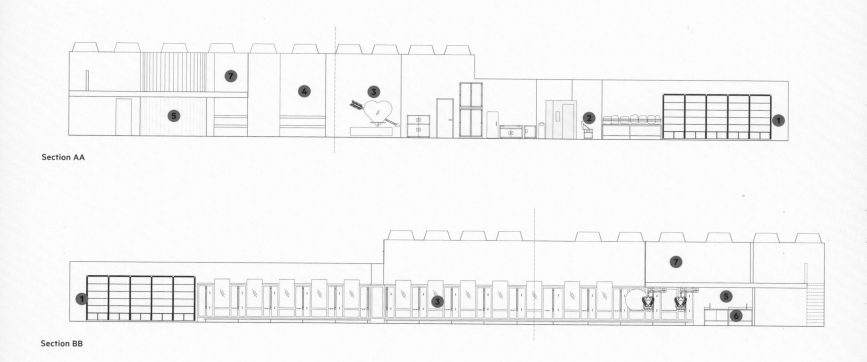

Section AA

Section BB

The client required a design that was highly professional but would put a smile on people's faces

The graphic design was also part of the assigment.

BOOKS
AND
MUSIC

148

OKS
ND
SIC

149

KIOSKOOL

by RÄL 167 AND SUMA+ESPACIO

★

1

WHERE Villalba, Spain WHEN March 2009
CLIENT Miguel and Jose Ignacio DESIGNERS Räl 167 (p.684) and Suma+Espacio (p.686)
TOTAL FLOOR AREA 200 m² SHOP CONSTRUCTOR Guardacantones
PHOTOGRAPHERS Yuri Pol and Ana Muller

In a small town, north west of Madrid, the owners of a newsagents and tobacconist realised the stagnation prevailing in the industry and decided to give their shop a facelift with the help of a group of young designers. The client brief was to re-evaluate the outdated concept of a tobacconists and create an establishment where the products are displayed as if they were precious jewels. The request was clear: to generate expectation, surprise, culminating in a final concept that is as far away as possible from what is conventionally understood as a business which sells cigarettes and newspapers. For the design team, inspiration came from lines of tobacco leaves, sinuous dancing smoke and the angular folds of newspapers. A black and white colour palette has been employed, with defined lines and glossy materials. The morphology of the internal space resembles two large twinned boxes, one with double height near the entrance where an architectural metaphor of swirling smoke is installed overhead. Aspects of this eye-catching structure extend and merge with parallel white lines on the walls which combine with overlapping planes to form the woodwork niches behind the cash desk. Such elements help to create a visual coherence within the space. Illumination is used as an important design aspect in its own right which subtly emphasizes the products and further enhances the gallery-like atmosphere of the store.

1 The shape of zigzagging newspaper stands was inspired by the folds of a newspaper.
2 The HLF light by Dab was selected for its resemblance with cigarette smoke.

3

The brief was to re-evaluate the outdated concept of a tobacconists

4

3 Since more than 500 customers visit the shop daily, the strength of materials used was paramount. The floor's finishing is an epoxy resin suitable for high traffic.
4 Morphology of the internal space resembles two large twinned boxes, though each has its own aesthetic and function.
5 Clear lines, simple shades and limited ornamental elements combine for a clean and luxurious atmosphere that's unique in a tobacco store.

5

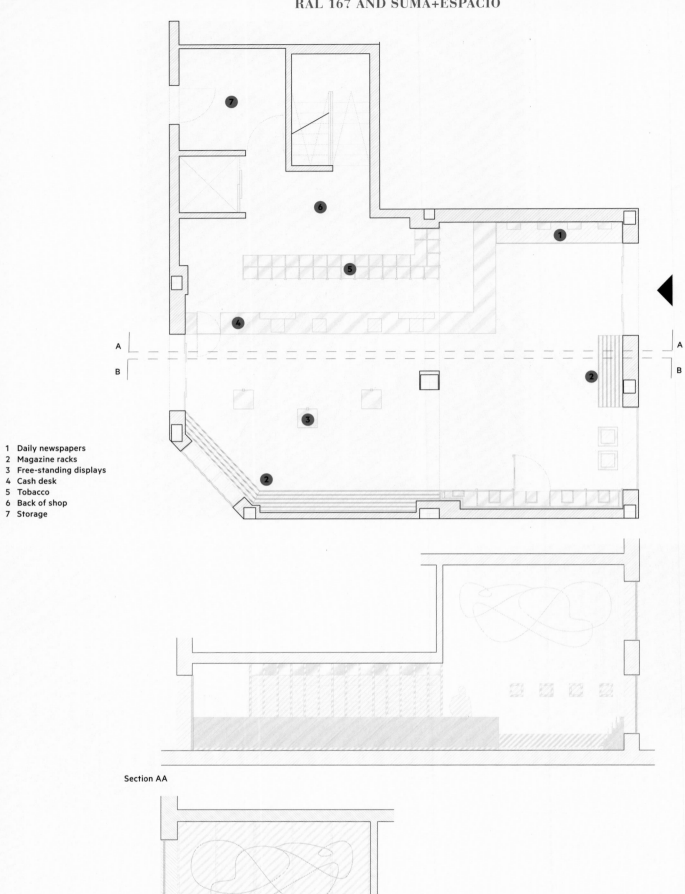

1 Daily newspapers
2 Magazine racks
3 Free-standing displays
4 Cash desk
5 Tobacco
6 Back of shop
7 Storage

Section AA

Section BB

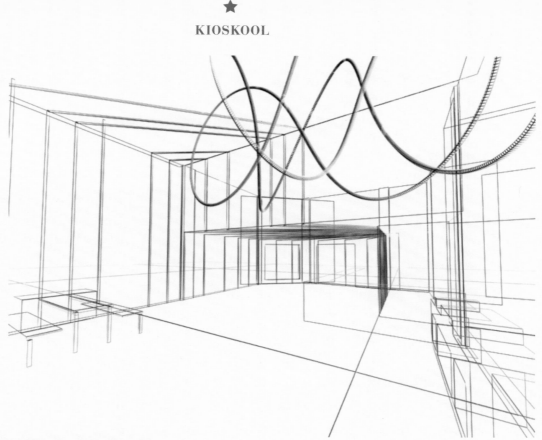

Sketches showing the lines springing from the cigarette display
behind the counter, running over the ceiling and down the walls;
a reference to lines on a tobacco leaf.

An architectural metaphor of swirling smoke is installed overhead

KUBRICK BOOKSHOP

by ONE PLUS PARTNERSHIP

★

1

WHERE Beijing, China WHEN January 2010
CLIENT Broadway Cinema China DESIGNER One Plus Partnership (p.682)
TOTAL FLOOR AREA 855 m² SHOP CONSTRUCTOR Design Delta
PHOTOGRAPHERS Ajax Law Ling Kit and Virginia Lung

In the Dongzhimen neigbourhood, adjacent to one of the gates of the of ancient city wall of Beijing, is the modern architectural landmark by Steven Holl, the Linked Hybrid complex. This 'contemporary celestial city' has eight residential towers, urban green spaces and a commercial zone on the ground floor which includes a cinema. Multifaceted spatial layers are defined by geometric buildings which are interconnected with elevated bridges creating a unique skyline feature. Alongside the MOMA Movie Centre is the Kubrick Bookshop, designed by Ajax Law Ling Kit and Virginia Lung of One Plus Partnership, which captures and combines the sensual stimuli of the exterior aspects of the building complex within the store. The space is divided between the movie bookshop on the ground floor and the information centre and library on the first

and second floor. A key aspect of the interior design is the random jumble of green box-like cabinets scattered throughout. Positioned against the grey concrete backdrop of the space, the custom made, bright green cabinets serve as bookshelves, cash desks, counters and storage. Overhead is an eye-catching installation of pendant lights which fills almost the entire ceiling space. The radial webs of electric cables not only respond to the shop's colour scheme but also as act a visual link between the old and new; localising the modern design of the shop with their appearance, the cables are also reminiscent of electric poles with their trailing wires which appear all over the old alleys of Beijing.

1 The cash desk near the entrance is constructed from the same bright green woodwork used for display cabinets.
2 Behind the cash desk, two screens integrated in a white wall show video clips related to movies playing at the cinema.
3 Webs of green electrical cords are spread throughout the entire shop space, forming a large light installation.
4 The LIB counter is a combination of cash desk, information and membership counter.

PROLOGUE

by MINISTRY OF DESIGN

★

2

WHERE Singapore, Singapore WHEN December 2009
CLIENT Popular Book Co. DESIGNER Ministry of Design (p.682)
TOTAL FLOOR AREA 1550 m² SHOP CONSTRUCTOR Design Delta
PHOTOGRAPHER Edward Henricks

The Popular Book Co. is a publisher based in Singapore with a large network of bookstores, specialising in English and Chinese books at affordable prices. The location of Prologue – its first foray into the higher-end market focused on a more lifestyle-oriented audience – is the ION Orchard, Singapore's premier luxury shopping mall. Ministry of Design is responsible for the shop's concept which redefines and updates the conventional bookstore experience. With its goal to 'question, disturb and redefine', the team focused on establishing a clear spatial hierarchy together with good visual zoning for distinct book categories allowing an ease of navigation for customers. Also key was to incorporate contemporary window and store displays, taking inspiration from fashion retail. In the design, a dynamic public element was incorporated via a vibrant cafe setting. Way-finding is prioritised with the colour-coded central spine that organises all the secondary zones and spaces. Curving sinuously through the black backdrop of the shop, the spine begins at the entry window display, continuing through the core of the space and culminating at the cafe and sculptural stairway leading to the store's stationery section. The entry zone has been defamiliarised by the creation of an installation art display starring a Godzilla-inspired creature unpacking books amongst towering piles of cardboard boxes which evolve into a cityscape of books as the customer enters the store.

1 To enhance visual distinction, each book zone is crowned with a colour-coded perforated metal canopy.
2 At the entrance, boxes of books are unpacked by a dinosaur in an installation that's reminiscent of Godzilla stampeding through New York's cityscape.

3

A colour-coded 'spine' curves throughout the space, indicating the various book categories

3 A cafe is located behind the bright red
   stairs which lead to the second level of
   the book store.
4 Experienced as a collective, the eight
   canopies create a dynamic ceiling-scape
   and clearly guide customers from one zone
   to another.
5 The flooring plays a significant role in
   the communication and identification of
   different zones.

RIJKSMUSEUM SHOP

by UXUS

★

1

WHERE Amsterdam Schiphol Airport, the Netherlands **WHEN** September 2010
CLIENT World of Delights **DESIGNER** Uxus (p.686)
TOTAL FLOOR AREA 161 m² **SHOP CONSTRUCTOR** Valk
PHOTOGRAPHER Dim Balsem

Schiphol Airport in Amsterdam handles between 100,000 and 150,000 passengers per day, making the airport terminal is a perfect conduit by which to communicate with its high-traffic audience. Uxus was commissioned to create a shopping destination and cultural experience to attract travellers at the airport wanting a taste of Dutch art and design. The shop is a new and innovative retail experience for Holland's premiere fine art museum, the Rijksmuseum. The interior has been conceived as a physical time line of creativity from the 'Golden Age' of Dutch masterpieces to the 'Concept Age' of contemporary Dutch design. This timeline is physically represented in the shop's design to help navigation through the diverse product range, which includes books and paintings to glassware and ceramics. The colour scheme also links to the

concept, with customers being able to literally take a step through time, starting with the golden hues of the 17th century artworks to the silvery metallic tones of the contemporary design zone. In addition to the timeline, a three-dimensional representation of Vermeer's masterpiece, *The Milkmaid*, as well as a reproduced self-portrait of Rembrandt attract the attention of passers-by, giving visitors to the airport an unexpected and exciting one-off photo opportunity, enabling them to experience some Dutch treasures without even stepping out of the airport.

1 A cut-out of Vermeer's *The Milkmaid* offers travellers a great photo opportunity.
2 Store fittings suspended from glass create a floating and translucent effect.
3 Images of Frans Hal's *Marriage Portrait* and Vermeer's *The Milkmaid* are printed on perforated steel and decorate the exterior of the shop.
4 Overview of the shop as seen from the 'Golden Age' section.

2

3

The interior has been conceived as a physical timeline of creativity

4

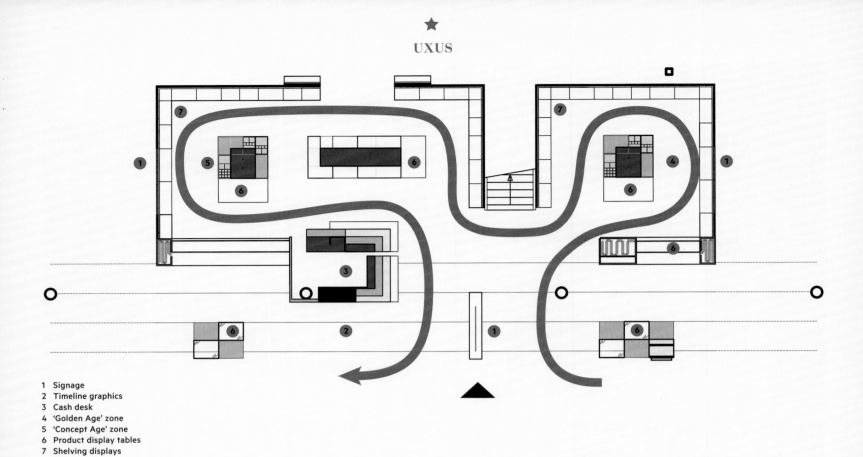

1 Signage
2 Timeline graphics
3 Cash desk
4 'Golden Age' zone
5 'Concept Age' zone
6 Product display tables
7 Shelving displays

The colour scheme helps navigation through the diverse product range

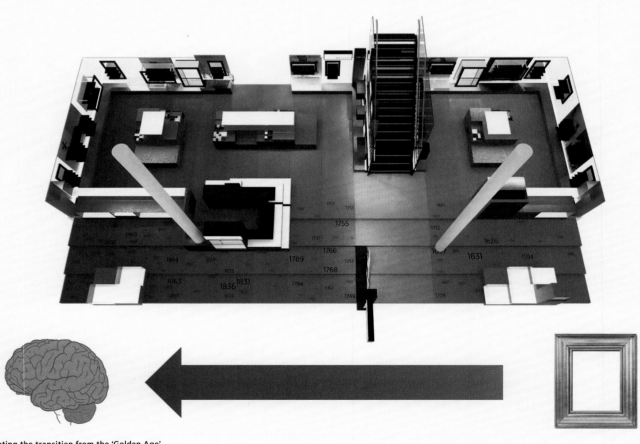

Rendering illustrating the transition from the 'Golden Age' in golden hues to the 'Concept Age' in grey.

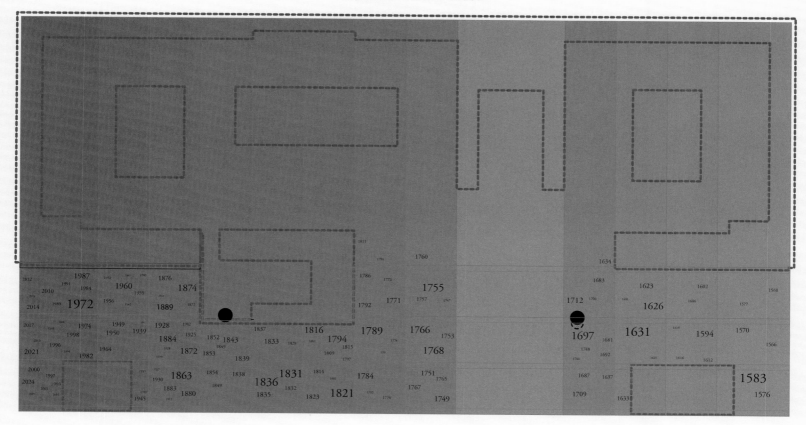

Drawing of the timeline carpet, also indicating the placement
of furniture.

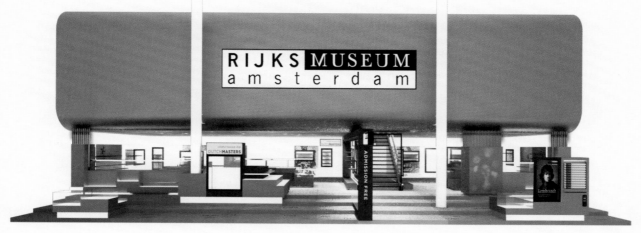

Rendering of the facade.

Whimsical signage featuring a Rembrandt self-portrait denotes
the location of the Rijksmuseum shop along the travellator.

SELEXYZ DEKKER

by MERKX+GIROD ARCHITECTS

★

1

WHERE Arnhem, the Netherlands WHEN October 2010
CLIENT BGN/selexyz boekhandels DESIGNER Merkx+Girod Architects (p.682)
TOTAL FLOOR AREA 1240 m² SHOP CONSTRUCTOR Keijsers Interior Projects
PHOTOGRAPHER Roos Aldershoff

With branches in 14 Dutch cities, selexyz is one of the larger bookstore chains in the Netherlands. The company aims to position its shops in special or monumental buildings and when the opportunity came to acquire the old post office (ca. 1890) right in the centre of Arnhem, Merkx+Girod architects was commissioned to undertake the transformation of the interior. The building has many grand aspects, such as extra high ceilings, monumental facades and original features. In designing the store, the team considered these characterful qualities of the building whilst coherently integrating the new corporate style into the space. The primary challenge was to create a clear directionality for customers when it came to moving around and between both levels of the store. The escalators become a focal point, with a curved timber-lined aspect overhead, emphasising the ceiling height on the first floor. In places, the original structure of the building is left uncovered with ceiling conduits being visible overhead. The furniture and fittings used in the interior follow the design previously developed for other selexyz shops, with some modifications to adapt to the building's features. A key aspect in this store is the design of the book display systems to accommodate the many windows which perforate the facade. The solution includes an integrated shelving system around the edge of the space which appears to be embedded within the wall itself.

1 A freestanding unit built around the escalators offers the necessary amount of shelving space.
2 Names of writers are used as graphics on escalator walls.
3 Freestanding modular display elements were modelled after furniture designs used in other selexyz shops.

4

The company aims to position its shops in special or monumental buildings

5

4 Computers in the space's centre invite
customers to place an order and have it
delivered to their home the next day.
5 From the escalator, narrow windows offer
views into the retail area.
6 A custom-made display system is embedded
in walls between windows, optimising
available space.

6

SECTIONS

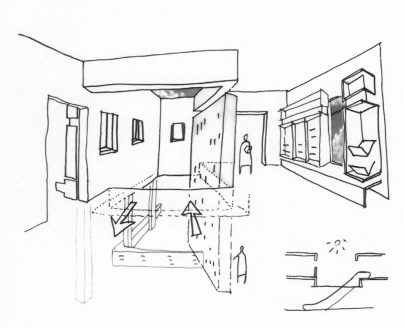

Preliminary daylight study of the first floor.

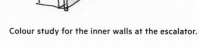

Colour study for the inner walls at the escalator.

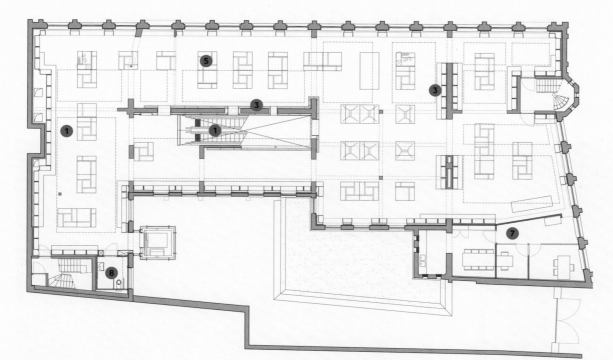

First floor

1 Escalator
2 Cash desks
3 Shelving displays
4 Multimedia zone
5 Table displays
6 Cafe area
7 Offices
8 Lavatory

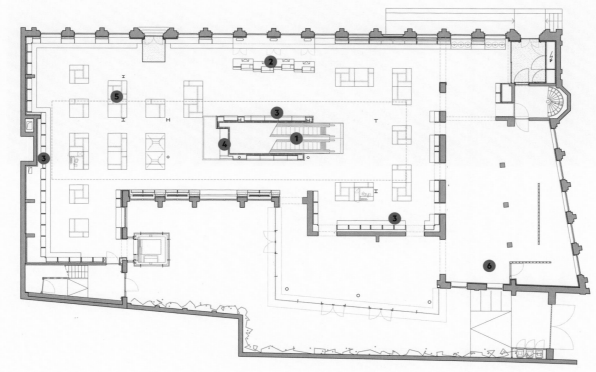

Ground floor

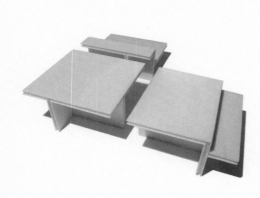

Model of display tables with three levels.

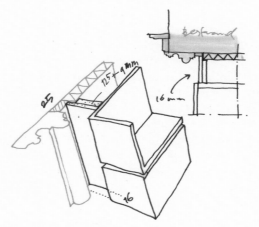

Sketch showing the integration of bookshelves
in the historic window frames.

SORAYUMEBAKO

by KRÄF•TE

———————————— ★ ————————————

1

WHERE Osaka, Japan WHEN November 2010
CLIENT Ken Nakahashi DESIGNER kräf•te (p.681)
TOTAL FLOOR AREA 43 m² SHOP CONSTRUCTOR Up Life
PHOTOGRAPHER Kiyotoshi Takashima

A unique space in a residential neighbourhood of Osaka, well away from the busy commercial centre, was commissioned of the studio of Yukio Kimura in 2010. The design was specifically conceived so as not to blend in with the surroundings, following the client's wish to reflect the meaning of the shop's name – Sorayumebako – in the actual design. In Japanese, *sorayume* means 'a fabricated dream' and so a place was realised that would make the locals wonder, did I just dream that? An other-worldly environment was created that was entirely orange; orange floors, walls, ceiling, furniture and fittings. Experiencing such a monochromatic interior can have a disorienting, dream-like quality as form and function are dematerialised and structures become unreal. The retail space can take on many guises, from bookstore to gallery to cafe, perhaps shifting on a daily basis. One thing that does not change is the vibrant colour, which was selected as it interprets the time between day and night, summer and winter, and yin and yang. The second part of the shop name, *bako* (the variant form of *hako*), means 'a box'. The shop is a box of delights of second-hand novels and unique artworks, displayed within a series of portal frames along the side walls. The only non-orange material in the shop is the mirrored table-top positioned in the centre of the room which forms striking visual reflections.

1 A box-like structure within the store incorporates bookshelves, tables, exhibition panels and projection panels, making the space suitable for various functions.
2 Customers can find second-hand books and unique art works in the store.
3 Only one colour was used throughout the entire interior, resulting in a disorienting, dream-like atmosphere.

STND/OHWOW

by ARCHITECTURE AT LARGE/RAFAEL DE CÁRDENAS

★

1

WHERE Miami Beach, United States WHEN December 2010
CLIENT OHWOW DESIGNER Architecture at Large/Rafael de Cárdenas (p.673)
TOTAL FLOOR AREA 21 m² SHOP CONSTRUCTORS Architecture at Large, CKA Construction Group,
Emmett Moore and Larry Newberry PHOTOGRAPHER floto+warner

OHWOW is a gallery, publisher and purveyor of special projects, all of which is fuelled by a creative community. A recent addition to its portfolio is a retail presence, with its first store opening in New York in early 2010. The design vision behind the store interior came from Rafael de Cárdenas whose team has now also designed the latest store, inside The Standard Spa Miami Beach. The shop sells a selection of specially curated products including exclusive art books and a range of accessories and other essentials which will catch the attention of the hotel guests. A minty fresh palette of glossy white and hints of turquoise permeates throughout the space, interrupted by the signature graphic stripes of Architecture at Large. Dramatic edges are incorporated into the space with its recessed pyramidal wedges and glass-top black

triangular columns that serve as impactful product pedestals. The display island in the centre of the store and the shelves which line the walls are constructed from enamelled plywood. Other materials used to decorate the interior include glass vitrines, terrazzo flooring and mirrored surfaces. The sci-fi-meets-art-deco vibe of the shop complements well with the holistic and relaxed atmosphere of the hotel and cultivates an artistic air which means the space is an ideal backdrop for book signings and events.

1 A terrazzo floor is laid throughout the space.
2 The shelves hold a selection of hotel guests' bare necessities – cotton swabs and toothpaste – plus products designed by a community of artists.

The space is an ideal backdrop for book signings and events

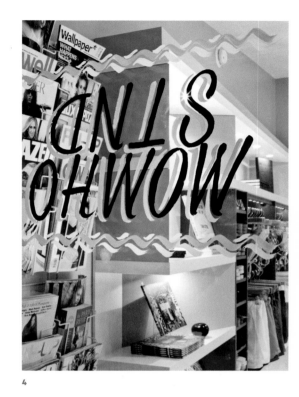

3 Triangular columns display jewellery below
   a glass top.
4 The store is located in The Standard Spa
   Miami Beach.
5 Books published by OHWOW are presented
   on the central display element.

VAN GOGH MUSEUM SHOP

by DAY

★

1

WHERE Amsterdam, the Netherlands WHEN September 2009
CLIENT Van Gogh Museum Enterprises DESIGNER Day (p.677)
TOTAL FLOOR AREA 550 m² SHOP CONSTRUCTOR Harmeling Interieurconcepten
PHOTOGRAPHER Jeroen Musch

The Van Gogh Museum in Amsterdam houses the largest collection of Van Gogh's paintings and drawings in the world. It was designed by Dutch architect Gerrit Rietveld in the early 1960s. As well as featuring the work of Van Gogh's contemporaries and other 19th century art, the museum has a shop selling an extensive range of books and merchandise relating to the permanent and temporary exhibitions. In order to ensure the shop reflected the international reputation of the museum, the design team at Day was brought on board to realise a redesign in 2009. Day's main requirements for the revitalised space was that the building's monumental status needed to be taken into consideration within an environmental design. Inspiration came from the building's original architect, with the concept for the new shop taking Rietveld's architectural grid and guidelines as the starting point. The main focus is a staircase-shaped iconic object in the centre of the store, with its domineering structural form which appears to float within the space whilst at the same time integrates into the building. The staggered white structure acts as a focal point and a product display system, allowing the colourful products to shine 'on stage'. The surrounding interior elements of integrated, elongated display systems and a cash desk, provide a dramatic contrast, utilising materials such as black coated wood and black stone floor tiles.

1 The focal point is a white corian display element with two mirrored staircase-like structures.
2 To avoid obstructing customer flow, the cash desk was placed in the centre of the space next to the display structure.
3 The museum is receiving more visitors than ever planned, therefore the redesign needed to create spaces for accommodating large groups of people.

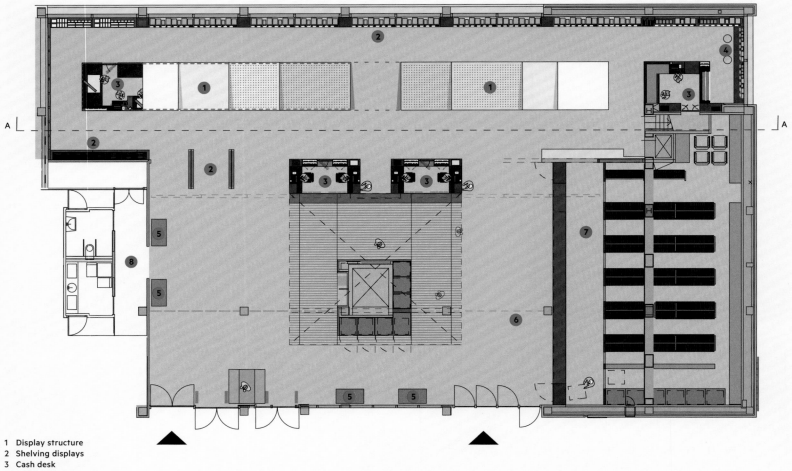

1 Display structure
2 Shelving displays
3 Cash desk
4 Reading desk
5 Seating
6 Rolling shutter
7 Museum cloakroom
8 Lavatories

Section AA

Rietveld's architectural grid and guide lines were the starting point for the design

MAIN DISPLAY STRUCTURE

Side view

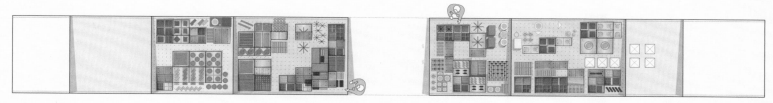

Top view

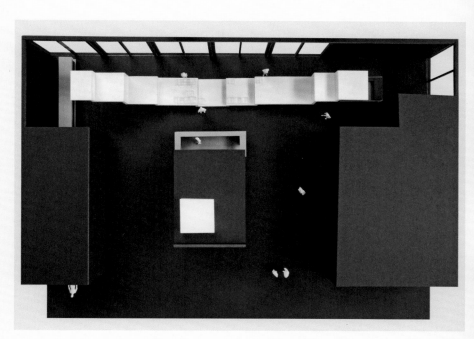

Images of the scale model, focused on the display structure.

FASH

182

HION

183

3.1 PHILLIP LIM

by LEONG LEONG

1

WHERE Seoul, Korea WHEN October 2009
CLIENTS 3.1 Phillip Lim and Shinsegae International DESIGNER Leong Leong (p.681)
TOTAL FLOOR AREA 543 m² SHOP CONSTRUCTORS Barun Structure Engineering and Dadam SD
PHOTOGRAPHER Iwan Baan

The designer label 3.1 Phillip Lim describes its fashion creations as 'everyday classics accented with a touch of madness'. The brand's flagship store in Seoul's premier fashion district, designed by Leong Leong, mirrors that description: a large textured white box, which some might see as a little crazy, with its interior decorated in classic materials such as wood, marble and gold panelling. The brief called for a design that could be incorporated into a global roll-out campaign. Aware of the inevitable requirement of brand recognition, the team thought the typology of a flagship store as being characterised by the simultaneous need for sameness and difference. A legible consistency was required in order to unify the existing stores in New York, Los Angeles and Tokyo and so diagrammatic manoeuvres from each shop were re-interpreted for the Seoul store. The building is wrapped in a blanket of white convex cells, with the different 60 x 60 cm concrete panel types progressively flattening as they climb the facade. On the interior walls, conical acoustic foam fixtures create a textured lining and a white backdrop, interspersed with touches of gold, for the product displays. A continuous curving wall is cropped into a smaller frame, creating four central enclaves, stacked to fit within the two levels of retail space. Each accommodates a different use – display, fitting rooms, storage and stairs to the upper level – and the design makes a distinguished use of mirrored surfaces to expand a continuous visual field of space in which the 'cropped' enclaves float.

1 The subtle texture of the 20-m-high facade
fades into the often overcast grey sky
above the city.
2 The conical texture on the walls consist of
acoustic foam.
3 Two of the enclaves were extended
vertically to cut out double-height spaces,
one of which became the new staircase to
the upper floor.

4

Capitalising the need for consistency, materials established in the brand's other stores 'evolved' in the Seoul store

4 The wallpaper is the result of an ongoing collaboration with artist Wook Kim, whose inspiration for the pattern was ancient Korean ceramics.
5 On the first floor, gold clothing rails suspend from the ceiling, giving the appearance that the garments are floating through the space.
6 Enhancing brand recognition, the herringbone floor pattern used in the Tokyo flagship store was transferred into this location. Beginning at the entrance, it slowly transitions through a gradient of grey tones.

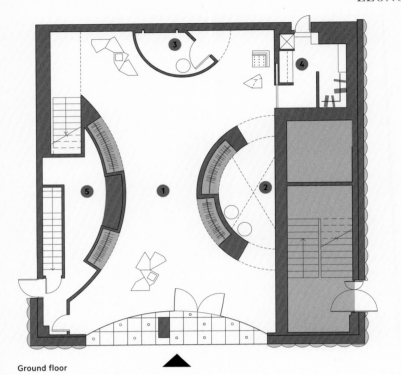

Ground floor

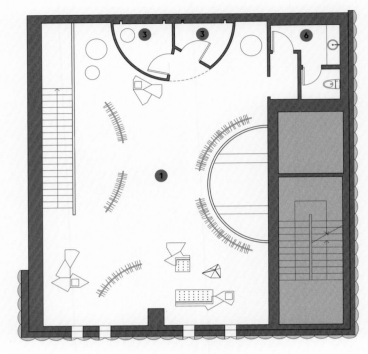

First floor

1 Main retail display
2 Feature display
3 Fitting room
4 Cash desk
5 Storage
6 Lavatory

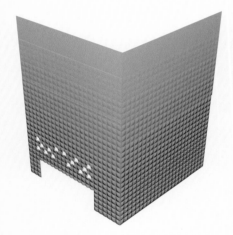

Facade contour analysis.

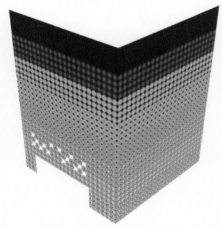

Guassian curvature analysis.

Panel 0   Panel 1   Panel 2   Panel 3   Panel 4   Panel 5   Panel 6

The facade panels progressively flatten
the higher they are installed.

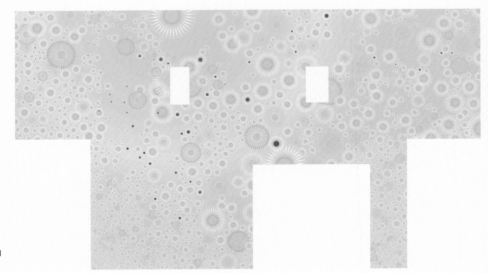

Drawing of the wallpaper used
in one of the retail spaces.

A subtle gradient of convex concrete panels
wraps the building.

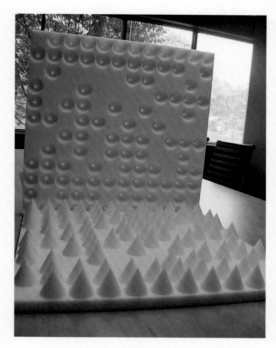

One of the acoustic wall panels. Some of the
cones were painted gold.

Drawing of the panel configuration of the
staircase wall. Five different foam panel types
can be organised into various patterns.

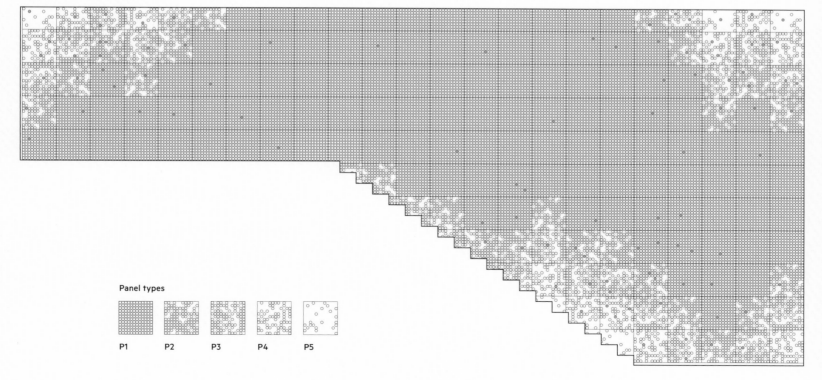

Panel types

P1   P2   P3   P4   P5

ADIDAS SLVR

by ÆDIFICA, SID LEE AND ADIDAS

1

WHERE New York, United States WHEN February 2009
CLIENT adidas DESIGNERS Ædifica (p.673), Sid Lee (p.685) and adidas
TOTAL FLOOR AREA 185 m² SHOP CONSTRUCTOR –
PHOTOGRAPHER Johannes Marburg

Adidas opened its first store dedicated solely to its SLVR fashion collection, a mixture of contemporary aesthetics and ecological conscience, in New York in 2009. The streamlined interior design was a collaborative effort between the creative teams of Ædifica, Sid Lee and adidas to represent the sportswear brand's values of simplicity, transparency and functionality. The concept embodies the principle of efficient sobriety and the design is a true ode to and a celebration of the pureness of the eco-chic elements of the SLVR range. Going from the gunmetal grey facade, the largely white interior decor is enhanced with touches of silver creating a unifying background for the collection. The narrow store is airy and free of unnecessary clutter, with men's and women's apparel divided cleanly along opposite walls.

With black concrete flooring underfoot, the walkway is divided into two channels with a central lower-level display area delineated with lighter-coloured plywood flooring. The materials used are an assortment of recycled items, such as wood and felt, as well as elegant finishes like glass and polished steel. Constructions made of irregular-length wooden planks strapped together by leather belts serve both as bespoke seating aspects when placed atop with industrial felt cushions or as display modules for precious products when encased in glass. The simple strip and spot lighting throughout the store is enhanced by the eye-catching clusters of clear tubular pendant lights suspended overhead.

1 On the central catwalk stands a bespoke plywood chair that has been covered with several layers of felt printed with striped patterns matching the collection.

2 Wall displays include an array of alternating hanging displays and shelving units aligned in groups of three, as a subtle reference to the iconic adidas three stripes logo.

3 More formal and structured product visual presentation is done within the glass cubes.

ALLA SCALA

by OOBIQ ARCHITECTS

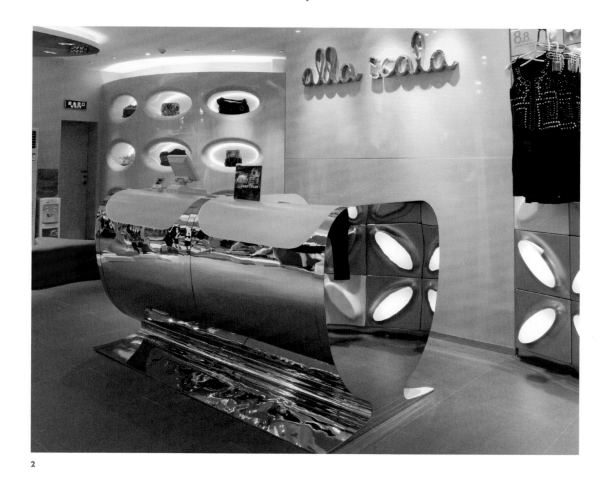

2

WHERE Shenzhen, China **WHEN** May 2010
CLIENT Alla Scala **DESIGNER** Oobiq Architects (p.683)
TOTAL FLOOR AREA 175 m² **SHOP CONSTRUCTOR** Oobiq Architects
PHOTOGRAPHER Courtesy of Oobiq Architects

Oobiq Architects designed the Shenzhen store in China of the womenswear fashion brand Alla Scala. Briefed to create a concept design for the new brand, the requirements from Alla Scala were very clear, as the client already knew its positioning in the market, having experience of previously bringing a successful brand to the market. The theme was inspired by strong visuals incorporating vibrant colours and a design that was reminiscent of pop art, like an Andy Warhol painting. Furniture pieces were constructed which had been directly influenced by that cultural atmosphere. A starting point in the team's approach was to devise a logo which incorporated familiar, flowing shapes and these would also run through the design of the store. With seamless continuity, these shapes morph into concentric ellipses – reminiscent of the curvy script of the letters in the brand's logo – and are incorporated into the different materials and finishes. There are no strict straight lines in the design, only sweeping shapes at every line of sight. The choice of materials includes a contrasting match of natural warm wood, shiny stainless steel and coloured lacquered panelling. Vibrant lime green colouring, in line with the brand's young dynamic image, is used for the wall coverings and recessed shelving is embedded with illuminated product offerings. A central column is located on the ground floor that draws the eye upwards to the mezzanine display area. This organic structure has a seating area incorporated on its back side, hidden from view from passers-by, creating a cosy enclave exclusively for customers.

1 Elliptical shapes predominate the design, from the free-standing display elements to the wall niches.
2 The pop-art inspired shapes are reflected in the stainless steel sales counter.

APC ROYALE

by LAURENT DEROO ARCHITECTE

1

WHERE Paris, France WHEN July 2011
CLIENT APC DESIGNER Laurent Deroo Architecte (p.681)
TOTAL FLOOR AREA 120 m² SHOP CONSTRUCTORS Ambiance Bois, Concept Bois,
Grésillon, Erwan Boulloud and CB Services PHOTOGRAPHER Olivier Placet

When a new store in the hometown of French fashion brand APC was to be opened, Laurent Deroo Architecte was the obvious choice to design the interior, having worked with the company on 30+ other projects across the world. The entrance-level floor area has a select display of goods and is considered as an appetiser before discovering the main collection downstairs. The challenge in such a narrow preliminary space was to propose an attractive entranceway. The concept is that of a 'bright corridor', lined with minimal elements on one side and by a detailed wooden wall on the other. The full-ceiling height presentation shelving is constructed from 5-cm wide blocks and integrates the cash desk with its smooth plywood panelling towards the back of the store. The white wall opposite has been given a rough relief and decorated with interesting display niches: small boxes hang on the wall with their golden lids propped open and products placed on top. A singular brass handrail, which starts at the entrance, guides customers through the shop. On the back wall – with a bright image of natural landscape, like a picture window – the brass rail continues beneath and becomes the handrail of the stairwell leading down to the lower level where a central brass display column stands proud like a bright, shining beacon. Sparkling reflections appear on the ceiling and soft lighting falls on the collection which swirls around the central element creating a curved circulation. With wood and brass decoration, the space has a golden glow and a warm atmosphere; the shop feels like a cosy wood-lined cabin that has display and seating niches embedded in the walls.

2

3

The entrance level is an appetiser before discovering downstairs

4

1 A rough wall coating made of paper fibre creates an interesting contrast with the smooth brass and wood finishing.
2 A larger retail space awaits customers in the basement where a large, shiny display column illuminates the space.
3 The handrail is made of 10-mm thick polished and waxed brass. With a high positioning near the entrance, it gradually slopes down the wall towards the back of the shop.
4 The cash desk is constructed from panels of Movingui wood.

APC SPECIALS

by LAURENT DEROO ARCHITECTE

1

WHERE New York, United States WHEN February 2011
CLIENT APC DESIGNER Laurent Deroo Architecte (p.681)
TOTAL FLOOR AREA 60 m² SHOP CONSTRUCTORS Face Design + Fabrcation and Hecho
PHOTOGRAPHER Will Calcutt

Already with one store in Lower Manhattan, French fashion brand APC wanted to open a new retail space in New York which was dedicated to selling special collections of its designer clothes. The shop was designed by the brand's long-time collaborator Laurent Deroo. The elevated situation of the small store – 1 m above the street – gives it a special status; passers-by cannot see directly into the store but they can look up through the tall windows and glass entranceway. For this reason, the ceiling of the store was given a treatment that would maximise the visual impact from the exterior. Pale oak solid boards have been laid in slim strips overhead, interspersed with elongated openings into which the light fixtures are integrated. Once inside the store, it is clear to customers that the ceiling actually is a reflection of the design of the wooden floor. The relationship between ceiling and floor introduces a 'mirror' theme, as a possibility to enlarge the perception and multiplicity of perspectives of the seemingly small space. A light atmosphere is created due to the oak plywood panelling used throughout. Polished-mirror aluminium panels create space-expanding reflections and also give materiality and intrinsic structural resistance to the shelves, presentation walls and furniture elements on which they are used. The wooden handrail that starts in the entrance stairway, continues as a product display rail and crosses each lateral window, becoming natural light frames on some elements of the collection.

1 Near the entrance, customers can relax and listen on headphones to music.
2 The mirror-top cash desk creates intresting reflections of the ceiling.
3 The shop is clad in oak board, from floor to ceiling and all the pieces of furniture.

BARNEYS NEW YORK CO-OP BROOKLYN

by ÆDIFICA

1

WHERE New York, United States **WHEN** October 2010
CLIENT Barneys New York **DESIGNER** Ædifica (p.673)
TOTAL FLOOR AREA 873 m² **SHOP CONSTRUCTOR** James Barb Construction
PHOTOGRAPHER Stephane Brügger

For its first Co-op in Brooklyn, Barneys New York wanted an environment that reflected the evolving neighbourhood outside. With Brooklyn being a base for emerging artists, Ædifica answered the brief with an artistic theme. The ground floor was designed to echo the ambience of an urban art gallery, with the raw industrial backbone of the building maintained and amplified. White-painted concrete blocks, pipework and exposed conduits – running across the walls and ceiling – are accompanied by blackened steel lighting elements and an expanse of white epoxy concrete on the floor. The large central staircase, with a solid metal framework which adds to the store's industrial look, leads to a basement inspired by an artist's loft. With reclaimed wood-clad walls and floors covering all exposed surfaces, the space is punctuated by couches, area rugs and vintage furniture pieces, giving the atmosphere of an artist-in-residence's living quarters. The changing rooms are also fitted with reclaimed wood slats, while the outer walls serve as the canvas for a collection of artists' illustrations and avant-garde artwork.

1 In the fitting room area, silhouette portraits are painted on-site by local artists, each with a personal statement such as 'Gabby roots for the underdog'.
2 Behind the cash desk, the building's main power conduits and panels are positioned. The number of pipes and panels was doubled to create an *in situ* sculpture.
3 Upon entering, customers immediately sense the raw industrial backbone of the building. A large staircase gives a glimpse of the wood-clad basement.
4 Next page: On the lower level, wood timber flooring and repurposed industrial tables cohabit with retro chairs and exotic wool scatter rugs.

2

3

The space
was designed
to echo the
ambience of
an urban art
gallery

BREDL BATHHOUSE WOMEN

by ATELIER 522

1

WHERE Ravensburg, Germany WHEN February 2009
CLIENT Bredl DESIGNER atelier 522 (p.674)
TOTAL FLOOR AREA 400 m² SHOP CONSTRUCTOR Gerhard König
PHOTOGRAPHER atelier 522

Back in 1993 when the fashion house Bredl began renovating its original store in Ravensburg, the remains of a medieval bathhouse were uncovered. Fast forward a couple of decades and this interesting fact was to become the inspiration for atelier 522 when the studio was commissioned to redesign one aspect of the store. The team took on the challenge to reinterpret the womenswear fashion area within the basement of the building, opting for a theme that had aquatic associations with bathing – with additional inspiration coming from the region's nearby Lake Constance. The basement location was to be a creative playground which would entice customers down to investigate its delights via the spiral staircase. Here interesting aspects instantly grab people's attention: painted swimming pool ladders serve as presentation for hanging garments. These lead the observing eye to 'the scene' beyond with its driftwood decoration and nostalgic summertime connotations, including the old-fashion sunloungers, timber-lined walls reminiscent of a pool fence and snorkelling decor within the haphazard dressing room constructions. Overhead a bright beam of light – like an illuminated protruding jetty – redirects the gaze of the customer throughout the extent of the store leading to the real gem: an authentic, retro motor boat acting as a unique product display element. These quirky decorative details give the concept a unique look and surprise, whilst also fulfilling a function, creating a memorable retail experience for customers.

1 Quirky elements are introduced to surprise the customers but each one also serves a functional purpose, such as the motor boat being used as a display element.
2 Snorkelers await the customers in the fitting rooms.
3 Sunloungers are neatly arranged in rows, just as they are on the beach.
4 At the base of the stairwell, merchandise is hung from multicoloured ladders.

2

3

4

The designers
were inspired by
uncovered remains
of a medieval
bathhouse

BRUNS

by BREIL + PARTNER INTERIOR DESIGN

◆

1

WHERE Oldenburg, Germany **WHEN** March 2011
CLIENT Gerhard Bruns **DESIGNER** Breil + Partner Interior Design (p.675)
TOTAL FLOOR AREA 3500 m² **SHOP CONSTRUCTOR** Hoffmann Ladenbau
PHOTOGRAPHERS Johannes Vogt and Tjaard M. Spiering

Breil + Partner Interior Design was engaged to create a unique design for the Bruns store in Oldenburg, Germany. The brand has been a menswear retailer in the region since 1896 and the Breil team focused on making a masculine statement for the integration of newly evolved house-style elements within the design framework. Being a traditional fashion house, visual communication orientates towards its local environs and symbolic elements run throughout the three floors in a consistent thread. Embedded in the interior architecture is a stylistic vocabulary created by the use of contemporary graphics for decoration, such as the character 'O' – referring to Oldenburg and its culture – which appears behind the cash desks. Also recurring are circular symbols such as bike wheels, which link to the preferred local means of transportation, the bicycle.

Every area is shaped individually for the specific target group. Especially accentuated is the young fashion section with vintage elements and reclaimed timber planks adorning the walls and ceilings, many of which are decorated with song lyrics. A wooden construction climbs up and over the men's casualwear section, forming a pinnacle overhead resembling a wooden sail which is stained a darker colour to emphasise the design. To complete the look, authentic beer crates from the 1950s, industrial scaffolding and display modules constructed from loudspeakers have been integrated into the space.

1 Lyrics from songs such as *It's my life* decorate the overhanging structure. All graphics in the store were done by Jork Andre Dieter from Berlin.
2 The graphic elements are linked to each other and to the city. A bicycle wheel depicted on the wall refers to the joy that locals get from riding their bikes.
3 A display table made from a stack of speakers furnishes the jeans area.

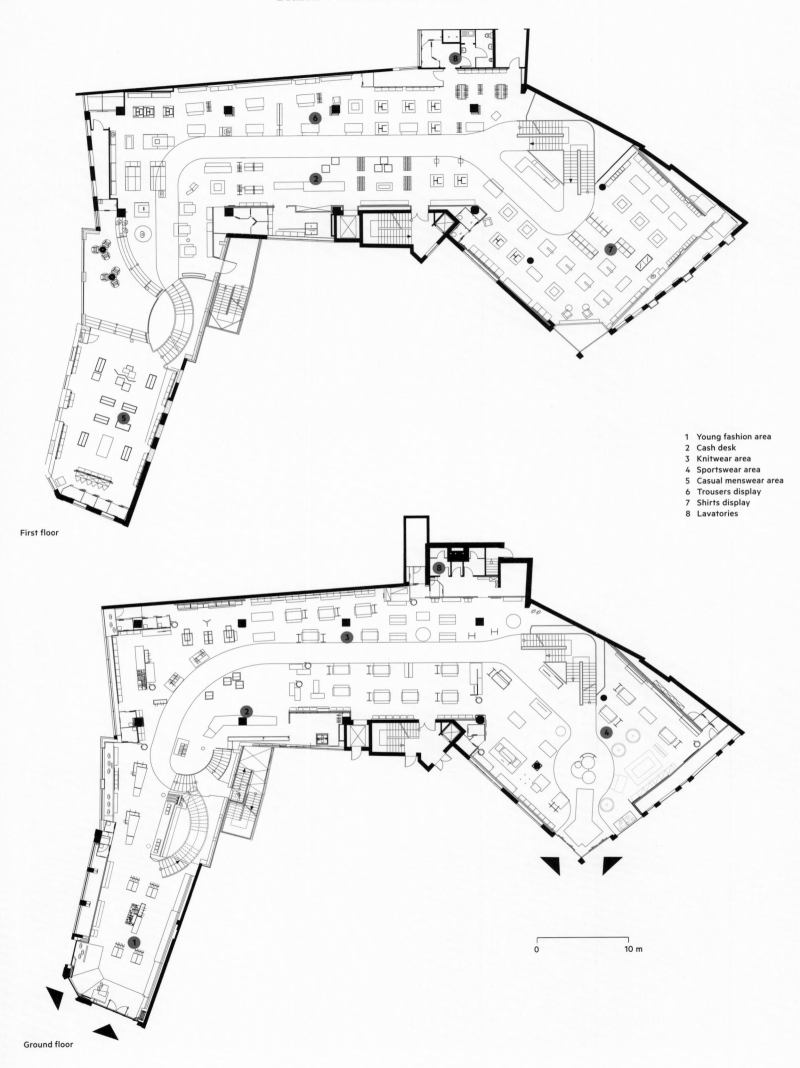

1 Young fashion area
2 Cash desk
3 Knitwear area
4 Sportswear area
5 Casual menswear area
6 Trousers display
7 Shirts display
8 Lavatories

First floor

Ground floor

0   10 m

Rendering of the entrance area where the young fashion department is located.

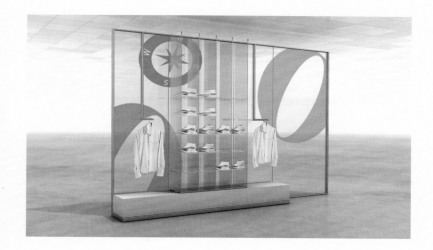

A stylistic vocabulary was created by the use of contemporary graphics

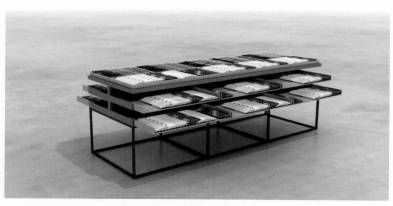

Renderings of several pieces of display furniture.

CANDIDO1859

by LOLA

◆

1

WHERE Maglie, Italy WHEN November 2009
CLIENT Candido1859 DESIGNER LOLA (p.681)
TOTAL FLOOR AREA 627 m² SHOP CONSTRUCTOR Giuliano Casaluci
PHOTOGRAPHER Francesco Prato

Candido1859 is a fashion store located in southern Italy in an impressive 18th century building, the three storeys of which recently underwent a complete renovation. Two floors were reworked separately before LOLA was brought on board to transform the menswear department. The building, formerly a private residence, is characterised by thick walls and high-vaulted ceilings but this floor – which was a later additional to the original structure – has very low ceilings, which was one challenge which the design team faced. Another was how to deal with the central area above the lower main entrance hall. This zone was transformed by incorporating an elevated patio area with a round table at its centre that has a double-faced mirrored and transparent glass top which actually acts as a skylight for the lower level, allowing

light to filter through to the entrance on the ground floor. The walls in this zone are painted an invigorating shade of blue which is in stark contrast to the crisp white palette of the rest of the decor. Surrounding this room, which is used as a private sales area, are four distinct mono-label collections. These are nestled in amongst the architectural spaces created within the building's original structure and also in illuminated niches hollowed out of the solid walls. Tubular display rails are positioned in every possible nook and cranny, creating intriguing sculptural forms in the stairwell. Reflective materials are used in the modular mirrored ceiling, composed of eight triangular elements, to give a feeling of height in the space. The team that was responsible for this design consisted of Rute Brazzao, Sandra Carito Ribeiro and Riccardo Cavaciocchi.

1 The circular counter has two forms and functions: it is a mirrored table; and it is a transparent skylight for the floor below.
2 One of the mono-label spaces seen from the central corridor that surrounds the patio and gives access to all the retail areas.

3 A mirror-clad ceiling makes the spaces appear larger than they actually are. The low ceiling height of this storey proposed quite a challenge to the design team.
4 Perforated metal is used for the white display tables.

The building used to be a private residence

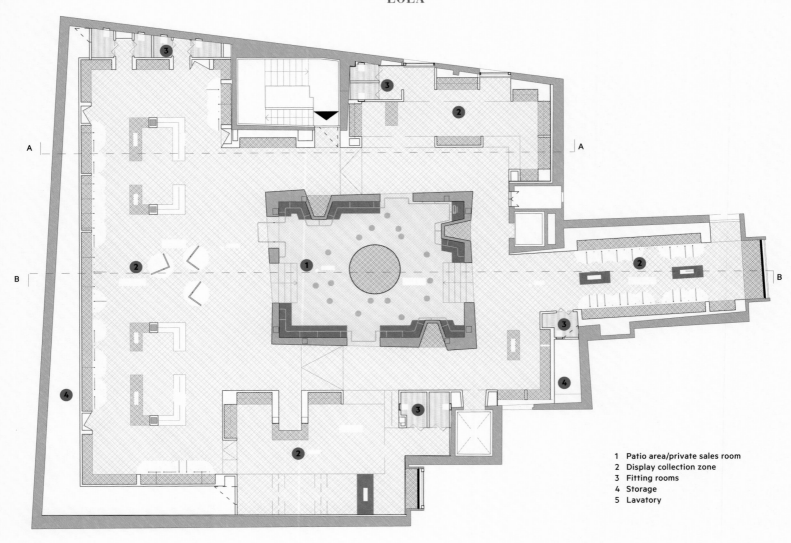

1 Patio area/private sales room
2 Display collection zone
3 Fitting rooms
4 Storage
5 Lavatory

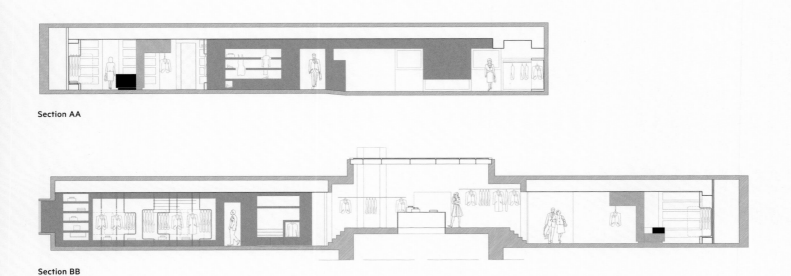

Section AA

Section BB

The very low ceiling was a challenge the design team faced

Section of the main staircase.

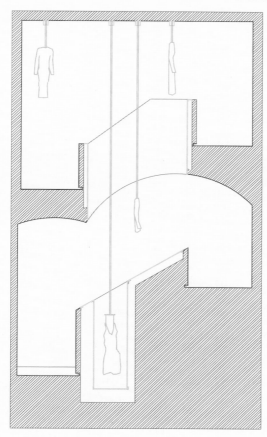

Photograph of the facade of the building, taken in the early 1900s.

Model of the patio.

Construction of the central table in the patio area.

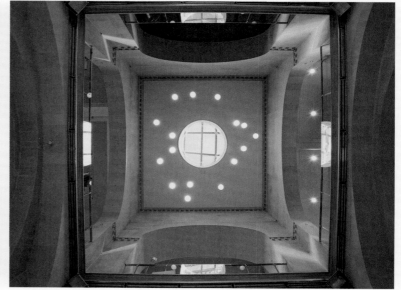

View of the skylight from the lower level.

COLLECT POINT

by LINE-INC

1

WHERE Tokyo, Japan WHEN November 2010
CLIENT Point DESIGNER Line-Inc (p.681)
TOTAL FLOOR AREA 963 m² SHOP CONSTRUCTOR Space
PHOTOGRAPHER Kozo Takayama

The new Japanese store of fashion brand Collect Point is located on a busy intersection in downtown Tokyo. This junction makes it hard for a new-kid-on-the-block to stand out amidst the hustle and bustle. This was certainly the case for the building – formerly a bank, with a rather drab and unimpressive appearance – where the new Collect Point shop would be located. The transformation by the Line-Inc team started with creating an open design, both in the interior and the storefront. The full glass facade allows passers-by to see straight into both floors of the shop and its bright and welcoming atmosphere is immediately obvious. Illuminated frames around the entrance doors are the first of many examples of contemporary lighting details within the store design that will be apparent to customers. The two floors are distinguished by the different lighting aspects that adorn the ceilings, from pendant lampshades, bare lightbulbs and fluorescent strips. Spacious floor plans have been incorporated according to a simple and neutral concept. An almost entirely white space is decorated with natural materials, such as wood, brick and tiles, to create scenes and sections utilising different approaches. A honeycombed pattern on the ground floor is mixed with patterned tilework on the structural columns and cash desk, with bare brickwork on specific walls. Varnished wood is used to accent furniture and fittings, as well as to highlight design features, such as lining the edges of the circular and mirror-lined recesses overhead. Such circular elements are a theme running throughout, from the display tables to the light fixtures on the first floor.

2

3

4

1 To emphasise the spaciousness and high
  ceiling of the ground floor, the designer
  installed suspended pendant lights.
2 Big circular lighting fixtures mask the low
  ceiling-height of the second floor.
3 Illuminated frames around the shop's
  entrance act as a beacon to shoppers on the
  busy intersection.
4 A mirrored back wall visually doubles the
  fitting room space.

DE BIJENKORF

by MICHELGROUP

1

WHERE Eindhoven, the Netherlands WHEN November 2010
CLIENT de Bijenkorf DESIGNER Michelgroup (p.682)
TOTAL FLOOR AREA 4000 m² SHOP CONSTRUCTOR Benschop The Retail Factory
PHOTOGRAPHERS Dirk Wilhelmy and Unit 300 (Silvain Wiersma)

The premium Dutch department store chain de Bijenkorf commissioned Michelgroup studio to design, together with Benschop to engineer and construct, the basement level of its Eindhoven store. The team aimed to create a stylistic vocabulary across the interior architecture of the 4000-m² lower level, which cohesively connected each of the distinct areas: the new men's fashion and shoe department, the childrenswear section and the books and media zone. Metallic bronze and silver were key decorative elements which were utilised in the clothing and footwear areas, with full ceiling-height metalwork screens and intricate meshwork panelling creating eye-catching patterns which catch customers' attention from across the store. These details are positioned alongside natural materials such as square stone tiles on the floor and

lengths of pale wood panelling overhead, which adds perspective to the vast floor space. The neutral palette is interspersed with orangey tones in the furnishings, from the copper-metal trolleys in the menswear section to the glass panels in the books and media zone. Here also, citrus-hues are included in the walls emblazoned with graphic letters which act as contemporary space dividers. The green winged lounging chairs provide a fresh colourful aspect. The chairs are positioned at the entrance of the customer service area, which is subtly branded with the honeycombed signature of de Bijenkorf, which literally means 'the beehive' in Dutch.

1 A dividing screen has honeycomb shapes in the metalwork (the translation of the Dutch word *bijenkorf* is 'beehive').
2 In the formal menswear section, brands like Armani and Hugo Boss are for sale.
3 A walk-in structure in the children's area appears to be constructed from giant white and yellow drinking straws.
4 The men's shoe department is located next to the customer service. Brownish tones strike the highest note in this area.

2

Metalwork screens and meshwork panelling create eye-catching patterns across the store

3

4

DESA

by KINNERSLEY KENT DESIGN

◆

1

WHERE London, United Kingdom WHEN January 2011
CLIENT Desa DESIGNER Kinnersley Kent Design (p.680)
TOTAL FLOOR AREA 160 m² SHOP CONSTRUCTOR Kad Retail
PHOTOGRAPHER Peter Cook

Desa is a premium Turkish designer brand which started out as a leather goods manufacturer in 1972 and has since evolved into a fashion label which includes luxury womenswear, accessories and shoes. The company wished to enter the local market via a stand-alone boutique format in order to launch, nurture and grow the brand's renown in the United Kingdom. Kinnersley Kent Design was briefed to create an elegant and intimate retail environment that could work in both boutique and flagship formats. 'Innovation through tradition' is the philosophy that the team wished to engrain within a stylish retail space, celebrating the heritage, craftsmanship and design of the brand. This was realised by the use of a muted, warm-toned brown and gold colour palette mixed with brass, marble and leather highlights. The lighting used has a theatrical edge in order to fully highlight the products which are positioned throughout the two-storey space on bespoke display systems. Recessed wall bays with contrasting linings, combining glossy with smooth, have lighting on each shelf. Luxurious detailing is included at every turn: furnishings edged with brass plates, leather clad pilasters with stitch detailing, marble table tops with branded brass legs and large integrated wall mirrors with illuminated surrounds. Behind the first floor cash desk, which has been traditionally hand-crafted with mirrored-panel detailing, is a textured wall which lines the stairwell with further product alcoves. The luxurious design concept lends itself for future roll-outs in Paris and New York.

1 Marcel Wander's Skygarden lamp suspends above the display table.
2 Pressed Glass Lights by Tom Dixon illuminate the cash desk, behind which a wall displays a pattern created from Desa's corporate logo.

A muted, warm-toned colour palette is mixed
with brass, marble and leather highlights

3 Recessed display niches with integral lighting showcase the merchandise like museum pieces.
4 Luxurious fitting rooms have vintage re-upholstered seating and product displays.
5 Rug details are laid in the herringbone patterned parquet floor throughout.

DETROIT

by ARKTEAM

1

WHERE Athens, Greece WHEN February 2010
CLIENT Tsouroukoglou Bros DESIGNER Arkteam (p.673)
TOTAL FLOOR AREA 60 m² SHOP CONSTRUCTOR Arcon Constructions
PHOTOGRAPHER Studio Vavdinoudis (Dimitriou)

For the design of its fourth store in Athens, the family-owned fashion retailer Detroit called upon the talents of Arkteam. Located in Kifissia, the bourgeois north suburb of Athens, on a street where there are already two other Detroit shops, a unique concept was required that emphasised the new store which is dedicated solely to menswear. Arkteam, having designed all the Detroit outlets, chose an experimental and bold approach for this rather conservative shopping district. The design plays a geometrical game with vertical and horizontal planes and the space is organised as a 'pattern' ready for merchandise to be added. Natural oak shelving is turned 90 degrees to deliver a vertical hanging system and, as a result, space and display systems are integrated to act as a singular entity, reinforcing the simplicity of the organisational gesture. All the materials – steel, natural oak, concrete, grey mirror and polished stainless steel – are part of an integral interior vocabulary. The ceiling is plain and the anthracite-cement floor tiles introduce a decorative 'carpet' as a reference to the residential past of the area. Red naval ropes accentuate the monochromatic ambience, adding a playful vibrant fixture that allows the display of clothing at different heights. Designer furniture and fittings complete the scene with a touch of glam, like a Michelangelo's *David* print on the cashier's table-top, which pays homage to Italian architect and designer Carlo Mollino. Chris Kabel's Sticky Lamps on the shopfront window panes obscure visual access for passers-by, arousing their curiosity to enter the store and explore the space.

2

3

1 Vertical and horizontal planes are used in the geometric design.
2 Hanging down one wall are red naval ropes affixed to the ceiling with rivets and pulley systems. These can be used to display merchandise at different heights.
3 Chris Kabel's Sticky Lamps playfully filter the view through the shop windows.
4 The large black foot is by architect, designer and artist Gaetanco Pesce and brings a sculptural note to the store.

The design plays a geometrical game with vertical and horizontal planes

4

DIAMANT NOIR HOMME

by LOGICA:ARCHITETTURA (RICCARDO SALVI + LUCA ROSSIRE)

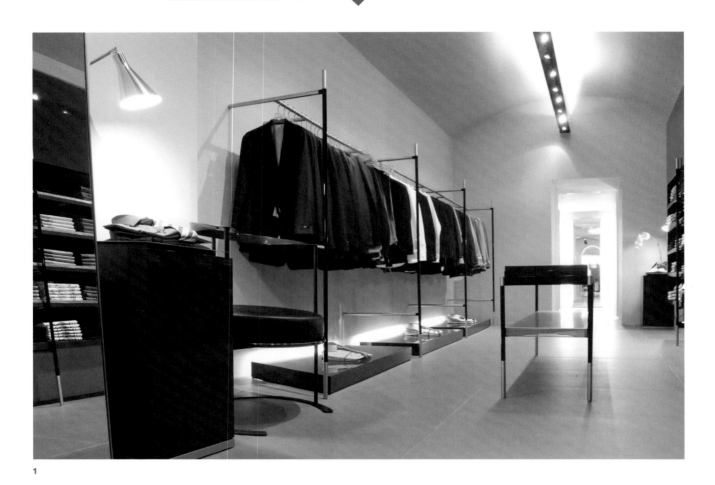

1

WHERE Ajaccio, France WHEN April 2009
CLIENT Diamant Noir Homme DESIGNER Logica:architettura (Riccardo Salvi + Luca Rossire) (p.681)
TOTAL FLOOR AREA 250 m² SHOP CONSTRUCTOR Sice Previt
PHOTOGRAPHER Logica:architettura (Marc Crawford)

The team at Logica:architettura was responsible for the renovation and decoration of the menswear boutique Diamant Noir Homme in Ajaccio, Corsica. The design follows a severity of expression and is mixed up with an attempt to rethink the production of the so-called 'Milanese architectural school'. In the redesign of the small retail store, the volumes of the original spaces have been kept intact and any juxtapositions made by previous interventions removed. Within the original shell of the building, the team wished to express a sensation of calm in a space characterised by a strong architectural identity. For this purpose, the materials chosen – natural brass, brushed glossy lacquer, leather upholstery – recreate a sense of classic elegance and sincere simplicity. A backdrop with simple and clean lines has been created by covering the

walls, ceiling and doorways in a smooth plasterwork and by positioning large square polished stone floor tiles underfoot. The pieces of furniture, distinguished by their simple elegance and refined details, represent and rediscover the values of 'artisan handmade' items and pursue the perfection of timeless realisation. The lacquered green display systems are accentuated with brass-meshwork shelves and the accompanying brass detailing and fittings add a crisp grandeur to the space. The lighting beams, incorporating recessed spotlights, were expressly designed for the boutique and were produced by Viabizzuno.

1 The designers of the store aimed to create a timeless design.
2 The lighting was designed by Viabizzuno.
3 Brass was one of the materials chosen to create a sense of elegance and simplicity.
4 All pieces of furniture in the shop were custom designed.

2

3

4

The design
expresses
a sensation
of calm

DODENHOF D-STRICT

by ATELIER 522

◆

1

WHERE Posthausen, Germany WHEN May 2009
CLIENT dodenhof DESIGNER atelier 522 (p.674)
TOTAL FLOOR AREA 895 m² SHOP CONSTRUCTOR Schrader
PHOTOGRAPHER atelier 522

Within the dodenhof shopping centre in Posthausen, the atelier 522 team was challenged to create an exciting new concept for its young fashion hall 'd-strict'. The target group for the featured brands is a young, hip crowd and the space called for an atmosphere that would be familiar to this audience whilst also enticing them to shop. The answer was to execute a trendy club feel, with an all-black facade decorated by graffiti artists. Dominating the interior space are dark colours on the walls and ceiling, with an expanse of bare concrete floor. The striking splash of colour comes from the vibrant red carpet which streaks through the space with its VIP connotations, drawing customers along to investigate the products on display beneath the glitter balls and spotlights. Sleek black curtains frame the space and act

as dividers between different product areas interspersed with obligatory nightclub paraphernalia, such as record players, speakers, chunky headphone cables and beer crates. Elsewhere, colourful urban artefacts become a stage for merchandise – from the wooden cable reels and metal barrels to an authentic canary yellow Chevrolet – which sit alongside a discarded motorcycle as it waits to be filled by a long-since-abandoned gas pump. Including these unusual objects in an out-of-context location creates an intriguing atmosphere for the young clientele to discover the latest fashion trends.

1 Unconventional product display elements like an old Chevrolet and painted steel barrels are used throughout the store.
2 A red carpet leads up to a 27-m² stage where regional bands occasionally perform. With glitter balls and spotlights, a trendy club fleeing was created.

DOM REBEL THREADS

by IGLOODGN

1

WHERE Montreal, Canada WHEN April 2009
CLIENT Dom Rebel Threads DESIGNER Igloodgn (p.679)
TOTAL FLOOR AREA 232 m² SHOP CONSTRUCTOR AXP Reno
PHOTOGRAPHER Pierre Arsenault

Based in Canada and retailing worldwide, Dom Rebel Threads is a men's fashion label that aims to bring a new element of excitement with a strong meaning and purpose behind each creation. The menswear company wanted to redefine and solidify its brand and commissioned Igloodgn to create a showroom with an exclusive line of upholstered furniture and display cases where buyers and private clients could experience the Dom Rebel lifestyle. Inspiration for the retail space stemmed from the brand's very own hand mounted Swarovski Crystal Collection, which is the whimsical manipulation of a beat up cotton t-shirt decorated with luxurious gems, a look that says style without pretension. The realised space embodies a contrasting concoction of the rugged and the refined, with the minimalist concept of an art gallery. The walls

and ceiling of the showroom received a coat of matt black paint to unify the space and create the perfect backdrop to showcase the merchandise. A striking feature are the fluorescent lighting strips suspended overhead, like floating lightsabers, creating shimmering reflections in the high-gloss lacquered wooden floorboards. The light fixtures were installed at varying heights and angles to create a voluminous sculpture which makes the most of the reclaimed loft space. A touch of luxury was injected with the use of brass, brushed gold and chrome in the additional contemporary pendant lights, bespoke product railings and display module fittings. Vast leaning mirrors and an inviting leather sofa add a cohesiveness to the space, created so that clients can have the opportunity to appreciate the brand culture while keeping their attention on the products.

1 An 18-feet-long leather couch adds luxury to the showroom and private retail space.
2 Located in a building that dates back to 1882, the original floors and painted ceilings provide contrast to the newly-added modern elements.
3 Oversized mirrors leaning against the wall aptly correspond to the height and scale of the space.
4 Tom Dixon's Bronze Copper Shades are hung above a custom-made Dom Rebel lifestyle display.

2

3

4

Fluorescent lighting strips are suspended overhead, like floating lightsabers

DOUBLE STANDARD CLOTHING BALABUSHKA

by PROPELLER DESIGN

2

WHERE Tokyo, Japan WHEN October 2010
CLIENT Film DESIGNER Propeller Design (p.683)
TOTAL FLOOR AREA 500 m² SHOP CONSTRUCTORS N2, Shift, Sogo Furniture and ZYCC Corporation
PHOTOGRAPHER Nacása & Partners

Double Standard Clothing, the fashion brand of Japanese designer Masahisa Takino, has various associated sub-brands: DSC, the womenswear line; Sov., a collection of grown-up elegance; D/him, a menswear brand; DSC accessories; and the newest brand line Wedding, a collection of dresses, made-to-measure suits and wedding rings. Its store in Tokyo's Shinjuku shopping district, located within one of the biggest department stores in Japan, incorporates all the sub-brands and their diverse styles. The Propeller Design team led by Yoshihiro Kawasaki created an environment that is full of contrasts, being both modern and classic, both cool and emotional, both casual and feminine. A cream and browny black colour palette is used, interspersed with dashes of vibrant red. Sumptuous textures and reflective materials unite the various aspects of the shop, which circulates around a central void. Surfaces are lined sometimes as a complete antithesis to what is expected, with ceramic tiles on the floor and herringbone patterned wooden parquet on the walls. Elsewhere, the origami-like screens of the window displays are continued into the interior and also used as wall coverings. Display units are made from metal and glass juxtaposed with furniture featuring wood and leather, providing yet another attractive contrast. All fixtures and fittings are based on straight lines but dividing walls curve gently at certain junctures. Lighting also creates unexpected visual patterns overhead – and down the walls – primarily playing with strips of illumination as well as circular halos of light.

1 The oval-shaped mirror positioned above the wedding collection has the effect of expanding the space upwards.
2 'Balabushka' has been added to the shop name in honour of George Balabushka, the legendary billiard cue maker.

5

Display units are made from metal and glass juxtaposed with furniture featuring wood and leather

3 The open entranceway of the men's section
   means the interesting range of decorative
   textures used in-store are immediately
   obvious to passers-by.
4 The overall decor of the store instils an
   atmosphere akin to a luxury salon.
5 Geometric shapes and angular lines are a
   key feature of the store design.
6 Contrasting patterns from the parquet tiles
   climbing the walls provide a distinctive
   backdrop for the merchandise.

6

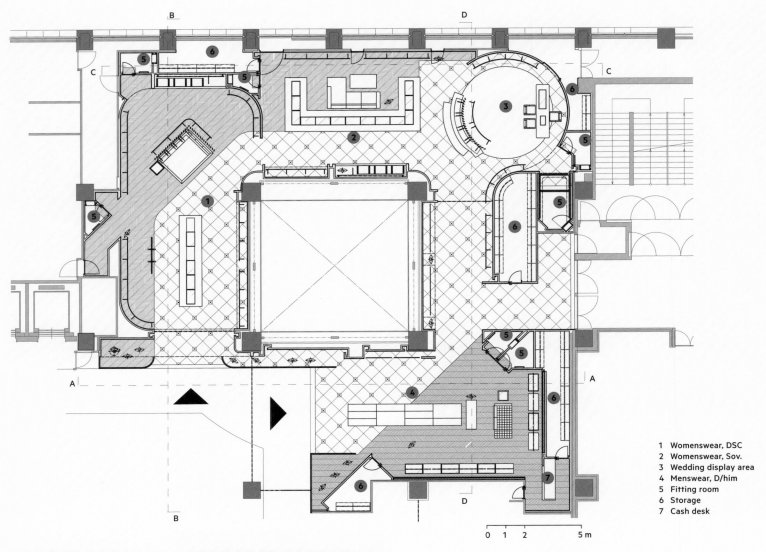

1 Womenswear, DSC
2 Womenswear, Sov.
3 Wedding display area
4 Menswear, D/him
5 Fitting room
6 Storage
7 Cash desk

0 1 2   5 m

Renderings of the women's section depicting
the textured origami-like wall coverings.

Rendering showing the two entrances of the store.

A neutral colour palette is interspersed with dashes of vibrant red

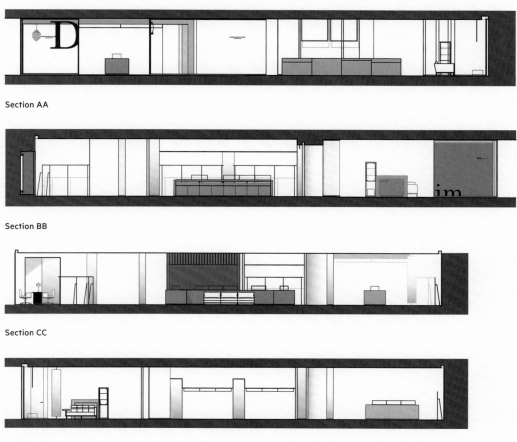

Section AA

Section BB

Section CC

Section DD

ENGELBERT STRAUSS

by PLAJER & FRANZ STUDIO

1

WHERE Hockenheim, Germany WHEN August 2010
CLIENT Engelbert Strauss DESIGNER plajer & franz studio (p.683)
TOTAL FLOOR AREA 750 m² SHOP CONSTRUCTOR schleifenbaum design & project
PHOTOGRAPHER diephotodesigner.de (Ken Schluchtmann)

Engelbert Strauss is one of the biggest workwear producers on the German market. It recently went through a transition of primarily being a mail-order company to opening its first ever retail store. The challenge for plajer & franz studio was to incorporate the world of various work professions in a realistic way without creating a 'boutique' fashion store. The architecture and interior of the first store represents modern, reduced and simple shapes. On the exterior, a bright red colour was contrasted with dark grey brickwork and natural wooden planks, which were also used piled-up at one corner of the courtyard to form an 18-m high pylon construction, visible from all directions. In the store, various elements and materials reflect the different work trades for which merchandise is available. The red, grey and light-coloured wood of the exterior is repeated and the shop is specifically structured to have a warehouse character with open ceilings and wide rafters. The 4-m high walling system is in its design similar to a high-bay storage and several smaller areas are laid out with a lamella structure. The nature of the fittings utilised have a raw and industrial feel, including textured bricks, fibreglass tiles and aluminium tool-boxes stacked against the walls or arranged as free-standing display modules, as well as metal meshwork detailing and painted wooden pallets. The fitting rooms look like corrugated containers and the cash desk is built in stretched metal with piled-up timber, which underlines again the roughness and honesty of the crafts in a witty way.

2

1 A raw concept is realised by the use of
   wooden planks and metal meshwork giving
   the shop an industrial feel.
2 The brand's first ever retail store
   incorporates a distinctive branding design
   on the exterior.
3 Construction materials are used in the
   decor, including a ceiling installation made
   out of different dimensions of pipework.
4 Red branded walls are a recurring feature in
   the store.

3   4

5

Various elements reflect the different work trades for which merchandise is available

6

7

5 The fitting rooms are clad in corrugated
iron, each illuminated by an industrial-style
pendant light.
6 The display wall in the shoes section is
made out of lime sandstone, laid vertically.
7 Stacked tool boxes form ideal shelving
displays on one wall in the accessories area.

ESPRIT

by CORNEILLE UEDINGSLOHMANN ARCHITEKTEN

2

WHERE Frankfurt, Germany WHEN September 2010
CLIENT Esprit Retail DESIGNER Corneille Uedingslohmann Architekten (p.676)
TOTAL FLOOR AREA 3600 m² SHOP CONSTRUCTORS Baierl & Demmelhuber Innenausbau and
Umdasch Shop Concept PHOTOGRAPHER Frank Alexander Rümmle

In 2010, fashion brand Esprit saw its new flagship store in Frankfurt take shape and become the company's largest shop worldwide. The project was undertaken by Corneille Uedingslohmann Architekten, giving the existing store a facelift and extending it to include an extra two floors. The sheer scope of the project was a challenge, particularly as the structural, facade and interior construction all needed to be completed within 4 months. The team succeeded in introducing a sophisticated and comprehensive design concept throughout. This was achieved in part by incorporating generous structural openings, which interconnect all floors and provide visitors with a vertical orientation within the building. Extending from the basement right up to the third floor, an extensive wood-frame construction – like an artificial towering tree – is an eye-catching feature that also offers seating and presentation platforms. The spatial division of each floor into smaller product areas uses a mixture of interesting textures, including black powder-coated steel and stained oak for the free-standing furnishings and unfinished steel, brick and concrete for the wall fixtures. Lighting accents provide product highlights throughout and illumination also arises from the polka-dot pixellated panels which are a recurring theme, appearing on the newly-built escalator which transports visitors directly to the menswear department on the second floor, and also on the striking facade. Polka-dot illumination on the shop's facade creates a dynamic shining beacon and impressive sight for passers-by on Frankfurt's famous Zeil shopping street.

1 Through a void overhead, the escalator can be viewed.
2 Over 14,000 computer-controlled LEDs behind perforated metal panels are used. From the street, an ever-changing light show can be seen across the full height of the shop's four storeys.

3

This flagship store has become the company's largest shop worldwide

4

5

3 One of the escalators runs directly from the ground floor to the second floor.
4 A timber construction connects the five floors and amid its 'branches' niche seating areas have been created.
5 The menswear department on the second floor can be reached using the escalator affectionately termed as the 'Men Express'.

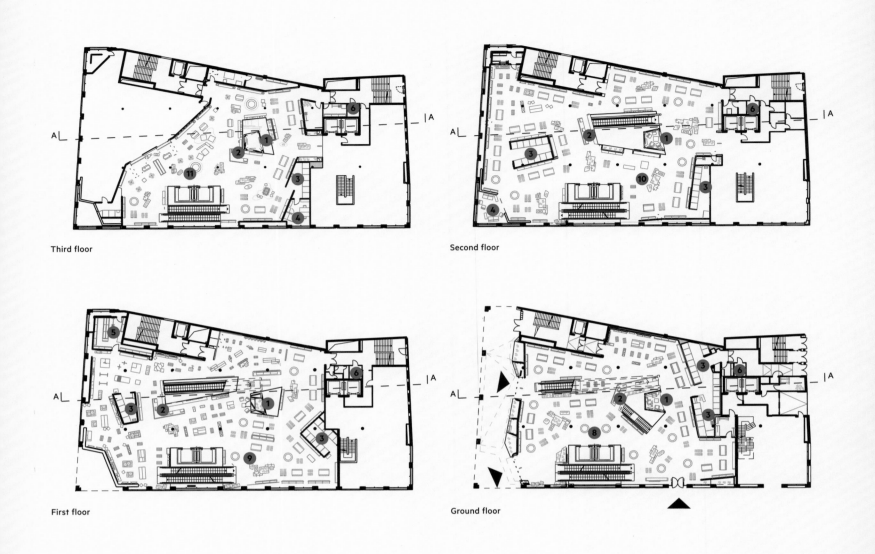

Third floor

Second floor

First floor

Ground floor

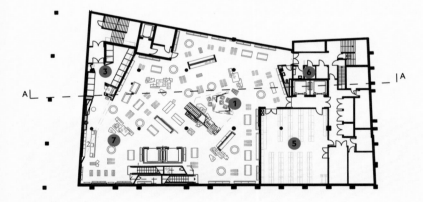

Basement

1 Central void/tree construction
2 Cash desk
3 Fitting rooms
4 Office
5 Storage
6 Lavatories
7 Women EDC
8 Women Casual/DeCorp
9 Women Accessories/Sportswear/Collection
10 Men Casual/EDC/Collection
11 Kid's World

Generous structural openings interconnect all floors with a vertical orientation

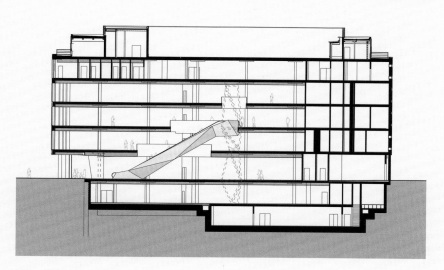

Section AA

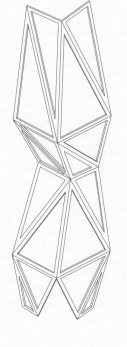

Isometric drawing of the towering structure that perforates the five floors of the store.

Drawing of the escalator that also features LEDs behind a perforated panel – like the facade.

GRACE

by HEIKAUS INTERIOR

1

WHERE Munich, Germany WHEN April 2010
CLIENT Grace Fashion House DESIGNER Heikaus Concept (p.679)
TOTAL FLOOR AREA 190 m² SHOP CONSTRUCTOR Heikaus Interior
PHOTOGRAPHER Uwe Spoering

The Grace Fashion House is a German retailer of multibrand womenswear. For the brand's existing Munich store, Heikaus Concept was brought on board to redevelop the 190-m² first floor storage area into a mezzanine retail space, extending the shop's sales area to over 1000 m². Accessed from the ground floor by a sweeping stairway with a glass handrail, the new upper level is saturated with a glistening and glamorous metallic gold decor. A long display wall presents merchandise which is interspersed with large geometric structures. These configurations are reminiscent of cut diamonds and have the sole purpose of highlighting individual accessories, which are encased in a glass box at the centre of each display module. A faceted language of shapes is consistently used throughout, exhibited also in the flooring – where

stainless steel strips divide the glistening floor covering into angular jewel-like shapes – and in the hexagonal central canopy overhead. Free-standing furniture and a bar counter repeat the same contours, with the architecture of the space being enhanced by sophisticated lighting. Two pendant crystal lampshades and strip lights under the prism-shaped furniture create particularly strong effects and striking shadows. Spotlights are also used to focus directly onto the presented pieces of clothing and accessories. A mixture of textures, materials and furnishings complete the luxurious look and feel of the space with its plush seating niches and leather-clad furniture.

1 For the lighting, Gaia and Stella II spotlights of Heikaus' own Professional Retail Light series are used.
2 A comfortable lounge area features Jaime Hayon's Showtime Armchairs.
3 The geometric wall structures appear to be 'cinched in at the waist' to present featured products in glass cases.
4 The bar counter repeats the same faceted shapes that are applied to the walls and display furniture.

2

The space is saturated with a glistening and glamorous metallic gold decor

3

4

HYUNDAI DEPARTMENT STORE

by HMKM

2

WHERE Seoul, South Korea **WHEN** August 2010
CLIENT Hyundai **DESIGNER** HMKM (p.679)
TOTAL FLOOR AREA 40,000 m² **SHOP CONSTRUCTOR** HMKM
PHOTOGRAPHER Jae-Youn Kim

Hyundai Department Store is one of the leading department store retail chains in South Korea. Its latest location is the prestigious Illsan Kintex Mall in the capital city Seoul. The HMKM team was asked to challenge the very typical design and layout that most department stores conform to, and create an exceptional retail destination. In order to reflect the Hyundai name as a provider of aspirational shopping experiences, a more European model was adhered to that would offer a significant point of difference with a unique and innovative design. Each floor has a distinctive look and feel and a coherent overall architectural palette, thus establishing a strong visual language throughout. On entering the store, customers first encounter the food hall with a monochromatic scheme of sparkling white floors contrasting with black ceilings which throw into lush relief the vivid hues of the fresh produce. A sensuous white bulkhead element wraps around the perimeter of the space, drawing customers in, and delineating product categories with its sinuous curves. This overhead design feature is a key aspect deployed on each floor as a distinctive and unifying envelope; its shifting form mutates to sit alongside specific splashes of colour which are used to enliven the monochrome display areas. A multitude of materials define each of the spaces, including pale grey stone, polished stainless steel-edged tiles and mirrored bronze panels. At many junctures, the ceiling element incorporates jagged, edge-illuminated strips against the black ceiling, which creates dramatic sight-lines throughout the store.

1 Bright-coloured, illuminated shapes are visible in the openings in the suspended white plasterboard panels, highlighting the walking route in the young fashion area.
2 The food hall has a Carrara marble floor.

3

4

3 The department store covers ten floors.
4 Brushed stainless steel, orange acrylic,
  glass and timber are used for the sneaker
  displays on the fifth floor, the level
  dedicated to sports and kidswear.
5 In the young fashion section, a stripped-
  back warehouse-style space was created.

5

The overhead feature acts as a distinctive and unifying envelope

ISSEY MIYAKE/STICKS

by EMMANUELLE MOUREAUX ARCHITECTURE + DESIGN

◆

2

WHERE Tokyo, Japan WHEN August 2010
CLIENT Issey Miyake DESIGNER emmanuelle moureaux architecture + design (p.677)
TOTAL FLOOR AREA 133 m² SHOP CONSTRUCTOR emmanuelle moureaux architecture + design
PHOTOGRAPHER Nacása & Partners

Fashion designer Issey Miyake commissioned Emmanuelle Moureaux to create an installation for his retail spaces in Tokyo's chic shopping district Aoyama. The idea was to make it look like the label's neighbouring shops, the Issey Miyake store and the Pleats Please store, were linked to each other with a core creativity. What was realised for the month-long exposition was a connection that came about by crafting a scenic union between the shops which echoed a sense of balance. With 411 wooden sticks, overlapping and floating, a new appearance was instilled with intermingled colours and shadows. The sticks, randomly positioned, created tensions and chance balances and ultimately became tangible forms. The concept was inspired by the children's game Mikado, which involves letting a handful of sticks fall

to the ground and then picking them up, one-by-one, without moving any of the others. Sticks of a larger dimension than would normally be used in the game were used to line the window displays and were also positioned around the interior, not only on the floors but also floating in space. It is as if the sticks had been thrown and suddenly everything had stopped – with time seeming to stand still whilst the sticks hovered in mid-air. The slender wooden batons were arranged either in monochromatic white bundles or in a rainbow of colours, interspersed amongst the product displays. It seems the slightest touch could send them all crashing down but, in fact, the installation was designed to be structurally balanced in spite of its unbalanced and chaotic appearance.

1 The installation was inspired by the game
Mikado, which is played by local children.
2 During one month, coloured and white
sticks decorated the shops.

3 The wooden sticks were coloured with
   urethane paint.
4 The installation visually connected
   separate, neighbouring Issey Miyake stores.
5 White sticks were placed in the shop
   window of the Pleats Please shop.

3

The scenic union between the shops echoed a sense of balance

4

5

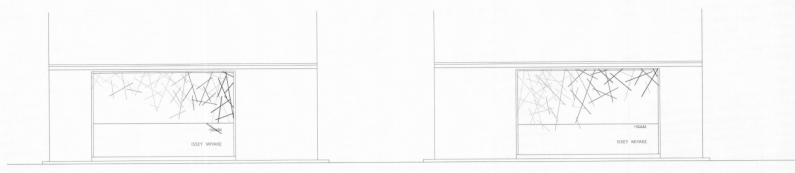

Front elevation

1 White sticks
2 Coloured sticks
3 Cash desk
4 Fitting room
5 Storage

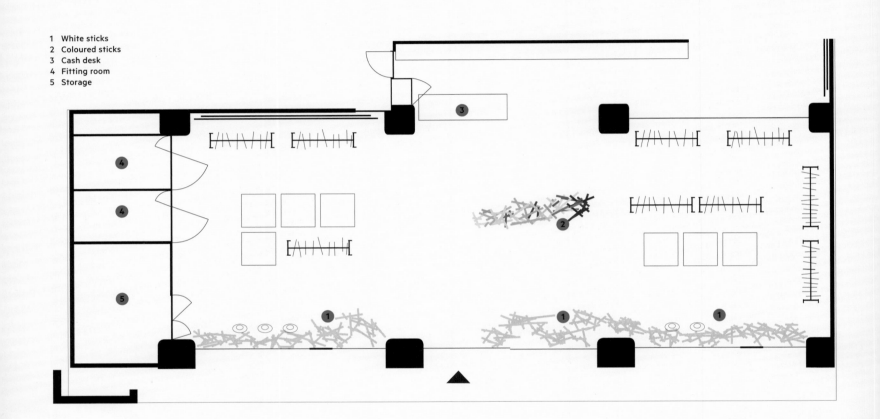

Time seemed to stand still whilst the sticks hovered in mid-air

Painted sticks are checked against the original colour samples.

A miniature study model at Moureaux's office.

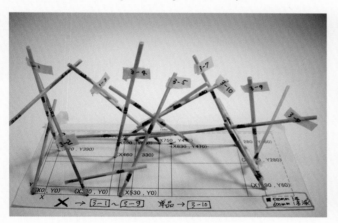

Model of the configuration of the sticks, used for construction.

Full scale model being tested at the office.

The making off the sticks at a small woodwork factory.

Construction of the installation on site.

JAEGER LONDON

by KINNERSLEY KENT DESIGN

1

WHERE London, United Kingdom WHEN November 2010
CLIENT Jaeger DESIGNER Kinnersley Kent Design (p.680)
TOTAL FLOOR AREA 160 m² SHOP CONSTRUCTOR Esprit
PHOTOGRAPHER Peter Cook

Established in 1884, Jaeger is a luxury British fashion brand. The Jaeger London collection is a uniquely-designed range diffused with aspects of the brand's catwalk collection. When Jaeger decided to expand the range, Kinnersley Kent Design was invited to design a retail format for roll-out into new stand-alone Jaeger London stores. The brief called for a boutique that would appeal to fashion-aware women who appreciate quality and design. The idea behind the concept was to create a sense of space, a clean, light backdrop and gallery-inspired environment. The result is a contemporary interpretation of classic style and quality. Interior elements range from the elegant framing of fixtures to etched panelling detail and texture on key walls, combined with lighting features to add a distinctive touch. Monolithic white ceramic flooring

and off-white chalk walls create a canvas against which the clothing can stand out. Bespoke panelling on the walls and quirky accents in the furnishings imbue a modern, urban feel but a softer, feminine feel was also important. To add a touch of colour, the cash desk was clad in 3form Chroma acrylic in a shade of dusty pink. Merchandise is displayed on angular metal stands and in black oak timber-framed fixtures with satin nickel inlay, angled to the walls at 10-degree angles. The flexible fixtures allows for outfit building to reflect the urban working woman's needs. The use of desirable furniture pieces from contemporary British designers, such as Benjamin Hubert's Pebble stool and Tom Dixon's Wingback chair, adds a traditional twist.

1 Droog's 85 Lamps illuminate the cash desk made of 3form Chroma.
2 Elegant and simple fixtures are used to display and – in some cases – frame the designer products.
3 Etched panelling adorns the architectural glass balustrade.
4 Benjamin Hubert's Pebble stool furnishes the fitting room.

2

3

4

1

JELMOLI

by BLOCHER BLOCHER PARTNERS

2

WHERE Zurich, Switzerland WHEN October 2010
CLIENT Jelmoli DESIGNER Blocher Blocher Partners (p.674)
TOTAL FLOOR AREA 34,000 m² SHOP CONSTRUCTORS Ganter, Glaeser Baden, Iringer,
Schweitzer and Vizona West PHOTOGRAPHER Nikolaus Koliusis

A principal shopping address in central Zurich is the Jelmoli department store, a brand name with historical connotations in the city. It was established in 1833 on Bahnhofstrasse and 177 years later saw the redesign of its original location unveiled, after undergoing an 18-month complete renovation. The design team of Blocher Blocher Partners created a new identity for the store, with the monumental building now protected behind a modern glass-fronted facade. A special highlight within the space is a central vertical void which slices through the floors giving customers the sensation of being right at the heart of the action. The store has the ambience and charisma of a fashion boulevard, along which customers can stroll from one department to the next. Attractive and clear-cut concepts for the presentation of merchandise

are consistently placed throughout the building with optimal function and a tasteful mix of materials and metallic earthy colours. An assortment of interesting textures are exemplified in the wall coverings by the use of perforated and laser-cut sheet metal, stretched rubber bands and oak panelling and, for the floors, natural stone combined with Royal Mosa tiles, rubber and hardwood. High-gloss reflective surfaces and curved or angled inset materials overhead ensure that there is always something interesting to catch the eye at every turn, particularly when illuminated by the custom-made lighting at feature focal points.

1 Some product areas are defined by black
  rubber flooring that contrasts with the tiles
  on the pathways.
2 The children's department spreads out over
  an area of 700 m².

3

4

3 Over 1000 brands are staged in the
department store.
4 Tom Dixon's Pipe Lights and Arne
Jacobsen's Egg Chair welcome the
customers into the formal menswear area.
5 Perforated metal walls form the backdrop
for the fragrances in the largest perfumery
in Switzerland.
6 A chandelier of champagne glasses points
out what customers can find at the J-Bar on
the ground floor.

5

6

The store has
the ambience and
charisma of a fashion
boulevard

JOSEPH AVENUE MONTAIGNE

by RAËD ABILLAMA ARCHITECTS

◆

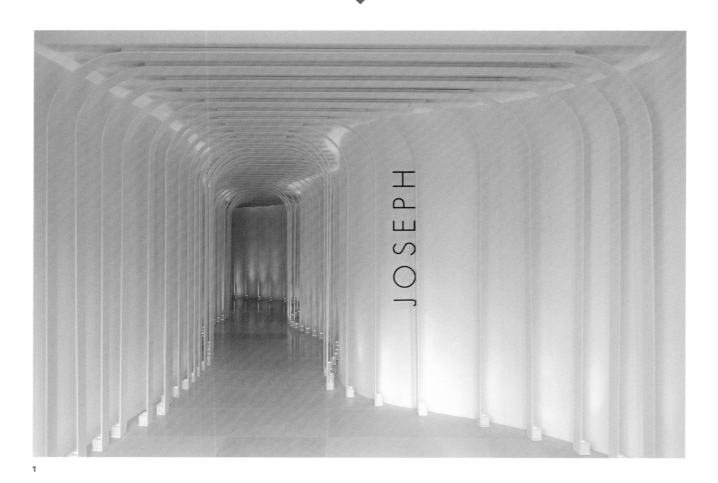

1

WHERE Paris, France WHEN December 2009
CLIENT Joseph Tricot DESIGNER Raëd Abillama Architects (p.684)
TOTAL FLOOR AREA 250 m² SHOP CONSTRUCTOR Teknisens
PHOTOGRAPHER Geraldine Bruneel

British designer label Joseph engaged with Raëd Abillama Architects to redesign the Paris store on Avenue Montaigne. The existing architecture of the shop was used as the principal guiding element for the project, with an overall ethereal quality being exuded thanks to the decor's crisp white palette. The area was divided into three main zones: the entrance, the skylight area and the curved wall area. To get people access the shop was a major problem since there is a long hallway to reach the retail area. The main challenge was to make entering the shop like a journey, leading customers down an attractive and intriguing path. The integration of white metallic arches gives this narrow walkway a rhythm and it becomes a unique architectural experience. The curved wall was continued deep into the shop, creating a circular and welcoming space with multiple purposes: lounge seating area, footwear section and fitting rooms. The building's existing U-shaped skylight became an integral part of the rebranded space. Metallic frames, used as hangers, are suspended to elevate the upper limit and give a three-dimensional impression to this zone. The frames, which are 3.2 m in height, can slide and turn along the length of the skylight, thus giving a desirable flexibility to the space. This zone is the brightest in the shop with a backlit stretched ceiling. All the furniture and finishing in the shop is mostly in white except for the counter that is in black rough metal and is designed and worked as a sculptural piece extending out of the rest.

1 The serpentine walkway, with its rhythmical white painted steel arches, leads customers from the entrance to the heart of the store.
2 View of the white high-frame hanger product displays.
3 The back of the shop is lit by the original U-shaped skylight.
4 Spherical aspects in the store include the fitting rooms and footwear section with its circular backlit illumination feature.

2

4   3

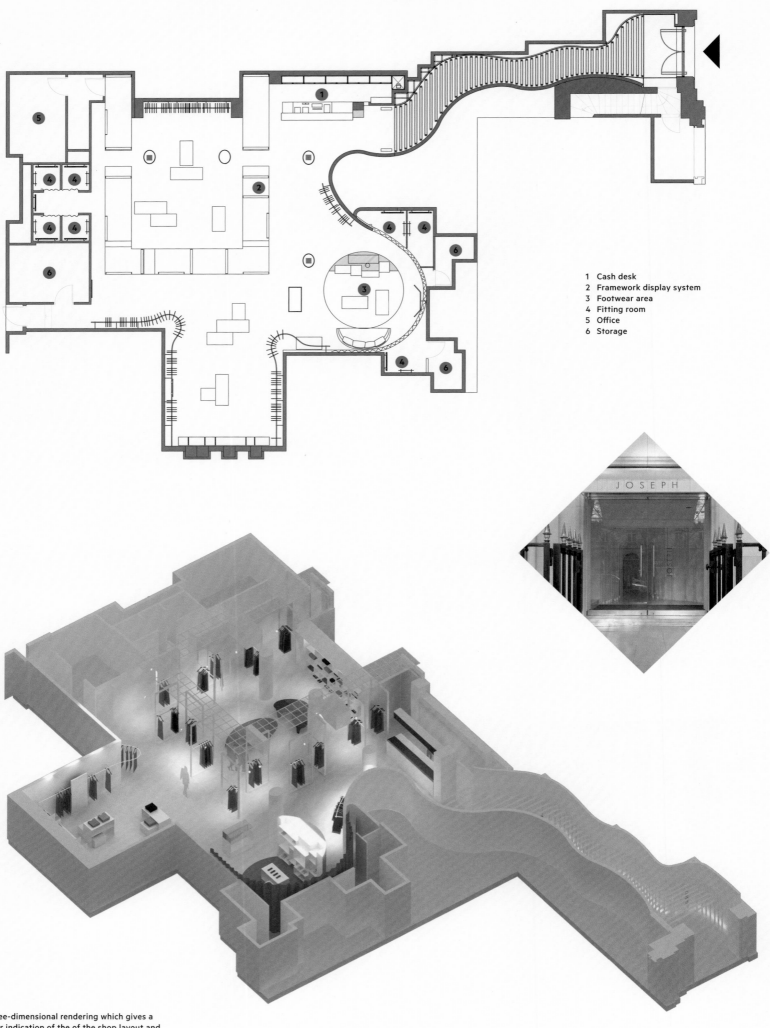

1 Cash desk
2 Framework display system
3 Footwear area
4 Fitting room
5 Office
6 Storage

Three-dimensional rendering which gives a clear indication of the of the shop layout and the U-shaped skylight.

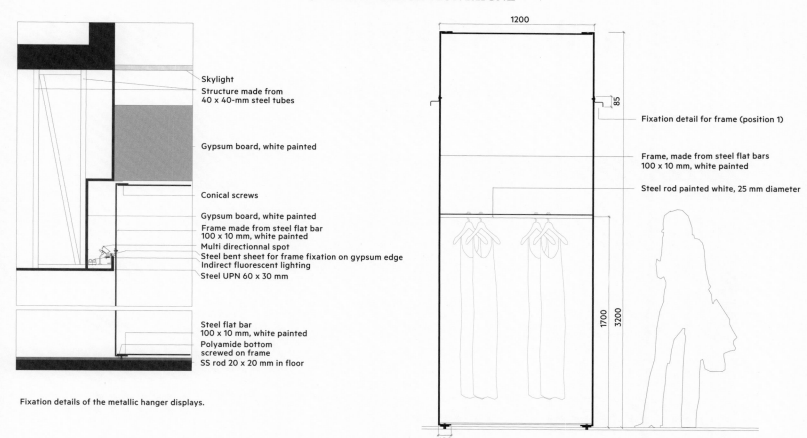

Skylight
Structure made from
40 x 40-mm steel tubes

Gypsum board, white painted

Conical screws

Gypsum board, white painted
Frame made from steel flat bar
100 x 10 mm, white painted
Multi directionnal spot
Steel bent sheet for frame fixation on gypsum edge
Indirect fluorescent lighting
Steel UPN 60 x 30 mm

Steel flat bar
100 x 10 mm, white painted
Polyamide bottom
screwed on frame
SS rod 20 x 20 mm in floor

Fixation details of the metallic hanger displays.

1200

85

Fixation detail for frame (position 1)

Frame, made from steel flat bars
100 x 10 mm, white painted

Steel rod painted white, 25 mm diameter

1700

3200

100

Front view of the metallic hanger displays.

0   200   400 mm

White metallic arches gives the narrow entrance walkway an architectural rhythm

Drawing of the store concept as viewed
looking towards the skylight and high-frame
hanger displays.

JOSEPH WESTBOURNE GROVE

by RAËD ABILLAMA ARCHITECTS

1

WHERE London, United Kingdom WHEN December 2009
CLIENT Joseph Tricot DESIGNER Raëd Abillama Architects (p.684)
TOTAL FLOOR AREA 590 m² SHOP CONSTRUCTOR Garenne Shopfitting
PHOTOGRAPHER Geraldine Bruneel

London is the historical home of womenswear label Joseph. With the establishment of a store on Westbourne Grove, Raëd Abillama Architects were brought on board to realise a high-end shopping experience. The architectural concept of the design is to display the clothing and accessories within a minimal, streamlined and light environment. The shop itself is treated as the main display area and there is a strict focus on the designer pieces. The window displays, which give an open and transparent view into the store for passers-by in the street, also create accessible product islands to customers in-store. With grey oiled wood flooring throughout and white walls and ceiling, the shell of the store is turned into a 'gallery' space ready for the material exhibits. The distinctive display units are self-contained and incorporate all the elements – lighting, modular hanging or shelving aspects and mirrors – required to exhibit the clothes under optimum conditions. The shelving systems are arranged to create a fluid circulation through the shop. As independent, freestanding components, their positions are flexible, thus allowing the space to be reshaped depending on the collection or the season. This modular character produces a highly adaptable tool for the retailer, with which a fresh and up-to-date feeling can always be created in-store. Mirrored and glass surfaces are used in the shop, with a main feature being the glass balustrade on the main stairwell leading down to the lower level. The glass above the floor level is clear and below it forms a sort-of frosted light box with a diffused glow streaming out.

1 The in-store product display islands double-up as window displays along the length of the store's facade.
2 All showcases are self-lit.
3 The stairwell to the lower floor has a wood-panelled banister painted gloss white.

1 Self-contained display units
2 Cash desk
3 Fitting rooms
4 Storage
5 Office
6 Lavatory

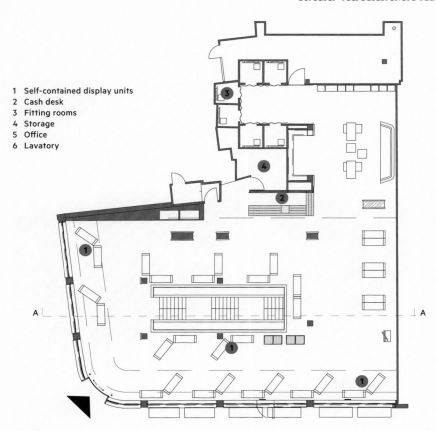

Ground floor

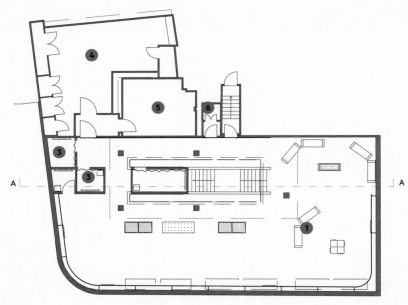

Basement

Layout of the various possible positions
for the display cases.

Section AA

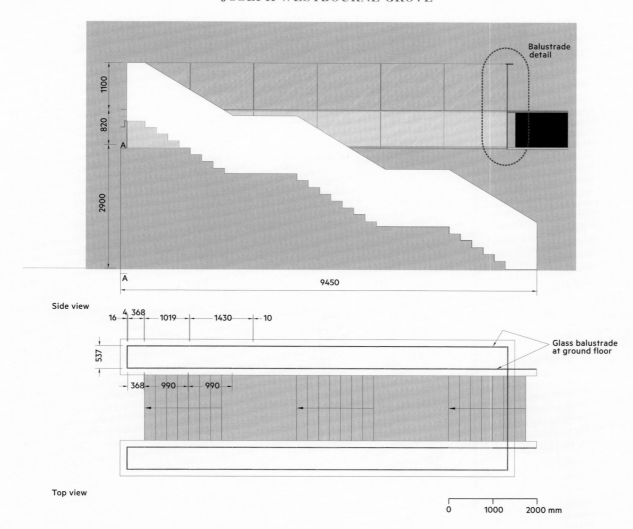

Balustrade
detail

1100

820

A

2900

A

9450

Side view

16 4 368 1019 1430 10

537

368 990 990

Glass balustrade
at ground floor

Top view

0   1000   2000 mm

The glass balustrade below the first floor forms a frosted light box with diffused light streaming out

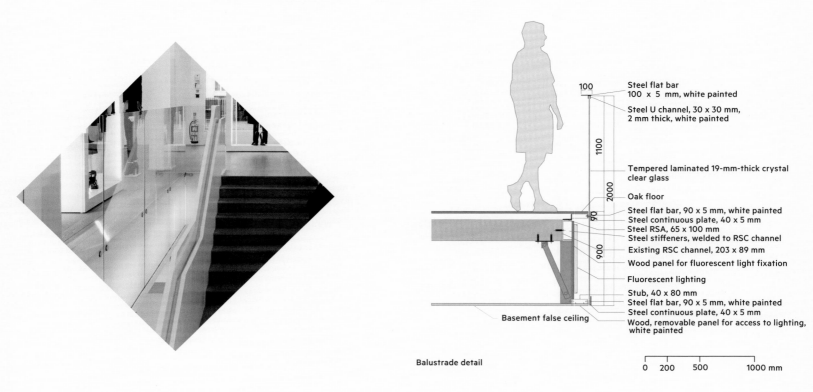

100

Steel flat bar
100 x 5 mm, white painted

Steel U channel, 30 x 30 mm,
2 mm thick, white painted

1100

Tempered laminated 19-mm-thick crystal
clear glass

2000

Oak floor

90

Steel flat bar, 90 x 5 mm, white painted
Steel continuous plate, 40 x 5 mm
Steel RSA, 65 x 100 mm
Steel stiffeners, welded to RSC channel

900

Existing RSC channel, 203 x 89 mm

Wood panel for fluorescent light fixation

Fluorescent lighting

Stub, 40 x 80 mm
Steel flat bar, 90 x 5 mm, white painted
Steel continuous plate, 40 x 5 mm

Basement false ceiling

Wood, removable panel for access to lighting,
white painted

Balustrade detail

0   200   500   1000 mm

KASTNER & ÖHLER

by BLOCHER BLOCHER PARTNERS

◆

1

WHERE Graz, Austria WHEN October 2010
CLIENT Kastner & Öhler DESIGNER Blocher Blocher Partners (p.674)
TOTAL FLOOR AREA 40,000 m² SHOP CONSTRUCTORS Ganter, Lauinger, Schlegel, Schweitzer,
Umdasch, Vizona and Visplay PHOTOGRAPHER Nikolaus Koliusis

To be Austria's largest, most modern but especially most beautiful fashion house – this was the ambition of retailer Kastner & Öhler and interior architecture studio Blocher Blocher Partners when working on the interior renovation and expansion of the department store in central Graz. With the building's prime location in this UNESCO City of Design, the team's concept was to create a unique atmosphere reminiscent of the time-honoured Belle Époque era. The filled-in atriums have been reconstructed lovingly to enhance many of the original features – with historical reconstruction of the attractive stucco decoration – and the addition of a striking roofing system floods ample daylight into the interior. Linking the various departments of the store with a coherent ambience was the challenge for the design team. The total floor space was increased by 10,000 to 40,000 m² with two escalators connecting all six floors in a well-apportioned arrangement. Throughout the shop, distinct landscapes have been created using natural materials, such as natural stone, slate and hardwood, to cover walls, walkways and ceilings with textured patterns and eye-catching angular aspects. Balconies overlooking the impressive atrium ensures customers are treated to striking vistas on every level as they journey upwards through the store – a taste of what awaits them at the pinnacle of the building where they are treated to a panoremic view across the city.

1 During the renovation, the area dedicated
  to fashion was almost doubled in size.
2 The department store takes up all six floors
  of the Belle Époque building. At the top is
  a roof terrace restaurant that allows for a
  magnificent 360-degree view of Graz.

3

5

3 In the natural cosmetics area, all materials were chosen to match the products. Wooden ceiling beams, large plants and stone flooring bring about the right atmosphere.
4 One of the highlight for customers is the champagne bar on the first floor. Relaxing in one of Arne Jacobson's Egg Chairs, they can listen to live piano music while enjoying a glass of bubbly.
5 Backlit onyx walls mark the perfume department on the ground floor.

The concept was to create a unique atmosphere reminiscent of the time-honoured Belle Époque era

LE CIEL BLEU

by NORIYUKI OTSUKA DESIGN OFFICE

2

WHERE Osaka, Japan WHEN May 2011
CLIENT Le Ciel Bleu DESIGNER Noriyuki Otsuka Design Office (p.682)
TOTAL FLOOR AREA 278 m² SHOP CONSTRUCTOR Hasegawa
PHOTOGRAPHER Hiroyuki Hirai

The design of the new Le Ciel Bleu fashion store in Osaka was undertaken by Noriyuki Otsuka Design Office. The brief called for a brilliant white space with a high degree of perfection, which suited the studio's own policy – 'Nothing is everything / Mixtures of transparency' – perfectly. The backdrop to the new store is a luxurious architectural space with a 5-m high ceiling. So as to not end up with an interior resembling a fashion retail megastore, the team proposed a design that housed another architectural space within the shop's own spacious floor plan. This was the crux of the design, as part of a concept that embodies a simple sparseness. A structure takes the form of an oval-shaped caged cylinder that is constructed from a self-supporting mesh. Due to the size of this feature, it was necessary to avoid integrating it too much with the surrounding space and so it was deliberately aligned off-centre from the axis of the building. This layout instils a sense of gravity, yet at the same time enhances the light and airy atmosphere that is created in the entirely white room. Custom-made light fittings run along the length of the see-through cylinder in order to make the interior space the primary focus of the design. In here, as well as on the surrounding walls of the shop, products are displayed on simple railings and elegant glass shelves, with accessories also positioned in the Perspex cubes which line one of the side walls.

1 A tunnel structure within the large space contained the fashion collection.
2 The shop was designed for a retail complex called Lucua, which was built as part of the redevelopment of a commercial district.

3

The designer proposed an
interior which housed another
architectural space within it

4

5

3 The customised floor is gold metallic.
4 The cylinder structure consists of a self-supporting mesh.
5 Transparent shoe racks are integrated in the wall outside the mesh structure.

LEVI STRAUSS

by CHECKLAND KINDLEYSIDES

◆

2

WHERE London, United Kingdom WHEN March 2010
CLIENT Levi Strauss & Co. DESIGNER Checkland Kindleysides (p.675)
TOTAL FLOOR AREA 793 m² SHOP CONSTRUCTORS CDS and Checkland Kindleysides
PHOTOGRAPHER Keith Parry

In charge of the redesign of the Levi's flagship store on London's Regent Street was the Checkland Kindleysides team, following a brief which called for a 'complete brand experience at the ultimate jeanswear destination'. The concept encapsulates an artisan's working environment, crafting a visually-captivating space where customers experience not only product offerings but also storytelling. Akin to a gallery in parts, the first aspect that greets customers as they walk in off the street is an 80-m²-curated space, showcasing everything from exclusive product collaborations to art exhibitions. Glass with a blue hue is a prominent aspect in the store, with a toughened-glass footbridge – which carries a product gallery – running over the main stairwell. As customers descend to the lower level, a sea of tailors' leg forms provides visual

impact, positioned proudly above the contemporary haberdashers' cabinets that display the corresponding denim finishes with their further product displays. A vault which holds 22 washes of the iconic Levi's 501 jean also awaits to be discovered in the basement. The challenge for the design team was to ensure that the building looked authentic and in-line with the concept. Attention to detail was examined in minutiae, from the reclaimed Regency bricks – laid in English-bond with lime-mortar – to sourcing the perfect recycled timber for the flooring; even subtle nods to the historical precursor of the 501 – the Levi's 'XX' jean, dated ca. 1880 – are expressed throughout in the architecture and furniture.

1 The basement warehouse focuses on the 22
different washes of the iconic 501 jean.
2 Upon entering the store, customers first
find themselves in a curated space called
the 'Origin' gallery.

3

4

The iconic Levi's 501 jean awaits to be discovered in the seemingly endless vault in the basement

5

6

3 In the 'inspection room', leg forms present different jean types while the available denim finishes are laid out below.
4 In the fitting rooms, walls are crafted with 'duck canvas', a reproduction of the original canvas that was used by Levi Strauss in the 19th century.
5 Reclaimed Regency bricks are used for the wall behind the cash desk.
6 A gallery runs over the staircase, telling seasonal product stories.

LEVI'S ICON STORE

by PLAJER & FRANZ STUDIO

1

WHERE Berlin, Germany WHEN July 2010
CLIENT Levi Strauss DESIGNER plajer & franz studio (p.683)
TOTAL FLOOR AREA 87 m² SHOP CONSTRUCTOR Skill Crew Event- und Bühnenbau
PHOTOGRAPHER diephotodesigner.de (Ken Schluchtmann)

The Levi's Icon Store in Berlin is a small concept store designed by plajer & franz studio. The challenge for the team was to redesign and transform the existing store in just 5 weeks before Berlin Fashion Week and, in addition, the project needed to be completed with a limited budget. The vision was to create a feeling of being in a typical old loft apartment filled with an industrial charm. Throughout the store, the Levi's brand merges with Berlin culture by using historic architectural elements in an artful manner. Aged window frames – with the original paintwork flaking off – have been utilised in a unique way. They are positioned around the edge of the store and form shelf structures and their metalwork bars becoming clothes rails. Some of the panes of glass in sections of the frames are original and others are glazed with acrylic panes that etches of 'places-to-be' in Berlin on them, providing customers with informative messages. Large old radiators also find a use in the shop, providing a base for the presentation table which takes pride of place at the centre of the store. Reclaimed wooden beams, like those used in the table, are also utilised as wooden supports and decoration elsewhere in the store, for instance the imposing cash desk which has been constructed from a mishmash of vintage wood and recycled door elements. Herringbone patterned parquet covers the floors and in the fitting room area, well-worn colourful rugs are scattered underfoot giving this space a cosy and warm atmosphere.

1 The two rooms of the original building are distinguished by different window styles.
2 Vintage furniture and original coving gives the shop the feel of a well-loved apartment.
3 Reclaimed wood has been used to construct the fitting rooms.
4 The etching on the panes act as personal invites to customers to check out some of the lesser know places in Berlin.
5 Next page: The wall between the two rooms has been removed to open up the space.

2

3

Some of the panes of glass have etches of 'places-to-be' in Berlin on them

4

LÓDZ

by ZOOM INDUSTRIES

1

WHERE Oisterwijk, the Netherlands **WHEN** January 2009
CLIENT Lódz **DESIGNER** Zoom Industries (p.687)
TOTAL FLOOR AREA 230 m² **SHOP CONSTRUCTORS** Bouwbedrijf Gelens and Trimet BVBA
PHOTOGRAPHER Gregor Ramaekers

Dutch fashion brand Lódz extended its retail reach in 2009 by adding a new boutique to its ranks in the Tilburg region of the Netherlands. The new store was designed by Zoom Industries as a subtly sophisticated transformation of the original architecture. Contemporary aesthetics and materials were employed to reflect the selection of high quality womenswear available in the store. The concept saw two important attributes of fashion – material and cut – being adapted and interpreted into the interior design. The tripartite division of the facade incorporates the existing floor tiles of the entrance way and the horizontal framework corresponds with the structural walls of the building. The entrance has an integrated central display window which, because of the stepped-back flanking windows, gives a feeling of extending into the promenade mediating between the indoor and outdoor space. Inside, parallel illuminated strips overhead draw the eye to span into the depths of the shop. The space is furnished simply with leather wainscoting and upholstered wall coverings in the entrance zone and at the very back of the shop. Here architecture meets fashion: the concept of wall covering becomes wall dressing. The consistent and minimalist geometric forms of the design creates a unified whole with its earthy palette of creams and browns. Subtle contrasts are exploited in the choice of materials from the powder-coated steel on the facade and the light travertine used for the counters to the combination of polished steel with large reflective surfaces and leather panelling used for the furnishings.

1 The travertine limestone counters tie in with the light colour palette of the store.
2 Parallel lighting strips overhead draw customers to the back of the store.
3 The shop's glass-fronted facade is framed with a dark powder-coated steel surround.
4 Walls and shelving systems are lined with brown leather-padded panels.

Architecture meets fashion: the concept of wall covering becomes wall dressing

2

4

MADHECTIC

by LINE-INC

◆

1

WHERE Tokyo, Japan **WHEN** September 2010
CLIENT World **DESIGNER** Line-Inc (p.681)
TOTAL FLOOR AREA 134 m² **SHOP CONSTRUCTOR** Space
PHOTOGRAPHER Kenzo Takaya

In the 1990s, at the time that the street culture of skating, music and graffiti was of great influence in Japan, the Hectic brand was founded in Harajuku, Tokyo, a place known for the gatherings of young people dressed in expressive styles. The creators – who were immersed in the popular street culture themselves – imported American street wear and also designed their own line. In order to expand their business, they opened a shop called MadHectic in 1994. A second store followed a little later and, in 2010, it was time for the grand opening of the third shop. The interior was designed by the Japanese design firm Line-Inc with a concept that has a raw feel. The left wall is panelled in unfinished wood, which continues up the full height of the building, crossing overhead as it sweeps across the ceiling of the upper level. This feature is reminiscent of a skate ramp and snaking across the wooden surface is a bold, black-and-white graffiti-like painting by the Japanese artist Oyama Enrico Isamu Letter which gives the space an energetic and dynamic impact. Upstairs, customers will even spot bicycles suspended from the wooden ceiling, hanging upside-down. Together with several pinball machines that have been installed, the bicycles give the store its playfulness. The concrete floor and rails that carry the clothing collection all match the skate park theme. As the entire facade is glass, the store's features can already be spotted from the street, communicating exactly what kind of clothing style can be found inside.

1 Clearly visible from the street is the wooden left wall that sweeps across the ceiling, shaped like a skate ramp.
2 The store has a rough, urban look.
3 Pinball machines add to the playfulness of the store.

MINÄ PERHONEN ARKISTOT

by TORAFU ARCHITECTS

1

WHERE Tokyo, Japan WHEN September 2010
CLIENT Akira Minagawa DESIGNER Torafu Architects (p.686)
TOTAL FLOOR AREA 108 m² SHOP CONSTRUCTORS Tokyo Studio and Masamune
PHOTOGRAPHER Fuminari Yoshitsugu

The team at Torafu Architects was brought on board to realise the interior design for the new store minä perhonen arkistot in Tokyo. This is a retail space for the fashion brand of Japanese textile and clothes designer Akira Minagawa. The word *arkistot* is Finnish for 'archive' and symbolises the concept of the store, which deals in items which the brand released in the past. Giving the merchandise a new lease of life, the shop was created as a free space that allows for change. The textiles and clothes are characterised by a romantic and appealingly naive style, with the interior of the shop having a similar feel. Having the depth of a typical house in this region of Tokyo, the shop has a long and fairly narrow footprint. Throughout the floor space mobile box-shaped displays of varying heights and sizes are positioned, which can

be moved to accommodate changing store layouts or events such as workshops. Removable shelf boards and hangers can be reconfigured to avoid restricting the arrangement of items. Each of the display boxes incorporates both a mirror panel and a green chalkboard on perpendicular surfaces. As the boxes can be faced in differing directions, the mirrors catch hidden angles and generate interesting reflections, creating a complex image of the surroundings that confers an expansion to the space.

1 One simple furniture unit design is utilised for the display modules and the cash desk counter. The chalkboard aspect means fun messages can be displayed throughout.
2 The store is designed as a space that defies seasons due to the fact that the layout can be changed quickly and easily.
3 The concrete floor and ceiling gives the space a raw feel.
4 On the windows, a wood-grain-effect film has been applied to tie in with the light wood materials used in the shop's simple style of furnishings.

Mirrors catch hidden
angles and generate
interesting reflections

MOSS BESPOKE

by HOUSEHOLD

1

WHERE London, United Kingdom WHEN June 2010
CLIENT Moss Bros Group DESIGNER Household (p.679)
TOTAL FLOOR AREA 180 m² SHOP CONSTRUCTOR John Richards Shopfitters
PHOTOGRAPHER Julian Abrams

The British brand Moss Bros has been synonymous with fine suits for well over a century in the United Kingdom. The Group's reputation in formal menswear and commitment to customer service saw the natural progression to create a new retail proposition: bespoke tailoring on the high street. Household was briefed to develop the brand architecture for the new bespoke suiting business. For many, the idea of getting a suit made might not have been an option previously, associated with high-end luxury and an equally high price tag. The challenge for the design team was to demystify the process of creating a bespoke suit and communicate the stages and price options available, whilst staying true to the magic, tactility and individuality of personalised suit-making. The 'bespoke' branding is highlighted with a distinguished choice of material – copper – which appears in the light fittings and decorative panels. Copper also forms the basis of the colour palette along with a particular shade of marine blue on the feature wall, where the copper thread lettering forms a simple yet striking visual signature. The core idea for the brand experience is the 'A to Z of suiting', incorporating an integrated journey for the customer which details the options available to them, beginning at the 'Alphabet Bar' with an online library of fabric and tailoring books. It is also an architectural element connecting the bespoke service feature between floors, creating additional privacy for the exclusive mezzanine lounge.

1 Branded signage was also part of the brief: copper letters appear to be stitched in the marine blue wall.
2 Graphic panels on one wall highlight to customers the key aspects of bespoke tailoring to create their unique suit.
3 The quality of the suits was communicated through the use of trusted and traditional materials, such as fumed oak.

2

3

The challenge was
to demystify bespoke
tailoring whilst
staying true to the
magic, tactility and
individuality of
the process

NIKE

by DAY

1

WHERE Paris, France WHEN August 2009
CLIENT Nike Europe DESIGNER Day (p.677)
TOTAL FLOOR AREA 100 m² SHOP CONSTRUCTOR Umdash
PHOTOGRAPHER Katrien Franken

Nike Sportswear is a division of Nike which includes collections based on timeless sports apparel and shoes. It has its own (sub) brand identity which encompasses images of classic gyms, used equipment and urban environments. Day was commissioned to design the pilot Nike Sportswear flagship store in Paris, the first of a chain throughout Europe. The brief required that sportswear retail designs from the United States be included within the shop, as well as exhibit and guerrilla store designs. The charismatic location – an old bookstore in Le Marais – offered a unique mix of classic Parisian beauty, wear and tear and performance gear. Enhancing the ambience, the relevant historic details and finishes of the building were maintained whilst being combined with the strong and iconic fixtures. Bespoke display modules were constructed with an amalgamation of used sports equipment, such as jump boxes, gymnastic rings and parallel bars, being given a new lease of life in a contemporary setting. The colour palette is a muted mixture of dusty browns, blues, greys and greens, with a splash of sunshine yellow on the original stair banister greeting customers as they reach the first floor. On the ground floor, a visual array of angles and shapes appears within the patterned carpet and in the paintwork, which seamlessly integrates the cabinets lining the front of the shop beneath the display window. On the walls are illustrations, which can be altered seasonally, portraying a graphical illustration of the concept and the brand.

1 View towards the entrance. The original
   floor tiles were kept intact.
2 The graphics on the staircase are by design
   duo Antoine + Manuel from Paris.
3 View of the cash desk and the fitting rooms
   located directly behind.

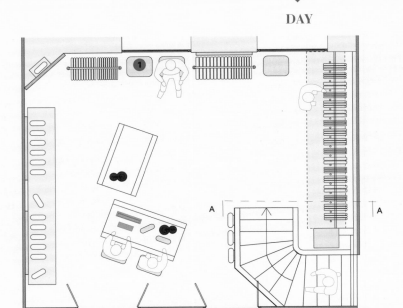

First floor

1 Seating
2 Cash desk
3 Fitting room
4 Storage

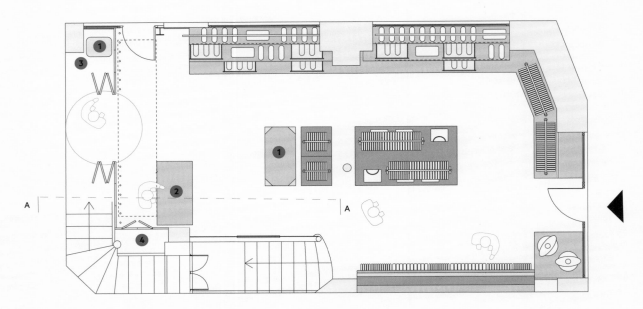

Ground floor

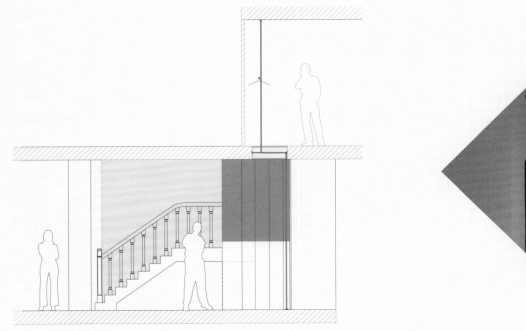

Section AA

Gym equipment was used for the furnishing of the new shop.

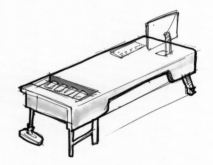

Illustrations on the walls can be altered seasonally

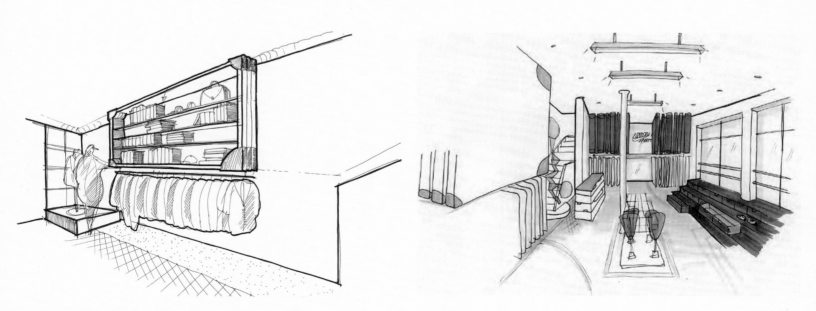

Sketches showing how the previous function of the space as a bookstore is subtly integrated into the design.

NIKE STADIUM

by ARCHITECTURE AT LARGE/RAFAEL DE CÁRDENAS

1

WHERE New York, United States WHEN May 2010
CLIENT Nike Sportswear DESIGNER Architecture at Large/Rafael de Cárdenas (p.673)
TOTAL FLOOR AREA 743 m² SHOP CONSTRUCTORS Tangram and Atomic Design
PHOTOGRAPHER Allen Benedikt

When the global sportswear company Nike decided to establish a Nike Stadium in the Bowery area of Manhattan, the space was to be a combination community centre, gallery and store. Bowery Stadium is a celebration of sports and the opening coincided with the FIFA World Cup in 2010. Rafael de Cárdenas collaborated with Nike on the design of the retail aspect of the space and football was the inspiration. The concept began with a football field which was rotated, revolved and replicated to give a unique pattern of directional lines. In the retail space, the pattern is applied to the floor to give it the dynamism of a football field, with a black and white palette together with the yellow and green colours of the Brazilian national team, integrating the designer's own Brazilian background. A slightly disorienting effect is realised when the graphic stripes are viewed in conjunction with the floating display elements around the edge of the space which play with visual ideas of gravity. Polygonal modular cells are dispersed throughout, constructed from an everyday material – pegboard – which is also used for the wall coverings. Backlit illumination creates further visual patterns within the angular niches which are cut out to incorporate product displays. In the gallery space, the triangular floor modules can be arranged to create micro-spaces within the larger context to enable installation art, games or exhibitions.

1 Patterned tape in Brazilian green and yellow on the flooring represents the dynamics on a soccer field.
2 Nike Stadium collaborated with artistic partners to deliver creative expressions of soccer, including the yellow and black design near the entrance by Allen Benedikt.
3 The main event space is designed to fulfil multiple functions, moving and changing like players on a field under a directional, pitch-like pattern of linear fluorescents.

1

At the end of the simulated runway lies a world of fashion

OLYMP & HADES

by CORNEILLE UEDINGSLOHMANN ARCHITEKTEN

2

WHERE Essen, Germany **WHEN** October 2009
CLIENT J.P. Jeans Palast Schmidt & Görgens **DESIGNER** Corneille Uedingslohmann Architekten (p.676)
TOTAL FLOOR AREA 1600 m² **SHOP CONSTRUCTOR** Dettmer Ladenbau
PHOTOGRAPHER Jan Poppenhagen

Olymp & Hades is an expanding German multi-label fashion concept which has almost 30 outlets nationwide. Its new store in Essen was designed by Corneille Uedingslohmann Architects. With the merger of several small areas to create the retail space, there were specific challenges which arose in the implementation of a consistent design concept. Difficult spatial realities, such as different floor levels, low ceilings and an unorthodox floor plan, required a custom-designed retail space. The creative team opted for a sleek and glossy environment: a dark space punctuated by shining light streams with an almost futuristic feel. At the entrance, the eye-catching rolling walkway which conveys customers up to the first-floor store is mysterious and intriguing and passers-by are enticed to step aboard. With the accompanying sleek black LED wall generating light and music to one side and the installation reflection in the parallel mirror wall, it's as if it is pulling customers through a vortex into the retail space. At the end of this simulated runway, they find themselves amidst a world of fashion. Different materials, furniture forms, lighting and flooring distinguish each autonomous area in the essentially black space and the vast showroom is divided up with various product islands. Highly-reflective materials – such as Corten steel and high-gloss laminate – are used for the furniture and fittings, with a feature aspect being the lustrous burgundy red canopy which wraps around the cash desk. The use of leather, faux concrete, brushed oak and wire mesh also further accentuates the diversity of each product area.

1   A rolling walkway transports customers from the entrance to the retail area on the first floor.
2   The bright red colour of the cash desk makes sure customer have no problem finding it.

3

It is as if it is pulling customers through a vortex into the retail space

4

3 The floor is treated with a concrete coating.
4 A generous seating area upholstered in genuine cowhide was created in front of the fitting rooms.
5 Suspended ceiling panels define the various product areas.
6 The 'Denim Corner' is set apart on a raised oak platform.

PADDOCK SHOP

by AHEADCONCEPT

◆

1

WHERE Nürburg, Germany **WHEN** July 2009
CLIENT MBA-Solutions **DESIGNER** AheadConcept (p.673)
TOTAL FLOOR AREA 780 m² **SHOP CONSTRUCTOR** Falckenthal Möbel
PHOTOGRAPHER Stefan Thomas Kröger

Nürburgring is a motor sport complex in Nürburg, Germany, that holds a modern Grand Prix Circuit and a much longer race track around the village. AheadConcept was asked to translate the exhilarating atmosphere of motorsport into a retail interior for the sale of multibrand clothing and merchandise associated with the racing lifestyle. The dynamic aspects of racing were at the core of the design concept, as well as key components of the racing circuit. A key aspect is the 100-m long ceiling panel of extruded PVC which mirrors the stylised circuit that seamlessly guides the customer through the space under the grandstand which goes up to a height of 7 m. The winding pathway is inlaid with several special PVC coatings which look like asphalt that sparkles enticingly beneath the spotlights. The space has a somewhat futuristic feel with its high-gloss white and silver surfaces. By using typical elements of racetracks – such as hairpin beds, chicanes, a pit lane, gravel trap and run-off area – customers are treated to an exciting journey around the store past the defined areas for the different fashion brands. The circuit also takes them past actual Formula 1 racing cars positioned amongst the product displays. Having a chance to get up-close to the stars of the racing world – the cars – creates a memorable experience and is the icing on the cake for many motorsports aficionados.

1 All furniture is made of coloured MDF with high-impact and abrasion-proof high pressure laminate in white high gloss.
2 Inside the hairpin bend is an actual a Formula 1 racing car, another one is positioned on the wall.

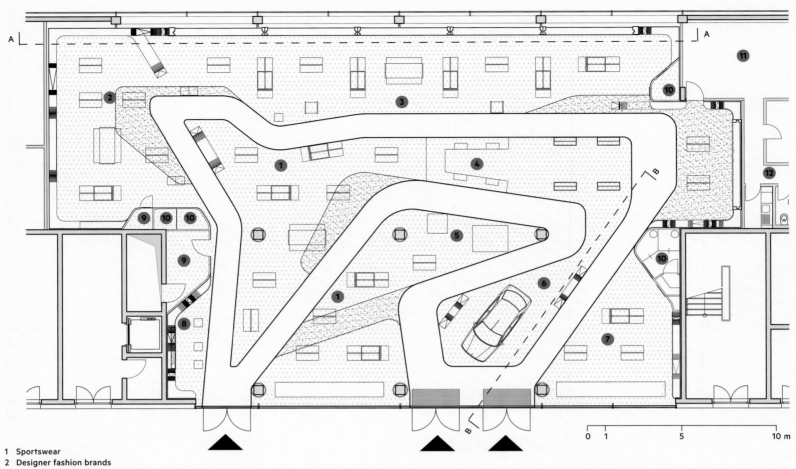

1 Sportswear
2 Designer fashion brands
3 Motorsport brands
4 Cash desk
5 Books
6 Event area
7 Nürburgring merchandise
8 Footwear
9 Storage
10 Fitting room
11 Office
12 Lavatory

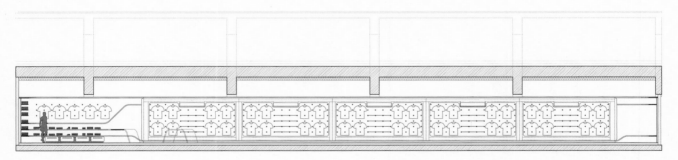

Section AA

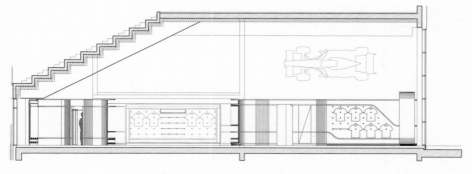

Section BB

Rendering of the MDF furniture and the ceiling
panel that mirrors the racetrack below.

The twisting pathway looks like asphalt that sparkles enticingly beneath the spotlights

The area below the Formula 1 race car that is
attached to the wall carries the assortment of
Nürburgring merchandise.

PRECINCT 5

by KUUB

2

WHERE Amsterdam, the Netherlands WHEN January 2010
CLIENT Precinct 5 DESIGNER Kuub (p.681)
TOTAL FLOOR AREA 300 m² SHOP CONSTRUCTOR Swider Bud
PHOTOGRAPHER Primabeeld (Marcel van der Burg)

Precinct 5 is a new store concept which was created in the centre of Amsterdam in an old canal house which once housed the old police station, hence the name of the shop. This is where fashion and lifestyle brands Stussy and Enplus have their base in the Dutch capital and this unique collaboration called for a unique store design, which is where the Kuub architects stepped in. The brief was to create a high-end fashion store and the team needed to employ creative design tactics in order to stick to the low budget and meet the tight deadline. The starting point was the structure of the building itself, with the overall design concept being to reveal the space, creating a luxury shell with a modular and flexible interior. The team plus industrial designer Pieter Kool worked with specific themes: modularity, flexibility, architectural lines, volumes and

space. Unveiling the constructive characteristics of the former precinct, the conditions were set for the black steel furniture to outperform in an inspiring industrial cathedral of fashion. In five weeks, the transformation was complete using the basic materials of concrete, steel, glass and paint. The main modular element in the space is the 'Kube', a tubular black steel framework that can be assembled into different spatial volumes. Each unit measures 129 x 43 x 43 cm (or 86 x 43 x 43 cm) and can be left as the skeleton steel cubes or lined with wood, glass or LED panels. Whether stacked high on the raw concrete floor or suspended from the open ceiling rafters, the sculptural forms fill the space with maximum visual effect.

1 A snake-like constellation of 'Kubes' entices visitors to explore the next level.
2 The stretched cubical elements with shoe storage space are suspended in the central void from the high ceiling of the shop.

3 One of the Kubes, wrapped in red shoelaces, gives a pair of Nike sneakers maximum exposure.
4 Dynamic signage was integrated in the interior design concept in collaboration with the graphic design studio Experimental Jetset.
5+6 For the Nike Stadium Amsterdam event, during the 2010 FIFA World Cup, the Kubes were used in the formation of a Nike experience 'room' which had a moveable roof that could be hoisted up into the ceiling space.

4

The space became an inspiring industrial cathedral of fashion

5

6

PUMA

by PLAJER & FRANZ STUDIO

◆

1

WHERE Paris, France WHEN April 2011
CLIENT Puma DESIGNER plajer & franz studio (p.683)
TOTAL FLOOR AREA 207 m² SHOP CONSTRUCTOR Dula-Werke Dustmann & Co.
PHOTOGRAPHER Puma (Manuel Schlüter)

Sportswear brand Puma's Paris store reopened after a complete redesign by plajer & franz studio in cooperation with Puma's Ales Kernjak. The concept was to instil a sense of joy into the retail environment while aiming at a sustainable and innovative shop design. In line with the four key aims of the brand – to be fair, honest, positive and creative – the new store displays a great mix of an ecological technology and numerous cutting-edge aspects allowing for interactive customer engagement. The first aspect that catches the customers' attention is the large installation in the shop window over the entrance with its illuminated multi-coloured stripe functions. This is crafted out of wooden strips into the shape of a large Puma shoe and integrates into the first floor shelving system. Wood blocks are used for sneaker

displays placed against the grey backdrop to give clear product category navigation within the distinct areas. A 6-m high wall in the brand's red colour is a vibrant feature, built out of separate and movable cubes which can be changed randomly. The wall acts as the connecting element between the two floors and the colour is also repeated in the fixtures, fittings and 'redworld elements', including the iPad wall framed by red transparent glass, the 'Puma peep-show' and the 'un-smartphone'. Throughout the store, iPads are also embedded into the furniture – on retractable arms where customers can interact with the brand browsing the online store, or using specially developed apps on the 'Puma joy pad' wall – adding to a sense of fun.

1 The shop is located on a busy intersection.
2 In the store concept, brand expression was by GBH, London and the creative technology elements were incorporated by Spies & Assassins, New York.
3 One of the fun aspects is the 'Puma joy pad', a wall framed by red transparent glass and with numerous iPads positioned for customers to play around with.

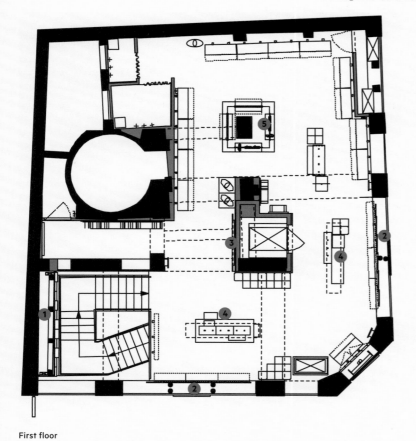

First floor

The concept aimed to instil a sense of joy into the retail environment

1 Brandwall
2 Puma shoe installation
3 iPad wall
4 Footwear display
5 Clothing display
6 Cash desk

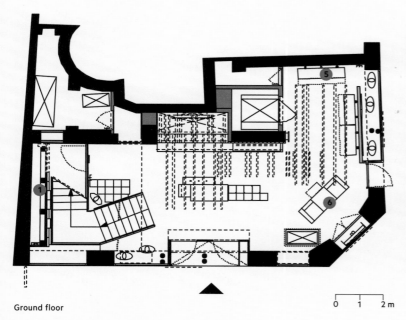

Ground floor

0 1 2 m

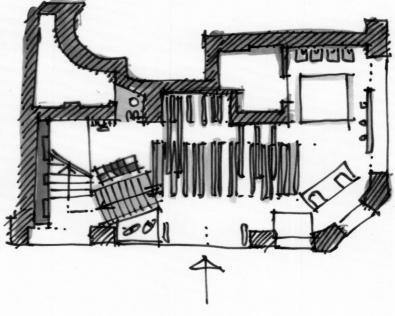

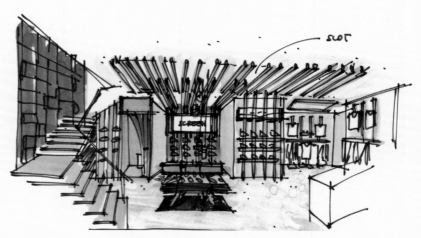

Sketch of the ground floor with its footwear wall system made from wooden slots.

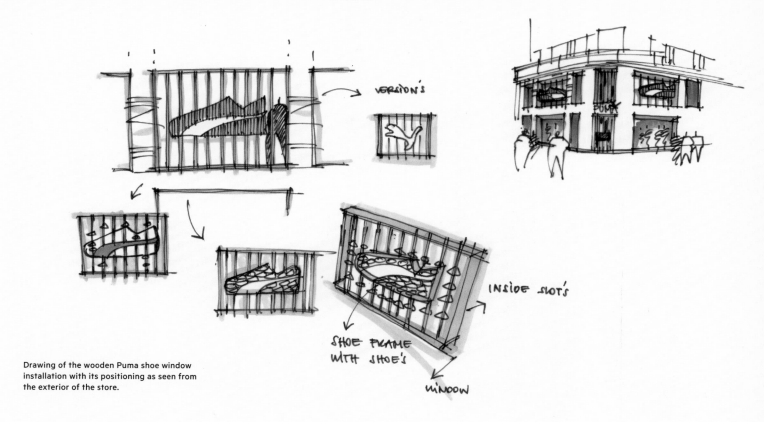

Drawing of the wooden Puma shoe window installation with its positioning as seen from the exterior of the store.

Sketch of the first floor view, indicating the iPad wall and the video screens on the ceiling.

RAZILI

by K1P3 ARCHITECTS

1

WHERE Tel Aviv, Israel **WHEN** January 2010
CLIENT Orit and Ya'ir Razili **SHOP CONSTRUCTOR** Gil Vaaknin (p.680)
TOTAL FLOOR AREA 100 m² **DESIGNER** k1p3 architects
PHOTOGRAPHER Daniel Sheriff

Tel Aviv's fashion enterprise Razili identifies fresh, new talent and gives upcoming Israeli designers a commercial platform in a retail boutique. For the shop design, k1p3 architects wanted to create a neutral display system which befits various different styles of product and could be adapted easily. The shop is situated within an assemblage of former small-scale factory buildings next to an abandoned train station. The individual structures of the compound are all preservation buildings and this particular space contained historic paintings on the inner walls which fell under the preservation category. The fundamental design guideline was the decision to develop independent, free-standing display elements which would not have to be connected to any existing wall and which would work with a narrow materials palette using basic, raw materials. A series of typologies was developed based on two modules, 50 x 50 cm and 150 x 50 cm cast concrete bases, supporting dark steel frames which in turn incorporate the various display elements. The jewellery collection is housed in two black cases which are cantilevered around an existing central column, with black steel supports on either side. The lighting is based on three rows of fluorescent tubes fixed on both sides of an existing double beam under the concrete ceiling, with individual custom-designed cylinder spotlights illuminating the mannequins.

1 Plywood display boxes, placed on either side of the structural column, contain the accessories collection.
2 As the preservation building contains historic paintings, the design team created free-standing displays that don't have to be connected to walls.
3 All display elements were placed on a square concrete base.
4 The original wall served as an artwork in itself, creating a dialogue between new display typologies and the historic context.

2

3

4

REISS BARRETT STREET

by D-RAW AND SQUIRE AND PARTNERS

2

WHERE London, United Kingdom WHEN August 2010
CLIENT Reiss DESIGNERS d-raw (p.677) and Squire and Partners (p.685)
TOTAL FLOOR AREA 850 m² SHOP CONSTRUCTOR Centreline Shopfitting Projects
PHOTOGRAPHERS Will Price and Richard Leeney

In the heart of London's busiest shopping district, nestled just behind Oxford street, stands the headquarters of British fashion retailer Reiss: an example of eye-catching architectural design dedicated to promoting brand values. Affectionately known as Reiss One, the central London flagship was collaboratively designed by two architecture agencies, d-raw and Squire and Partners, as a one-stop destination for Reiss' entire manifesto. A retail beacon spread across seven storeys, the space is required to perform multiple, simultaneous functions including housing the brand's global flagship store, design ateliers and central office hub, plus the penthouse apartment of company founder David Reiss. Its most distinguishing feature is its imposing facade – a pavement-to-roof surround consisting of 10-cm-thick panels of a serrated acrylic substrate – which can be both back- and under-lit to reveal a glowing second skin. Pre-programmable with an infinite range of colour changes, the facade has been designed to track the mood of the moment as succinctly as the changing fashion seasons. The concept for the interior design of the space revolves a gallery-style canvas of raw concrete, allowing for experimental interchanges of fixtures and fittings. Metallic silver and gold accents punctuate a neutral decor of stone, glass, marble and wood and just two windows, flanking the entrance, offer passers-by a glimpse inside. Dispensing with the usual show-and-tell of window displays or ostentatious visual merchandising to entice consumers in, this is a store that instead relies on its architectural bravado to do its talking.

1 The building can be lit to any required shade allowing it to shift seasonally or according to new in-store developments or events.
2 The store has a herringbone patterned marble floor laid underfoot.

3

Metallic silver and gold accents punctuate the product display areas

4

5

3 Three storeys of the building are used for
the flagship store.
4 Look books are laid out on the display
tables throughout the store.
5 Display units made from brass scaffolding
are placed in the centre of the space. A
silver colour is used for the rails which line
the walls.

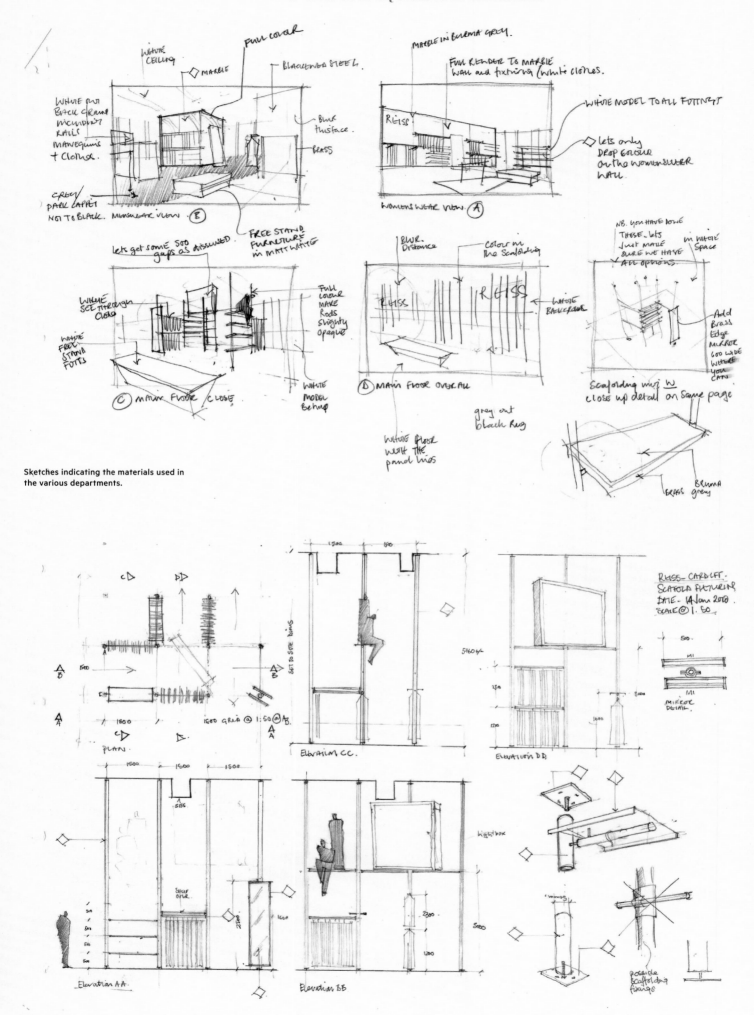

Sketches indicating the materials used in
the various departments.

Sketches of the brass scaffolding
display construction.

Sketch of the womenswear department indicating the different wall finishes.

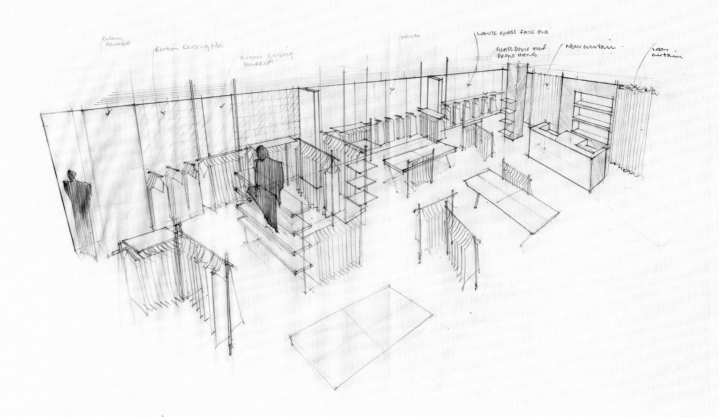

A gallery-style canvas of raw concrete allows for experimental interchanges of fixtures and fittings

Sketch of the suspended ceiling panel that consists of slats concealing the light sources.

REISS ROBERTSON BOULEVARD

by D-RAW

2

WHERE Los Angeles, United States WHEN June 2009
CLIENT Reiss DESIGNER d-raw (p.677)
TOTAL FLOOR AREA 900 m² SHOP CONSTRUCTOR Team CIS
PHOTOGRAPHER Eric Laignel

When British fashion brand Reiss opened its first store in California – at the time, only its second in the United States – in 2009, the project brief called for a store that would redefine the retailer's existing identity for a US audience. Architectural consultancy d-raw took inspiration from both the natural and the synthetic in order to make a bold yet inviting statement space at the foot of the Hollywood Hills. Drawn from a neutral palette, the interior is based on a strong, sculpturally-influenced repertoire of flowing shapes and solid materials, including marble, wood and resin, while the facade is composed almost exclusively of glass. This gives the building a sleek, dark frontage in stark contrast to the other shops on the tree-lined boulevard. The outer glass layer is punctuated with a swathe of large-scale, pixellated graphic shapes which cast patterns onto the floors and walls inside the store as the sun traverses its perimeter – a dynamic scheme which is re-invented hour-by-hour, along with the naturally fluctuating interplay of light. The dappled light adds to the already texture- and shape-laden interior design, with its shimmering silk-thread curtains and delicate wall graphics. These aspects help to delineate the different areas within the shop and the triple-tiered, semi-opaque dividing curtains, which appear to literally slice through the floor from above, also act as a surface onto which films can be projected. It is these subtle inflections, visual motifs that echo the city's rich cinematic heritage, plus a boutique-within-boutique-style VIP area toward the back of the upper level that affirms the brand's commitment to its Hollywood location.

1 The pixellated shapes of the facade are repeated in-store as a delicate swirling graphic on the white wall.
2 The store's exterior demands as much impact from the road as it does from the sidewalk, essential for a car-oriented city such as Los Angeles.

3

Semi-opaque dividing curtains appear to literally slice through the floor from above

4

3 Spotlight illumination orchestrates a shimmering sheen on the silk-thread curtains, echoing the interplay of light and shade used throughout the store design.
4 Monochromatic reflective furnishings are used, including black-and-white trestle tables positioned for optimum with featured product displays.
5 The sun shining through the glass facade causes pixellated patterns to be reflected in-store.

5

First floor

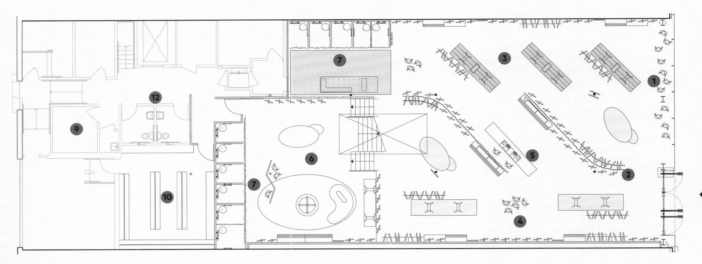

Ground floor

1 Window display
2 Dividing curtain
3 Menswear area
4 Womenswear area
5 Cash desk
6 Accessories area
7 Fitting rooms
8 VIP area
9 Office
10 Storage
11 Kitchen
12 Lavatories

0 1   5 m

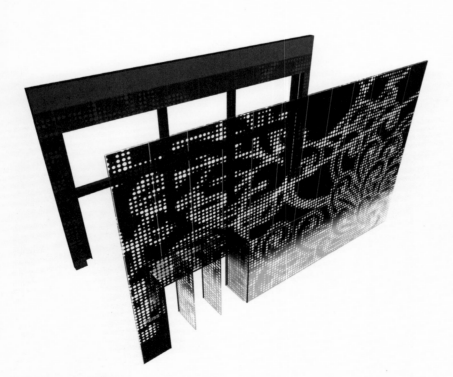

Rendering that shows the design for the
glass-fronted facade covering the full height
of the two-storey building into the concept.

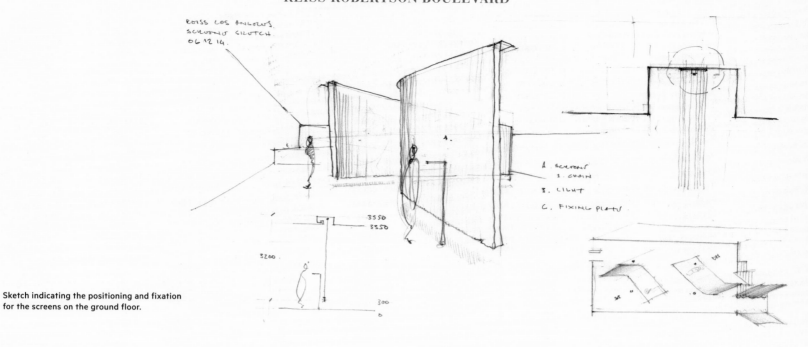

Sketch indicating the positioning and fixation for the screens on the ground floor.

The outer glass layer is punctuated with a swathe of large-scale, pixellated graphic shapes

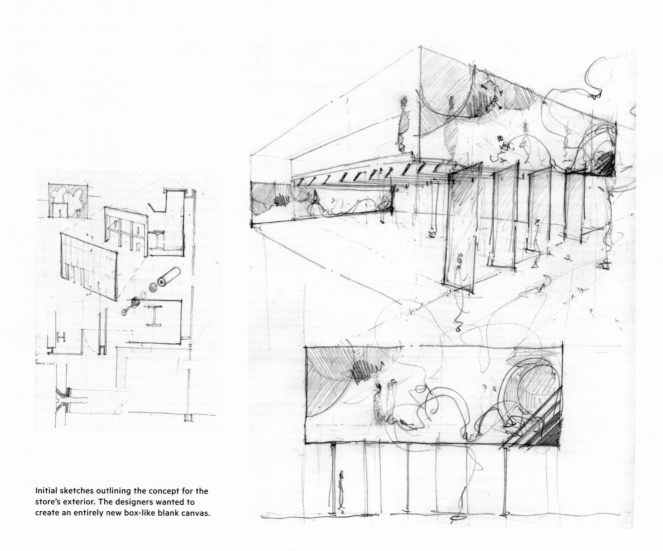

Initial sketches outlining the concept for the store's exterior. The designers wanted to create an entirely new box-like blank canvas.

RENAISSANCE

by GLENN SESTIG ARCHITECTS

◆

2

WHERE Antwerp, Belgium WHEN September 2010
CLIENT Princess DESIGNER Glenn Sestig Architects (p.679)
TOTAL FLOOR AREA 650 m² SHOP CONSTRUCTOR Descamps
PHOTOGRAPHER Jean Pierre Gabriel

The Belgian luxury business group Princess conceived a unique initiative with the opening of a new store, Renaissance, in the heart of Antwerp in 2010. The brief for this multibrand store was that it should be a haven of cosmopolitan living, merging directional fashion with fine dining. The 650-m² boutique was realised by Glenn Sestig Architects to also include an intimate restaurant incorporated in the one setting. The building dates back to 1894 and also houses ModeNatie, which includes the Flanders Fashion Institute, the fashion museum 'MoMu' of and the fashion department of the Royal Academy of Fine Arts. Staying true to the historical nature of the store's location, the atmosphere created is one that delivers bold statements in light, colour and atmosphere beneath the distinguished dome of the ModeNatie building.

Sweeping lines and a monochrome decor provide a striking backdrop for the designer collections, with the interior becoming a sculpture in its own right. Different zones that maintain a perspective view between them have been incorporated within the high-gloss white environment, with its white epoxy resin on the floors and huge slabs of veined white marble used in the display modules and counters. The shop layout pivots around a central juncture within the two angled avenues of the store. At the mid-point of the retail space, geometric volumes and midnight-blue lacquered panels on the cash desk creates a striking feature. The restaurant has been designed with the same architectural aesthetic of the attached boutique.

1 Renaissance was designed as an environment to surprise and stimulate, with interesting sight-lines incorporated.
2 The black and white space generated around a midnight blue metallic desk which forms the welcome area.

3

A haven of cosmopolitan living,
the store merges directional
fashion with fine dining

4

5

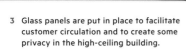

3 Glass panels are put in place to facilitate customer circulation and to create some privacy in the high-ceiling building.
4 Red strips of neon lighting indicate the availability of fitting rooms.
5 Large panes of glass shield off the restaurant from the retail area to invite people inside whilst simultaneously avoiding the smell of food and restaurant noise to enter the shop.

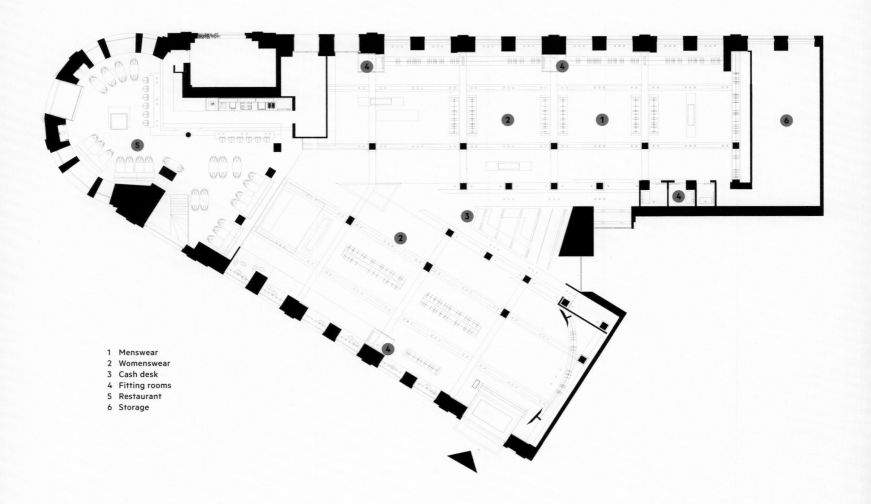

1 Menswear
2 Womenswear
3 Cash desk
4 Fitting rooms
5 Restaurant
6 Storage

Sweeping lines and a monochrome decor provide a striking backdrop for the collections

Renderings showing the various store divisions.

Front elevation   Side elevation

The rounded front of the building stands as a lighthouse for fashion, housing the multi-brand store, the restaurant, a museum and a bookshop.

RHUS OVATA

by K1P3 ARCHITECTS

◆

1

WHERE Tel Aviv, Israel WHEN March 2009
CLIENT Einav and Hadas Zucker DESIGNER k1p3 architects (p.680)
TOTAL FLOOR AREA 95 m² SHOP CONSTRUCTOR Yossi
PHOTOGRAPHER Daniel Sheriff

Rhus Ovata is a fashion brand of two Israeli sisters which has its flagship store located on the Dizengoff shopping street in Tel Aviv. Identifying itself as a subversive brand, a shop location was chosen that was set-back from the sidewalk. The concept devised by k1p3 architects for the shop was inspired by this positioning, with an aim to accentuate the span of the shop by including an aspect of horizontal layering, parallel to the street. The shop facade was redesigned and replaced, using steel on the lower and upper parts of the vitrine, framing the shop window along the full length of the shop front – as a continuous horizontal strip – which highlights fully the interior to passers-by. The materiality was kept minimal and basic in its nature, narrowed down to painted white steel and natural MDF for the furnishings, with herringbone parquet on the floor. Display modules and counters were designed with a style that draws references from contemporary art. The merchandise is organised in the space according to the layers concept, with the majority of the fashion collection hanging on a singular, continuous metal axis across the entire width of the space, with three passageways crossing it where the steel profile is set down to floor level. The various bespoke lighting elements generate a dialogue with the floor plan to highlight its orientation and creating a hierarchy in the space. In particular, the short rod-like incandescent strips appear like a floating 'highway' of lights in alternating positions above the clothes display.

1 The different layers of the store are designed to be parallel to the street.
2 A wall installation with vintage scarves is located next to the angular MDF cash desk with a Carrara marble top.
3 Passageways are incorporated into the clothes rail that spans the width of the store.

ROSA CHA

by STUDIO ARTHUR CASAS

1

WHERE Rio de Janeiro, Brazil **WHEN** August 2010
CLIENT Rosa Cha **DESIGNER** Studio Arthur Casas (p.685)
TOTAL FLOOR AREA 265 m² **SHOP CONSTRUCTOR** Lock
PHOTOGRAPHER Leonardo Finotti

Rosa Cha is a fashion brand, well known in Brazil for its beachwear products. Studio Arthur Casas was commissioned to design its first store in Rio de Janeiro which would showcase, in addition, the brand's new lines in casual wear and lingerie. The concept for the store was to create three distinct ambiences for each of the product ranges. The background colour palette for the entire concept is 'nude', with cream-coloured surfaces throughout, including the floors, walls and ceiling. What distinguishes each space are the surface treatments and materials that have been used: mainly concrete tiles and acrylic paint for swimwear and beachwear; craft paper and silk fibre-textured wall and ceiling coverings for casual wear and accessories; and acrylic paint, carpeting and niche linings of silk, leather, metallic gold and suede in the lingerie room. From the street, customers get a sense of the shoreline in the window displays, with wavy graphic lines representing the sea and the screens behind the mannequins textured almost like grains of sand. On entering the store, the space is bright and open. Recessed lighting panels overhead act as giant light boxes, creating the atmosphere of a sunny day on the beach. Moving into the next space, there is a darker-coloured decor lit by overhead spotlights positioned on parallel rungs in the ceiling, with backlit product alcoves. From here, the ceiling height doubles and entering into the lingerie section the pièce-de-résistance is the imposing wooden display system and its intriguing drawers propped open and filled with delectable products.

1 Textured wall and ceiling coverings imbue a cosy atmosphere in the casual wear and accessories area.
2 The beachwear section is light and airy.
3 A bronze mirrored wall gives the feeling of expanding the narrow walkway that leads to the lingerie room.
4 Customers enter a walk-in wardrobe dedicated solely to lingerie.

2

The background colour palette for the entire concept is 'nude'

3

4

SISTE'S

by BONGIANA ARCHITECTURE

◆

1

WHERE Milan, Italy WHEN September 2009
CLIENT Siste's DESIGNER Bongiana Architecture (p.675)
TOTAL FLOOR AREA 220 m² SHOP CONSTRUCTOR Mens Costruzioni
PHOTOGRAPHER Marco Righes

The Italian women's fashion brand Siste's wanted a flagship store in Milan that communicated a fresh, unique and up-to-date non-conformist image. The challenge for the Bongiana team was to successfully convey this ethos to the target customers by creating a space which allowed an expression of freedom from dictated fashion. Emphasising the characteristics of choice and distinctiveness, the interior design focused on utilising a few select, simple elements. All fixtures and fittings were designed to fit in with the clear-cut aesthetic, with metal tubing being shaped to construct the individual elements. A neutral palette was chosen as a backdrop for the collections with the elegant calligraphy-like graphics painted on the walls were in a darker hue. The aim was to create a fluidity throughout the two-storey space, ensuring a connection between both levels. This was achieved by removing the many columns which fragmented the original building and opening up a central void which acted like a mezzanine, so customers on the ground floor could catch glimpses of the merchandise on the lower level, and vice versa. This feature was made even more distinctive with the installation of a yellow cage, a stand-alone structure that was a focal point for customers in-store and an intriguing enchantment for passers-by, encouraging them to step inside for a closer look. The neutral space is interjected with additional vibrant bursts of colour which create a striking impression, such as the green counter at the cash desk, behind which is positioned a black-and-white, branded glass wall.

1 The bright yellow wire structure disappears in an opening in the floor, enticing visitors to find out what's downstairs.
2 Behind the cash desk a foil-covered glass panel communicates the name of the shop in a jumble of letters.
3 Metal tubes painted in neutral colours make up the custom-designed furniture.
4 The opening in the ceiling that lets in the large tube structure also allows the windowless basement level to be filled with natural daylight.

2

4

3

The aim was to ensure a connection between the two levels

STYLEXCHANGE FAUBOURG

by SID LEE ARCHITECTURE

1

WHERE Montreal, Canada **WHEN** April 2010
CLIENT Concept Wear **DESIGNER** Sid Lee Architecture (p.685)
TOTAL FLOOR AREA 375 m² **SHOP CONSTRUCTOR** Sajo
PHOTOGRAPHER Sid Lee

Stylexchange Faubourg is a fashion retail outlet located in a shopping centre close to Concordia University's campus in downtown Montreal. It is a young and vibrant student area and the boutique – designed by Sid Lee Architecture – blends seamlessly into the urban landscape of this diverse, multicultural part of town. A simple and flexible design showcases the contemporary fashion offerings in a linear commercial space, with low ceilings, surrounding an open plan, two-level space in the centre of the store, which is classified as 'the workshop area'. The aesthetic of this new atelier space is part design studio and part trendy, second-hand boutique. The team wanted to embrace the industrial history of Montreal by using materials that were as basic and natural as possible: plywood, steel, glass, visible screws and unfinished wood. The architectural plan called for the use of colours like black and charcoal grey to create a sense of continuity throughout the store. In this way, all the subdivisions and structural columns in the space have been painted uniformly, as well as the original floor, which features a mixture of tiles from different eras, thus recalling the history of the space. One central wall acts as a creative canvas, with a special chalkboard finish being applied which allows local artists to decorate the boutique in ever-evolving graphic art creations. The dominating white steel structure in the centre of the store is like a work of art in itself. The space acts as a workshop and draws the attention of customers to focus on the work of the in-store stylist who puts together noteworthy combinations of clothes and accessories.

1 The chalkboard wall overhead wraps around the double-height space which gives the space an urban gallery feel.
2 The central workshop area recalls the urban landscape of the store's neighbourhood.
3 When fashion shows take place in-store, the white steel structure is transformed into a DJ booth.

SUSIE STONE

by HMKM

1

WHERE London, United Kingdom WHEN June 2010
CLIENT Susie Stone DESIGNER HMKM (p.679)
TOTAL FLOOR AREA 112 m² SHOP CONSTRUCTOR HMKM
PHOTOGRAPHER Duncan Smith

Susie Stone is a new bespoke womenswear shop in London which is centred around style, sophistication and individuality. The HMKM team was brought on board to create a new brand positioning and retail vision for the fledgling business, a bespoke dressmaking service. A professional and feminine spirit needed to be embodied at the heart of the brand to reflect the owner's own personality and her love of vintage glamour. A starting point for the team was to design a feminine marque from her initials. A yellow and white colour palette is utilised for the brand that is acutely modern but with a befitting retro-feel. The swirling white logo and mustard yellow backdrop has been used to decorate the entire front of the store. The brightly coloured glass facade catches the attention of passers-by as they approach the shop and they can peek inside thanks to one central piece of the window being left uncovered. Within the Bermondey Street boutique, there is a strong visual direction for the retail concept, with distinctive zones incorporated to reflect the journey and process associated with the creation of a bespoke garment. By appointment only, the client arrives at the welcome area and moves through to the consultation zone, then on to the design studio with its fabric and mannequin displays. There is also a fitting room that includes a contemporary mix of lighting and furnishings. A mix of found furniture and vintage pieces is used throughout which brings an intimate warmth to the space.

1 Dummies dressed in Calico fabric are lined up in the main design studio and consultation area.
2 On the shop front, interlocking initials of the dressmaker form a heart which offers a peek inside the shop.
3 Wheels attached to the walls make it easy to relocate the fitting room.
4 A mirror in the welcome area reflects the inspiration wall.

2

3

4

TALLY WEIJL

by DAN PEARLMAN

1

WHERE Basel, Switzerland **WHEN** March 2009
CLIENT Tally Weijl **DESIGNER** dan pearlman (p.676)
TOTAL FLOOR AREA 713 m² **SHOP CONSTRUCTOR** Trockenbau Schult
PHOTOGRAPHER diephotodesigner.de (Dirk Dähmlow and Ken Schluchtmann)

Established in Switzerland in 1984, the women's fashion label Tally Weijl recently called upon the dan pearlman design team to develop a new interior concept for its stores to be rolled out across the globe. The brand has a young target market and the team opted to present glamorous spaces for interactivity which would be attractive to its teenage audience. The interior layout is spatially open and inviting to customers, with mirrored mosaic areas, spotlights, disco balls, text wall graphics, highly polished surfaces and glitter. It has a vibrant pink colour palette throughout and the entire decor reflects the motto of the label: totally sexy. The philosophy behind the project is to manifest a feel-good factor in the store with the primary aim of making the female customers feel confident in their fashion choices. Modeled on the atmosphere of a lady's boudoir in an 18th century French castle – reinforcing the femininity of the concept – a theatrical interrelationship of elements emerges. One set of curvaceous stairs, leading from the ground floor to the first level, are wide and sweeping and incorporate a heart-shaped format. Other various zones are defined within the two-storey space, each exuding their own character and personality. These are decorated with furniture such as chrome light boxes and oversized loudspeakers. By contrast, there is the lounge and chill-out fitting-room area, which invites the customers to sit, relax and dream, perhaps lounging on the Chesterfield-style seating.

1 The whole store oozes glitter and glamour.
2 The fitting rooms are covered in pink carpet and positioned around a sparkly column with lined with mirrored-mosaic tiles.
3 Glamorous stairs transform the teenage customer into the star of the show, the queen of the club.
4 Oversized loudspeakers, covered in glitter, add to the club design.

2

3

4

THE CONTEMPORARY FIX

by JAMO ASSOCIATES

1

WHERE Tokyo, Japan **WHEN** July 2010
CLIENT Pariya **DESIGNER** Jamo associates (p.680)
TOTAL FLOOR AREA 110 m² **SHOP CONSTRUCTOR** Alpha Studio
PHOTOGRAPHER Kozo Takayama

Director Yuichi Yoshii has for a number of years been involved with various boutiques and restaurants in Tokyo, each of which has defined a certain moment in the recent Japanese cultural landscape. When he decided to completely transform the building which at the time housed his fashionable lunch stop Pariya into a retail concept store, Jamo associates were brought on board to realise this vision. The new shop, The Contemporary Fix, brings together a mixture of fashion, culture and cuisine, specialising in of-the-moment items as a primer to Tokyo street fashion. Every inch of the shop expresses the design concept, being created in the image of an artist's home with rooms each recalling the atmosphere of an artist's living room, dining room, bathroom, closet, kitchen and terrace. The shop occupies half the ground floor

space – the remaining space comprises a cafe – and the whole of the first floor. The design takes a gallery approach, installing changing exhibitions that spotlight individual brands against a stripped-down backdrop. Skeleton ceilings, concrete surfaces and exposed brick are keyed with simple plywood constructions for the fittings and product displays. As customers explore the simple space, with its bright scatter rugs and cutesy wall decorations, they encounter the various rooms which highlight a host of designer collections of clothes and accessories. Each area fulfils a distinct function for the store and the concept succeeds in bringing together fun elements to realise a space that is both comfortable and edgy.

1   The ground floor houses a cafe, as well
    as the entrance to the shop. The first
    floor focuses on menswear and a diverse
    collection of accessories.
2   A spiral staircase takes visitors to the first
    floor retail space.
3   The spaces were created in the image of the
    rooms in an artist's home.
4   Black steel clothes racks are used to display
    the garments.

2

3

4

4

TOPMAN

by DALZIEL AND POW

1

WHERE London, United Kingdom WHEN September 2009
CLIENT Arcadia Group DESIGNER Dalziel and Pow (p.676)
TOTAL FLOOR AREA 2200 m² SHOP CONSTRUCTORS Patton Group
PHOTOGRAPHER Andy Townsend

With the opportunity to double its retail space by expanding an extra floor above, the men's fashion brand Topman wanted to make a bold statement for the relaunch of its Topshop Oxford Circus flagship store. The team at Dalziel and Pow was requested to create a retail environment that would be a beacon for the brand and a template for future openings. A multitude of textures and patterns, lighting and colours were manipulated, managed and mingled to create a distinct atmosphere and signature statements across the two showroom floors. Zoning the product offerings was a vital aspect to ensure precise customer orientation, devoting the entire ground floor to denim and casualwear and concentrating exclusively on tailoring and guest brands on the first floor, along with the footwear department. The general floorspace allows for large-scale statements, with the fixed product displays being emphasised with colour block enclaves and sculptured ceiling elements. Bold navigation signage is used throughout and the strong treatment of the feature staircase, with its vibrant and fun contemporary graphics and colourful accoutrements, continued through to the stylist lounge and the fitting room area. The directories use a combination of quirky typefaces and the monotone signage scheme is striking in the energetic environment full of the ever-changing product offerings.

1 Overview of the first floor.
2 The staircase walls inform customers of the Topman CTRL blog, dedicated to music.
3 The personal stylist lounge features a bar, several changing rooms and even mood boards that help the stylists with their client consultations.

4 An escalator leads up to the two floors of men's clothing. The lower three levels are reserved for Topshop, the separate womenswear store.
5 Long high-gloss cash desks are found on every storey.
6 Several areas are reserved for seasonal 'pop-up' spaces.
7 The colours orange, black and white dominate the footwear department.

Zoning the product offerings was a vital aspect to ensure precise customer orientation

TOPSHOP

by DALZIEL AND POW

◆

1

WHERE London, United Kingdom WHEN April 2010
CLIENT Arcadia Group DESIGNER Dalziel and Pow (p.676)
TOTAL FLOOR AREA 7000 m² SHOP CONSTRUCTOR Patton Group
PHOTOGRAPHER Andy Townsend

After successfully creating a vibrant new concept for Topshop's store in New York in 2009, it was a natural progression that Dalziel and Pow should be commissioned to translate this design into the Oxford Circus flagship store of this women's fashion retailer. A vital part of the brief stated that the store must remain trading during the redesign with minimal disruption to customers and a phased-in plan ensured that no more than a corner of the store was closed at one time. Spread over three floors, the main showroom areas offer flexible spaces for merchandise displays. The white ceiling rafts and chunky wooden-framed furniture stand out against a matt black backdrop. Contrasting light and dark floor tiles create clear routes in the store, echoing the ceiling architecture above. Illuminated navigational signage portrays a colourful and playful approach which clearly assists customers circulate through the space, with vibrant neon cubes, letters and strip lighting being recognisable recurring elements helping to define the different aspects. New in-store features have been introduced, such as the shopping and style advice service which has a crisp design – with a combination of high gloss flooring, diamond cut mirrors and white leather sofas – giving a premium feel to the personal consultation area. This is stepped up a notch for VIP guests, where two premium cubicles offer the ultimate hospitality in a self-contained area, decorated with premium natural finishes in golds and off-whites.

1 Customers who have booked a complimentary personal shopping appointment can relax in the lounge.
2 Cubes and texts constructed from fluorescent lighting tubes decorate the entrance area.
3 View of the make-up department.

4

Contrasting light and dark floor tiles create clear routes which echo the ceiling architecture

4 Large mirrors and comfortable sofas furnish the footwear department.
5 View of the personal shopping reception.
6 A long line of cash desks ensures that customers don't have to wait in line for a long time.

DALZIEL AND POW

Ground floor

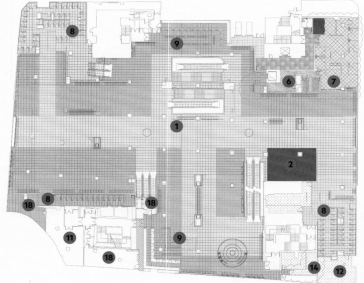

First lower level

1 Information point
2 Boutique area
3 Apparel area
4 Footwear area
5 Feature wall
6 VIP style advice area
7 Style advice area
8 Fitting rooms
9 Cash desk
10 Refund & exchange desk
11 Display studio
12 VM room
13 DJ booth
14 Press room
15 Seating area
16 Kitchen
17 Lunch room
18 Storage
19 Lavatories

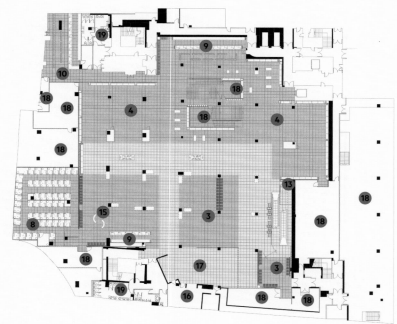

Second lower level

Illuminated navigational signage portrays a colourful and playful approach

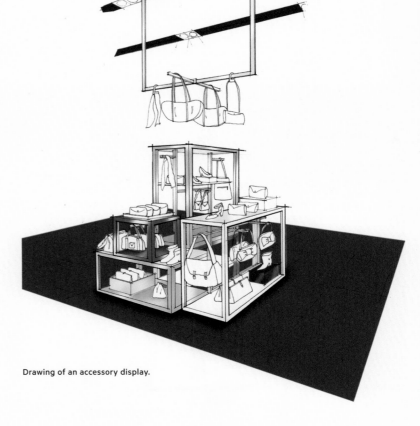

Drawing of an accessory display.

Drawing of one of the in-store display windows that are scattered throughout the store.

Rendering of the personal shopping reception.

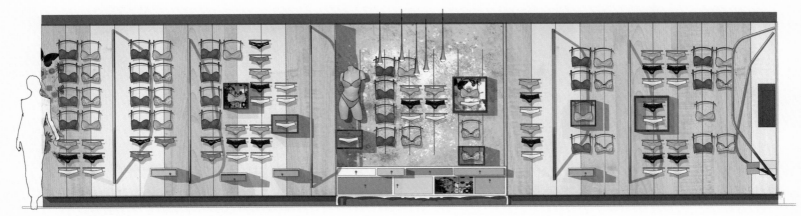

Rendering of the lingerie wall display.

TRAGBAR.PURE

by ATELIER 522

◆

1

WHERE Esslingen, Germany **WHEN** August 2009
CLIENT Tragbar (Klaus Fischer and Antje Hammelehle) **DESIGNER** atelier 522 (p.674)
TOTAL FLOOR AREA 140 m² **SHOP CONSTRUCTOR** Ladenbau Scholz
PHOTOGRAPHER atelier 522

To complement its existing shops, the German fashion brand Tragbar launched a new conceptual fashion store, tragbar.pure, which offers higher priced ranges. Featuring a select collection high-fashion brands with accompanying accessories, shoes and perfumes, the shop was designed by atelier 522. The store is a perfect backdrop to the quality merchandise available thanks to the concept that was executed which is based around one topic: raw. The 'stripped-back theme' means that no extraneous architectural flourishes or knick-knacks were needed in the design of the interior. The team made the most of the original features within the shop space, with the existing stone floor, walls and ceiling all being left in their original 'raw' condition resulting in an earthy palette throughout. A combination of both old and new elements as well as high-quality materials were utilised in their natural form – solid wood, glass, leather and steel – to create an exclusive but also warm and comfortable atmosphere. The bespoke product rails are made of uncoated metal tubing, which appears to snake around the shop and in places is suspended from the ceiling rafters. At the back of the store, behind the monumental steel counter, a wall of plants adds a fresh, and contrasting, dimension with its curtain of foliage.

1 Glamour was combined with raw materials to created an unique shopping experience.
2 The existing stone walls, floor and ceiling remained intact.
3 Behind the cash desk counter – made of steel – the eye-catching planted green wall is flooded in purple-hued light.
4 Made-to-measure, unconventional middle-room furniture and product racks made of steel-tubes wind their way through the room and up the walls.

2

3

VAN ZUILEN MODE

by BENSCHOP THE RETAIL FACTORY

2

WHERE Gorinchem, the Netherlands **WHEN** August 2010
CLIENT Van Zuilen Mode **DESIGNER** Benschop The Retail Factory (p.674)
TOTAL FLOOR AREA 1500 m² **SHOP CONSTRUCTOR** Benschop The Retail Factory
PHOTOGRAPHER Unit 300 (Silvain Wiersma)

The renovation of the multibrand fashion store Van Zuilen Mode in the small Dutch village of Gorinchem required a considered approach due to the historical nature of the building complex in which it is housed, which includes a listed 14th-century church. The repositioning of the brand within the newly-transformed retail interior was the task of the Benschop design team. The brief called for a warm and inviting concept which respected the historical setting, interpreted by the incorporation of a myriad of unique design features to enhance the character and distinguished atmosphere of the space. Many of these included antique showcases and vintage pieces with as much history as the building itself – such as doors from a former Belgium monastery – which were positioned in the shop alongside original oak beams on the ceiling and the floors. Adding a contemporary air is the bespoke custom-made furniture with dark steel fittings and a high-gloss Corian bar, complemented the latest merchandise collections. Maintaining many of the building's original features, special attention was given to the circulation plan which included opening up voids in the building to link horizontal and vertical movement. There are also many focal points and junctions as customers make their way around the store, not least within the nave of the historic church where spotlights affixed to the rafters provide illumination for the menswear section. The two floors featuring womenswear and footwear is also an interaction between old and new, with some of the off-white plastered walls being stripped back to expose the original brickwork.

1 The fitting rooms, located in the back of the men's shoe department, are made out of hot-rolled unfinished steel.
2 Vintage factory lamps illuminate 'Uno Duo' women's department.

3

4

5

3 Off-white plasterwork was applied around the historic brick wall. Through careful consideration to the historical value of the church, a unique and inspiring retail concept was achieved.

4 In the women's contemporary fashion department on the upper floor, the historic ceiling is a real eye catcher. Patchwork carpets and display units made from stainless steel, Zebrano veneer and high-polished white surfaces all add a contemporary touch.

5 Kartell's Charles Ghost Stools are placed around the high-gloss lacquered coffee and juice bar.

6 The wooden ceiling beams add to the distinguished atmosphere in the formal menswear department.

6

The building complex includes a 14ᵗʰ-century church

WERDER BREMEN FANWORLD

by SCHWITZKE & PARTNER

1

WHERE Bremen, Germany WHEN November 2010
CLIENT Werder Bremen Fan-Service DESIGNER Schwitzke & Partner (p.684)
TOTAL FLOOR AREA 635 m² SHOP CONSTRUCTOR Schwitzke Project
PHOTOGRAPHER Oliver Tjaden

Supporters of Werden Bremen can find all the necessary outfits and accessories to encourage their soccer team at the new fan shop, designed by Schwitzke & Partner. The main goal was to create a space that would express the easy-going atmosphere that characterises the sports club. An artificial grass carpet welcomes the customers into this branded soccer world. Large prints of a cheering crowd and logos of the team's sponsors adorn the walls of the entrance hallway that leads to the women's and children's department. Words of 'soccer wisdom' and quotes are written on the walls. The focal point of this floor is the back wall covered in hexagon-patterned leather reminiscent of a soccer ball. Another highlight is the wall where the traditional fan scarves are displayed in an organised fashion as ties would be in a chic department store. The cash desks are fitted-out in the green club colour, which makes an appearance throughout the entire store. By going up the concrete stairway, which is accentuated by a green-illuminated mesh wire embroidered with the club logo, customers reach the floor dedicated to menswear and home goods. Here, the fitting rooms are furnished with plastic stadium seats on a concrete block and shielded from the retail area by a wooden wall that features images of professional soccer players. At the place of one of the heads, is a hole through which the customer can peek through to be photographed amidst objects of his admiration.

1   Football-related cartoons have been drawn
    on the blackboard-painted columns.
2   The cash desk follows both the form and
    colour of the club logo.
3   The old bicycle of the stadium's green
    keeper is casually placed against a fence at
    the end of the artificial grass carpet.
4   The mesh wire is reminiscent of the netting
    of a soccer goal.

2

3

4

The space expresses the
easy-going atmosphere that
characterises the sports club

FOOD
BEVE

370

AND
RAGE

371

DUMON CHOCOLATIER

by WITBLAD

1

WHERE Kortrijk, Belgium WHEN October 2010
CLIENT Dumon Chocolatier DESIGNER witblad (p.687)
TOTAL FLOOR AREA 50 m² SHOP CONSTRUCTOR Descamps Interieur
PHOTOGRAPHER Rien van den Eshof

Dumon Chocolatier sells handmade chocolates and the company wanted an interior for its new shop that reflected the craftsmanship and passion that the owners have for their products. Dumon already had two shops in the Belgian cities of Bruges and Torhout. This third shop in Kortrijk is situated in the main shopping street and had to fit well in the design environment and image of the city of Kortrijk. The shop concept by witblad is based around treating chocolates as jewellery, as the Dumon handmade delicacies are as pleasing to the eye as gemstones. The entire length of the main counter is molded into angular shapes, with facets referring to diamonds. The large gloss-painted triangles differ in shape and size and reflect the light in a multitude of ways. Working their way from one side of the shop to the other, customers can view the

confectionary behind a glass partition. Complementing the molded counter are the Rock lamps from Diesel with Foscarini which hang overhead. The entire colour scheme of the shop – white, black and green – ties in nicely with the confectionary within; white and dark chocolate with, perhaps, a hint of fresh mint. The interior has been designed as a shop window in order to be inviting to customers and to entice passers-by into the store. Two, originally separate, shops have been combined into one space with a totally open facade which means, from the street, the entire product range can be viewed.

1 The shop's main counter is designed to resemble the flat and polished surfaces of a cut diamond.
2 The main colours of black and white are based on the corporate identity. The striking green is an accent colour that can be changed seasonally.

2

The main counter is molded into angular shapes, with facets referring to diamonds

EARL'S GOURMET GRUB

by FREELANDBUCK

2

WHERE Los Angeles, United States WHEN April 2010
CLIENTS Yvonne McDonald and Dean Harada DESIGNER FreelandBuck (p.678)
TOTAL FLOOR AREA 100 m² SHOP CONSTRUCTOR Vandermeer Construction
PHOTOGRAPHER Lawrence Anderson

In 2010, a new and exclusive food franchise was opened in the Mar Vista area of West Hollywood in Los Angeles. Earl's Gourmet Grub is an artisanal deli serving gastronomic sandwiches. It is located on an urban highway and geared to the takeaway trade, amidst a proliferation of other eateries. The owners commissioned FreelandBuck to create a contemporary architectural identity which also evoked the rustic appeal of the food. As the name suggests, the outcome is a hybrid: basic fare that is served with care in a space that was shaped by cutting-edge technology and inspired by early expressions of modernism. The team employed a rich material and a muted colour palette to evoke both technological refinement and the more rustic feel of alpine landscapes and Viennese cafes. Conceived as a variable and shifting space defined by a series of torqued ceiling surfaces and light 'scoops', the linear store is animated by the three illuminating apertures overhead, one of which is a skylight and the other two are artificially lit. High-gloss white paint was applied to the scoops to reflect as well as to channel the light over the white-marble serving counter. The sophisticated sculpting continues with the angled baffles of bleached plywood which form a canopy overhead, merging into the angled scoops at the mid-point of the store. On the side wall, created by inscribed digital patterns, is a mosaic mural which abstracts an image of the Alps, evoking neither pure landscape nor pure technology.

1 Geometric patterns imbue the store with a unique interior landscape.
2 The concept for the store employs a sophisticated design to stand out from the crowd and generate attention for its artisanal sandwiches and groceries.

375

3 The west wall, which spans the entire depth of the space, is embossed with an image of the Alps abstracted as a series of rectangular computational 'bits'.
4 The ceiling design creates an airy, light-filled canopy.
5 Seating aspects are incorporated along the wall for use by customers.
6 The rhythmic undulations overhead both subdivide the linear space into a series of spatial pockets and produce dynamic continuity from front to back.

The contemporary architectural identity evokes the rustic appeal of the food

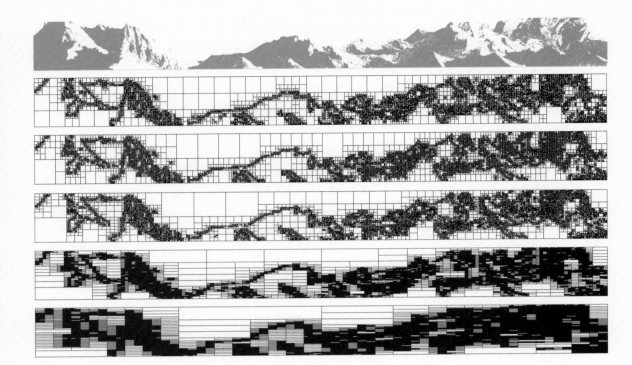

Study into the digitisation of an alpine landscape.

A mosaic mural abstracts an image of the Alps

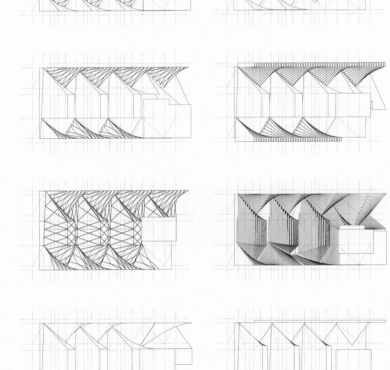

LIGHT SCOOPS

Skylight scoop

Artificial light scoop

Reflected ceiling plan

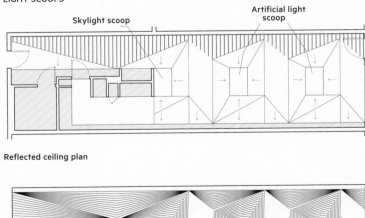

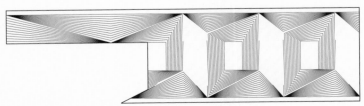

Ceiling contours

Digital designs were mocked up at different scales and experiments conducted to see how far the gypsum board could be bent to create curvilinear surfaces on the suspended frames.

1 Marble counter
2 Open kitchen
3 Seating/display
4 Cash desk
5 Back kitchen
6 Lavatory

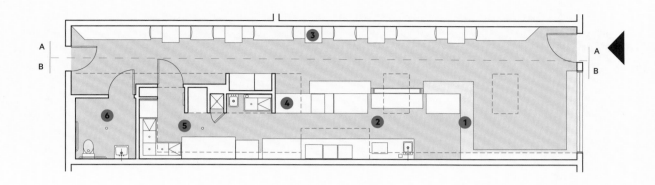

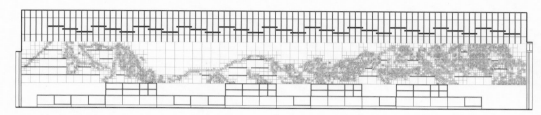

Section AA

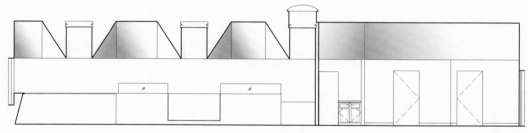

Section BB

Construction photos of the ceiling light scoops.

ELEKTRA

by STUDIOPROTOTYPE

2

WHERE Edessa, Greece WHEN November 2009
CLIENT Elektra Bakeries DESIGNER Studioprototype (p.686)
TOTAL FLOOR AREA 35 m² SHOP CONSTRUCTOR Studioprototype
PHOTOGRAPHER Spyros Paloukis

Elektra is family-run bakery business located in Edessa in northern Greece. Studioprototype had the opportunity to redefine the look of the entire chain of stores, with the first task being to refurbish a shop which occupies a strategic corner on the main pedestrian high street in the city of Edessa. The main challenge was how to redesign the layout so as to maximise its prime location, as well as making the most of the small space. The team worked with the narrow floor plan, installing a long marble counter to act as a monolithic focal point of the spatial arrangement. A key aspect in the design also is the illumination of the shop, from the strategically-placed pendant lights to the natural daylight that pours in from the large window which runs the length of the store. It acts as a picture window so, when viewed from the street, it

neatly frames and accentuates the food items on display inside. Exquisite materials such as marble, cedar wood and brass serve as the backdrop for all the freshly-baked goods, instilling the rustic and artisan aspect of bread making. A sense of craftsmanship is imbued, with the exterior wall clad in vertical cedar boards. Punctuating the cedar cladding on the long facade, a black powder-coated steel window box projects outwards beyond the 'crust' of the shop, expanding the space to serve as a seating area and bar for customers inside and outside the store.

1 Light and luminosity fill the interior accentuating the food items displayed on the Carrara marble food counter.
2 The large window box frames the interior elements of the shop.

5

The long marble counter acts as a monolithic focal point

1 Food counter
2 Display
3 Window bar
4 Seating area
5 Service counter
6 Coffee counter
7 Fridge
8 Preparation area
9 Lavatory

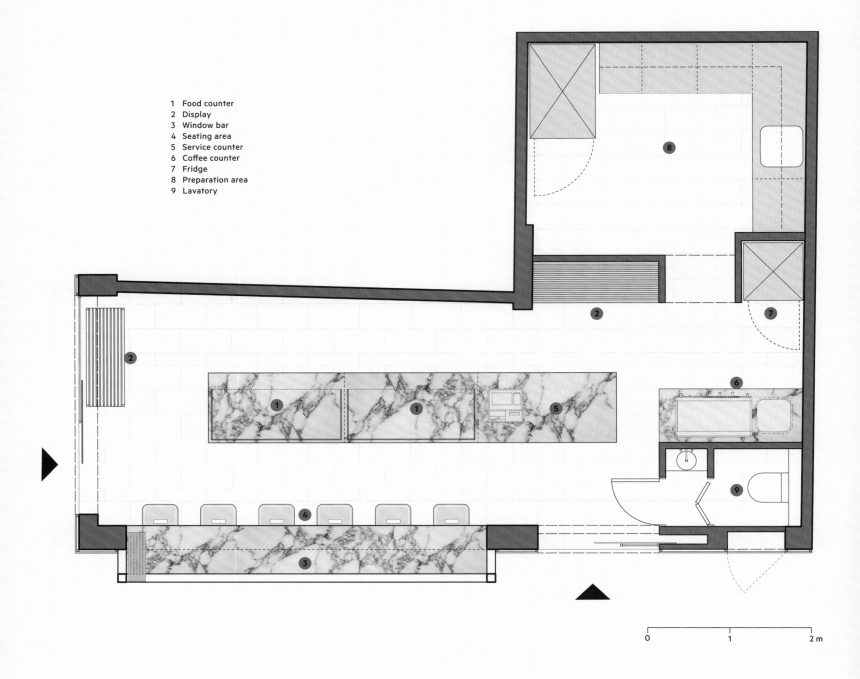

0   1   2 m

The bakery prior to refurbishment.

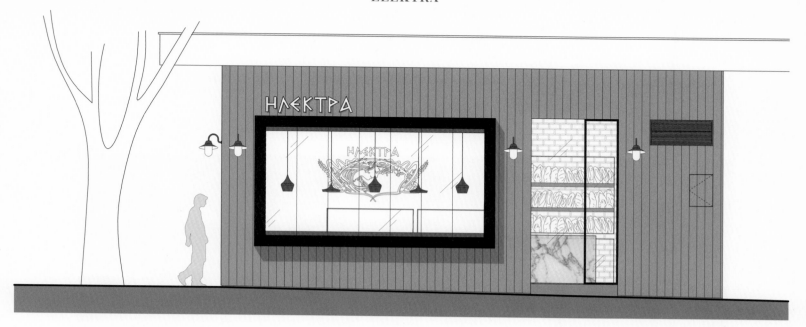

Side elevation

Hand-drawn sketch of the shop's exterior.

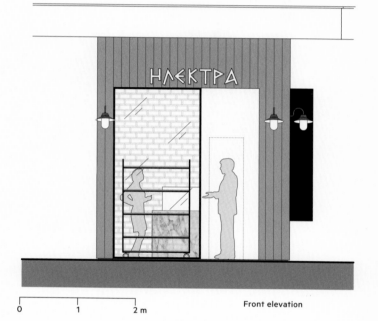

Front elevation

0   1   2 m

A picture window frames the food items on display

Rendering showing the corner positioning of the bakery.

EMPORIUM

by PORTLAND

1

WHERE Dubai Airport, United Arab Emirates WHEN December 2010
CLIENT Diageo DESIGNER Portland (p.683)
TOTAL FLOOR AREA 190 m² SHOP CONSTRUCTOR Bond Interiors
PHOTOGRAPHER Gulfpics/Motivate Publishing

Diageo is a global drinks business, with a large collection of brands across spirits, beer and wine under its remit. When the company commissioned a store to be opened in Terminal 3 of Dubai Airport, Portland was brought on board to create a new travel retail experience. Called Emporium, the objective of the project was to create a space that would encourage and allow customers to fully engage with the brands in-store in a meaningful way. The design team wanted to create something unique, with an international feel, yet inspired by and fully respecting Dubai and the Gulf region. A visually-enticing environment with a consistent tone was required to give Emporium the edge over other liquor stores within the duty free domain of the airport terminal. The display elements were crucial to this, as was the rich colour palette of golds and metallic browns used throughout the store. A gallery area near the front is where premium products are displayed on elegantly engineered tables to elevate their status to objects of beauty. Pleated fabric wall panels overlap to form apertures for product display, creating a warm neutral backdrop to the feature elements within the space. A central faceted gold-coated stainless steel bar creates a strong focal point, and a touch of retail theatre is added at the 'Taste Experience Table' to the rear of the space where world-class mixologists create cocktails to the delight of a select audience.

1 A wide glazed facade gives a clear view of the bar positioned at the entrance.
2 A feature chandelier with a cluster of acrylic rods provides focused illumination over the 'Taste Experience Table'.
3 There is gallery area at the front of the store with rare and premium products displayed in glass cases.

2

Pleated fabric wall panels overlap to form apertures for product display

3

HEINEKEN WORLD OF BEERS

by UXUS

1

WHERE *Viking Line Ferry* WHEN February 2011
CLIENT Viking Line Ferry DESIGNER Uxus (p.686)
TOTAL FLOOR AREA 18.5 m² SHOP CONSTRUCTOR The Set Company
PHOTOGRAPHER Dim Balsem

In 2010, Uxus won the commission of a Scandinavian ferry company to create an innovative new beer category destination within the duty free domain. The brief was to increase visibility and showcase Heineken as well as other premium beer brands owned by Heineken. A unique shelving system has been designed, which was inspired by the shape and angle of the Heineken logo where each letter 'e' is tilted backwards slightly, making them look like they are smiling. The configuration of the powder-coated steel shelves is such that at certain angles and degrees of elevation, a further 'smiling' effect has been created. Taking the natural hues of beer as a starting point, as well as the Heineken brand palette, the space is organised following a series of colour-coded elements as a backdrop to each beer brand. This is a key aspect of the design which allows customers to navigate the multiple brands on offer. In addition, interactive touch-screens, as well as the ability to scan the given QR code with a smartphone, were integrated within the space. As emphasis was put on presenting a variety of types of products to encourage trial and purchase, a 'Mix Your Own' element was included where consumers have the opportunity to create their own custom six-pack of speciality beers.

1 The bespoke wall and shelving system is made out of powder-coated steel with acrylic sheets, monitors, magnetic strips and Trespa panelling.
2 Interactive touch-screens allow shoppers to discover what food complements their choice of beer.

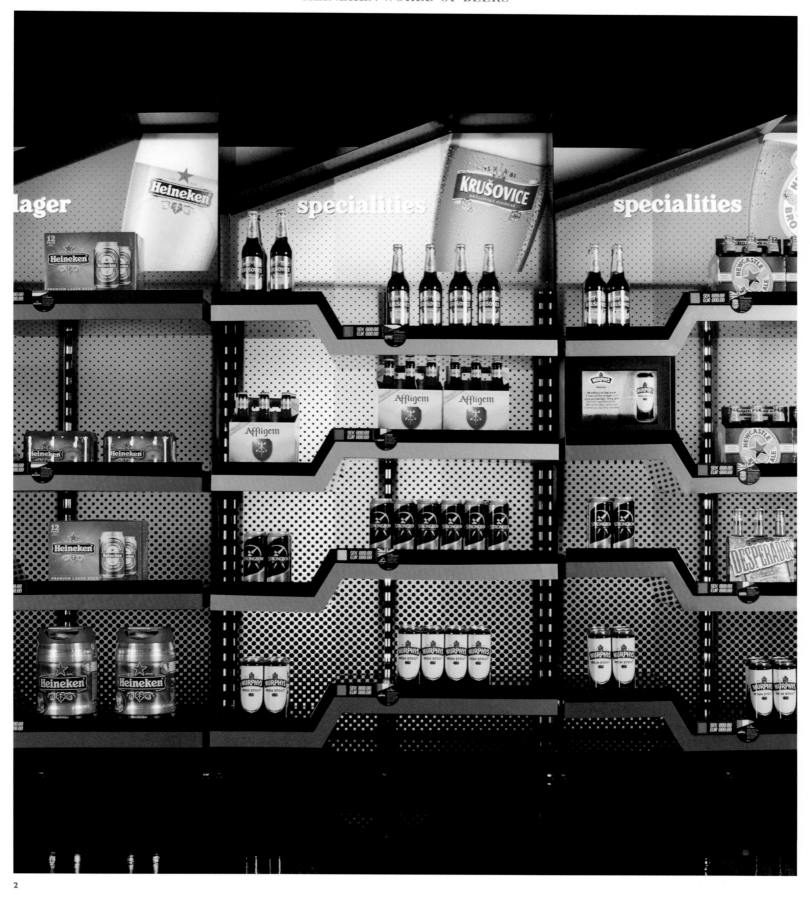

2

The space is organised following a series of colour-coded elements

Renderings showing close-up details of the shelving system.

Each panel is branded and colour-coded, which can be easily altered according to the brands of beer being sold at any one time.

Designs for the wall and shelf system. Stability was an important aspect to be considered due to the swaying motion that could be encountered once the ferry is in motion.

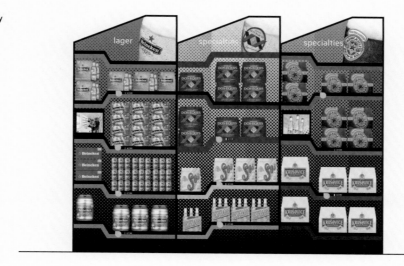

Extended shelf edge for stability

The natural hues of beer were taken as a starting point

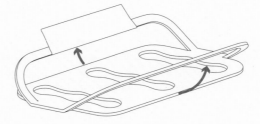

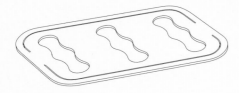

Drawings of the carrying handles for the 'Mix Your Own' element.

KIN NO TUBASA

by TONERICO

2

WHERE Tokyo Haneda Airport, Japan **WHEN** October 2010
CLIENT Japan Airport Terminal Company **DESIGNER** Tonerico (p.686)
TOTAL FLOOR AREA 318 m² **SHOP CONSTRUCTOR** Sogo Design
PHOTOGRAPHER Satoshi Asakawa

Kin No Tubasa is the name given to the store selling exclusive cakes and confectionery located in Terminal 2 of Haneda Airport in Tokyo. The brief to Tonerico was to design a space where five of each Japanese and Western pastry shops would be located, with a special focus on each of the manufacturers' original merchandise to be staged near the entrance. The challenge for the design team was to not end up with a space that was disjointed, with a cluster of shops lacking coherence. It was decided to make a primary use of materials to distinguish between the different realms, utilising the basic elements such as flooring, wall coverings and ceiling. With a common passageway as a line of symmetry between the two sections of the shop, the Japanese space is delineated by the use of sandstone and wood, and the space for the Western shops by the use of marble. The two zones are contrasted also by differentiation in lighting, fixtures and fittings. Each pastry company is positioned within a carved wall space. By carefully weighing the balance of the space as a whole and the carved individual spaces within each zone, the coexistence of the different patisserie personalities within the overall space is achieved. As well as accessing the two aspects of the store through the linking passageway, each zone has its own main entrance where a feature display showcases products from each of the five represented companies.

1 Speciality products from all the confectioners featured in the store are presented to customers.
2 The use of marble materials for the floor and the walls delineates the Western confectionery realm in the shop.

3

There is a coexistence of different patisserie personalities within the space

4

5

3 Sandstone and wood is used to decorate the Japanese area.
4 The brass mirror-finish chandelier creates a shimmering halo above each of the showcase tables.
5 At the entrance of each zone, a special presentation table is positioned to highlight certain products.
6 The presentation table appears to float at the entrance of the Japanese zone.

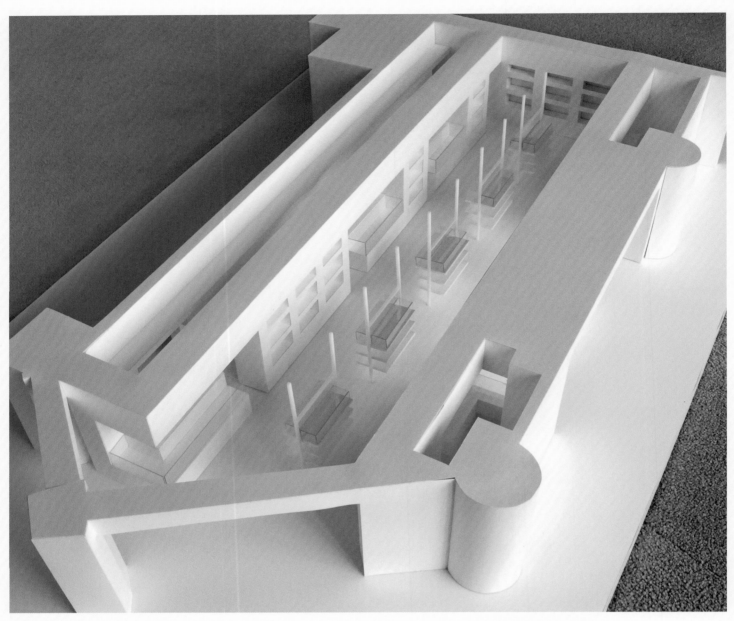

Three-dimensional model showing the layout
of one of the two realms.

Models showing different views of the interior
of the store.

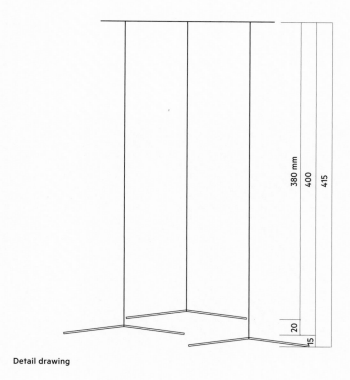

380 mm
400
415
20
15

Detail drawing

CHANDELIER

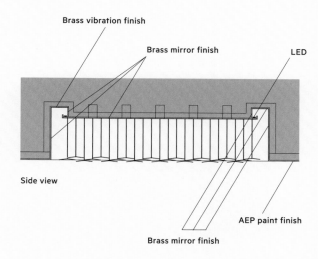

Brass vibration finish

Brass mirror finish

LED

Side view

AEP paint finish

Brass mirror finish

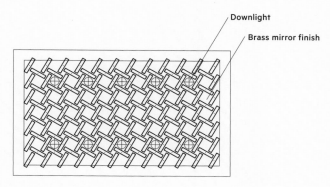

Downlight

Brass mirror finish

View from underneath

Chandelier model

The concept uses different materials to distinguish each of the realms

1 Adjoining passageway
2 Japanese confectionery
3 Western confectionery
4 Feature display case
5 Wooden display shelves
6 Glass display case

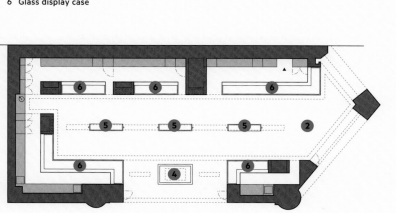
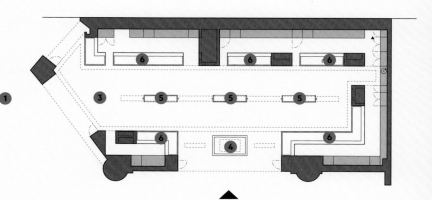

KLEINER

by STEFAN ZWICKY ARCHITECT

1

WHERE Zurich, Switzerland **WHEN** September 2009
CLIENT ZFV-Unternehmungen **DESIGNER** Stefan Zwicky Architect (p.685)
TOTAL FLOOR AREA 100 m² **SHOP CONSTRUCTOR** Pfister Ladenbau
PHOTOGRAPHER Heinz Unger

The Kleiner company has been baking bread in Switzerland for over 90 years. A business division of the ZFV group of companies, Kleiner recently wanted to revise its product range whilst maintaining its focus on natural, quality ingredients. At the same time, the company intended to radically redesign the appearance of its premises, with the creative vision of Stefan Zwicky and his team. Kleiner makes use of traditional baking methods and the concept for the interior design reflected this, both complementing and contrasting the variety of products on display. The main characteristic of the design is an extensive sales counter that stretches the entire length of the store right up to the facade, where it becomes the display window. The sales counter has an unusually high sales surface of 90 cm which places the products closer to the customer. The objective was to create a large, continuous presentation surface with an arrangement reminiscent of traditional market situations. The materials used in the interior have been chosen for their authentic qualities, reminiscent of the ingredients in the freshly-baked goods on sale. The walls are covered with split oak panels representative of slices of bread, whilst the rough iron panels of the display cabinet and shelves stand for fire and ash of the baking oven. Products are presented on woven willow mats or in baskets, on wooden grids or on baking paper directly in baking trays.

1 Split oak panels, lining the self-service wall with its seasonal gifts positioned on glass shelves, represent slices of bread.
2 The Gothic quill-style font used in the shop name makes reference to the ancient tradition of the baker's trade and is befitting of a company with such a history.
3 iGuzzini's Pixel Plus recessed luminaires draw attention to the products.

LE VIGNE

by MADLAB

1

WHERE New York, United States **WHEN** July 2009
CLIENT Carlo Orrico **DESIGNER** Madlab (p.681)
TOTAL FLOOR AREA 56 m² **SHOP CONSTRUCTORS** Madlab and Spurse
PHOTOGRAPHER Petia Morozov

Greenwich Village is the location of the wine store Le Vigne. Just as Wall Street began its downward tumble in the fall of 2008, a maverick sommelier Carlo Orrico followed a series of timely hunches that led to the opening of his New York wine shop. After a chance discovery of a vacant retail space, the next task was to commission Madlab to design a store that would break the mould in wine shopping and which had a fast, cheap and ingenious outcome. The Madlab team worked along with the artist collective Spurse on a design–build enterprise of creative problem solving on the fly. When the space was stripped back, what was found was an austere yet genuine space, with its painted plaster walls, brick fireplaces, hardwood floors and tin ceilings, worn but intact. It was decided to work with the excavated space as it was. Armed with tools, truckloads of thrift shop furniture and a knack for experimental carpentry, the team members moved in to hack, carve and create the look and feel of the store as they went along. Recycling and radically repurposing second-hand furniture was the primary design approach to discovering new forms and functions. Tables, drawers and chairs, all painted white, provide a backdrop that gives the discarded objects a new lease of life. Chairs are stacked high in nooks and crannies, and bottles of wine from the in-store cellar play a starring role in the delightfully hotchpotch presentation.

1 Built on-site, the store's wall unit not only displays and stores wine, it also acts as a conventional point-of-purchase incorporating the cash register.
2 At almost 8 m in length, the store's central table is the main focus, with its undulating form that hints at the complex geologies behind the store's artisanal Italian wines.

LOVE SWEETS ANTIQUE

by GLAMOROUS

1

WHERE Tokyo, Japan WHEN August 2010
CLIENT Club Antique DESIGNER Glamorous (p.678)
TOTAL FLOOR AREA 17 m² SHOP CONSTRUCTOR Space
PHOTOGRAPHER Nacása & Partners

Love Sweets Antique is a specialised store which will appeal to those customers with a sweet tooth and a taste for fairy tales. Selling products that are as visually pleasing as they are in taste and texture, the company's product development process is a story in itself. For instance, the 'Toronama doughnuts' range was inspired by imagining the sweets of fairies in a forest. The Glamorous team gobbled up the brief for a new store in Aoyama with gusto. The designers wanted the concept to be more than just a regular store design, striving further to create an impressive new landmark on Aoyama Street – arguably the most famous, trend-setting and high-fashion street in Tokyo. From an *Alice in Wonderland* perspective, Glamorous wanted to create a 'happy surprise' for shoppers, to entice them to stop for a sweet snack. Toronama doughnuts

are the major products sold at the shop and the team used these as the inspiration for the design. The vivid palette comes about from the multi-coloured hues of icing used to smother the doughnuts. The doughnut motifs with cheerful glazes are used as decorations on the candlestick, signage and even on the imposing shop facade, which towers above the store like a shining beacon. Glamorous imagined the iconic chandelier as if it were presented on a table and dressed the building not as a simple box, but as the shop signature to catch the eyes of customers both in distance and on the street.

1 On the day of the shop's opening, the designers heard a little boy say, 'Wow…look mum – it is like Disneyland. I want to go!'
2 Behind the sales counter sits a white ceramic bunny in a mirror-lined box, continuing the fairy tale theme.

PANSCAPE

by NINKIPEN!

2

WHERE Kyoto, Japan WHEN August 2010
CLIENT Tetsuya Kubo DESIGNER ninkipen! (p.682)
TOTAL FLOOR AREA 27 m² SHOP CONSTRUCTOR Gouda Kogyo
PHOTOGRAPHER Hiroki Kawata

Panscape is a Japanese bakery run by Tetsuya Kubo where the freshly-baked bread is the star attraction. With a new store in Kyoto planned, the ninkipen! studio was commissioned to design a space that complemented the rustic food being baked in-house. Situated in a completely rebuilt area which lacked a certain charm, the design studio sought to recreate the appeal of a traditional shop. The ninkipen! concept was all about creating a particular atmosphere. Just as the process of bread making and the kneading of dough takes time, the design team wanted customers to take their time in choosing their daily bread. A non-rushed and quiet ambience was called for and so a simple space that is quiet enough for a mouse – a Zen mouse – was created. The chosen lot had all the right ingredients, but needed to be stripped back as a starting point for the design team. Raw materials like wood, metal and stone were chosen for their robust, perennial qualities. The original expression of the building is evident, with new functional architectures and textures incorporated, with the focal point being a timber railway sleeper as a display for the bread. The long, aluminium and concrete counter serves as a second display point and forms a modern contrast with the window display. The remaining walls and floor have been painted either white or concrete grey, giving the space a rather industrial feel.

1   The metal sheet on the end wall – which
    is a door to conceal pipework – provides
    a golden reflection of the rustic display of
    bread in the shop window.
2   The design team aimed to instil an original
    expression by replacing the entire front of
    the store with a glass-fronted facade set in
    wooden sashes.

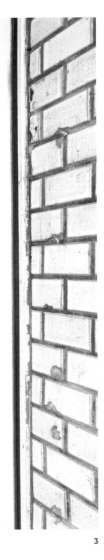

3

3 The design of the client's logo which appears on the entrance door was inspired by a freshly-baked loaf of bread.
4 Illumination is positioned in the wall so that light spills out of the 'mouse hole', capturing the attention of customers.
5 The long counter, with its 10-mm-thick aluminium surface, contrasts with the antique cabinet and wooden beam – weighing 500 kg – which showcases the bread at the front of the store.
6 Simple metalwork spells out the shop name at the store's threshold.

5

The original building is evident with new functional architectures and textures incorporated

6

NINKIPEN!

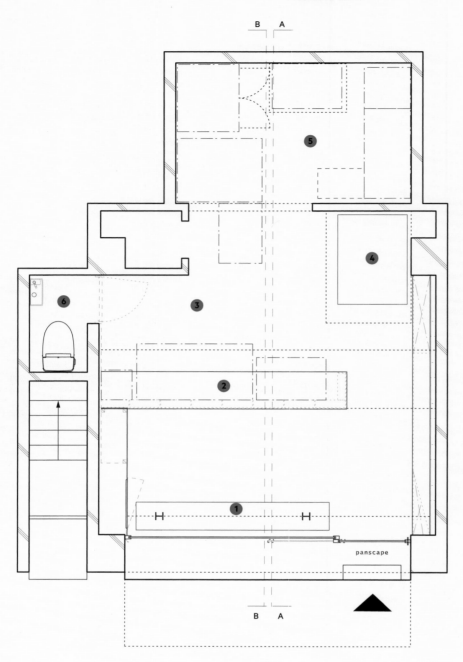

1 Window display
2 Counter and cash desk
3 Service area
4 Oven
5 Back office
6 Lavatory

panscape

BREAD DISPLAY

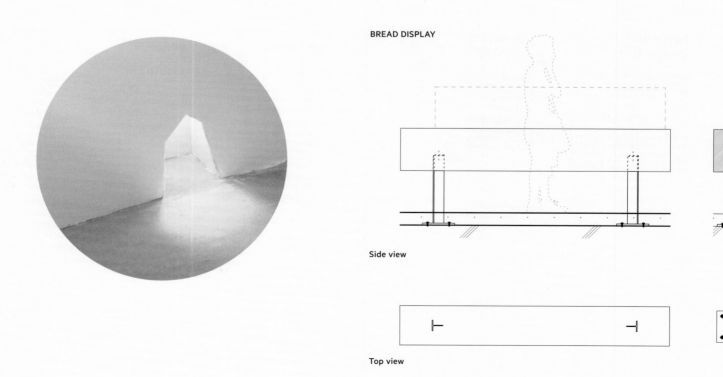

Side view

Top view

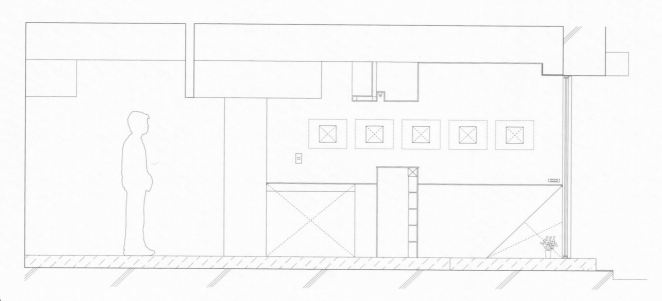

Section AA

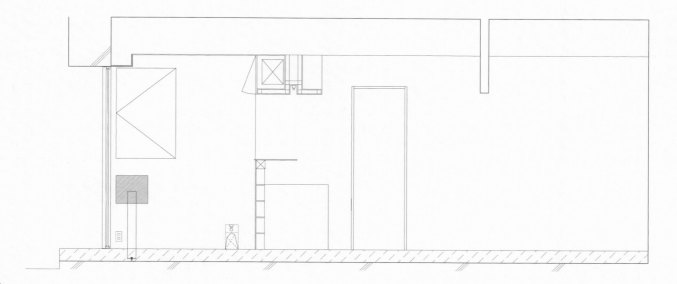

Section BB

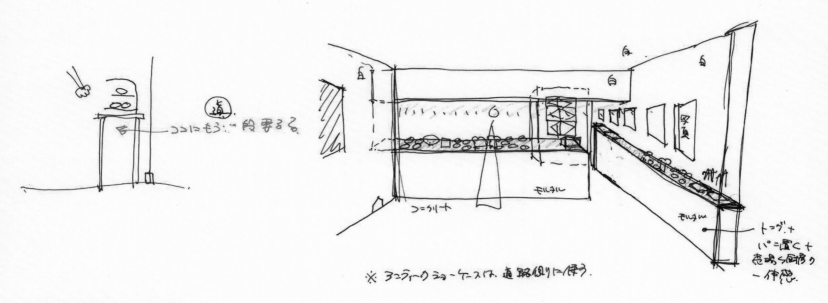

Hand-drawn sketch with the designer's notes
outlining the concept.

POMME SUCRE

by FRANCESC RIFÉ STUDIO

2

WHERE Oviedo, Spain **WHEN** September 2009
CLIENT Pomme Sucre **DESIGNER** Francesc Rifé Studio (p.678)
TOTAL FLOOR AREA 27 m² **SHOP CONSTRUCTOR** Pomme Sucre
PHOTOGRAPHER Fernando Alda

Pomme Sucre is a company founded by Julio Blanco which aims to bring together in one setting the latest trends and different European sweets and pastries, all manufactured in its workshop. To reflect the production quality and craftsmanship of its products, its new store in northern Spain required an innovative design. Francesc Rifé and his team conceived an interior concept that was representative of the three main ingredients used by the confectioner: flour, eggs and cocoa. This was interpreted in the use of materials – white opal acrylic, yellow resin and dark smoked surfaces – which give the store its colour palette and provide its reflective qualities, which help to visually expand the long narrow space. The three core elements have been incorporated into the walls, floors and product display systems. Illumination of the store was an important consideration, in particular of the display cases. These were designed as both recesses and protrusions from the walls, and are either chilled or at ambient temperature. In order to minimise heat exchange which could otherwise damage the products on display, it was necessary to install some cold temperature lamps and integrated systems to protect against condensation. Along the side walls, small yellow niches contrast with the white walls and are used to exhibit the brand's pre-wrapped products.

1 The design creates an interesting optical illusion where the dark-smoked glass mirrors the opposite wall, making the shop feel wider than it is.
2 The walls are like the contrasting dark and white colours of chocolate on sale in the quality confectioner's shop.

411

3 The sleek facade has a black-coloured
phenolic coating, juxtaposed with the more
traditional adjoining buildings in the street.
4 The recessed display cabinets are back-lit
with fluorescent lights.
5 White opal covers the entire ceiling and
walls of the store.

3

4

The interior concept was representative of a confectioner's main ingredients: flour, eggs and cocoa

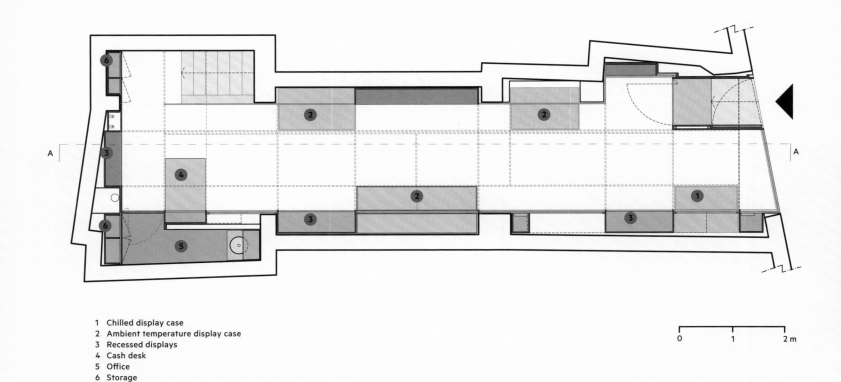

1 Chilled display case
2 Ambient temperature display case
3 Recessed displays
4 Cash desk
5 Office
6 Storage

Display case

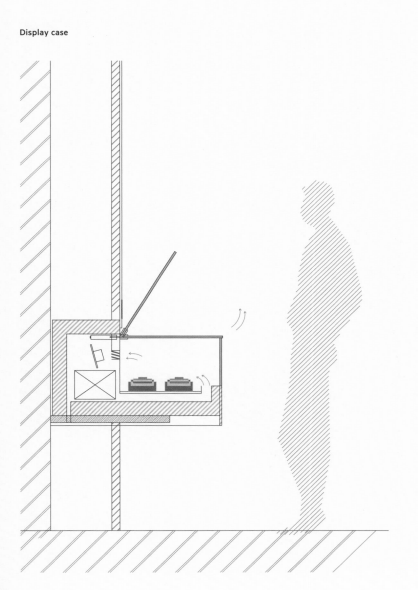

Reflective qualities
help to visually expand
the long space

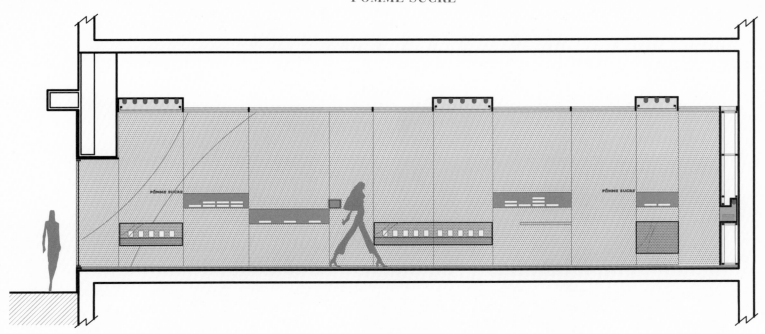

Section AA

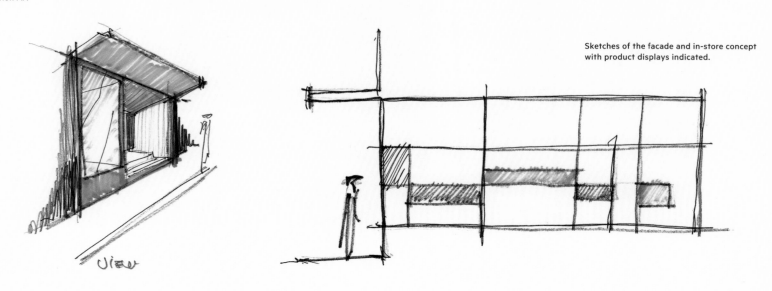

Sketches of the facade and in-store concept with product displays indicated.

Renderings of the entrance, viewed from both the outside and inside of the shop.

PUSATERI'S

by GH+A

1

WHERE Toronto, Canada WHEN October 2010
CLIENT Pusateri's Fine Foods DESIGNER GH+A (p.678)
TOTAL FLOOR AREA 915 m² SHOP CONSTRUCTOR Jasper Construction
PHOTOGRAPHER Philip Castleton

Pusateri's is an emporium of fine Italian imported and prepared foods with two other locations in Toronto. The design mandate for this new store was to create a space that reflected the refined tastes and lifestyles of Pusateri's clientele. GH+A opted for a modern approach to gourmet food shopping, creating an environment with clean architectural lines using sophisticated materials. The concept of 'food is fashion' was a guiding principle in the design approach where food is presented within a visually uncluttered and simple setting. For the large footprint store, the elegance of the design is enhanced by the use of luxurious materials forming the backdrops for the various departments. In the product presentation zones, all the walls are treated with either glass, veined white marble or natural stone. In keeping with the store's structured aesthetic, signage

and graphics are minimal. The ceiling, with its fully integrated lighting and rectilinear configuration, has a design that follows simple, yet eye-catching geometry. Warmth is introduced into the store via dark stained wood in the furniture and checkout area walls, evoking a boutique hotel lobby aesthetic. The storefront is noteworthy for being fabricated entirely from glass. The black frame surrounding the entrance is back-painted glass, as is the green glass surrounding the cheese display fridge.

1   Merchandise is integrated in the storefront thanks to the glass-fronted facade.
2   Marble slab counter tops, espresso-stained wood and white large polished floor tiles contribute to the sense of refinement of the product offerings.
3   From outside the store, passers-by can see straight into the fully-operational cheese fridge, with the Parmagiano-Reggiano wheels towering above them.
4   The white patterned ceiling demarcates the fresh produce section of the store.

2

3

The concept 'food is fashion' was a guiding principle

4

The storefront, at over 30-m wide, has two entry points each designed with restrained sophistication to make the shopper feel like a special guest.

The checkout area is meant to emulate the concierge desk of an exclusive hotel. Marble slab counters are used instead of traditional cash desks.

1 Fresh produce section
2 Cheese display
3 Cafe
4 Pastry area
5 Demonstration area
6 Deli/sandwich area
7 Fish area
8 Meat area
9 Freezers
10 Dairy area
11 Bread area
12 Cash desks
13 Office
14 Staff area

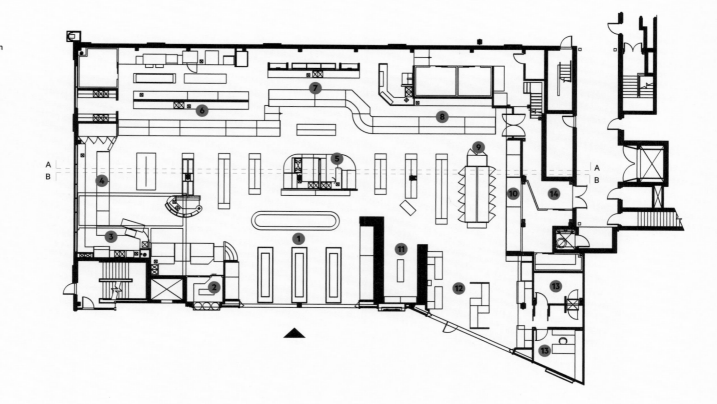

The elegance of the design is enhanced by the use of luxurious materials

Expressed through the highly reflective surfaces, the designers applied a merchandising approach often found in high-end department stores dedicated to fashion.

Throughout the white space, the different merchandise zones are distinguished according to the application of refined wall materials.

SAQ SIGNATURE

by ÆDIFICA, SID LEE AND SAQ

1

WHERE Quebec City, Canada **WHEN** January 2010
CLIENT Société des Alcools du Québec **DESIGNERS** Ædifica (p.673), Sid Lee (p.685) and SAQ
TOTAL FLOOR AREA 511 m² **SHOP CONSTRUCTOR** JCB Entrepreneurs Généraux
PHOTOGRAPHER Corinne Fortier

SAQ Signature is the high-end banner of the Société des Alcools du Québec, a state-owned corporation responsible for the trade of alcoholic beverages in the province of Quebec. Its clientele includes wine connoisseurs and aficionados looking for exclusive and prestigious wines. In an effort to enhance the shopping experience as a whole and to develop a richer, deeper and more modern retail environment, a new store concept was required. For the interior design, Ædifica, Sid Lee and SAQ teamed up and collaboratively drew inspiration from the ambience of an authentic French chateau's wine cellar. Realised within the foundation walls of the building, existing buttresses and pillars add a sense of rhythm to the space. The first floor store is accessed by the main steps or a blackened steel spiral staircase; as customers ascend, they notice the space getting darker and cooler to provide optimal conditions for the preservation of wine. Noble materials, coats of arms and quotations from famous poets decorate the slate walls and floors, while the wine is displayed in recessed alcoves. Simple wooden crates on reclaimed birch podiums display 'new arrivals' and an oak wood table, strategically positioned at the back of the store, allows for leisurely or organised wine tastings. As a centrepiece, two custom-made suspended glass cases house the most prestigious bottles (some fetching up to 26,000 CAN$) in a climate-controlled environment that is impervious to vibrations.

1 The store has an earthy polished concrete floor, dark slate walls and natural finish birch wood fittings.
2 Cases of newly-arrived wines are positioned in two central islands in the store.
3 The alcoves are lined floor to ceiling in dark slate tiles.

2

Quotations from famous poets decorate the slate walls and floors in recessed alcoves

3

4

5

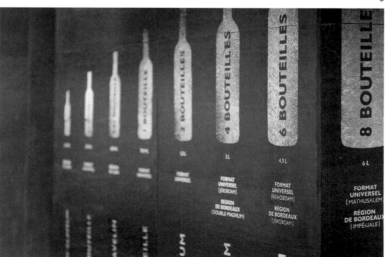

4 White quartz is inset into the long table at the back of the store, providing a neutral background for customers to appreciate the colour of the wine during tasting sessions.
5 Information for visitors is written in chalk-effect graphics on the slate walls.
6 Intimate alcoves have been created amidst the building's pillars to display wines by region and vintage.
7 The champagne section has a different decor, with wood-lined shelving being positioned in the limestone-tiled wall.

6

Existing buttresses and pillars add a sense of rhythm to the space

7

Sketch illustrating the alcoves which would surround the special presentations of new arrivals and vintage showcases.

The shop has an ambience of an authentic French chateau's wine cellar

Rendering of the central display area.

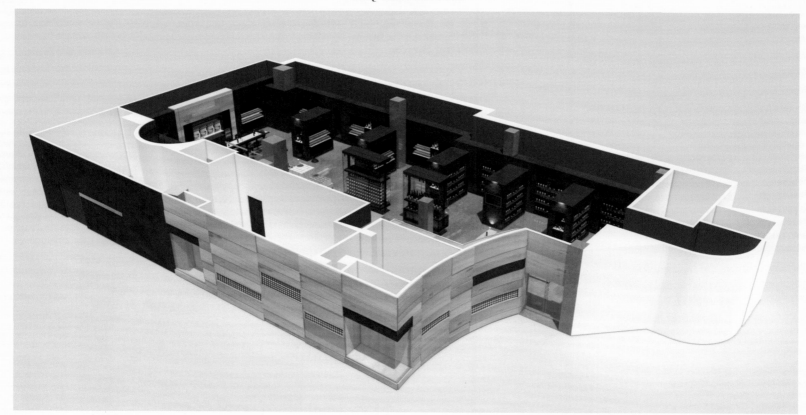

Three-dimensional view which distinguishes the black-walled store from the storage and office areas.

1 Cash desk
2 Champagnes
3 New arrivals
4 Suspended glass display cases
5 Spirits
6 Wine alcoves
7 Bottle formats chalk illustration
8 Wine tasting lounge
9 Sommelier's station
10 Storage
11 Office

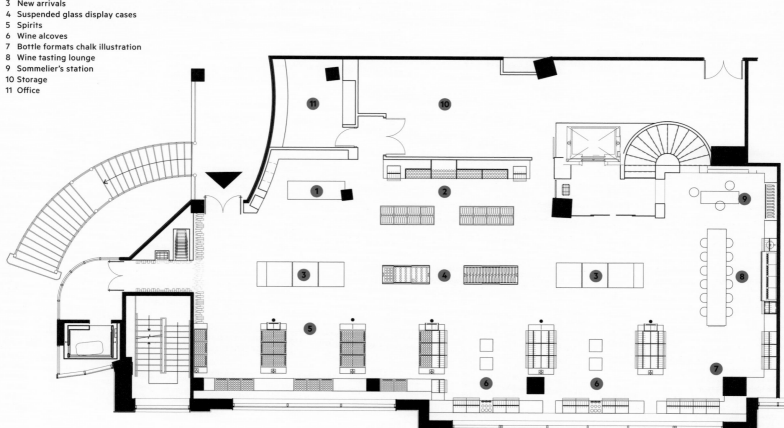

SPRÜNGLI

by STEFAN ZWICKY ARCHITECT

1

WHERE Zurich, Switzerland WHEN September 2010
CLIENT Confiserie Sprüngli DESIGNER Stefan Zwicky Architect (p.685)
TOTAL FLOOR AREA 180 m² SHOP CONSTRUCTOR Pfister Ladenbau
PHOTOGRAPHER Heinz Unger

The Sprüngli name is synonymous with fine chocolates and the company has an assortment of pastry shops across Switzerland. A family-run business, the Sprüngli flagship store in Zurich has been trading for over 175 years at the same location, which recently underwent a major refurbishment. That redesign was headed by Stefan Zwicky, who was next commissioned to give a facelift to another key Sprüngli destination in the city. The challenge for this latest transformation was to coherently translate the corporate design into the existing building. The facade was completely renovated; its upper section consists of a frameless pre-tensioned glass skin which has divisions incorporated to reflect the structure of the building. The plinth section consists of perforated, flush-fitting metal that guarantees the functionality of various ventilation inlets and outlets. Two former entrances have been reduced to only one at a central axis giving prominence to feature display windows on either side. The interior of the store has a clear-cut, symmetrical design. Two parallel sales counters guide the customer to a self-service section at the back of the space. The floor consists of a marble diamond-shaped design and represents the tradition of the house of Sprüngli. The woodwork on the walls and shelving display systems has a dark reddish tone, whilst the metal components have a warm nickel colour tone, all of which complement the dark chocolate confectionary on sale in-store perfectly.

1 The rejuvenated logo wraps around the entire length of the facade at intervals and is a new interpretation of traditional reverse glass inscriptions incorporating elements of screen printing, gold leaf and LED lighting.
2 Jordi Veciana's Lewit t pendant lampshades are positioned over the sales counters.

2

The interior of the store has
a clear-cut, symmetrical design

THE CUPCAKE BOUTIQUE

by DITTEL ARCHITEKTEN

1

WHERE Stuttgart, Germany **WHEN** June 2010
CLIENT The Cupcake Boutique Cafe **DESIGNER** Dittel Architekten (p.677)
TOTAL FLOOR AREA 60 m² **SHOP CONSTRUCTOR** Nazor Innenausbau
PHOTOGRAPHER Dittel Architekten

The Cupcake Boutique stands for quality, fresh products and flavour combinations with a twist. It is the brainchild of Vanessa Forcelli, who approached Dittel Architekten to develop the corporate design for her cupcake concept. Following on from the opening of the first store in 2009, the Dittel team was again commissioned to design the Stuttgart boutique. The brief called for a true representation of the brand encompassing its unique and fun character, as well as its tagline: sweet and chic. Tying in with the corporate identity, the store colour scheme is like a chocolate cupcake with pink frosted icing. Cupcakes are, not surprisingly, the star attraction within the space. A large glass cabinet in the middle of the long counter, adjacent to the cash desk, showcases the full range of mouth-watering morsels. The choice of an understated white design for the service counter forms a further key element of the store concept. Customers can take their cakes away or eat them in-store in the seating areas which are symmetrically framed by the interior design aspects. Niches are hollowed-out of the white walls to act as display shelving, painted dusty pink inside to contrast with the imitation cakes on display here, cakes which are equally as colourful and almost as delectable-looking as the real thing. The cupcake theme is playfully reflected throughout from the flower-shaped wall graphics to the quirky signs on the doors, and even the lampshades are evocative of fairy cake cases.

1 The pink and white decor encapsulates the sweet and chic theme.
2 A cupcake graphic is incorporated as a flower motif of differing dimensions on the shop walls.
3 The products are showcased in a glass cabinet presenting a tower of delectable delights for the customers to choose from.
4 Seating is symmetrically aligned with the shop windows giving each booth a continuous frame.

2

3

4

1   Seating area
2   Display area
3   Cash desk
4   Cupcake glass display case
5   Service area
6   Storage for crockery and cutlery
7   Coffee machine
8   Fridge
9   Dishwasher
10 Shelves
11 Salad/sandwiches area
12 Kitchen
13 Lavatories

Section AA

Section BB

Section CC

Section DD

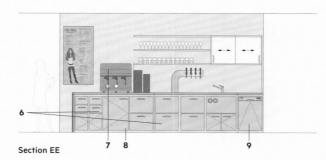

Section EE

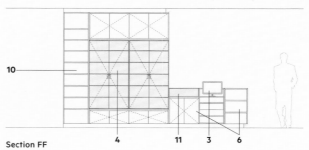

Section FF

Door icons

GIRLS   BOYS   KITCHEN

The store colour scheme is like a chocolate cupcake with pink frosted icing

Renderings illustrate both the colour scheme and the layout in-store when viewed from the counter (above) and from the entrance (below).

THE SALAD SHOP

by ASYLUM

1

WHERE Singapore, Singapore WHEN December 2009
CLIENT The Salad Shop DESIGNER Asylum (p.674)
TOTAL FLOOR AREA 139 m² SHOP CONSTRUCTOR Nestspace
PHOTOGRAPHER Lumina Photography (Teck Lim)

Salad is a type of food which is stereotypically described as an option only for vegetarians or the health conscious amongst us. The owners of a new food and beverage outlet in Singapore, which is all about the green stuff, wanted to change this misconception. The brief called for a fresh identity to be conceived that encompassed the fact that salad can be a hearty meal in everyday life for everyone. Asylum developed the interior design of the shop around the strategy 'Salad for Everybody' tagline. A light-hearted culinary approach was used to emphasise freshness, variety and taste. The brand philosophy was echoed throughout the collaterals using silhouettes of animals, reflecting the fact that salad can be for herbivores, carnivores and everything else in-between. From the street, customers are greeted with a plywood feature screen with cut-outs of oversized forks and spoons, behind which glimpses of the interior are revealed. Inside the shop, alongside white surfaces and cement screed flooring, plywood is the primary material used which gives the space an organic touch. The furniture and fittings have been customised by the Asylum team, from the stools imprinted with animal graphics to the rows of customised fabric lampshades with scenic views, imbuing the space with a breath of nature.

1 The store's window display includes giant cutlery shapes that have been cut-out of a plywood screen.
2 Cutlery silhouettes also make an appearance as the relief on the plywood wall next to the condiments station.
3 Ikea stools have been customised with vinyl stickers, giving a splash of colour against the neutral palette of the store.
4 The customised lampshades show scenic views, which add to the healthy atmosphere in the store.

2

3

4

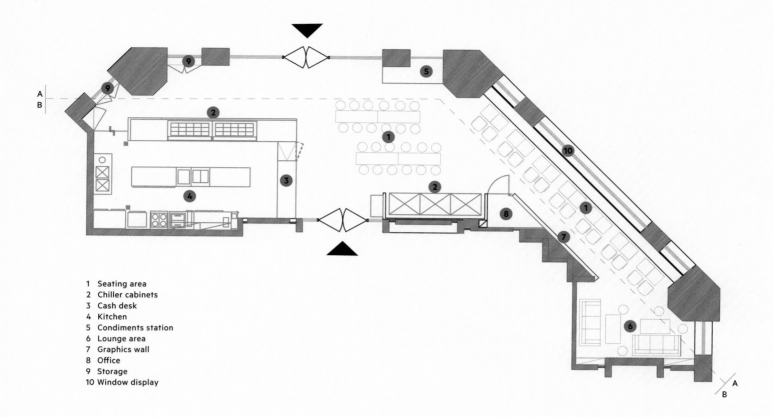

1 Seating area
2 Chiller cabinets
3 Cash desk
4 Kitchen
5 Condiments station
6 Lounge area
7 Graphics wall
8 Office
9 Storage
10 Window display

Section AA

Section BB

Asylum also designed the brand identity of The Salad Shop. The
business cards have the tagline cut out, while the tray features
animal silhouettes overlaid on a bed of lettuce.

SHOP SIGNAGE

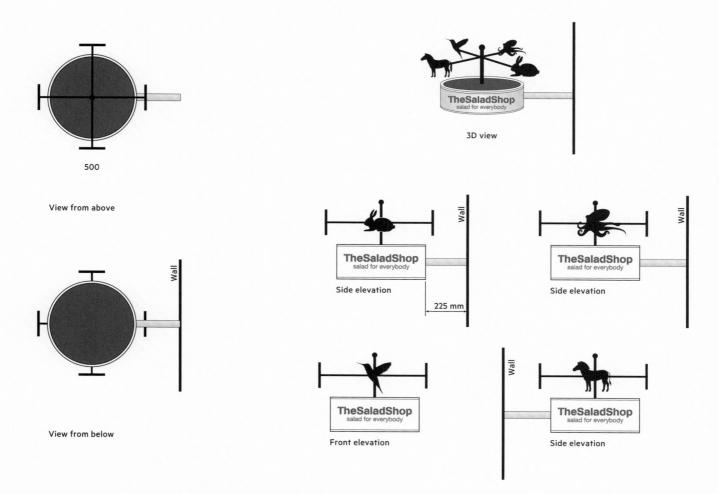

500

View from above

View from below

3D view

Wall

Side elevation

225 mm

Side elevation

Wall

Wall

Front elevation

Side elevation

Wall

Silhouettes of animals reflect the fact that salad can be for both herbivores and carnivores

The brand's message – 'Salad for Everybody' – was incorporated into the shop signage, which was designed like a weather vane.

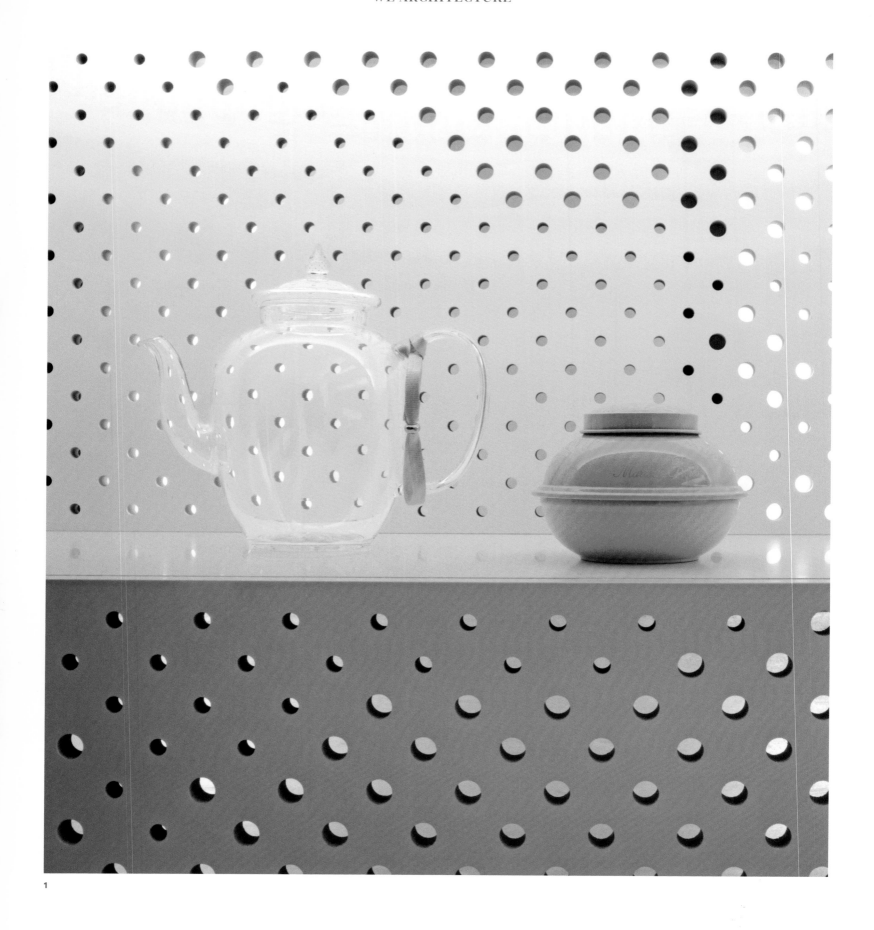

1

From the street, the perforated holes provide
an illusory 3D image of a large teapot

T-MAGI

by WE ARCHITECTURE

2

WHERE Copenhagen, Denmark WHEN October 2009
CLIENT T-Magi DESIGNER WE Architecture (p.687)
TOTAL FLOOR AREA 60 m² SHOP CONSTRUCTOR Jönsson
PHOTOGRAPHER Enok Holsegaard

T-Magi is a speciality tea shop right in the heart of Copenhagen for the exclusive French tea brand Mariage Freres. The owners asked WE Architecture to create a store with a distinctive design with a touch of magic. The teapot – an object universally associated with tea – was utilised as the motif for the shop, as well as the logo and PR material. Whilst many shops tend to have a clear distinction between storefront and interior, the design of T-Magi is intended to allow the shop itself to be perceived as the display window. The fascinating features within the interior are the backlit display shelves and counter which are punctured with tiny holes in different sizes. The entire back wall and the front of the cash desk have this perforated design. When viewed from the street, the illuminated punctured openings provide an illusory three-dimensional image of a large teapot. Moving closer, the teapot distorts into smaller light fragments. Inside the shop, the space is intentionally designed to have a laboratory feel, which comes across in the clinical white furnishings. One side is dedicated to a scent wall where all the 40 different tea varieties are exhibited in small glass flasks with cork stoppers. With the visual and olfactory senses stimulated, customers are invited experiment, smelling and tasting their way to discover their favourite red, green or black teas in-store.

1 When inside the shop, the teapot motive dissolves into an abstract pattern of illuminated perforations.
2 The image of a shining teapot attracts the attention of passers-by and leaves no doubt about what kind of product T-Magi sells.

The store is an experimental space where customers can discover their favourite tea

3

3 The scent wall gives a distinctive aroma
  to the shop, stimulating the senses and
  tantalising the taste buds.
4 It appears at first glance that the flasks on
  the illuminated wall are floating in space.
5 The wall's punctured holes can be seen as
  metaphors for the perforations of a teabag.

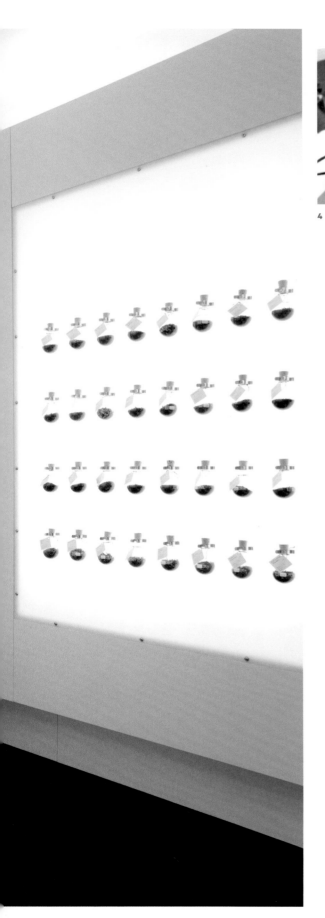

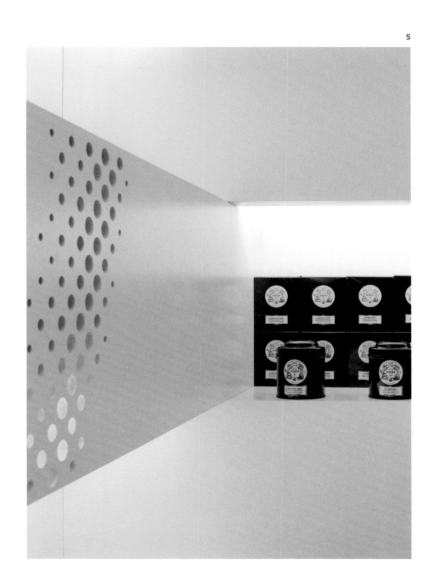

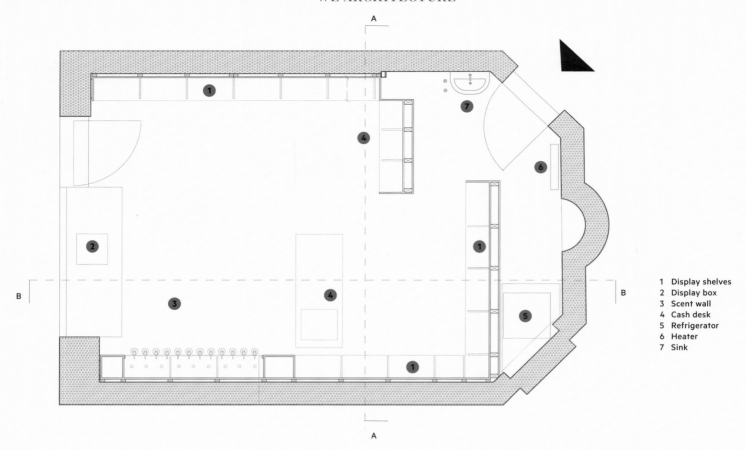

1 Display shelves
2 Display box
3 Scent wall
4 Cash desk
5 Refrigerator
6 Heater
7 Sink

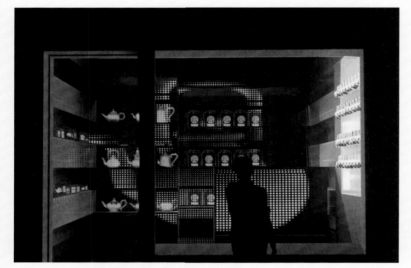

Rendering that shows the customer's
perspective of the store from outside the shop.

CASH COUNTER

Fluorescent tube

Electric
outlet and
cabels plug

Section

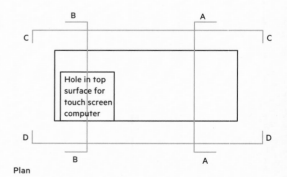

Hole in top
surface for
touch screen
computer

Plan

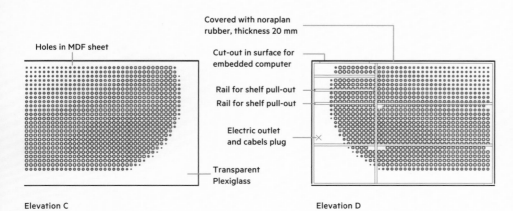

Holes in MDF sheet

Covered with noraplan
rubber, thickness 20 mm

Cut-out in surface for
embedded computer

Rail for shelf pull-out

Rail for shelf pull-out

Electric outlet
and cabels plug

Transparent
Plexiglass

Elevation C

Elevation D

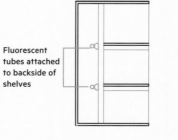

Fluorescent
tubes attached
to backside of
shelves

Section AA

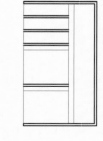

Section BB

440

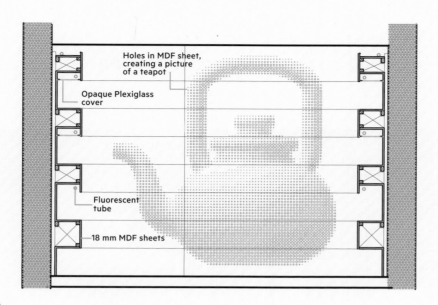

Holes in MDF sheet, creating a picture of a teapot

Opaque Plexiglass cover

Fluorescent tube

18 mm MDF sheets

Section AA

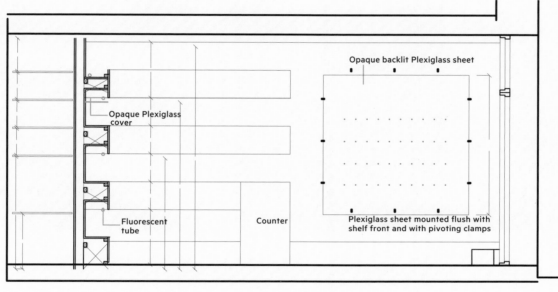

Opaque backlit Plexiglass sheet

Opaque Plexiglass cover

Fluorescent tube

Counter

Plexiglass sheet mounted flush with shelf front and with pivoting clamps

Section BB

Moving closer, the teapot distorts into smaller light fragments

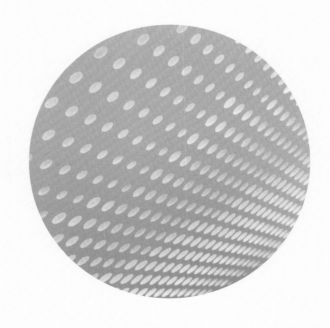

VOLKHARDTS WEIN

by TOOLS OFF.ARCHITECTURE

1

WHERE Munich, Germany WHEN October 2008
CLIENT Gebrüder Volkhardt München DESIGNER tools off.architecture (p.686)
TOTAL FLOOR AREA 155 m² SHOP CONSTRUCTOR tools off.architecture
PHOTOGRAPHER Lothar Reichel

Volkhardts Wein is a German wholesale business for wines from across the world. When a retail space was commissioned just outside Munich, tools off.architecture conceived a design which incorporates the two seemingly incongruous essential properties of wine: simplicity and complexity. Translating this concept into the interior design, the team created a complex static installation – a spatial glass design – which forms a dramatic backdrop to the product displays. From outside the store, a curtain of coloured glass allows only a selective view into the shop which arouses curiosity of the customer, enticing them to enter. Light from inside and outside creates the impression that the glass curtain is glowing on its own; it generates a changing light pattern depending on the time of day. The materials of the interior decoration bring to mind the key elements that play a crucial role in wine production and storage, such as earth, glass and wood. By encapsulating such robust and reliable materials in the store design, an authentic atmosphere is created. Floor, ceiling, walls and furniture complement each other in form and material. An inviting landscape is composed where the products are presented either in timber boxes, piled together as display cases in the centre of the store, or in the wine rack wall with its sliding doors of iron and steel.

1 The bottle installation in the store window attracts the attention of passers-by.
2 A little bistro in the back of the store gives customers the possibility to enjoy their selected wines straight away.
3 iGuzzini spotlights provide illumination for the product offerings positioned amidst the dark metal and light wood furnishings.

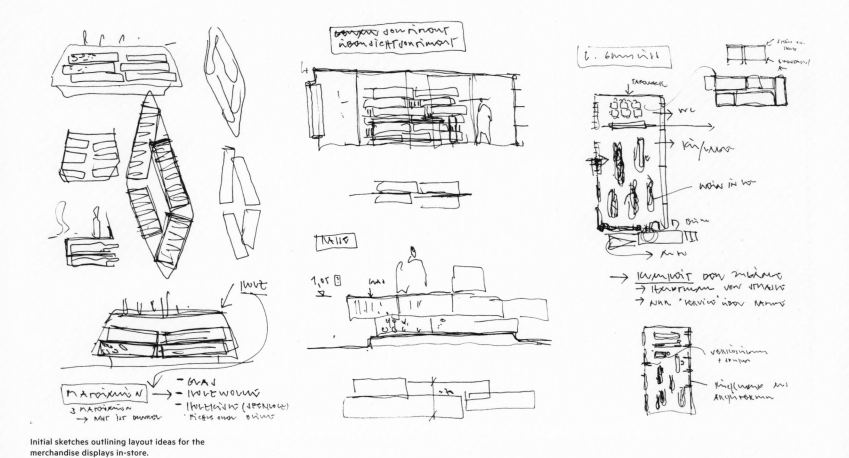

Initial sketches outlining layout ideas for the merchandise displays in-store.

Materials bring to mind key elements that play a crucial role in wine production

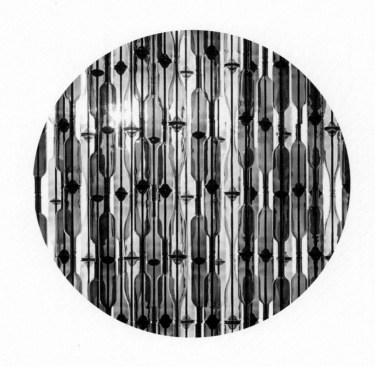

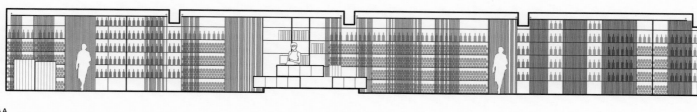

Section AA

Section BB

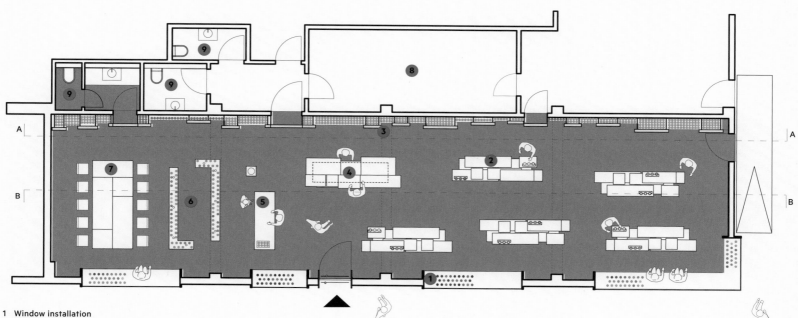

1   Window installation
2   Pine box display cases
3   Wine rack wall
4   Cash desk
5   Tasting desk
6   Tasting display
7   Workshop area/bistro
8   Staff room
9   Lavatories

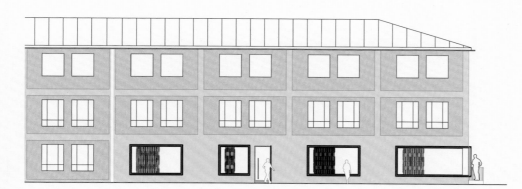

North elevation

West elevation

445

FURN
AND
PROD

446

TURE
HOME
UCTS

447

@BTF

by BUTTERFLY-STROKE

1

WHERE Tokyo, Japan WHEN August 2009
CLIENT butterfly-stroke DESIGNER butterfly-stroke (p.675)
TOTAL FLOOR AREA 202 m² SHOP CONSTRUCTOR butterfly-stroke
PHOTOGRAPHER Eiji Ohda

The @btf shop opened in Tokyo in 2009 to sell original products of the creative agency butterfly-stroke, as well as selected items from local and international artists. The concept for the store created by Katsunori Aoki was one in which visitors could retrace their footsteps to places filled with fond memories, unexpectedly stumbling across items that spark a recollection which had otherwise long since been forgotten. The design store also needs to double-up as an exhibition and event space where artists from various fields unleash the powers of their imagination, creating and unveiling their own personal histories using unique methods and approaches. The retail interior is a creative junction that invites customers to crave things that reflect the essence of who they are, as represented by the past and the present. Those things should be precious and conjure up a sense of nostalgia, as well as be aesthetically pleasing. In the shop space there is an array of unusual items, ranging from rare artworks and exquisite mass-produced merchandise to sought-after dead stock items. Placed against a white backdrop is this unparalleled showcase of products which satisfies the interests of those who may have grown tired of simply purchasing expensive brand items. A wall which divides the retail from the exhibition space has intriguing gaps along its length that appear to have just been hammered out, giving visitors a glimpse of what lies beyond.

1 The space is a creative junction that includes a shop combined with a gallery and exhibition area.
2 There are no regular doors connecting the shop and the gallery, only intriguing openings and walkways.
3 In the event space, artists from various fields unleash their powers of imagination.
4 In the D.I.Y. Department, customers can purchase ordinary items like hammers, buckets or fire extinguishers that have been transformed into works of art.

2

3

4

BARLETTI

by RON VAN LEENT

2

WHERE Amsterdam, the Netherlands WHEN February 2010
CLIENT Barletti DESIGNER Ron van Leent (p.684)
TOTAL FLOOR AREA 650 m² SHOP CONSTRUCTOR Beerens Tilburg
PHOTOGRAPHERS Rene van der Hulst and Ron van Leent

Barletti is a retailer of exclusive kitchens which are created by three young designers in the Netherlands. The brand comprises five distinct kitchen collections, each corresponding to a different way of life. Within the new Amsterdam flagship store, a showroom was required which housed the different kitchen styles whilst encapsulating the essence of the brand in a coherent space. Already familiar with the Barletti signature, Ron van Leent answered the brief with a concept that was very restrained and which let the specific product ranges speak for themselves. A Barletti lifestyle experience was created with the kitchens set in an open space alongside playful and frivolous items, a far way from the regular kitchen showroom format. There are no walls for partitioning but instead elements such as PVC ribbons, floating sales corners,

glass mosaic tiled columns and book cases are used. A luxurious atmosphere is created in the aspirational settings, each of which is defined and enhanced by the choice of lighting, with downlighters, coloured LED panels and theatre lights on steel structures adding dramatic illumination throughout. Whilst each area is decorated according to its collection's own style, the fabric of the showroom has a raw, almost industrial feel. To tie in with the colour of the natural concrete floor, the exposed mechanical systems of the ceiling space have been painted a dusty grey.

1 A spiderweb-like PVC ribbon wall – a twist on the classic 1930s room divider – has been used at the entrance to one kitchen area in the showroom.
2 In between the kitchens, there are several living room style spaces which establish a homely setting.

5

Each kitchen collection corresponds to a different way of life

6

3 One area is furnished as an almost entirely all-white environment illuminated by designer lighting, including Izar ceiling lights by Gerd Couckhuyt.

4 A frivolous atmosphere has been created in the baroque-style sales corner, decorated in black velvet and gold.

5 Theatre-style lighting creates interesting shadows across the grey concrete floor and wooden worktops.

6 Comfortable seating areas with deep-pile rugs and fringed curtains are available for customers to relax and take stock.

BOX SHOP

by EDGE ARCHITECTURE + DESIGN

2

WHERE London, United Kingdom WHEN July 2010
CLIENT Rocket Van DESIGNER Edge Architecture + Design (p.677)
TOTAL FLOOR AREA 50 m² SHOP CONSTRUCTOR The Garage Woodworks
PHOTOGRAPHER John Stewardson

Rocket Van is a London-based furniture removal and delivery company. Having spotted a niche opportunity in the market, the company wanted a one-stop-shop with everything needed to arrange a house or office move. Edge Architecture + Design was briefed to work closely with brand agency Bear to produce an integrated retail experience that embedded the company identity within the interior design of the space. Encapsulating the light-hearted and approachable personality of the service-focused business, the design team created a concept for the store which is summed up in its name, Box Shop. A raw and basic aesthetic was incorporated by essentially using a singular material choice – MDF that resembles cardboard – throughout the small space, which is nestled under a railway arch in central London.

Box Shop is a unique proposition that uses the tools of the removals trade to generate the store's visual appearance. Bold, black graphics adorn the walls, with messages and information reminiscent of 'this way up' symbols which can appear on the core component for sale in the shop, cardboard boxes. There is the 'rocket science' information service providing tips and advice about moving, and a 'consultation area' where customers can plan everything for their move, even selecting wall graphics for the children's new room. Playful and colourful decorations from this aspect spread out into the shop, from the aeroplane suspended from the corrugated ceiling to the space invaders climbing the back wall.

1 The store's concept is immediately obvious to passers-by, thanks to the 'open box' design incorporated into the facade.
2 Traditional box-print themed way-finding graphics appear on the walls.

3

4

3 The design studio also created a brand logo for the removals arm of the business.

4 An engaging box-themed children's activity area is located in the back.

5 Customers are taken on a 'merchandise journey' along which they can buy any kind of item that could be needed for a move.

Bold, black graphics portray the
light-hearted personality of the store

457

ESPAÇO SANTA HELENA

by JAYME LAGO MESTIERI ARCHITECTURE

1

WHERE São Paulo, Brazil WHEN December 2010
CLIENT Espaço Santa Helena DESIGNER Jayme Lago Mestieri Architecture (p.680)
TOTAL FLOOR AREA 700 m² SHOP CONSTRUCTOR Souza Lima Construction
PHOTOGRAPHER Ary Diesendruck

Espaço Santa Helena is a chain of department stores in Brazil selling home and kitchenware products. For the new store in São Paulo, Jayme Lago Mestieri and his team had to create a space for 15,000 products, divided into more than 20 categories. The biggest challenge in designing an interior for such a variety of merchandise was maintaining a coherent aesthetic whilst succinctly orienting the visitor flow and product placement. Strong architectural lines achieve this goal, in conjunction with an eye-catching construction at the entrance of the store. This comes in the form of a giant expanded walk-in cube which creates a significant impact – not surprising given its proportions. It is a key design feature with a primary function of establishing the starting point for the customer. The cube, which is full ceiling height, appears as if it has been pulled apart and inside customers can discover a selection of luxury brands. Above its entrances are wooden slats which reflect the ceiling configuration. The shop-in-shop cube aspect has an organic shape with curved edges, as well as graphics and a colour palette based on brand principles. This continues throughout the store in the product presentation booths around the edge of the space where materials such as steel and glass proliferate, along with laminate and lacquer coatings. The back of the shop embraces a cosier atmosphere thanks to the a predominance of walnut wood in the display units.

1   A singular floor covering of large porcelain tiles with a concrete texture has been laid throughout the store.
2   The 10 x 10 x 6-m-high cube positioned at the entrance created appeal from outside the store.
3   Overhead, lengths of white wood laminate were placed 25 cm apart with spotlights positioned in-between. Above the wood ceiling, a black acoustic covering was set.

The shop space had to display 15,000 products, divided into over 20 categories

4   Walnut-laminated furniture marks the 3-m-high kitchenware area.
5   The shelving units feature embedded fluorescent lighting and product information screens.

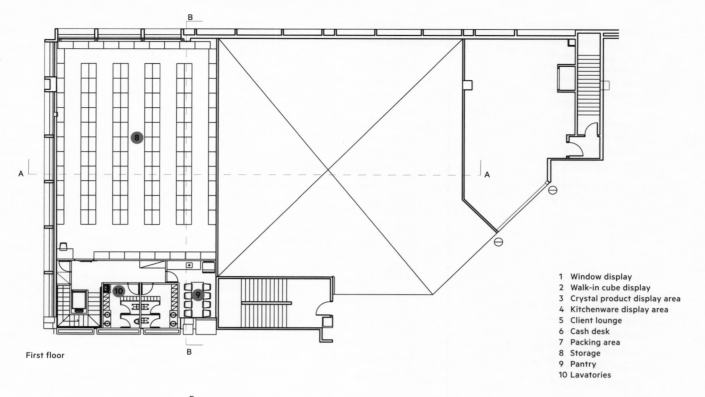

First floor

1   Window display
2   Walk-in cube display
3   Crystal product display area
4   Kitchenware display area
5   Client lounge
6   Cash desk
7   Packing area
8   Storage
9   Pantry
10 Lavatories

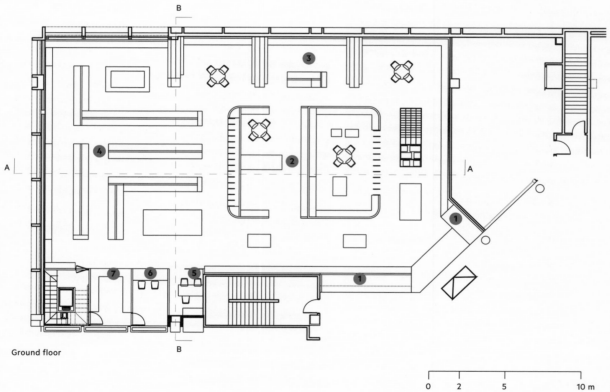

Ground floor

0   2   5   10 m

Rendering of the showroom with the kitchenware display area
on the left, the central double-height aspect of the space and
the entrance at the right.

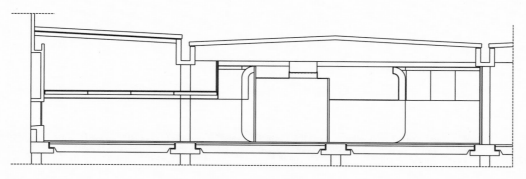

Section AA

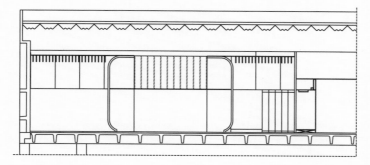

Section BB

A giant expanded walk-in cube creates significant impact

Sketches showing the muted colours of the store as well as the potential customer traffic flow.

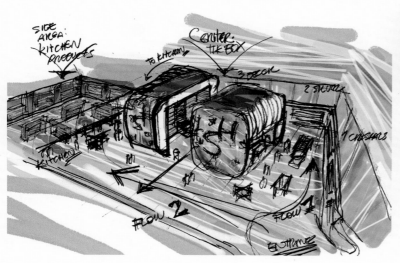

FRANCFRANC NAGOYA

by GLAMOROUS

1

WHERE Nagoya, Japan WHEN October 2010
CLIENT BALS Corporation DESIGNER Glamorous (p.678)
TOTAL FLOOR AREA 1388 m² SHOP CONSTRUCTOR Nomura
PHOTOGRAPHER Nacása & Partners

Francfranc is a Japanese-based retailer of furniture and interior goods with outlets across Asia. The new department store in Nagoya was designed by the team at Glamorous and debuts the theme of 'Lifestyle with Art'. The concept encapsulates the idea that art should be brought closer and enjoyed as part of everyday life, whilst having the opportunity to shop in an environment that has its products displayed akin to exhibits in a museum. The black and white corporate colours of the Franfranc brand is engrained across the three floors of the store, both inside and out. For customers approaching the shop, the impressive facade has a distinctive curb appeal with its differently-shaped windows scaling the full height of the building's frontage surrounded by what appear to be illuminated-picture frames. On entering the store, a low-hung and large-scale chandelier is an immediate eye-catcher. The merchandise is laid out around the circumference of the ground and first floor levels leaving way for the black central staircase to be a key feature. Neatly stacked rows of merchandise nestle into the space beneath the stairs. This is in contrast with the jumble of black letters which spell out the brand name on the glass paneling above, as well as the cluttered white-painted wooden chairs which are strewn and squeezed into crevices beneath the ceiling. Both these aspects emphasise the double-height space of the ground floor level, as do the delightful little painted animals that can be seen scurrying up the walls and across the mishmash of chairs.

1   The outlet consists of three floors, designed to be an elegant Francfranc-like museum.
2   The facade was designed by Yasumichi Morita and is a unique take on the phrase 'picture windows'. The artworks within the frames are painted by Japanese artist Masataka Kurashina.

FRANCFRANC XINTIANDI

by GLAMOROUS

1

WHERE Shanghai, China WHEN December 2010
CLIENT BALS Corporation DESIGNER Glamorous (p. 678)
TOTAL FLOOR AREA 411 m² SHOP CONSTRUCTOR JRS International
PHOTOGRAPHER Nacása & Partners

Francfranc, the Japanese home furnishing brand, extended its reach across Asia with the opening of a flagship store in the Xintiandi district of Shanghai at the end of 2010. The store, designed by Glamorous, ushers in the brand's 'casual stylish' concept to the Chinese market with a delicate and elegant design style. A largely white colour palette in the interior, along with accents of black and silver, gives the two-storey shop a spacious and light feel. A stunning feature staircase dominates the ground floor level, flanked by two oversized contemporary chandeliers. These bell-shaped illuminations in addition act as product display modules, with all-white home products suspended around their circumferences. Towards the back of the ground floor, there is an open-plan aspect. The unobstructed space beneath the stairs is left as a walkway

with a strikingly-visual mural painted in silver overhead. This design subtly reflects the animal theme that occurs throughout the store: here a reindeer appears out of the swirls of paint, on the laser-cut wood-fronted cash desk other wildlife can be seen lurking and at the top of the stairs are two giant bunnies that watch over customers as they explore the store. The building's facade includes a 3-m diameter backlit logo and a curtain of shimmering metallic-coloured squares, a feature which also appears on the wall behind the cash desk and throughout the store. The window displays at the main entrance feature another pair of large lampshades, this time with black products suspended. The base is made from numerous precariously-positioned products of Francfranc which have been customised by artists to become 'a symbolic artwork of the brand'.

1 Two custom-made chandeliers are positioned near the entrance so as to perfectly combine space and light and present a surreal visual effect.

2 A total of 25,000 small plates of plastic resin were used to create the shimmering curtains in-store, hung behind the cash desk and in the shop windows.

3 Surrounding the glass banister at the top of the stairs on the first floor are ten candles, symbolic of the monochrome art of the store. These objects are 1.2 m in height and are made of fibreglass-reinforced plastic.

On the laser-cut wood-fronted cash desk, wildlife can be seen lurking

HAAZ DESIGN AND ART GALLERY

by GAD

1

WHERE Istanbul, Turkey WHEN December 2010
CLIENT Haaz Art and Design Gallery DESIGNER GAD (p.678)
TOTAL FLOOR AREA 200 m² SHOP CONSTRUCTOR SFG Architecture
PHOTOGRAPHER Ali Bekman

Haaz Design and Art Gallery is a retail space that combines furniture, design objects and art. When the owners Ozlem Avcioglu and Murat Patavi wanted to relocate their concept to Tesvikiye, an exclusive shopping district of Istanbul, a two-storey building was chosen. A complete renovation was required and the GAD team used a primarily architectural approach to produce varied articulations of the space whilst at the same time giving it a familiar and cosy feel. In keeping with the brief, a sense of space was instilled to ensure the showroom was as flexible as possible – it was to have a dual purpose of displaying products as well as being a location for events. Materials like wood and stone have been utilised within the interior, with a mixture of black steel and lead tubes on the facade to attract attention from the street. The sunken ground floor is reached via five stairs which also extend into a display for the products. The floor continues in solid oak wood herringbone, with a black and white colour scheme used for covering surfaces and fixtures, which included Haaz graphics as wallpaper. Cantilevered steel stairs to the first floor help to enhance the sense of space and allow a clear view from the street to the back of the shop. Upstairs, the old cladding and residual layers on one of the walls was removed to leave an interesting backdrop for the presentation of lighting products and art pieces.

1 The gallery is located on the first two floors of an apartment building.
2 Bruno Gecchelin's Iguzzini Tecnica spotlights are positioned within circular ceiling recesses.
3 Herringbone parquet – a traditional housing floor material in Turkey – was used throughout the space.

2

The showroom has a sense of space that allows for varied articulations

3

4

5

4 Haaz graphics are used on the walls, sliding panels and steel-concealing panels.
5 The original cladding on one wall has been removed revealing an interesting backdrop for artworks, such as those by Zhu Fadong and Song Yang. Alongside is positioned Jurgen Bey's St Petersburg chair.
6 Antique pieces sit alongside designer items in the gallery, such as Tom Dixon pendant lamps and Moroso's Bohemian armchair by Patricia Urquiola.

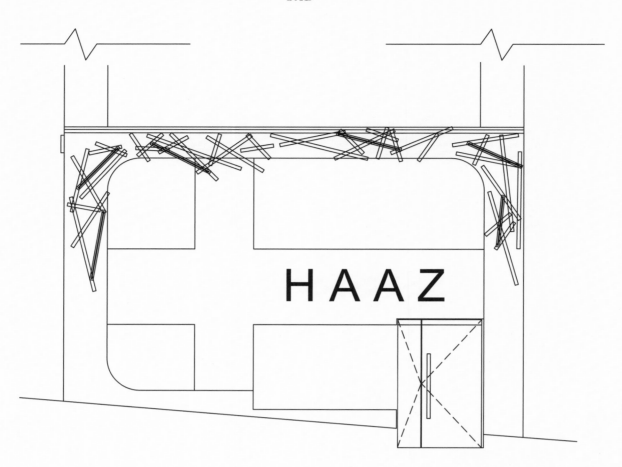

Front elevation

A mixture of black steel and lead tubes on the facade attract attention from the street

View of the facade showing the sunken aspect of the ground floor.

Rendering of the first floor depicting the large window at the front of the store.

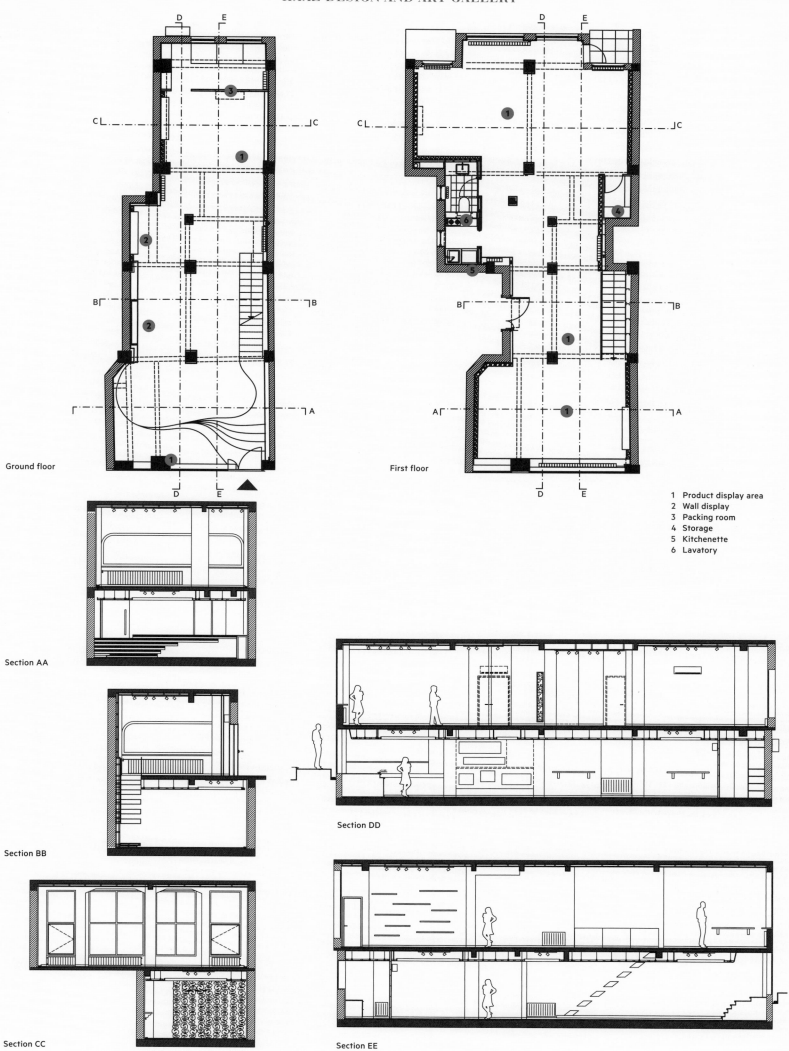

Ground floor

First floor

1 Product display area
2 Wall display
3 Packing room
4 Storage
5 Kitchenette
6 Lavatory

Section AA

Section BB

Section CC

Section DD

Section EE

I FIND EVERYTHING

by MAKOTO YAMAGUCHI DESIGN

1

WHERE Tokyo, Japan **WHEN** May 2010
CLIENT I Find Everything **DESIGNER** Makoto Yamaguchi Design (p.681)
TOTAL FLOOR AREA 24 m² **SHOP CONSTRUCTOR** Denkoubou
PHOTOGRAPHER Koichi Torimura

The new retail premises for I Find Everything – a shop that sells jewellery, objects d'art, hats and photographs – was realised after the renovation of a single unit of a Tokyo apartment building that was built 40 years ago. Hidden away, passers-by do not notice the presence of a commercial space; customers already need to know about the shop or else be prepared to hunt it out, following the small sign placed on the street alongside some nearby stairs. The design concept that Makoto Yamaguchi opted for is extremely simple, creating an elegant and uncomplicated ambience. A key challenge was to give the room a feeling of space, which was achieved by manipulating both the horizontal and vertical dimensions starting with exposing the ceiling rafters to give an extra 1.2 m in height. Clean lines and discrete storage are the focus of the shop which is decorated with white painted walls and scaffold wood planking on the floor. A gallery-like space has been created with a sleek central counter that helps customer circulation. Balancing the small scale and intimate atmosphere, the design team incorporated a mirrored-surface onto each side of this counter, which creates intriguing reflections of the floor, making the counter appear to be made of the same material. From certain angles, the counter even seems to disappear, which confuses the eye and gives the illusion that the size of the room is much larger than it actually is.

1 The use of mirrored-surfaces on the central counter produces a reflection of the opposite wall and floorboards, which tricks the mind and makes it look like the counter has disappeared.
2 The wooden ceiling was originally hidden by flat board, which was removed to give extra height in the shop.

JOINWELL

by CHRIS BRIFFA ARCHITECTS

1

WHERE Qormi, Malta WHEN January 2009
CLIENT Joinwell Group DESIGNER Chris Briffa Architects (p.675)
TOTAL FLOOR AREA 4000 m² SHOP CONSTRUCTORS Joinwell and JS Dimech
PHOTOGRAPHER Chris Briffa Architects

The Joinwell Group is one of the oldest furniture makers in Malta. Established in 1947, over two generations the company has grown from a small joinery shop to an industrial set-up manufacturing both contract and licensed furniture. When it was decided to move the high-street showroom to a 15,000-m² factory site, the intention was to demolish the front end of the factory to make way for a contemporary showroom, which would be integrated with part of the old factory. Chris Briffa was brought on board to manage the interior design of the furniture showroom, as well as a home ware shop and the company's offices. The showroom was to sell a variety of imported quality furniture brands bringing about the need for a single unifying gesture. With the site consisting of two main environments – a concrete 1960s factory and a new steel–glass structure – the architect's first concerns centred around how to deal with the edge between the two aspects. The resulting design was based around a connecting space with trees bathed in natural light. This green division, analogous with the environmental concerns of the company, greets customers with its unorthodox reception area, which is more akin to a conservatory than a furniture shop. A 110-m timber fence consisting of undulating slats of varying thicknesses and lengths, frames and links the mezzanine floor. Hovering above the entire shop, the tree-house platform showcases Joinwell's artisan and logistic capabilities.

1 The reception area is positioned in a garden terrace with the cantilevered tree-house platform overhead.
2 Snaking around the railings and staircases of the first floor, the timber division delineates between new and old buildings.
3 The timber 'curtain' consists of more than 1,200 different pieces of wood.
4 Detail of the floating timber staircase.

2

3

4

The tree-house platform showcases Joinwell's artisan and logistic capabilities

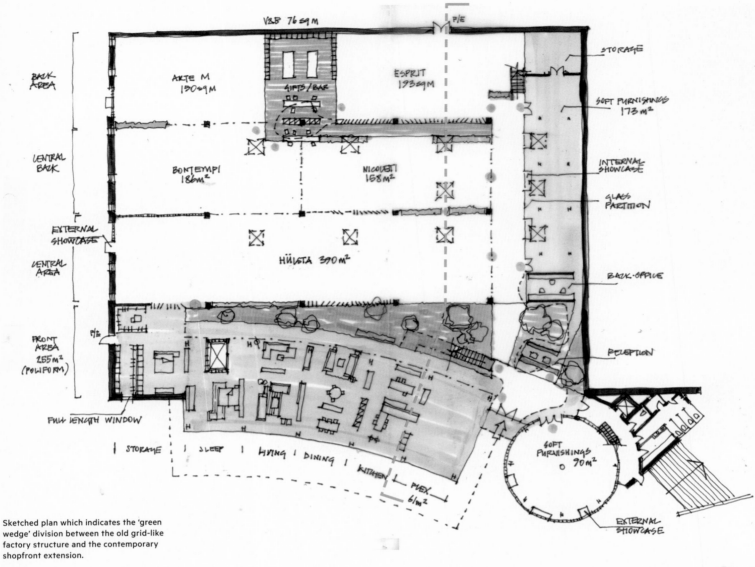
V&B 76 SQ M   P/E

BACK AREA

AKTE M 130 SQ M

GIFTS/BAR

ESPRIT 193 SQ M

STORAGE

SOFT FURNISHINGS 173 M²

CENTRAL BACK

BONTEMPI 186 M²

NICOLETTI 158 M²

INTERNAL SHOWCASE

GLASS PARTITION

EXTERNAL SHOWCASE

CENTRAL AREA

HÜLSTA 390 M²

BACK-OFFICE

FRONT AREA 255 M² (POLIFORM)

P/E

RECEPTION

FULL LENGTH WINDOW

STORAGE | SLEEP | LIVING | DINING | KITCHEN

FLEX 61 M²

SOFT FURNISHINGS 90 M²

EXTERNAL SHOWCASE

Sketched plan which indicates the 'green wedge' division between the old grid-like factory structure and the contemporary shopfront extension.

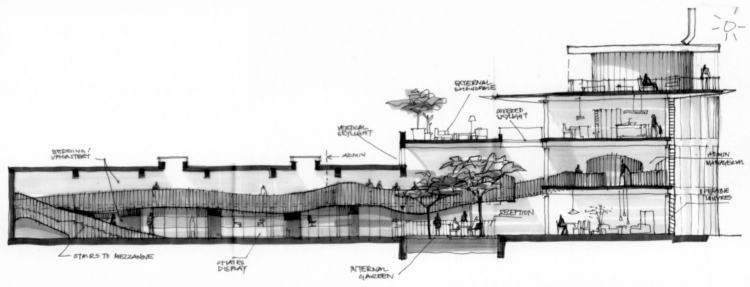

EXTERNAL SHOWCASE

VERTICAL SKYLIGHT

COVERED SKYLIGHT

ADMIN

ADMIN MANAGERIAL

BEDDING / UPHOLSTERY

OPERABLE LOUVRES

RECEPTION

STAIRS TO MEZZANINE

CHAIRS DISPLAY

INTERNAL GARDEN

Section which depicts the positioning of the undulating wooden platform.

A 110-m timber fence frames and links the mezzanine floor

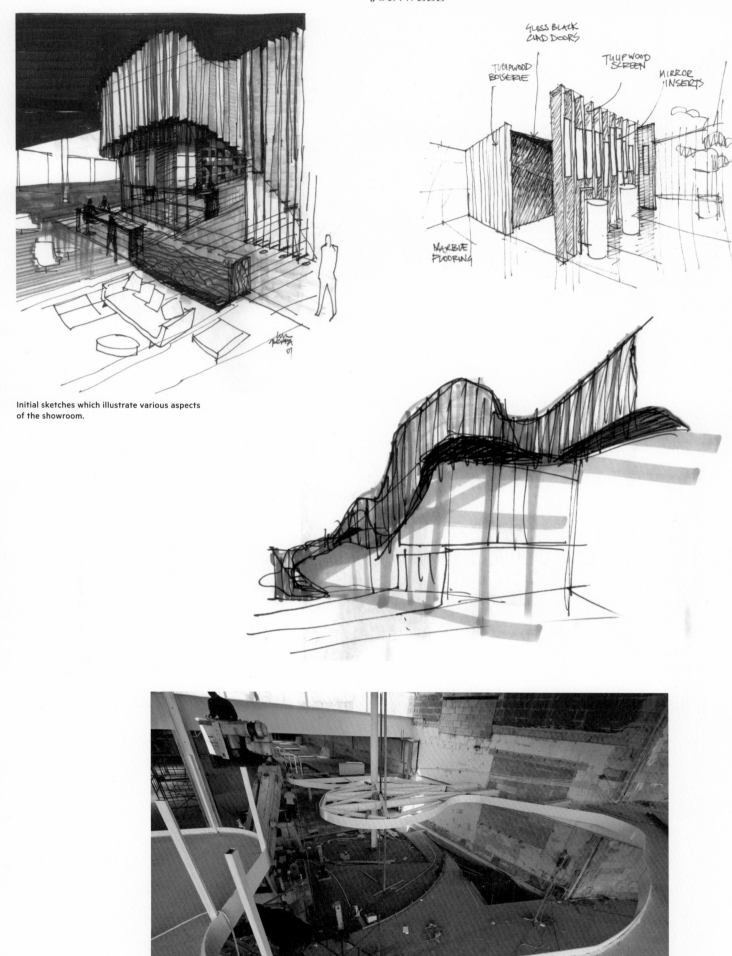

Initial sketches which illustrate various aspects of the showroom.

Construction photo showing the platform taking shape.

L2 DESIGN GROUP

by TRIGUEIROS ARCHITECTURE

2

WHERE Stockholm, Sweden WHEN February 2010
CLIENT L2 Design Group DESIGNER Trigueiros Architecture (p.686)
TOTAL FLOOR AREA 95 m² SHOP CONSTRUCTOR Huskvarna Snickeri
PHOTOGRAPHER Mattias Lindbäck

L2 Design Group is an interior design company founded in 2002. The small, fast-growing group established itself in several local markets in the south of Sweden before being ready to take on the challenge of Stockholm. In order to make a stand in the Swedish capital, the input of the team at Trigueiros Architecture was called upon to create a unique showroom in the middle of the new design district at Torsgatan. The brief asked for a neutral environment that would highlight the L2 interiors, furniture and products. The result is very urban and Scandinavian: white-painted concrete floors, spray-painted ceilings, stark white walls, exposed pipes and installations. Clean, minimalistic and modern, but beyond the expected and strictly conventional, awaits something more profound. The showroom is also designed as a flexible platform

with space and energy for the company to create an all-encompassing experience for its customers. The small, bright and efficient room has been equipped with a number of large screens which balance on white insect-like steel legs. The positioning of these screens alongside the products creates a basic but very versatile stage for all sorts of exhibitions. The rigid ash wood frames are bespoke pieces crafted by a local carpentry studio and incorporate a stretched, technical fabric. As an eye-catching overhead feature, the screens have been reinterpreted and sculpted into different geometrical shapes which fit together like a random jigsaw.

1   The store, which showcases designer furniture such as the Harry Bertoia leaf-shaped wire chair, is divided by the movable structural screens in ash wood frames.
2   Suspended from the ceiling and positioned within the shop, the wood-frame screens can be spied from the street.

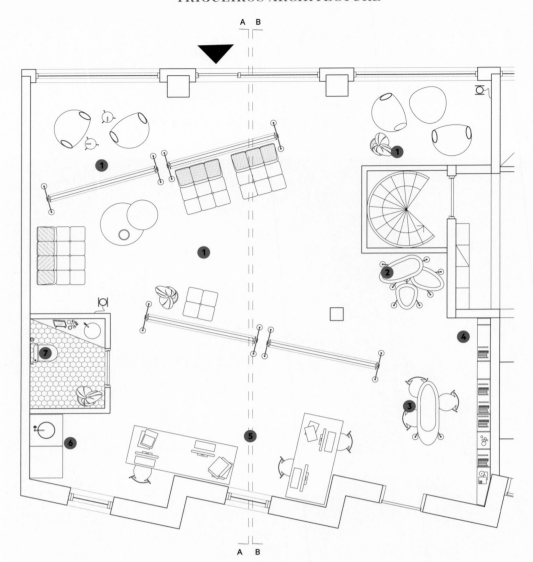

A B

A B

1 Showroom
2 Seating podium
3 Meeting area
4 Material library
5 Back office
6 Kitchenette
7 Lavatory

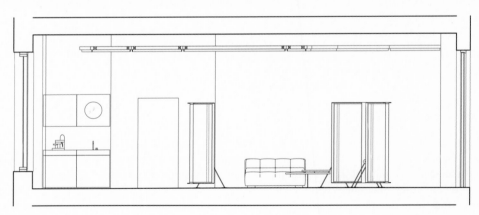

Section AA

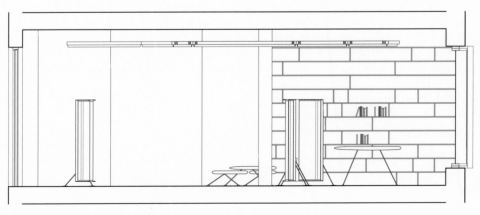

Section BB

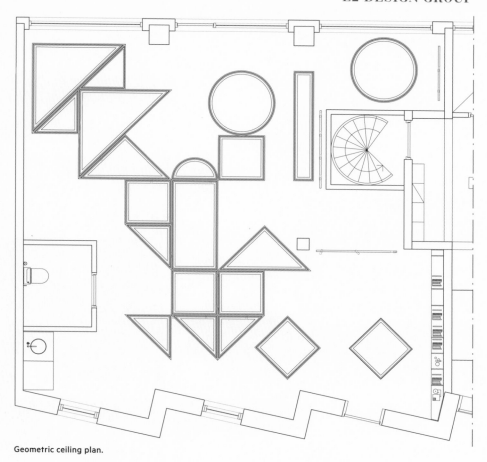

Geometric ceiling plan.

Large screens balance on white insect-like steel legs

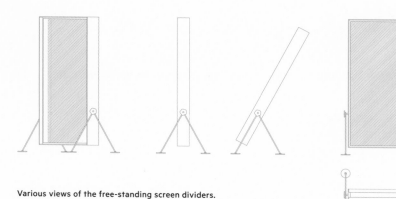

Various views of the free-standing screen dividers.

Rendering show the initial concept idea where the screens on the ceiling could be seen as windows to the sky.

PINO

by BOND

2

WHERE Helsinki, Finland WHEN December 2009
CLIENT pino DESIGNER Bond (p.674)
TOTAL FLOOR AREA 100 m² SHOP CONSTRUCTOR Pekka Koivikko
PHOTOGRAPHER Paavo Lehtonen

Pino is a marketplace for design objects. The brief was to design a holistic graphic and interior concept for pino and its new helsinki store. In order for the brand to be able to expand at some point in the future, the store design had to be adaptable and simple enough to be repeated in different locations. Aleksi Hautamäki and Jesper Bange at Bond created a concept based around the shop name pino – meaning a 'pile' or 'stack' in finnish – which is taken visually and applied to the new logo as well as the design of the fixtures and fittings. The stacked shelving system was designed to have lots of different dimensions to display the merchandise which varies substantially in size. The layout has been kept simple and all the mid-floor displays are low, maintaining clear sight-lines around the space. The fixtures are uncomplicated constructions, made from pine wood planks and finished with gloss paint. A muted colour palette is evident in the interior, working as a crisp background for the fresh, colourful identity and products. A stripped-back effect is also evident in the lighting used, from the industrial spotlights to the bare pendant light-bulbs of differing sizes. An eye-catching feature is the large branded graphic incorporating the stack concept which has been positioned on the wall behind the cash desk.

1 The ceramic floor tiles are an original
   part of the building, dating back to the
   1900s, and were discovered beneath 1960s
   linoleum flooring.
2 A large cash desk allows space for packing
   and merchandising.

The store design had to be adaptable and simple enough to be repeated in different locations

3 Varied lighting systems provide illumination for the design objects in-store.
4 The Bond design team was also responsible for the graphic concept which was incorporated into branding materials.
5 The stack shelving along the walls creates an interesting silhouette.

RBC DESIGN SHOWROOM

by JAKOB + MACFARLANE

1

WHERE Lyon, France WHEN September 2010
CLIENT RBC DESIGNER Jakob + MacFarlane (p.680)
TOTAL FLOOR AREA 900 m² SHOP CONSTRUCTOR Sort & Chasle
PHOTOGRAPHER Nicolas Borel

RBC is a purveyor of contemporary furniture and design. The company's showroom on the banks of the river Saône in Lyon was created by Jakob + MacFarlane. The realisation of this project was all about bringing together a world of design objects inside one larger design object, the design duo's architectural project 'The Orange Cube'. The showroom is dominated by a sheer white wall that wraps around the double-height ground floor space. The whole structure, designed to mimic the river flowing alongside, acts as a virtual 3D-waterway which carries along with it the design objects. As an extrapolation of the building's facade design, the wall is pitted with large polygonal cavities which become distinctive display cabinets. As the focus of the space, the 60 angular holes are filled with pieces of contemporary furniture. The alveoli are unique in size and form, thus allowing an intimate and private view of each design piece. The imposing porous structure acts to define the circulation in the showroom. Customers can move from the spectacular entry wall towards more intimate spaces around the showroom, where grey platforms on the floor are imagined like islands that become stages for different thematic presentations.

1 'The Orange Cube' project came about as a part of an urban planning project to replenish the docks of Lyon.
2 The designer team took the language of the building's exterior, which is based on the fluid movement of the River Saône, and incorporated this movement into the showroom space with the flowing wall.
3 From the showroom, customers can look out and see building's exterior orange metalwork. The bright orange shade is an abstraction of lead paint, an industrial colour often used for harbour zones.

2

The imposing porous structure acts to define the circulation in the showroom

3

5

6

A sheer white wall wraps around the double-height showroom space

4 The volume of the space is emphasised by the imposing wall being used as a unique display platform.

5 The porous envelope around the building allows natural daylight to stream in, creating shadows that can mirror the shape of the holes in the wall.

6 Spotlights positioned inside the wall's alveoli provide maximum illumination for the products.

Living

Kitchens + Design

SNAIDERO

by GIORGIO BORRUSO DESIGN

2

WHERE New York, United States WHEN October 2010
CLIENT Snaidero USA DESIGNER Giorgio Borruso Design (p.678)
TOTAL FLOOR AREA 310 m² SHOP CONSTRUCTOR Omara
PHOTOGRAPHER Magda Biernat

When Italian quality kitchen brand Snaidero was looking to open a showroom in New York, Giorgio Borruso Design was brought on board to sculpt the space. This project was the continued exploration of a concept that inspired two previous Snaidero showroom locations in Miami and Los Angeles. In the presentation of the product, the kitchens are displayed without a direct simulation of a domestic space. Instead, a tool is used that has the same effect produced by walls and ceilings, to compress or decompress the space. In this showroom, a type of 'fossil imprint' is the basis of the design, with staggered thick black strips in the form of horizontal panelling that envelops the space akin to geological striations of previously defined layers; like a trace of what might have been before. These strips, with a special chalkboard finish, wrap around the walls of the corner office and into the conference room, where they also form display shelving. The focal point of the overall white showroom lies in the series of long panels that jut-out horizontally from one wall into the space, displaying a varied collection of coloured material samples. This eye-catching aspect is the origin from where further striations radiate from, cutting black and orange lines into the expanse of white gloss-tiled floor. Angled walls, ceiling elements and strip spotlights also radiate from this central point and it appears the structural columns and beams are deformed by the force of the radial system, with torqued effects created where column and beam meet.

1 Directional striations are incorporated into the floor and ceiling giving the impression of exploding lines originating in the corner of the store.
2 The showroom is an overall white canvas in which the kitchens are positioned.

Structural columns are deformed by the force of the radial system creating torqued effects

3

4

3 The material samples, set in black jutting-out panels on one wall, are like a point of confluence directing visitors through the store. From this point, everything emerges in a universal rhythm.
4 Streamlined fixtures and fittings in the showroom create an almost futuristic setting for the domestic appliances.
5 In the living zone, the sculpted white space creates a perfect setting for the products.

5

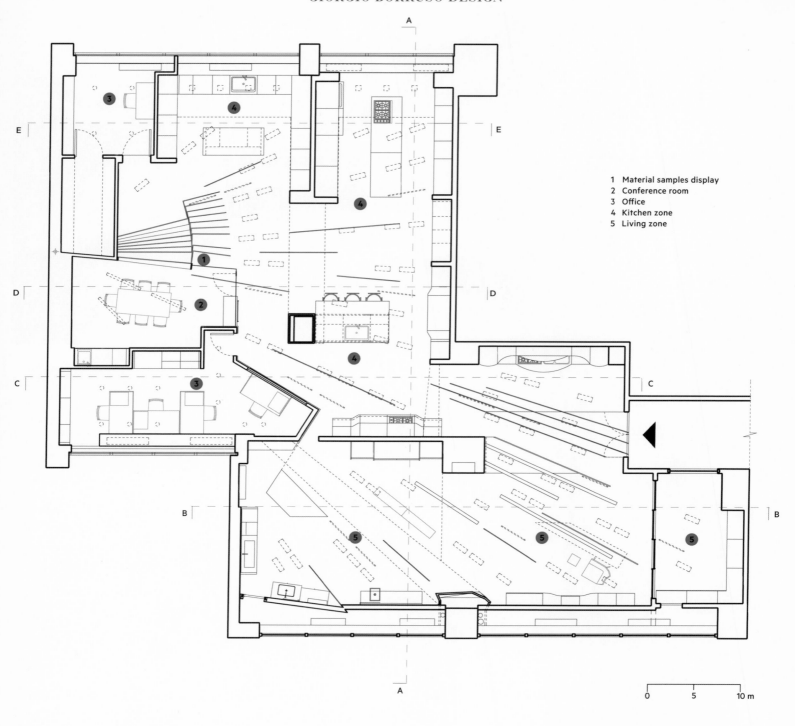

1 Material samples display
2 Conference room
3 Office
4 Kitchen zone
5 Living zone

0   5   10 m

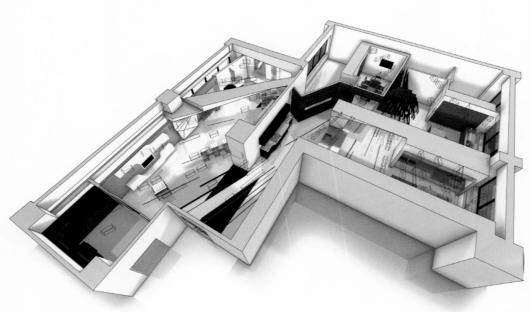

Three-dimensional drawing giving an overall
view of the showroom.

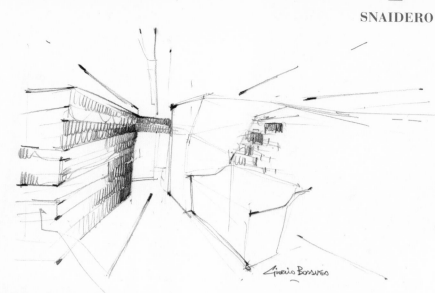

The kitchens are displayed without a direct simulation of a domestic space

Initial sketch exploring the design concept where the striations idea can be seen on the ceiling and the floor.

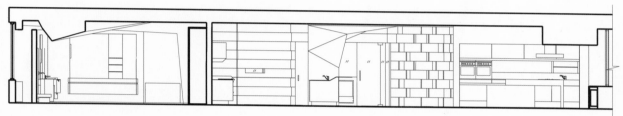

Section AA

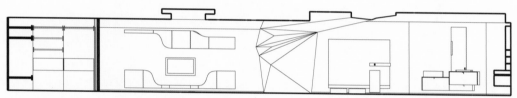

Section BB

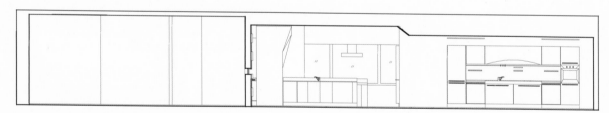

Section CC

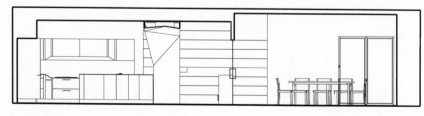

Section DD

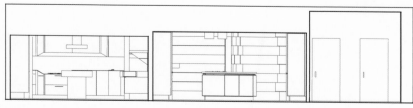

Section EE

SUXXAR

by JAYME LAGO MESTIERI ARCHITECTURE

2

WHERE São Paulo, Brazil WHEN June 2011
CLIENT Suxxar DESIGNER Jayme Lago Mestieri Architecture (p.680)
TOTAL FLOOR AREA 610 m² SHOP CONSTRUCTOR Souza Lima Construtora
PHOTOGRAPHER Ary Diesendruck

Suxxar is a Brazilian brand selling kitchen appliances and a wide selection of accompanying kitchenware. Tasked with designing a flagship store in São Paulo that could then be rolled out to other locations, Jayme Lago Mestieri and his team was responsible for the architectural project as well as the interior design. Inspiration for the concept came from the brand name, with the letter 'X' becoming a recurring architectural theme; on the exterior, this aspect generates inclinations and pillars as well the external shutter-like white patterned grid outside the windows giving solar protection to the building's facade. One wing of the store is raised up and appears to balance on giant X-shaped steel structures, which have been painted in a corporate red. Along with the red colour, concrete and wood is used within the interior creating a jointly rustic and contemporary feel. Rubber with wood finishing is applied to the inner part of the inclined walls and on the back wall concrete tiles create an eye-catching pattern. The furniture throughout is mounted with MDF and framed in steel with architectural and angled shapes creating a visual consistency. Circulation around the space is controlled by the customer and their own interface with the products. In particular, the store promotes a interaction within the kitchen gourmet centre, the virtual catalogue and the exposition tables.

1 The building's facade of laminate glass and aluminium framing has solar protection coming from the external white shutters. In-store, the ceiling and its conduits are kept visible, with a white acrylic paint applied.
2 Red illuminated letters spell out the store's name in the window display area on the ground floor.

3

Concrete and wood is used within the interior creating a jointly rustic and contemporary feel

5

3 The surfaces of the angular counters and shelving systems are covered in various textures and materials in the different product zones.
4 The furniture was specifically designed for each product area.
5 The slanted wall at the end of the building gives the store a geometric aspect.

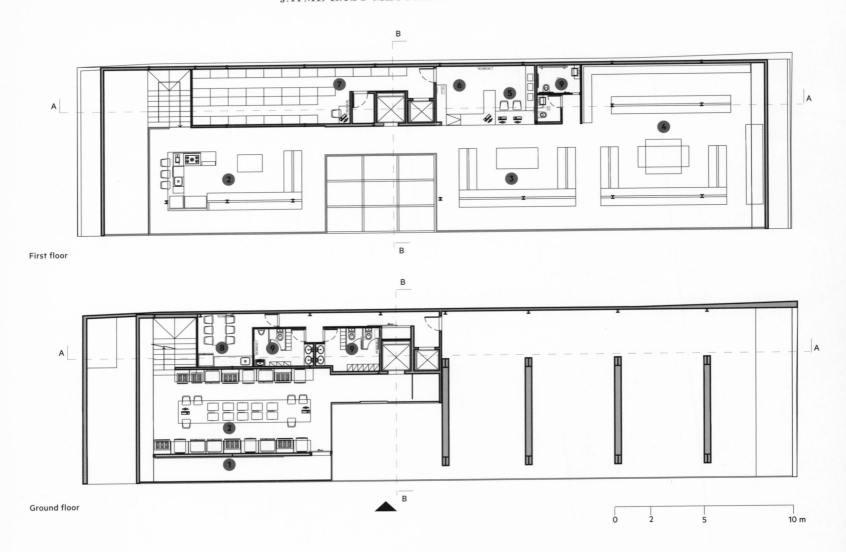

First floor

Ground floor

0   2   5   10 m

Renderings showing the front elevations of the building.

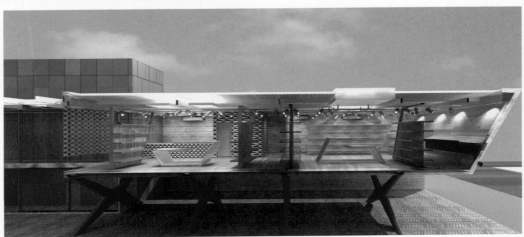

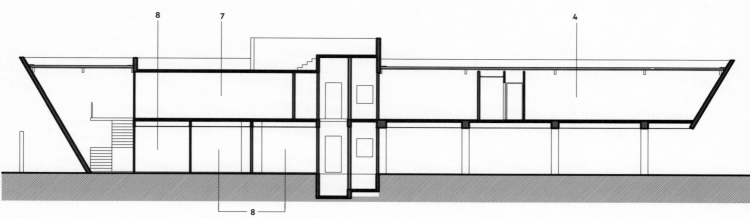

Section AA

1 Window display
2 Kitchen appliances
3 Decor line
4 Kitchen products
5 Cash desk
6 Packing area
7 Storage
8 Staff room
9 Lavatories

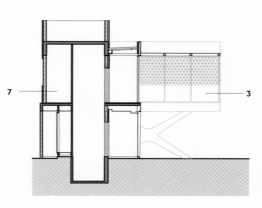

Section BB

The letter 'X' becomes a recurring architectural theme

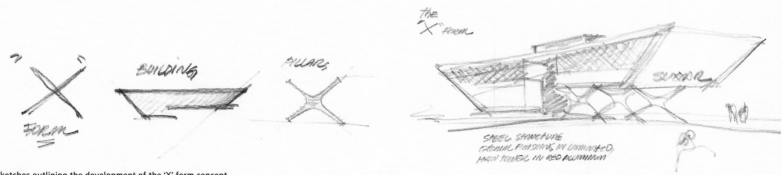

Sketches outlining the development of the 'X' form concept.

'T JAPANSE WINKELTJE

by NEZU AYMO ARCHITECTS

2

WHERE Amsterdam, the Netherlands WHEN April 2010
CLIENT 't Japanse Winkeltje DESIGNER Nezu Aymo Architects (p.682)
TOTAL FLOOR AREA 55 m² SHOP CONSTRUCTORS Gerrits en Sinnige and Roord Binnenbouw
PHOTOGRAPHER Jeroen Musch

Since 1976, there has been a shop selling various Japanese products in the heart of Amsterdam called 't Japanse Winkeltje (which is Dutch for 'small Japanese shop'). When the time came to revitalise the retail space, a brief was issued to give the shop a total makeover. Nezu Aymo took on board the task as a parallel investigation into material use and Japanese-ness. Based on analysis of shop display principles, the design team proposed a concept for the shop which was classified as 'tactile space', with a major challenge being to arrange the long and narrow space in as open a manner as possible. Taking as a starting point the different items sold in the shop combined with different materials and textures, the approach incorporated creative ways to present the merchandise. The display systems became an exhibition of Japanese crafts which were as much a part of the shop as the kimonos and ceramics on sale. Ensembles of materials were thoroughly examined and numerous prototypes produced by hand before the final pieces of 'haute couture architecture' were set in place. From the knitted paper yarn loops to the strips of white textile layers which are draped along the side walls to fashion integrated displays, the ceiling too is covered in a craft-like construction of paper-thin bamboo veneer sheets. The careful selection of soft, natural textures in combination with white, grey and natural colours creates coherency, richness and a calm, quiet atmosphere.

1 The material choices reflect the fragility and lightness of the items sold in the shop.
2 Knitted paper yarn loops veil fragile ceramics, half concealing, half exposing the items.

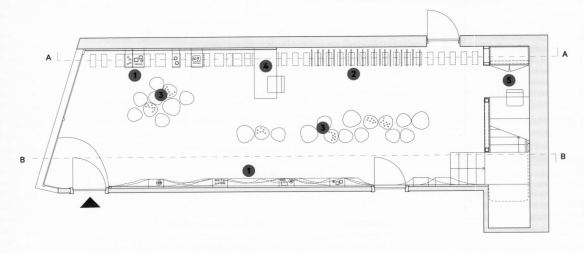

1 Shelf display
2 Hanging display
3 Table display
4 Cash desk
5 Office

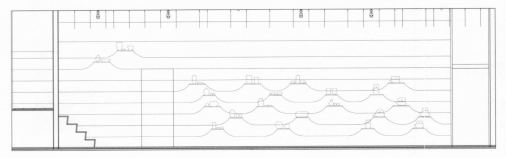

Section AA

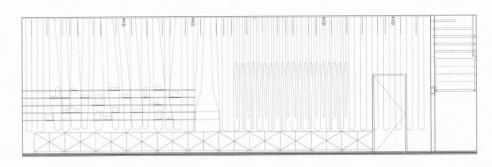

Section BB

Natural colours create coherency, richness and a calm, quiet atmosphere

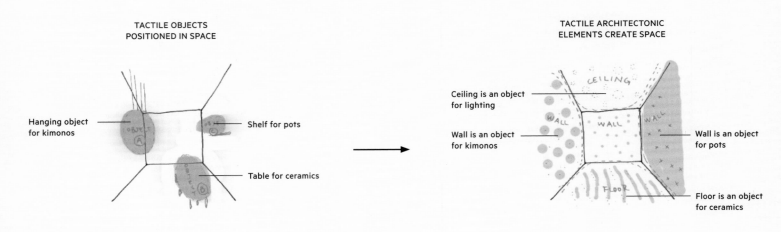

TACTILE OBJECTS
POSITIONED IN SPACE

TACTILE ARCHITECTONIC
ELEMENTS CREATE SPACE

Hanging object
for kimonos

Shelf for pots

Table for ceramics

Ceiling is an object
for lighting

Wall is an object
for kimonos

Wall is an object
for pots

Floor is an object
for ceramics

Concept sketch showing the development of the 'tactile space'.
The basic architectonic elements – walls, floor and ceiling –
become display objects.

1 Strip wall
2 Trunk floor
3 Paper yarn wall
4 Bamboo veneer ceiling
5 Fabric wall
6 Glass facade

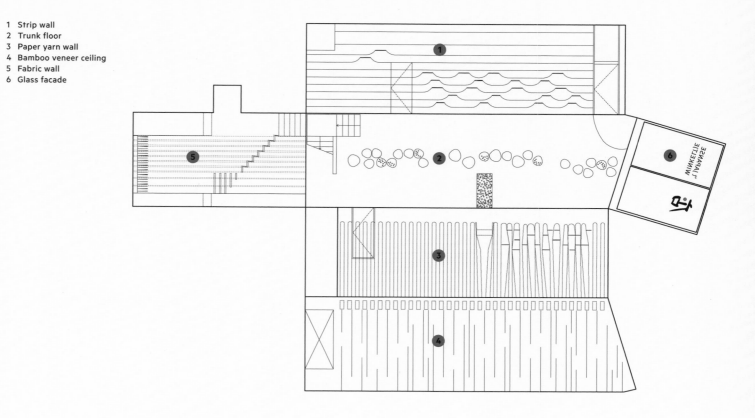

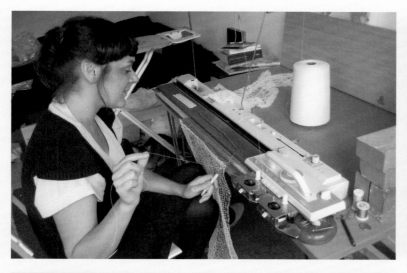 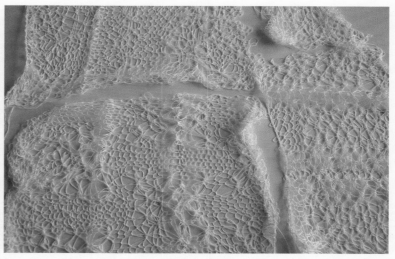

The knitted strips of paper yarn loops taking shape; 200 m of
yarn loops were specially produced by hand and soaked in rice
water to guarantee stability (photos by Nezu Aymo Architects).

MOBI
508

LITY

509

A.D.I. SYSTEMS

by ROTH TEVET EXPERIENCE DESIGN

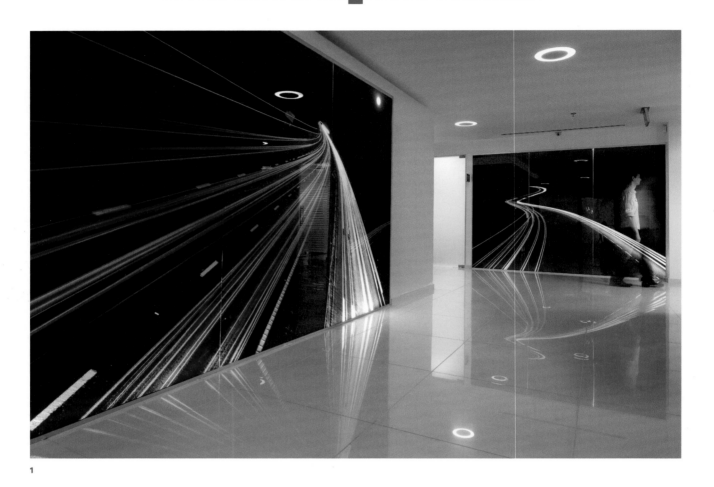

1

WHERE Rishon LeZion, Israel WHEN November 2010
CLIENT A.D.I. Systems DESIGNER Roth Tevet Experience Design (p.684)
TOTAL FLOOR AREA 1800 m² SHOP CONSTRUCTORS Ben-Ariel, Gisha-Shona and Motti Shpeizer
PHOTOGRAPHER Shai Epstein

Auto parts retailer A.D.I. Systems imports, sells and installs premium car accessories, plus audio and multimedia products. A requirement of the company's new store was that it should express the firm's advanced technological approach, and bring out the quality of the brands on sale. Roth Tevet created a new experience for customers which was far removed from the grungy garage workshop experience in the former shop. The concept was that of a car accessories boutique, realised by the design team headed up by Roy Roth and assistant architect Eyal Sudai. Automotive hi-tech gadgetry is presented inside glass boxes resembling jewellery display cases. The multimedia accessories are presented on transparent acrylic shelves, highlighted by hidden LED lightings, positioning them as prestigious floating objects. The interior design incorporates sharp precise angles and triangular planes. The main wall and ceiling are divided by three dominant grooves housing the spotlights, hinting to imagery of highways and car lights. Greeting customers entering the shop is a chandelier of car headlights. Out of context, these simple car parts demonstrate artwork-like aesthetics. Having the customers' experience in mind, and taking into account the great bond they are likely to have with their cars, the design team installed a vast window between the waiting area and the workshop, making the firm's service as transparent as possible. Alongside the showroom are offices and peripheral rooms, with splashes of colour in the mostly white interior coming from the car-paint-coated reception desk and the abstract night-time traffic images, positioned in light boxes along the hallways.

2

Out of context, car parts demonstrate artwork-like aesthetics

3

4

1 Illuminated abstract images of car light trails adorn the walls in the first floor office space.

2 Whilst browsing the store, customers can also watch the work on their cars in progress through the viewing wall.

3 The sculpted reception desk boasts a Bordeaux red tone, picked from a Cadillac colour catalogue.

4 The space is decorated with bespoke display modules and lighting elements such as the chandelier made from car headlights.

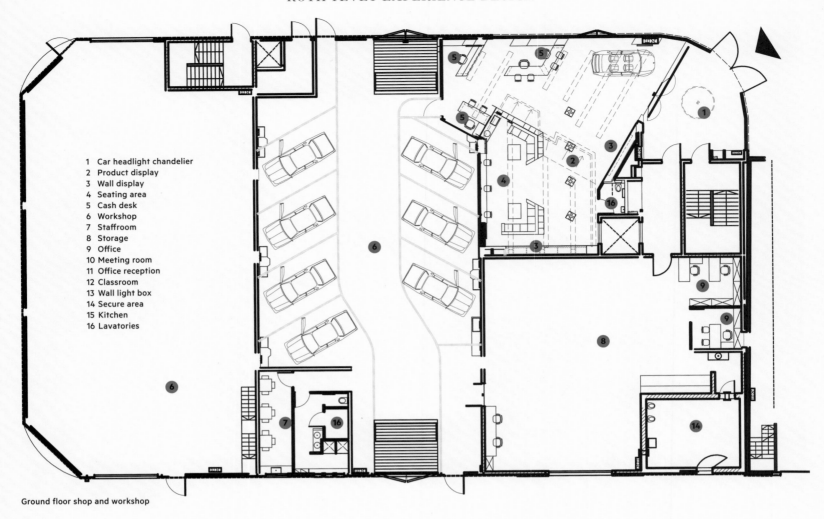

1 Car headlight chandelier
2 Product display
3 Wall display
4 Seating area
5 Cash desk
6 Workshop
7 Staffroom
8 Storage
9 Office
10 Meeting room
11 Office reception
12 Classroom
13 Wall light box
14 Secure area
15 Kitchen
16 Lavatories

Ground floor shop and workshop

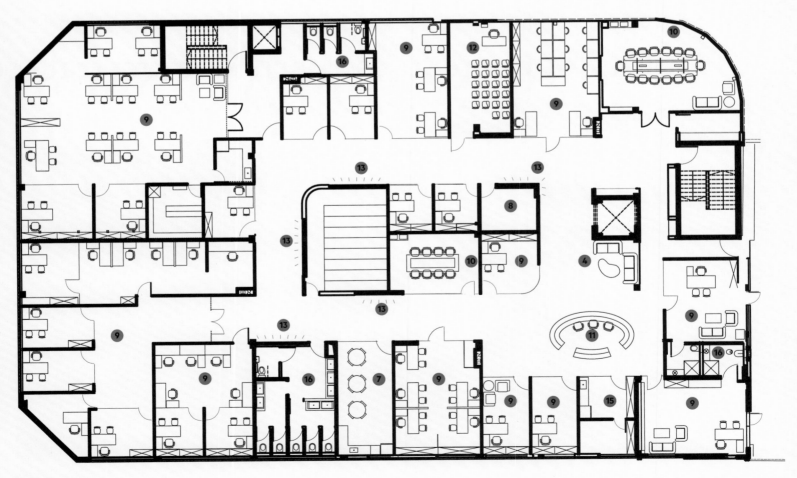

First floor office space

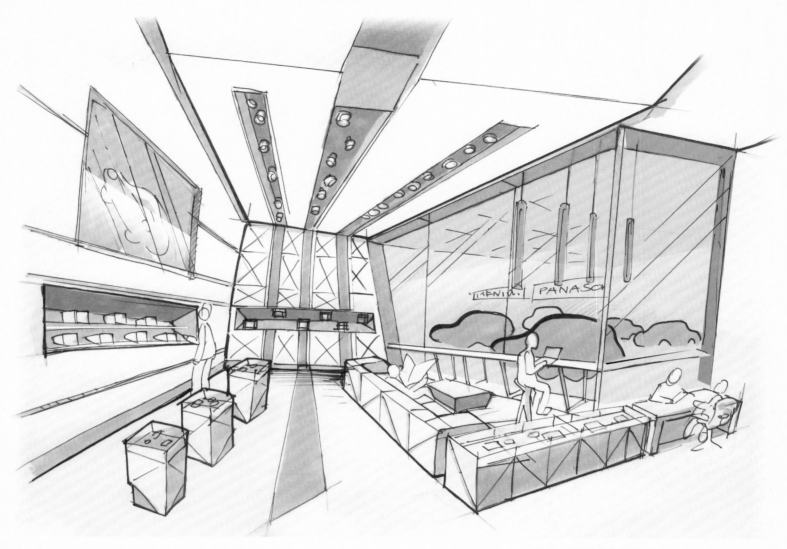

Sketch of the basic design concept incorporating sharp precise angles and triangular planes.

The spherical reception desk was imagined as a minimalist UFO that landed in the space.

Car headlights turned into artwork: above, the initial design resembled a flower petal; below, visualisation of the construction.

AUTOSTELLA

by SUPERMACHINE STUDIO

2

WHERE Bangkok, Thailand WHEN May 2009
CLIENT Autostella DESIGNER Supermachine Studio (p.686)
TOTAL FLOOR AREA 539 m² SHOP CONSTRUCTOR –
PHOTOGRAPHER Wison Tungtunya

Autostella is a small import car business located near a busy expressway in Bangkok. For its new showroom, a boutique space was required where its range of fun, small cars would be presented. In response to this, Supermachine Studio came up with a concept that was also fun and one which was as far removed from run-of-the-mill car showrooms as possible. Going back to basics, Supermachine Studio – led by Pitupong Chaowakul – wanted to reintegrate automotives and architecture. For the design team, inspiration came from classic examples of architecture such as Fiat's Lingotto factory in Turin in which the test track was located on the rooftop of the building. In the Autostella showroom, cars and lifestyle are integrated. The concept does not focus on the stereotypical aspects of automobiles, such as their speed or dynamic features. Instead, the fact that they can be termed as everyday accessories, much like the mobile phone, is the main focus. Cars become part of the furniture in the showroom, with the interior setting resembling a house which has cars randomly dotted around. The architecture of the building is that of a long red box which has been pulled and distorted into an angular shape. Internally it is divided into four interconnecting rooms, each with large windows in differing dimensions. The plan is to redecorate the rooms to suit the mood of the new models of cars that are on show in the future.

1 The building's architecturally-striking shape and bright red exterior creates an eye-catching roadside silhouette.
2 A cosy corner with floral wallpaper and upholstered seating is set beneath the overhanging first floor office.

3   4

3   Positioned next to the vast windows, cars
    parked inside the showroom are clearly
    visible from the outside.
4   The inside of the elongated light units are
    painted yellow, orange and pink, as are
    some of the coloured wooden strips which
    line the side wall.
5   View of the seating area and the kitchen.
6   The slender stairwell that leads from the
    office to the showroom also features homely
    flower-motif wallpaper.
7   The different rooms, delineated by dividing
    walls, are interconnected throughout
    the space.

5

6

7

Supermachine Studio wanted to reintegrate automotives and architecture

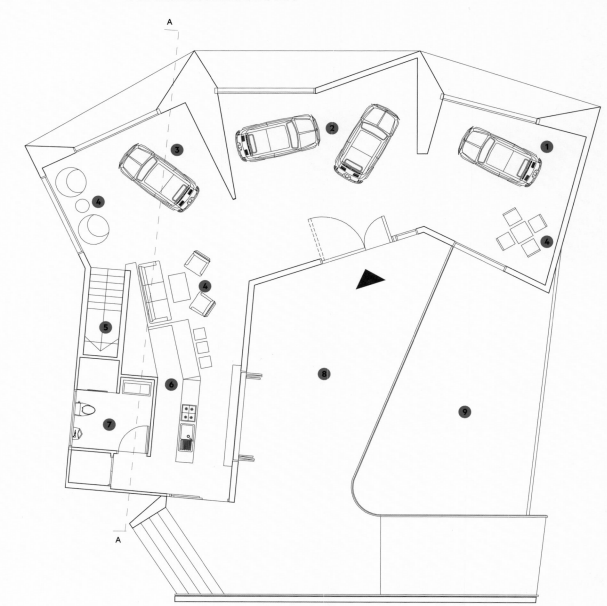

1 Showroom I
2 Showroom II
3 Showroom III
4 Seating area
5 Stairs to office
6 Kitchen area
7 Lavatory
8 Terrace
9 Fish pond

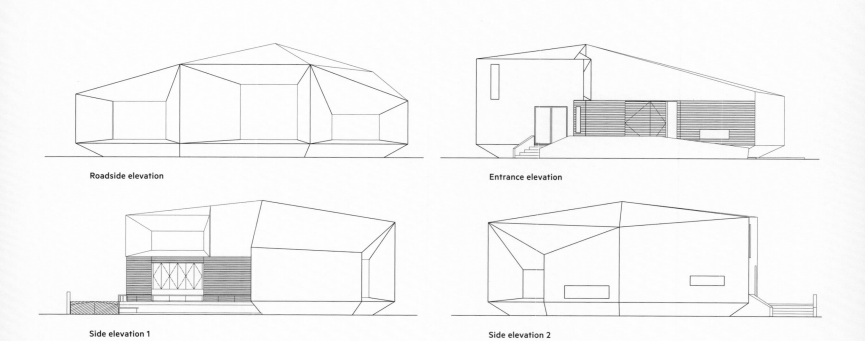

Roadside elevation

Entrance elevation

Side elevation 1

Side elevation 2

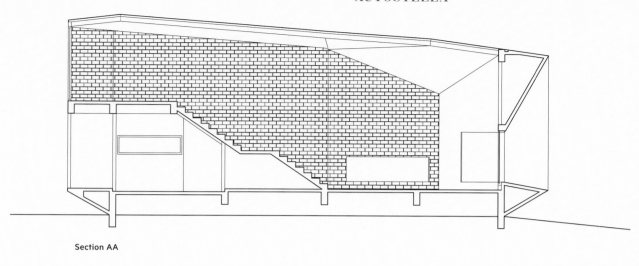

Section AA

Cars termed as everyday accessories, are the main focus

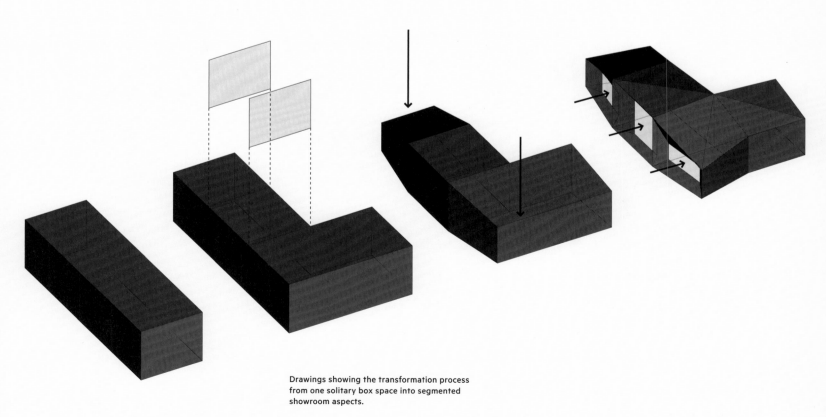

Drawings showing the transformation process
from one solitary box space into segmented
showroom aspects.

JAGUAR LAND ROVER

by PHILIPS DESIGN

1

WHERE Singapore, Singapore WHEN September 2010
CLIENT Jaguar Land Rover DESIGNER Philips Design (p.683)
TOTAL FLOOR AREA 847 m² SHOP CONSTRUCTOR Stag
PHOTOGRAPHER Philips Design

The period of transformation that Jaguar Land Rover has undergone since its takeover in 2008 has seen new products launched and business revitalised. Jaguar required a new showroom in Singapore that portrayed the freedom the brand had been given by its new ownership, as well as providing space for the addition of Land Rover models. In response to the brief, Philips Design wanted to realise a showroom that captured the contemporary luxury of the brand but was devoid of eliteness. The aim was to create a friendly space for prospective customers whilst also enabling an emotional connection to be generated. A luxurious clubhouse was the basis of the concept, with generous sofa areas combined with open spaces and a welcoming reception area. Over the entire length of two walls are screen projections which allow films depicting open-air scenes to be shown, consistently refreshing the customers' sense of space. Within the pristine white environment, the vehicle presentations are enhanced by the use of Philips Ambient Experience coloured lighting, with LED-lit displays allowing key products to be highlighted. Customers are left with a sense of awe on leaving the showroom thanks to a uniquely personal experience in the delivery suite. Here, the newly-purchased car is positioned on a turntable in complete darkness. As the space is slowly illuminated, the car is revealed to its new owner. On stepping inside the vehicle, it is then rotated to face the wall where doors slide open to reveal the outside world.

1 The blue square of light overhead connects all four corners of the main showroom area.
2 The 'Hero car display' with its canopy of light overhead provides a prominent impression from the street, particularly at night.
3 In the delivery suite, with the movement of the car turntable, the sequence of changing lighting colours are orchestrated to create a personalised delivering experience.

2

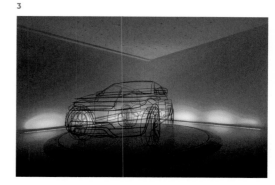

3

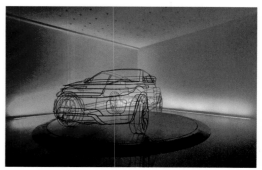

A luxurious clubhouse was the basis of the concept

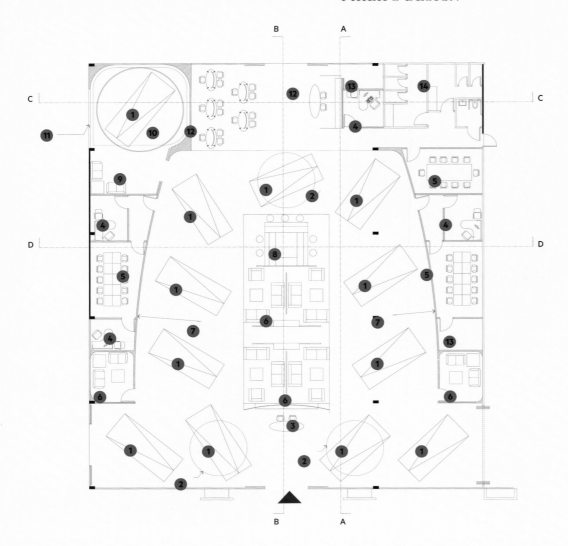

1 Vehicle presentation
2 Ceiling light structure
3 Reception
4 Meeting room
5 Office
6 Seating area
7 Film screen
8 Bar
9 Delivery suite
10 Motorised turntable
11 Motorised rolling shutter
12 Service area
13 Utility space
14 Lavatories

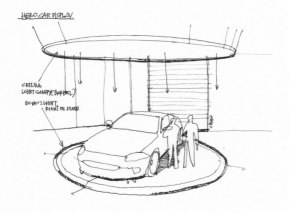

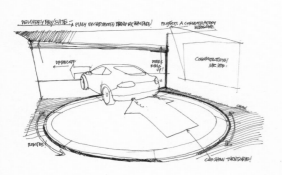

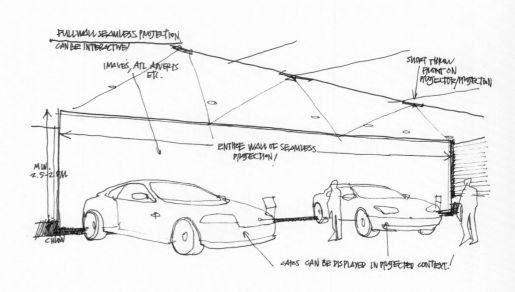

The 'Hero car display' concept uses a translucent Barrisol 3D system to integrate the lighting into an architectural form (top). The car delivery suite (bottom).

Sketches of the seamless wall-to-wall projection surface.

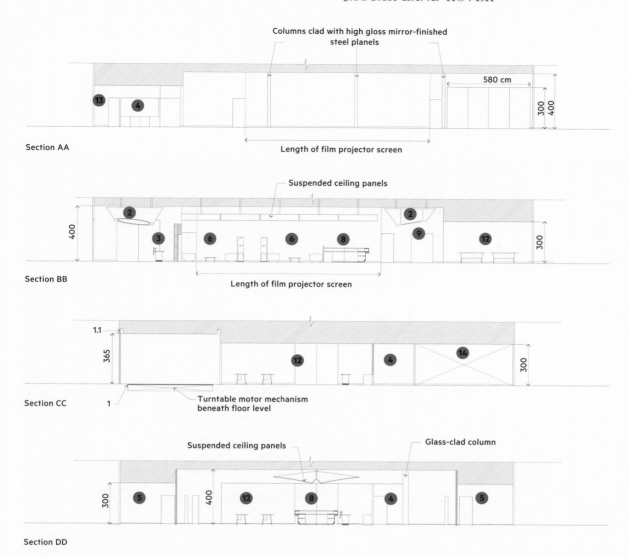

Columns clad with high gloss mirror-finished steel planels

580 cm

300
400

Section AA

Length of film projector screen

Suspended ceiling panels

400

300

Section BB

Length of film projector screen

1.1

365

Section CC   1   Turntable motor mechanism beneath floor level

300

Suspended ceiling panels   Glass-clad column

300

400

Section DD

The space generates an emotional connection

Renderings showing the delivery suite concept with its incorporated lighting systems. A congratulatory message is projected onto the wall as a parting gesture.

Congratulations! Mr. Lee

JAGUAR LOUNGE

by WIT DESIGN

1

WHERE Beesd, the Netherlands WHEN May 2010
CLIENT Jaguar Land Rover The Netherlands DESIGNER Wit Design (p.687)
TOTAL FLOOR AREA 150 m² SHOP CONSTRUCTOR De Bouwers
PHOTOGRAPHER Jamy Vodegel

After a recent takeover, the car manufacturer Jaguar wanted to strengthen its brand identity and, when a number of new models were simultaneously introduced, the company wanted to emphasise this in its showrooms. In the Netherlands, Wit Design developed a shop-in-shop concept in order to visualise the positive developments and to give the new models extra attention and substance. The design team wanted to create an energetic and contemporary environment that would appeal to today's young, successful professionals. The resulting Jaguar Lounge includes a luxurious 'black box' being positioned within the existing showroom to convey the appropriate sentiment for the Jaguar brand. In effect, the lounge provides a reinvigorated energy for the new models, which are displayed alongside iconic Jaguar imagery.

High quality materials are important to the concept, consistent with the premium market position of the brand. A sumptuous black space was created with high-gloss tiles and deep-pile carpet on the floor and matt paint across the walls and ceiling. To accentuate the premium products on show, the additional use of steel, mirrors and reflective materials throughout creates a dramatic atmosphere, especially with the crisp white furniture of Dutch manufacturer Gelderland standing in vivid contrast against the black backdrop. At the rear of the space, a strategically-placed large mirror over the vehicle presentation provides a eye-catching feature.

1 Matt paint wraps a blanket of black around the central area within the showroom, a concept that can easily be applied to the other showrooms in the Netherlands as well.
2 The contrasting white presentation area at the back of the showroom incorporates eye-catching reflections in the overhead mirror.
3 The brand wall confirms the manufacturer's successful history.

2

A sumptuous black space was created with high-gloss tiles and deep-pile carpet

3

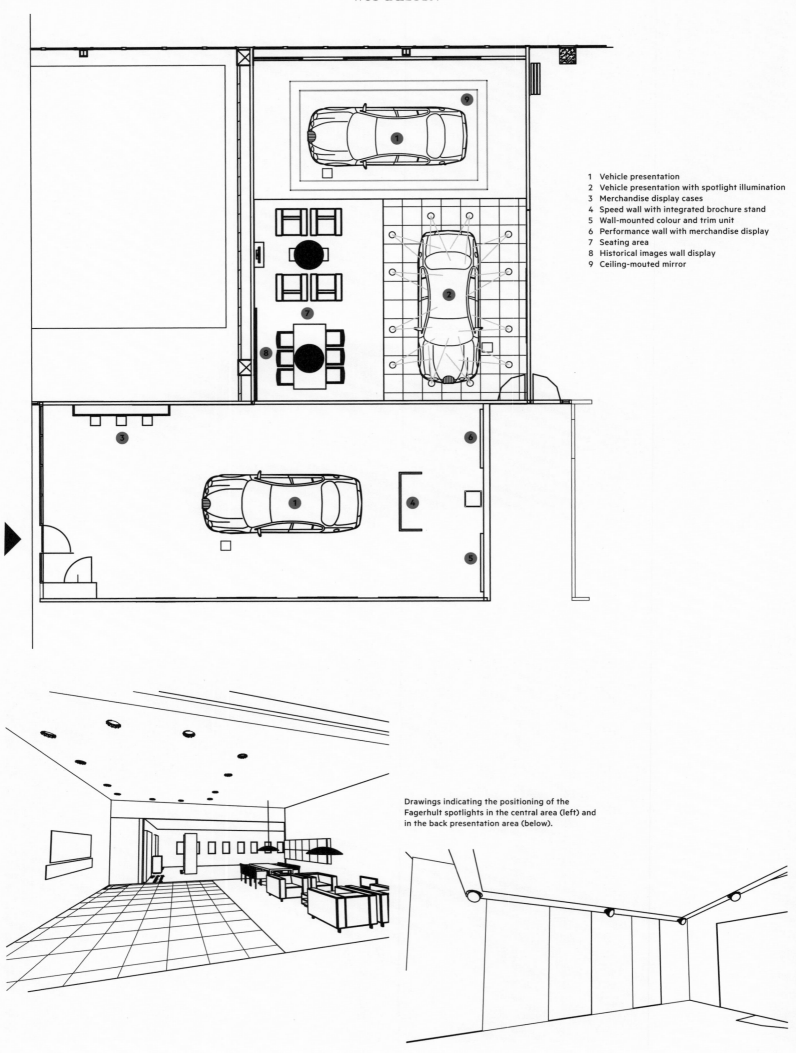

1 Vehicle presentation
2 Vehicle presentation with spotlight illumination
3 Merchandise display cases
4 Speed wall with integrated brochure stand
5 Wall-mounted colour and trim unit
6 Performance wall with merchandise display
7 Seating area
8 Historical images wall display
9 Ceiling-mouted mirror

Drawings indicating the positioning of the
Fagerhult spotlights in the central area (left) and
in the back presentation area (below).

Renderings of the different views of the showroom
indicating the distinct demarcations of the black
and white areas.

MERCEDES-BENZ GALLERY

by KAUFFMANN THEILIG & PARTNER AND ATELIER MARKGRAPH

2

WHERE Berlin, Germany WHEN October 2009
CLIENT Daimler Mercedes-Benz DESIGNERS Kauffmann Theilig & Partner (p.680) and Atelier Markgraph (p.674)
TOTAL FLOOR AREA 1430 m² SHOP CONSTRUCTOR Ernst F. Ambrosius & Sohn
PHOTOGRAPHER Andreas Keller Fotografie

In 2009, Mercedes-Benz launched a new generation of 'brand embassy' galleries. These showrooms sited in a number of major European cities, are all designed in a spatially distinctive way. The brief was to create forums where the brand could exchange ideas with an urban public. Architecture office Kauffmann Theilig & Partner and spatial design office Atelier Markgraph collaborated on the design of the galleries. The facade offers a showcase of maximum transparency, with vehicle presentations visible over two floors. The double-height branded space of 1500 m² is defined by a sculpturally fluid wall which has a glossy black finish and an eye-catching perforated pattern. Graphical elements and display cabinets are integrated into the wall, which is a central interface with its looping media feeds and dynamic lighting effects. Throughout the showroom, the wall sets the atmosphere and also connects the themed zones. It transforms the space into a walk-through stage set where customers discover exhibits and interactive stations outlining the brand themes of safety, comfort, design, quality and sustainability. The finish of the glossy wall and the quality of craftsmanship resemble the impression of a grand piano. The use of natural wood for the flooring and furniture completes the high quality appearance of the showroom, reflecting the values and standard of manufacturing of the Mercedes-Benz brand. The Berlin gallery provides a full customer experience; there is a restaurant on-site and the space hosts exhibitions and events on current brand-related topics or cultural themes, making it a vibrant meeting point in heart of the city.

1 Rich, emotional brand films were created especially to illuminate the background and act as 'impulse' generators.
2 From the entrance deep into the showroom space, the flowing media wall leads visitors through thematic areas.

3

4

The sculptural
wall communicates
the brand themes
through abstract
motion graphics

5

3 The bistro with the 'Stars & Cars' exhibition acts as an integrated part of the inner city showroom, making it a vibrant urban place to stay.
4 The transparent facade opens up the showroom to the prominent boulevard 'Unter den Linden'.
5 Over two storeys, the wall defines the space and the different areas for presentation.
6 An exclusively-designed content management system allows the personnel to adapt the presentation on the sculptural wall easily. Perforations and illuminations of the flowing media wall intensify effects of depth and spatial movement.

6

1 Vehicle presentation
2 Reception
3 Information desk
4 Restaurant
5 Advisory service
6 Shop
7 Office
8 Air space
9 Courtyard
10 Kitchen
11 Lavatories

First floor

Ground floor

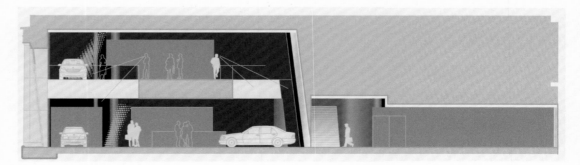

Section AA

Full-scale model of the perforated wall section
with LED modules positioned behind.

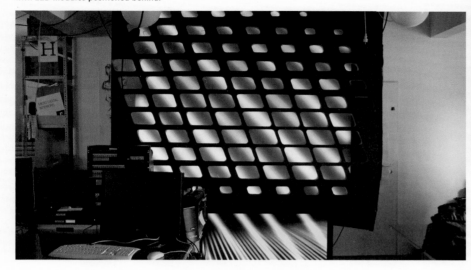

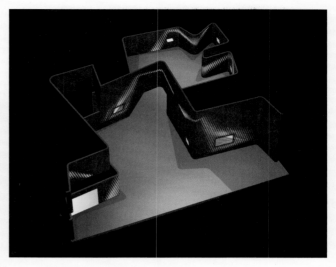

Three-dimensional model of the sculptural wall
showing the interconnectivity of the space.

The facade offers a showcase of maximum transparency

Construction photos of the wall being
assembled (photo courtesy of Atelier
Markgraph). The wooden material Kerto was
used for the perforated panels, with LED
modules and a reflection surface positioned
behind. Wooden embrasures of various depths
generate suspenseful views from the outside.

MINI DOWNTOWN

by RAW

1

WHERE Toronto, Canada WHEN April 2010
CLIENT BMW Canada DESIGNER Raw (p.684)
TOTAL FLOOR AREA 1851 m² SHOP CONSTRUCTOR Urbacon
PHOTOGRAPHER Tom Arban

Mini Downtown has the distinction of being Canada's first stand-alone Mini dealership. The showroom was realised by Raw as a companion to another project in its portfolio, the neighbouring BMW Toronto complex. The building, which features extensive glazing, has helped breathe new life into an post-industrial area of the city. It is situated at the base of a major highway affording passing drivers a panoramic view of the displays inside. The Mini showroom design has a striking graphic aesthetic, conceived as a playful jumble of cascading cubes which are each framed in the trademark colours of the Mini brand. It features distinctive box-like showroom platforms, which customers can easily interact with from both inside and outside the building. Citrus-hued cubes are also embedded within the interior design in differing dimensions, from the information desk and display modules to the framework of the office entrances. Mirroring Mini's fuel-efficient environmental outlook, the showroom features a green roof, a solar thermal hot water system and efficient insulation system. The building also incorporates an extensive loading bay and service area where the colour themes continue.

1 Extensive glazing and illuminated cubes allow customers to easily interact with product displays from both the inside and outside of the building.
2 From the first floor mezzanine, the transparency of the showroom can be fully appreciated.
3 Aluminium composite material panels are used for the wall coverings, adorned with branded imagery.
4 The cube design of the building is also integrated into the interior.

2

The showroom is conceived as a playful jumble of cascading cubes

3

4

Mini's striking graphic aesthetic breathes new life into a post-industrial area of the city

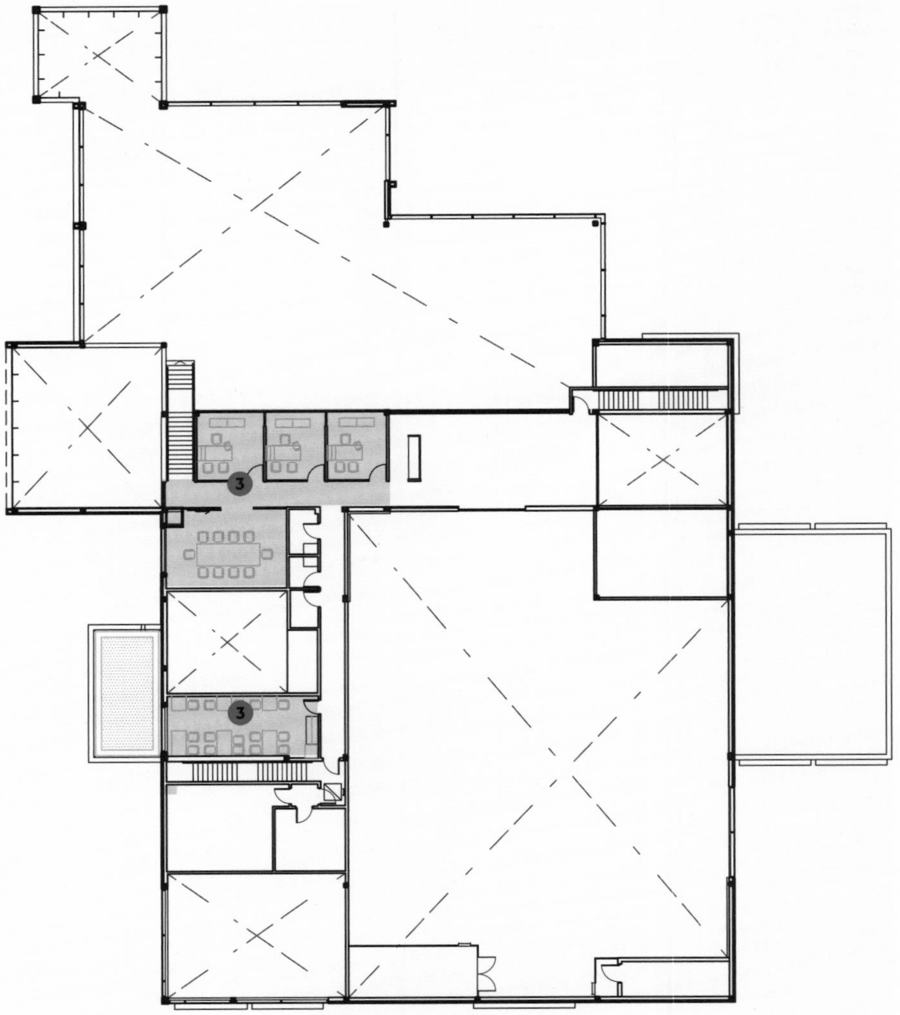

Mezzanine floor

1 Showroom
2 Customer service
3 Offices
4 Information and cash desk
5 Accessories shop
6 Service shop
7 Parts storage
8 Lavatories

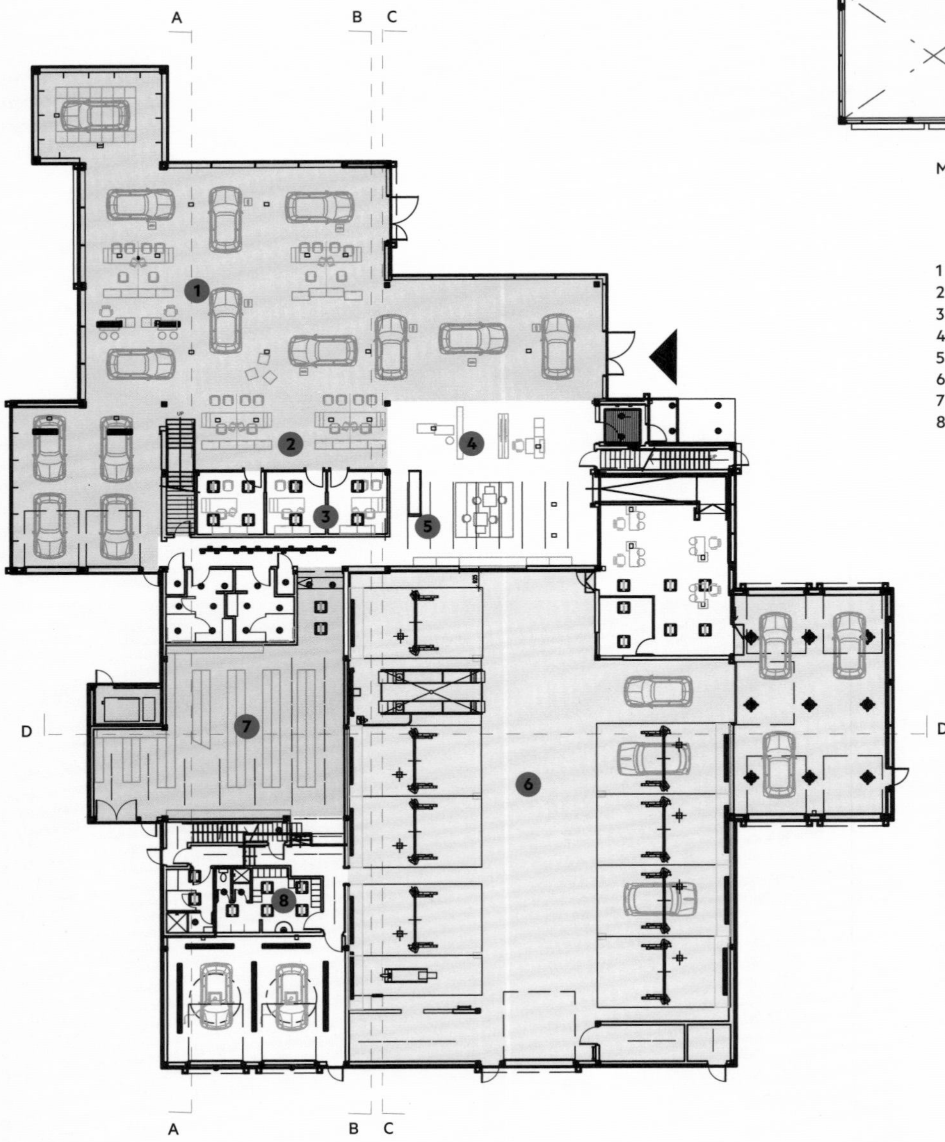

Ground floor

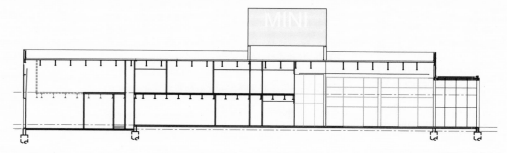

Section AA

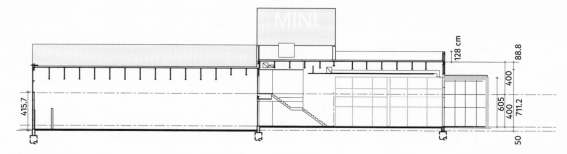

128 cm
88.8
400
605
400
711.2
415.7
50

Section BB

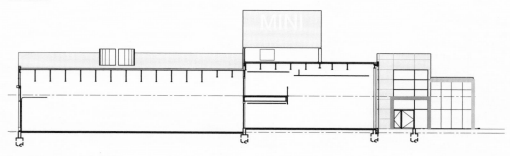

Section CC

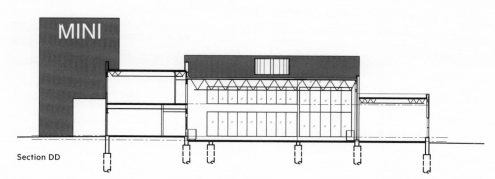

MINI

Section DD

Almost half of the ground floor area is dedicated to the service shop.

MISSION BICYCLE

by GRAYSCALED DESIGN COLLECTIVE

■

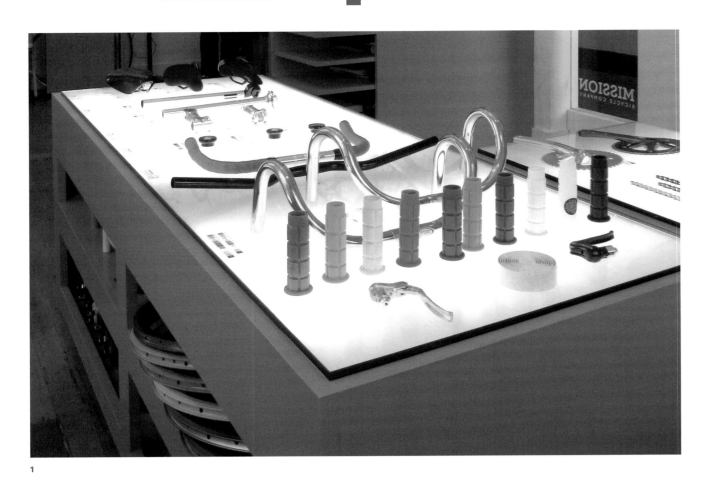

1

WHERE San Francisco, United States WHEN April 2010
CLIENT Mission Bicycle DESIGNER Grayscaled Design Collective (p.679)
TOTAL FLOOR AREA 56 m² SHOP CONSTRUCTOR Mackie Builder
PHOTOGRAPHER Sarah Hobstetter

Mission Bicycle started as an online company and passion project for San Francisco-based web developers Zack Rosen and Matthew Cheney. When the time came to open a physical store that reflected the successful identity already established in the digital realm, the Grayscaled team was brought on board for the interior design. Creative thinking was key to answering the brief which called for something different to make the store stand apart from regular bike shops which tend to be very cluttered. The concept which was realised came about by treating the space as if it were a gallery, approaching the project like an exhibition. The design team had a primary focus of utilising space and light to emphasize the beauty of the individual bike parts being presented. In the store, wheels, frames and handlebars are displayed as pieces of art. Bicycles suspended and offset above the tables convey the dynamic experience of riding a bike through space. A cycling narrative emerges above the digital interface zone in one corner of the shop where customers can design their own unique Mission bikes. Gurney-sized light tables at the centre of the shop display the anatomy of a bicycle as an exploded diagram, dissecting the bike into components to be selected by the customer. An open assembly work area allows customers to watch their bicycles being built, and learn about the process and upkeep.

1 All the parts required to make the customers' bespoke bicycles are stored on top or within the central table.
2 A space was created where customers could appreciate the simple beauty of each aspect of a fixed-gear bicycle.

How to build your Mission Bicycle

First, choose a frame color and size

Then, choose wheels and components

As you decide, fill out a build kit

When you're done, order at this kiosk

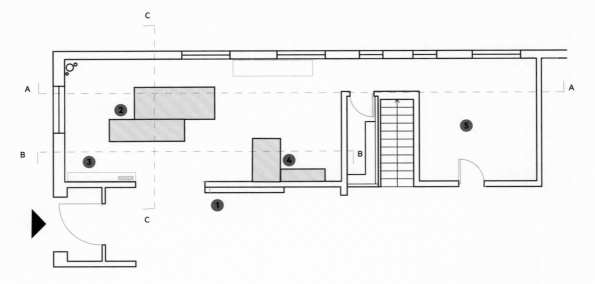

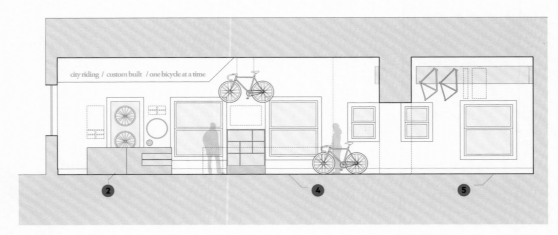

1 Sliding internal door
2 Bicycle anatomy table
3 Bike design /
   digital interface zone
4 Open assembly zone
5 Storage

Section AA

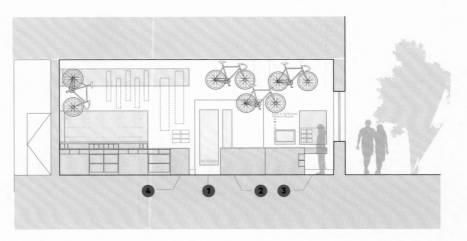

Section BB

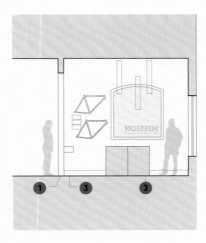

Section CC

Wheels, frames and handlebars are displayed as pieces of art

BICYCLE ANATOMY TABLE

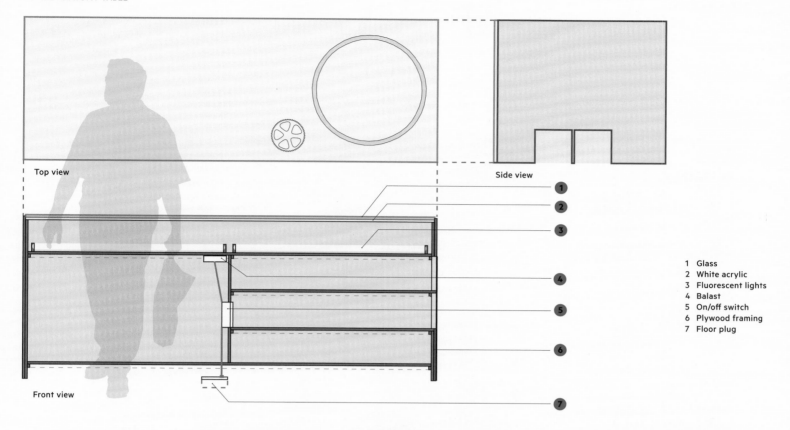

Top view

Side view

1 Glass
2 White acrylic
3 Fluorescent lights
4 Balast
5 On/off switch
6 Plywood framing
7 Floor plug

Front view

Bicycles – or their constituent parts – are affixed to walls and ceilings, hung from wire as installation pieces.

The wall graphics and signage were designed by Adaptive Path.

How to build your Mission Bicycle

First, choose a frame color and size

Then, choose wheels and components

As you decide, fill out a build kit

When you're done, order at the kiosk or online at www.missionbicycle.com

M-WAY

by DESIGNCULTURE

1

WHERE Zurich, Switzerland WHEN October 2010
CLIENT m-way DESIGNER Designculture (p. 677)
TOTAL FLOOR AREA 279 m² SHOP CONSTRUCTORS Designculture and Macroplan
PHOTOGRAPHER Alain Bucher

In 2010, the Swiss retailer Migros launched its m-way brand which is built around a new concept of electric mobility. This venture required a new store to be realised in Zurich and Designculture was brought on board for the project, in association with Brandpulse to create the branded materials. It was not only the retail aspects of the concept that were important to the design team but also the opportunity to orchestrate an eco-friendly experience based around a sustainable lifestyle. The outcome is a competence centre for electric mobility. Alongside the exhibited electric vehicles, such as the latest scooters, bicycles, cars and related accessories, are numerous information hubs all based around green transport, including interactive 'infotainment' modules and installations pertaining to the history of e-mobility in Switzerland.

These are linked to video screens showing clips offering further explanation about the displayed items. Visitors can test out an electric scooter on the store's interactive simulator, fully engaging themselves with the virtual urban environment that is projected onto a screen. Additional highlights involve 'mood drops' hanging from the ceiling, showing sustainable topics in video loops, as well as a modular green curtain wall and a colourful columnar construction made entirely from 9-V batteries which add to the atmosphere of the store.

1 Electro-vehicles are presented alongside information panels on green mobility.
2 In front of the 3D-wooden wall by Dukta are 'mood drops' with integrated video screens.
3 The lighting in-store is varied and includes a clear plastic inflatable installation representing clouds.
4 The infotainment system and media content was provided by Bildflug.
5 Customers can go for a ride through a virtual environment on the interactive e-scooter simulator.

2

3

The store is a complete centre for electric mobility

4

5

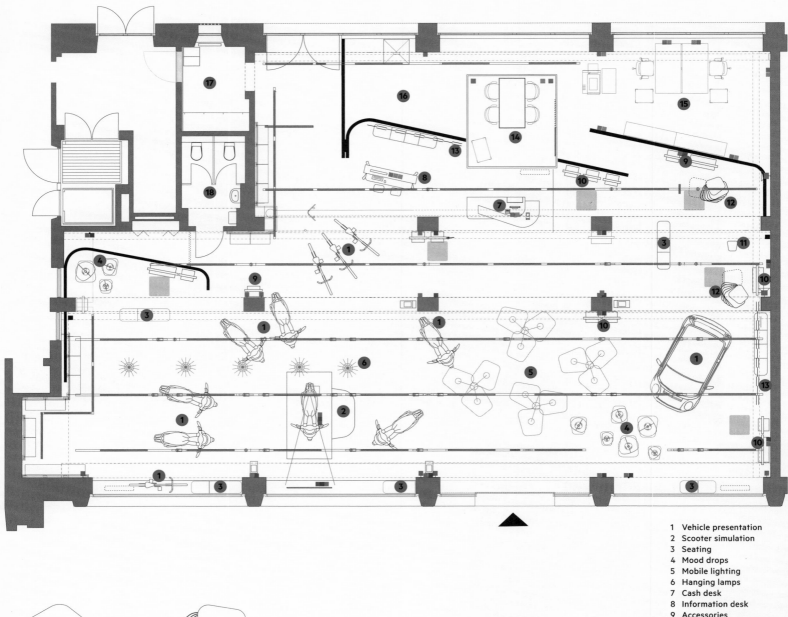

1 Vehicle presentation
2 Scooter simulation
3 Seating
4 Mood drops
5 Mobile lighting
6 Hanging lamps
7 Cash desk
8 Information desk
9 Accessories
10 Display panels
11 Battery sculpture
12 Display tower
13 Green curtain
14 Meeting room
15 Office
16 Storage
17 Kitchen
18 Lavatories

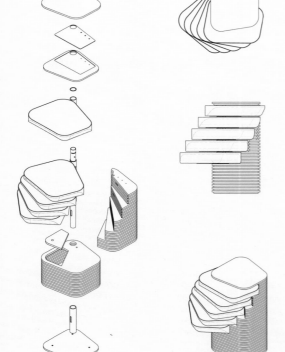

Exploded view drawing of the display tower
that holds items pertaining to the history of
electric mobility in Switzerland.

Initial sketches incorporating the 'mood drops'
and the inflatable light installation, as well as
the interactive scooter simulator.

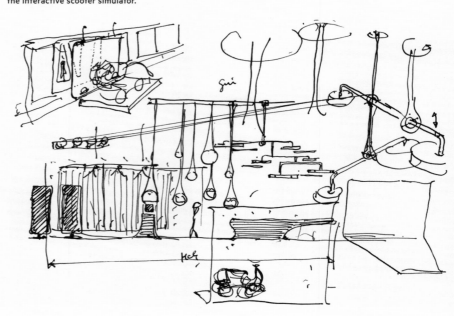

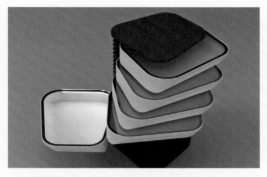

Renderings showing the swing capabilities of the drawers of the display tower.

A simulation of the bespoke inflatable lighting mobile.

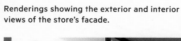

Renderings showing the exterior and interior views of the store's facade.

Pendant lights were constructed from the cutouts of the green curtain wall.

546

DES

547

BUZZER BEATER

by SLADE ARCHITECTURE

1

WHERE New York, United States WHEN January 2011
CLIENT Buzzer Beater DESIGNER Slade Architecture (p.685)
TOTAL FLOOR AREA 45 m² SHOP CONSTRUCTOR Bronze Hill
PHOTOGRAPHER Tom Sibley

Buzzer Beater is a high-end consignment store in New York's Greenwich Village that specialises in rare sneakers and apparel. There is no back-inventory – everything on display has its own unique history. Slade Architecture designed the store to reflect the nature of its eclectic collection, recognising the importance of the interaction within the store's community. Because the store's sales are made on consignment, buyers can become the sellers and sellers can become the buyers, and so the design concept was to be equally as engaging. Existing walls and dropped ceiling are covered in steel panels to create a continuous surface for magnetically-displayed merchandise, allowing a varied density and type of product to be presented in an almost graphic way. The bold tags attached to the stock introduce a repetitive rhythm, with a solitary red wall behind the cash desk repeating the vibrant colour of the tags. At the back of the store, the surfaces were stripped back to reveal the brick walls and existing pipes and ducts. Extra pipework was introduced, adding an architectural effect whilst also creating scaffolding for display. An exposed rail above the cash desk provides a place for merchandise to hang while it is being purchased, adding elements of ritual, convenience and conversation to the customers' checkout experience.

1 The long and narrow shop displays products up the walls and across the ceiling.
2 The black cash desk has rubber surfaces which offer a playful connection to the texture of athletic equipment.
3 Concrete, steel and exposed brickwork give the shop a raw aesthetic.
4 The shape of an original structural column emerges from the bold red wall behind the cash desk.

548

Buyers can become the sellers and vice versa

CAMPER

by RONAN & ERWAN BOUROULLEC

1

WHERE Paris, France WHEN July 2009
CLIENT Camper DESIGNER Ronan & Erwan Bouroullec (p.675)
TOTAL FLOOR AREA 70 m² SHOP CONSTRUCTOR Studio Bouroullec
PHOTOGRAPHER Studio Bouroullec

The belief that identity and diversity always go together is a key concept to the global footwear brand Camper. Every store needs to be different with its own personality, even more so for the Camper Together stores where designers collaborate with the brand to create a unique environment. The Bouroullec brothers made their debut as Camper collaborators in 2009, designing the store located beside Paris' imposing Centre Pompidou. They had a clear-cut idea of wanting to realise a space that was evident and at the same time surprising space. With the use of different shades of red throughout, along with textile interventions and a furniture collection designed for domestic rather than commercial use, the design duo created a store that was able to produce special sensations: the use of red adds warmth, the fabric textures muffle sounds and give depth, and the household furniture confers an air of simplicity. The felt-like textiles, which are also appear in citrus-hued oranges and greens, consist of backstitched blankets that partially cover the walls and certain furniture and decorative elements. They are hung in an irregular fashion and their relatively bright colours contrast with the red tone that pervades the entire store. The shelves, tables and chairs are uniquely designed to be a vital component aspect of the creative concept and act as display elements for the products in the space where customers can easily view and try on the footwear.

1 Metal rivets hammered into the felt wall panels provide an added textural dimension.
2 The Steelwood shelf system, designed by the brothers for Magis is positioned along the side wall to showcase the products.

CARLO PAZOLINI

by GIORGIO BORRUSO DESIGN

2

WHERE Milan, Italy WHEN October 2010
CLIENT Carlo Pazolini DESIGNER Giorgio Borruso Design (p.678)
TOTAL FLOOR AREA 386 m² SHOP CONSTRUCTOR Chiavari
PHOTOGRAPHER Alberto Ferrero

Carlo Pazolini is a Russian company, launched in 1990 by Ilya and Marina Resnik, which sells Italian-made shoes of high quality. Beginning its foray into the West, it was a must that Italy was the first destination for the company and a flagship store – with an impressive facade – was opened in Milan in 2010. Giorgio Borruso was commissioned to conceive a design that had the power to impress fashion centres and bring the brand to a higher level. Borruso began to sketch forms that could serve as display shelves and seating, finding inspiration in the beauty and flexibility of his small son's feet. He wanted to achieve a continuity of shape and texture between the shelves on the wall and the seating around the store. To achieve this, he collaborated with furniture designer Paola Lenti who utilised blended polymer and wool felt to create shapes

that are light, yet resilient, and have a sharp-edged profile that seem to float in the space. These furnishings have a citrus colour palette and dominate the women's section of the store. Two thirds of the rear wall is clad in narrow strips of black wood on which the shelves are clustered along the full height. The men's section to the right of the entrance is more austere. The rear wall is a curved expanse of white plaster, broken only by cantilevered aluminium cabinets and shelves. The vibrant colour accents of the sculpted wall and seating elements in this otherwise monochromatic interior creates an impressive vista when viewed from the street, maximising the impact of the concave glass in the expansive display windows.

1 Bonding polymer and wool felt, without glue, produced a hard shell that could be worked into interesting shapes for shelving and seating elements.
2 The Russian brand took over the lease for the space from McDonald's, earning the mayor's gratitude for 'liberating' the site.

3

3 Mirrors lining the end wall create space-expanding reflections.
4 Coloured felt could be applied to the top or on the underside of the sculpted platforms.
5 The only thing that survived the extensive renovation is a pair of cast-iron Corinthian columns from the original structure.

4

Blended polymer and wool felt create
shapes that are light, yet resilient, and
have a sharp-edged profile

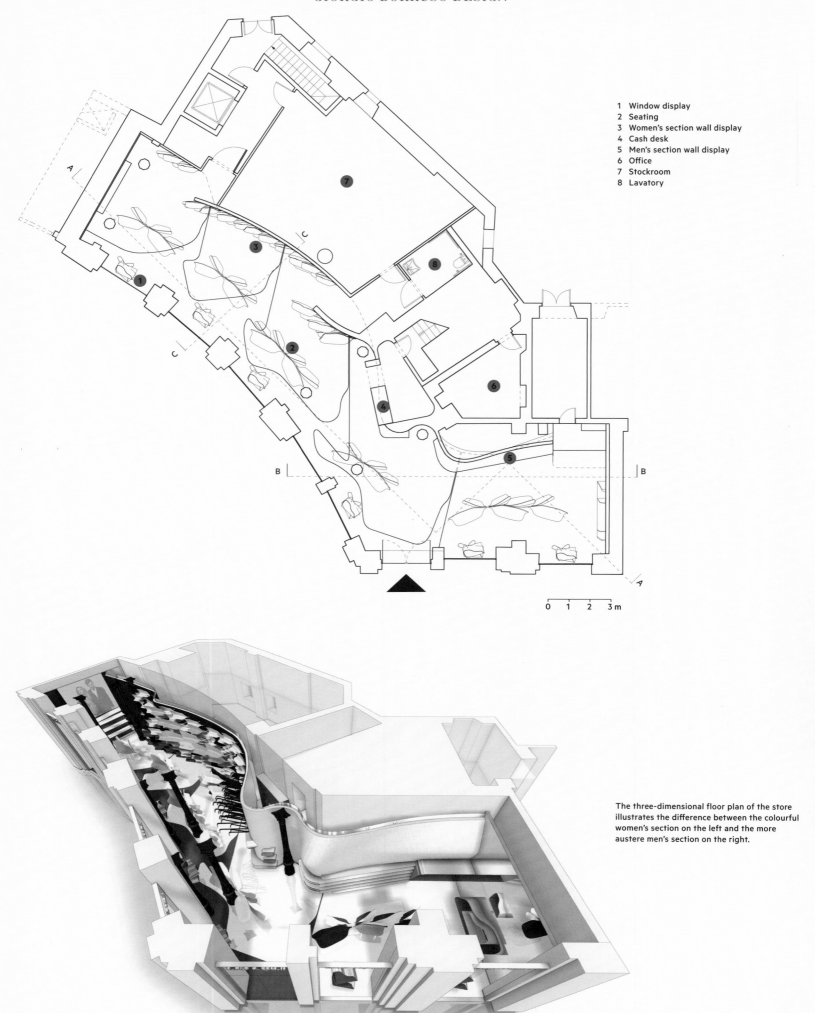

1 Window display
2 Seating
3 Women's section wall display
4 Cash desk
5 Men's section wall display
6 Office
7 Stockroom
8 Lavatory

0 1 2 3 m

The three-dimensional floor plan of the store illustrates the difference between the colourful women's section on the left and the more austere men's section on the right.

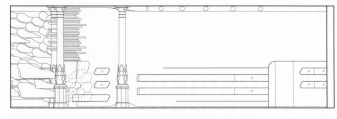

Section AA

Section BB

Section CC

Borruso began to sketch, finding inspiration in the flexibility of his small son's feet

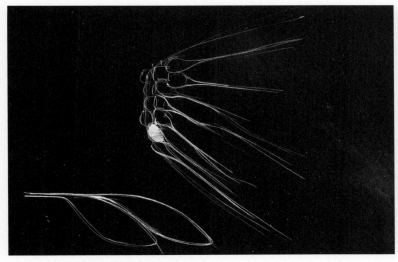

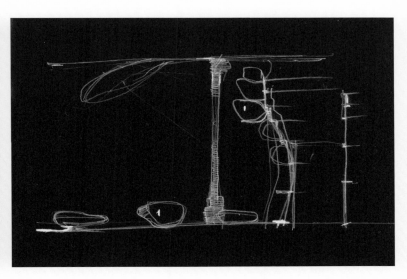

Initial sketches (above) of the forms which would morph into display shelves and seating (below).

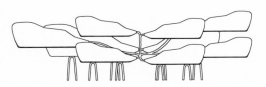

Back view

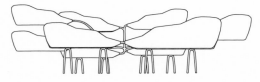

Front view

Top view

0   1 m

CHRISTIAN LOUBOUTIN

by HOUSEHOLD

1

WHERE London, United Kingdom WHEN September 2010
CLIENT Christian Louboutin DESIGNER Household (p.679)
TOTAL FLOOR AREA 93 m² SHOP CONSTRUCTOR Clements Retail
PHOTOGRAPHER Julian Abrams

The high-end women's footwear brand Christian Louboutin is available in exclusive boutiques across the world, including the Selfridges Shoe Galleries in London. The brief required a luxury concession to be developed which had a high level of theatre and personality inherent in the retail space. The concept was realised by Household and gives an insight into the life of Christian Louboutin, drawing inspiration from his own Parisian apartment. The challenge for the design team was balancing the theatrical with the practical; the importance of making a memorable experience, driving foot-fall and word-of-mouth appeal whilst at the same time considering stock level and seating option requirements in line with the high-traffic retail environment of Selfridges. The outcome is a bespoke boutique which is both sumptuous and seductive, inviting customers to kick their shoes off, as much as try a pair on. The backdrop to the apartment concept is a statement wall offering an intimate portrait of the shoe designer through family photographs and inspired personal artefacts. Ivory-cracked walls house the designer's signature shoe niches, with trompe l'oeil stairs leading nowhere and arched doorways leading to discrete alcoves. Amid a sea of striking red carpet, a velvet- and satin-upholstered seating centrepiece offers space for a luxurious trying-on experience, as does the exclusive product showcase beneath the intricate leaded window. Throughout, vintage furnishings are mixed with brass and gilded fittings as well as bespoke furniture, all selected as a representation of Christian Louboutin's eclectic and original taste.

The boutique is both sumptuous and seductive

1 The 'apartment' is divided into two, bringing an authentic domestic feel of walking from one room to another. Through the metal archway, the second 'room' takes on a richer, more indulgent personality.
2 The doorway leads to the 'invisible payment' area within a secluded chamber to further enhance the luxury feel.
3 The seats are layered with patchwork fabrics that have caught the client's eye on his travels around the world, embracing his eclectic and original taste.
4 The stairway actually leads nowhere and is just an illusory effect.

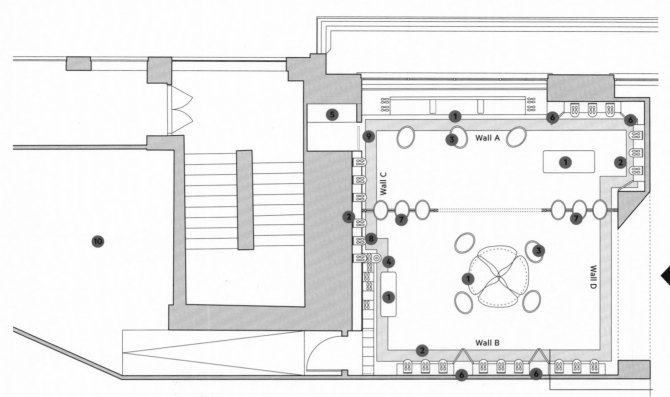

1 Seating
2 Product display wardrobes
3 Host trolley
4 Feature stairs
5 Cash desk
6 Stock
7 Product screen display
8 Tromp l'oeil wall
9 Grille door
10 Back of house

The theatrical space is inspired by Christian Louboutin's own Parisian apartment

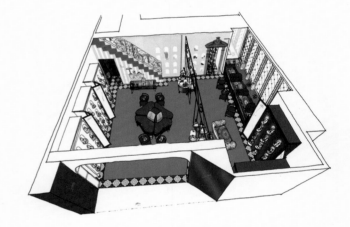

Colourful collage showing the sparkling vintage Murano chandelier above the plush sofa where customers can try on shoes.

Wall A

Wall B

Wall C

Wall D

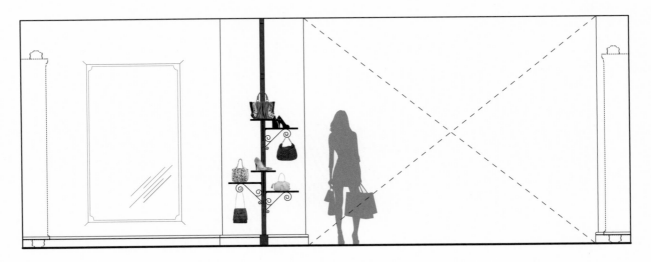

DR MARTENS

by CAMPAIGN

1

WHERE London, United Kingdom WHEN August 2009
CLIENT Dr Martens DESIGNER Campaign (p.675)
TOTAL FLOOR AREA 180 m² SHOP CONSTRUCTOR Triplar
PHOTOGRAPHER Hufton + Crow

Dr Martens is a heritage footwear brand with attitude, ever since the DM boot was catapulted from a British working-class essential to a global countercultural icon in the 1960s. Campaign tapped into this legacy when responding to the client's brief to design a pop-up store which had to uniquely reflect the brand and be replicable in any city in the world at a very low cost. The store was designed with a no-frills aesthetic using inexpensive construction materials which are readily available and quick to assemble. Combining off-the-shelf industrial fittings with customised elements, Campaign created a shop which was more akin to a warehouse depot, an area usually out-of-bounds to the customer. The stockroom vernacular included Gypframe metal wall systems, construction site lamps and loading palettes that were stacked to form impromptu display units and a cash desk. Salvaged furniture and objects, such as ladders and stools, were also shrink-wrapped and could be found dotted throughout the store. The trademark yellow of the Dr Martens brand was vigorously expressed in the space, from the positional markings on the concrete floor to the back display wall illuminated with fluorescent lighting. Adding to the vibrant yellow glow emitting from the store was the 18 x 3.5 m heavy-duty PVC curtain which divided and enlivened the shop floor.

1 Constructed in just six days and using inexpensive construction materials, the temporary retail interior was achieved at very low cost.
2 The loading palettes, piled-up to form product display islands, were illuminated with industrial lamps.

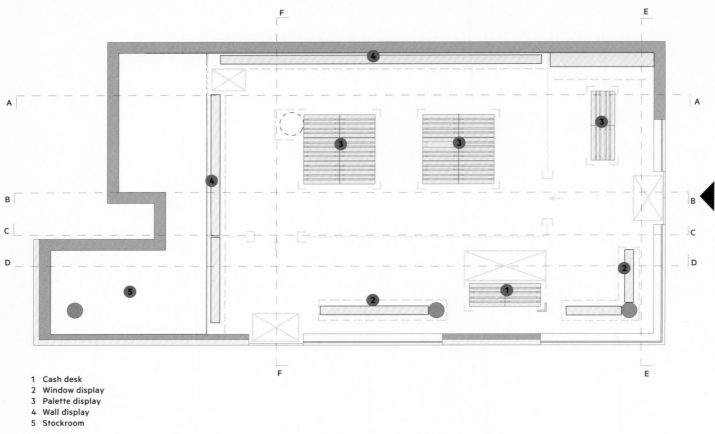

1 Cash desk
2 Window display
3 Palette display
4 Wall display
5 Stockroom

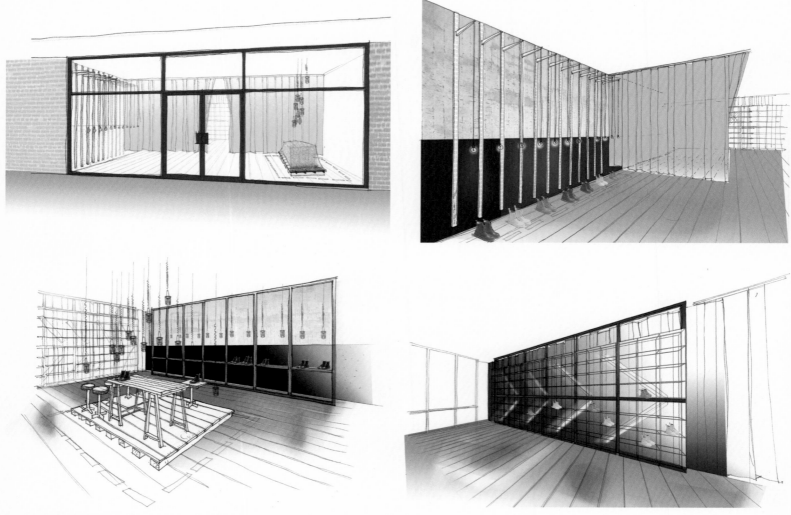

Sketches of the shop design which encapsulates a minimal and utilitarian character, in keeping with a back-to-basics trend.

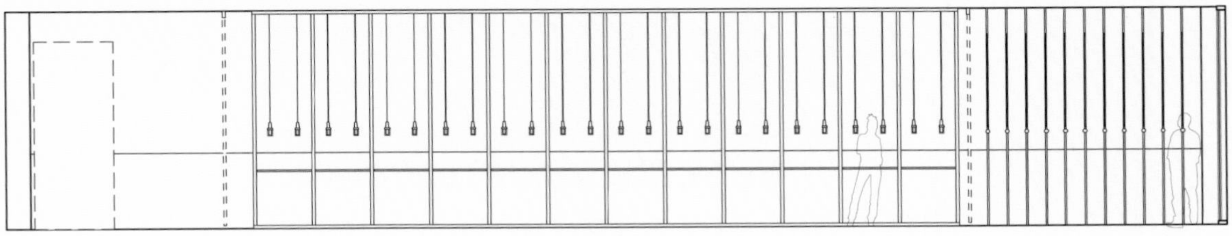

Section AA

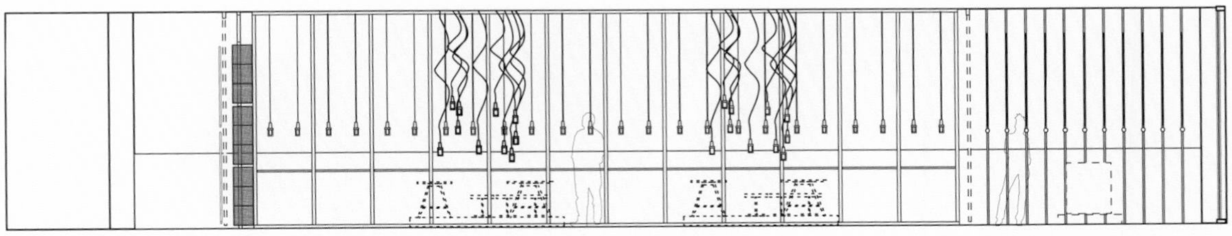

Section BB

Section CC

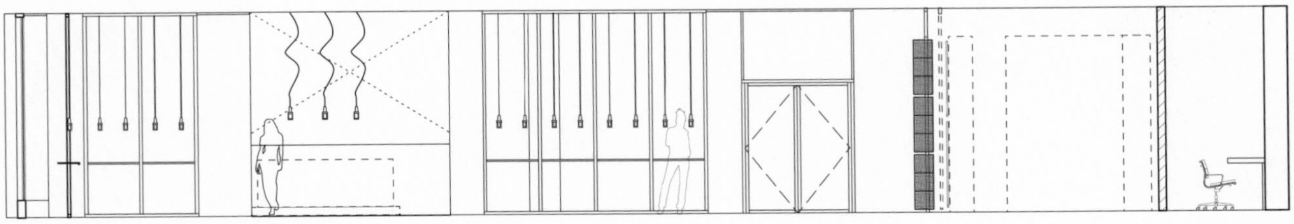

Section DD

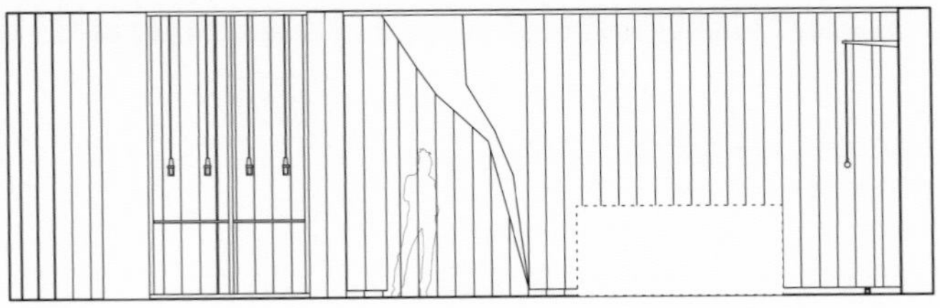

Section EE

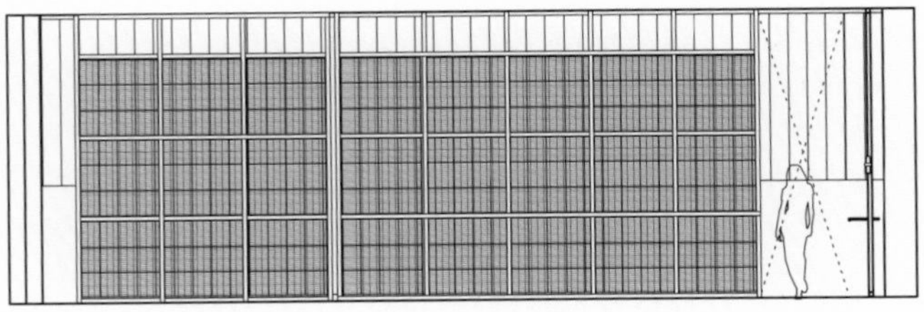

Section FF

A no-frills aesthetic combines industrial fittings with customised elements

FLIGHT CLUB

by SLADE ARCHITECTURE

1

WHERE New York, United States WHEN October 2010
CLIENT Flight Club DESIGNER Slade Architecture (p.685)
TOTAL FLOOR AREA 250 m² SHOP CONSTRUCTOR Bronze Hill
PHOTOGRAPHERS Slade Architecture and Tom Sibley

Flight Club, a high-end consignment sneaker store, sells a diverse collection of sports footwear and apparel products. The brief was to create a flagship store in a loft-style building in New York City's Greenwich Village. The goal for Slade Architecture was to create a clean, authentic urban space within the existing shell of the building using a strategy that minimised the amount of new material used and, thus, keeping costs down. The design team used as a reference the neighbourhood basketball courts and playgrounds, as well as urban spaces that skaters and bikers appropriate for recreation and sports. A raw concept was implemented, stripping the elongated space back down to its structural elements and leaving exposed brickwork on the walls and structural steel beams uncovered overhead. The products are displayed along the full length of both side walls. Large glass pivot doors define the exterior enclosure which is recessed from the sidewalk to create an open frame, presenting the product almost right into the street. The only facade branding comes from the orange custom door plates, which incorporate basketball leather and rubber. Inside the store, basketball references continue – from the materials used for the cash desks and bench to the integrated custom hoop and backboard, which doubles as a projector screen during store hours. After hours, the owners, staff and friends play on the court, continuing the cycle of appropriation.

1 The products are inherently colourful and tactile and treated almost as architectural elements in themselves. The wall of sneakers comes right out to the street creating a perspective of colour from the front to the back.

2 Customers can browse for sportswear and then shoot some hoops in the shop.

FOOT PATROL

by BRINKWORTH AND WILSON BROTHERS

1

WHERE London, United Kingdom WHEN July 2010
CLIENT Foot Patrol DESIGNERS Brinkworth (p.675) and Wilson Brothers (p.687)
TOTAL FLOOR AREA 50 m² SHOP CONSTRUCTOR Mentha Halsall
PHOTOGRAPHER Louise Melchior

Foot Patrol has a history of supplying exclusive sneakers and offering special make-up versions of new and classic sports shoes, limited editions and rare stock, as well as own-brand products and accessories. For the relocation of its London store, Foot Patrol commissioned a collaborative approach between Brinkworth and the Wilson Brothers to create a store which was as much a one-off as the products on sale within. Despite its small footprint, the shop was to be both adaptable and flexible, as well as distinguished and memorable. The team created a space which gives customers a sense of discovery as they enter. With an almost anonymous glass-fronted facade, visitors must first walk through a dark-walled entrance vestibule. This is lit by a white neon glow coming from the Foot Patrol gas-mask logo, in an aged metal frame, and

from the light from the interior shop which has been assembled within the shell of the space. With the floors, walls and ceiling constructed from an urban palette of recycled wooden planks, the designers took inspiration from the hidden and tiny boutiques of Japan. A mirrored end wall accentuates the intimate scale of the inner store, playfully reflecting the linearity of the design as an optical illusion, that appears to extend the store rearwards as an infinite space. Concealment of lighting and services behind the pitched roof cladding, allows for the bespoke 'library-style' display system. These sliding black steel fixtures can be extended along the whole length of the store, or nested at either end to leave space for special events or promotions.

1   A blend of modularity and function is offset
    with an aged backdrop to create a perfect
    stage for the merchandise.
2   Customers enter through a 'transition'
    space, an intriguing antechamber where the
    outer and inner aspects of the store meet.

2

The space gives customers a sense of discovery as they enter

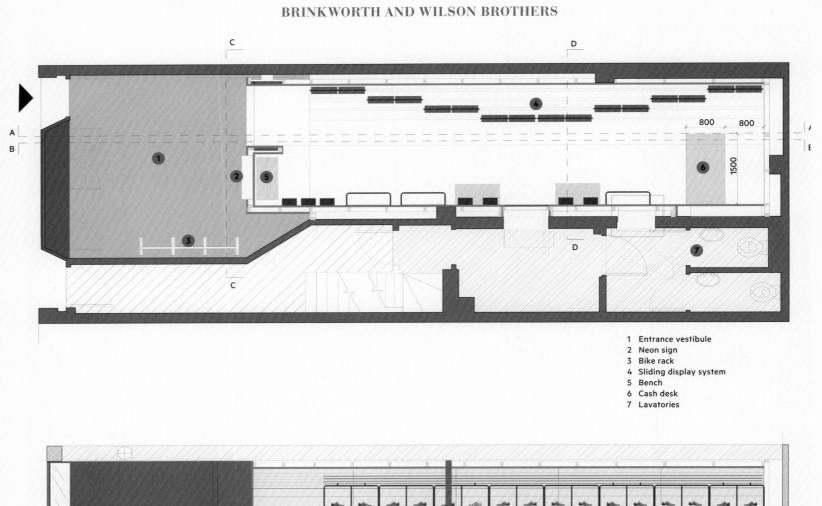

1 Entrance vestibule
2 Neon sign
3 Bike rack
4 Sliding display system
5 Bench
6 Cash desk
7 Lavatories

Section AA

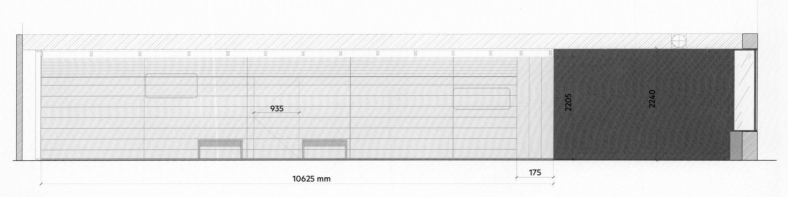

Section BB

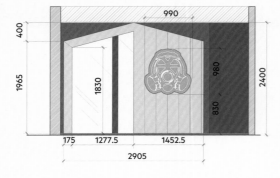

Section CC

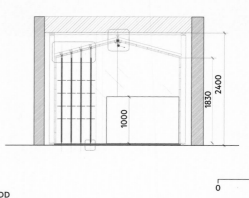

Section DD

0   1 m

The shelving system can be retracted, giving extra space for events to take place in-store.

The floors, walls and ceiling are constructed from an urban palette of recycled wooden planks

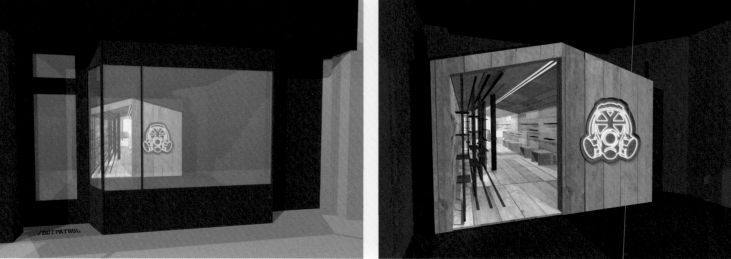

Renderings of the entranceway. The darkened vestibule comprises almost 20 per cent of the footprint of the small shop.

KURT GEIGER

by FOUND ASSOCIATES

1

WHERE London, United Kingdom WHEN August 2010
CLIENT Kurt Geiger DESIGNER Found Associates (p. 678)
TOTAL FLOOR AREA 400 m² SHOP CONSTRUCTOR B Batch Group
PHOTOGRAPHER Guy Archard

For the design of its new store in the heart of London's Covent Garden, luxury shoe retailer Kurt Geiger commissioned Found Associates. The two companies worked together previously to realise a number footwear stores internationally and this project was also created in close collaboration. The concept – to provide a 'jewellery shop of shoes' – was optimised by the input of visual display expert John Field, who enhanced the visual merchandising to its peak and set a benchmark for all other Kurt Geiger stores. The challenge for the Found team was to fulfil the chic and luxurious dictates of the brand and the expectations of its existing customers, whilst also drawing in a younger and equally brand-aware clientele. The store occupies a double-fronted corner unit which was designed to obtain maximum brand awareness,

with a raised window and a red neon sign at high level, intended to be clearly visible above the crowds of the Covent Garden piazza. To entice customers into the main trading area on the lower ground floor, a grand staircase and display area is incorporated at the entrance, visible from the street. Critical to the design is the sense of space created by the use of reflective materials, with a mirrored stretched film on the ceiling and mirrored walls creating symmetrical reflections of the visual merchandising throughout.

1 Mirroring on the ceiling and end wall creates a perspective which appears to enhance the store space lengthways.
2 The shoe chandelier was designed by John Field and manufactured by Elite Metalcraft. Its illuminated stainless steel and Perspex structure can display an impressive 250 individual shoes.
3 The impact of the design is magnified by the use of highly reflective surfaces, as well as natural elements such as wood and stone tiles on the floor.

2

3

The new shop was to draw in a younger but equally brand-aware clientele

Ground floor

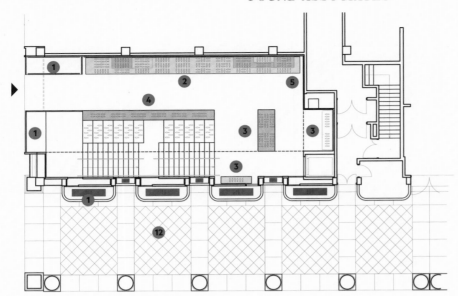

1 Window display
2 Low-level display plinth
3 Mid-level display plinth
4 Full-height display shelves
5 Mirror
6 Cash desk
7 Internet
8 Seating area
9 Stockroom
10 Staffroom
11 Lavatories
12 Piazza

Lower level

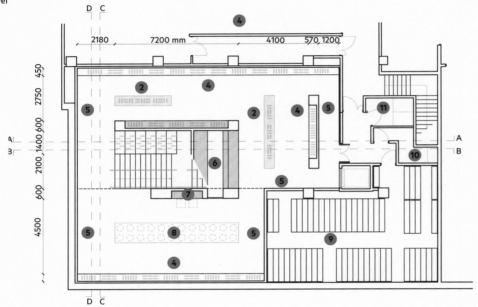

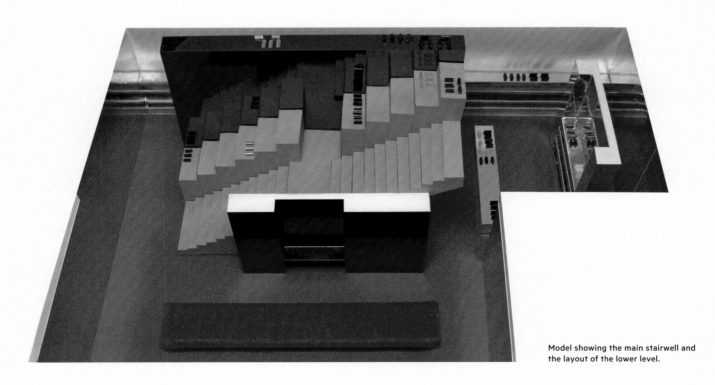

Model showing the main stairwell and the layout of the lower level.

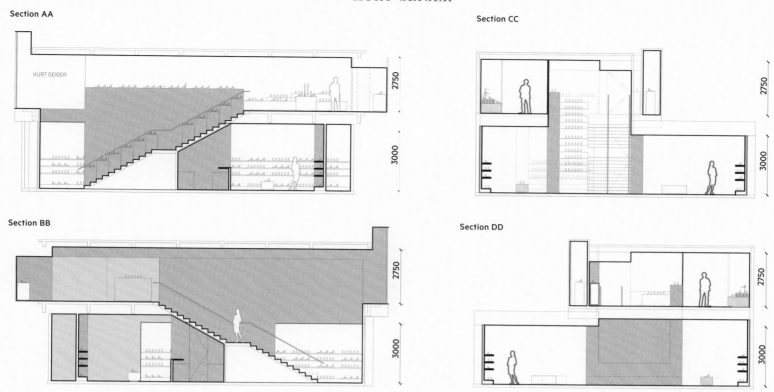

Section AA

2750

3000

Section CC

2750

3000

Section BB

2750

3000

Section DD

2750

3000

Optimum brand awareness comes from the red neon sign on the facade

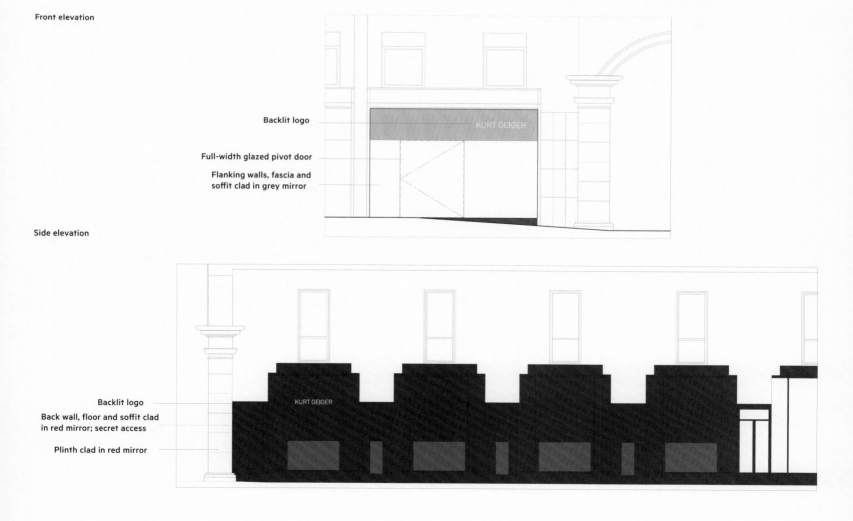

Front elevation

Backlit logo

Full-width glazed pivot door

Flanking walls, fascia and
soffit clad in grey mirror

KURT GEIGER

Side elevation

Backlit logo

Back wall, floor and soffit clad
in red mirror; secret access

Plinth clad in red mirror

KURT GEIGER

MOERNAUT

by B-ARCHITECTEN

1

WHERE Dendermonde, Belgium **WHEN** January 2010
CLIENT Moernaut **DESIGNER** B-architecten (p.674)
TOTAL FLOOR AREA 739 m² **SHOP CONSTRUCTOR** Inter-Fast
PHOTOGRAPHER Jeroen Verrecht

Moernaut is a family-run business in Dendermonde, Belgium, which sells multi-brand shoes. During the major renovation and expansion of its flagship store, the company continued trading by opening a temporary retail space alongside. B-architecten was in charge of the entire design project and was briefed to provide the client with a completely new look and feel for the overall concept. A temporary shop was created within the newly-built stockrooms of the main shop where, by the very nature of the space, the finish was bare and purely functional. The concept was to create a warm atmosphere as a radical contrast to the raw nature of the space. Cosy enclaves were crafted throughout, with each area decorated with specific categories of furniture, flooring and lighting. The various product collections were presented in stage-like themed settings, such as vintage and retro furnishings or cardboard box constructions. The temporary nature of the project – it was only in place for three months – was also integrated and enhanced, with counters and walls encased in plywood into which peep-holes were cut to reveal discrete product displays. A vast billboard on the facade of the building announced to passers-by that the store was still trading. By following the red graphic arrows, side-stepping the scaffolding along the way, a homely experience awaited inside.

1 The facade of the building delivered a clear message to customers, directing them to enter the temporary store.
2 The general lighting in the space was fluorescent tubes, with each product setting having its own lighting that strengthened its character.
3 Vintage record players were used as surfaces on which to position the merchandise.

2

As a radical contrast to the raw nature of the space, cosy enclaves were crafted throughout

3

NIKE HARAJUKU

by WONDERWALL

2

WHERE Tokyo, Japan **WHEN** November 2009
CLIENT Nike Japan **DESIGNER** Wonderwall (p.687)
TOTAL FLOOR AREA 946 m² **SHOP CONSTRUCTOR** D. Brain
PHOTOGRAPHER Kozo Takayama

The Harajuku section of Tokyo, an influential epicentre of the capital where style and culture blend, was chosen as the location for the first Nike flagship store in Tokyo, the largest of its stores in Japan. The concept for the expanse of retail space – 946 m² over three floors – came from the interior design firm Wonderwall. Going beyond innovative product offerings, the store is a playing field for various experience-based activities rooted around running and athletics. The imposing glass facade gives visitors an intriguing glimpse into the Nike world, with hundreds of pairs of shoes lining the windows. Inside, the use of natural wood in the furnishing and fittings throughout creates a relaxing ambience, set against the innovative and energetic installations. A grained oak running track wraps around the ground floor alongside product displays with decorative elements all related to running, such a wall created from the rubber soles of 1600 shoes and an installation of race bibs suspended from the ceiling. In the stairwell to the first floor, a chandelier-like creation made from almost 500 pairs of white sneakers is hung from the wood-beamed ceiling. The interior expresses the joy of sports, engaging customers to get involved either technically by analysing their running strides or creatively in the NikeiD studio where unique designs can materialise.

1 A cloud-like installation of sneakers floats above the heads of customers as they ascend the main stairwell.
2 The flagship store has the largest iD studio of any of Nike's retail outlets in Japan.

The interior expresses the joy of sports, engaging customers to get involved

3

CUSTOMIZE YOUR

3 The athletic track marked on the floor links in with the runner's studio positioned beneath the stairs where customers can have their running strides analysed.
4 On the first level, the mortar floor is painted with graphic lines and old oak beams in the ceiling are left uncovered.

4

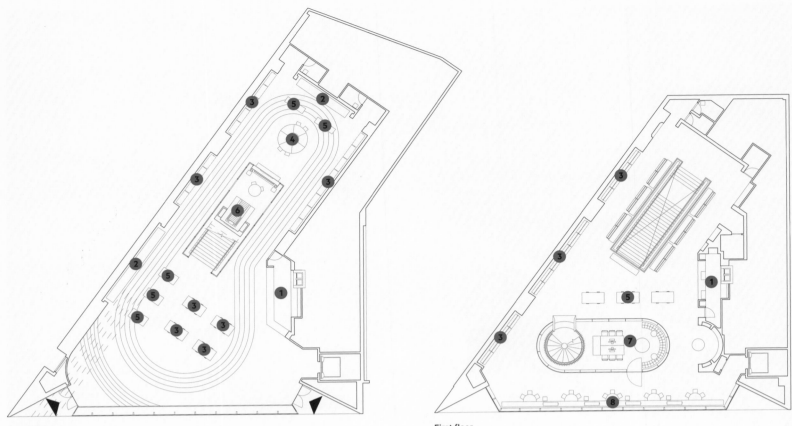

Ground floor

First floor

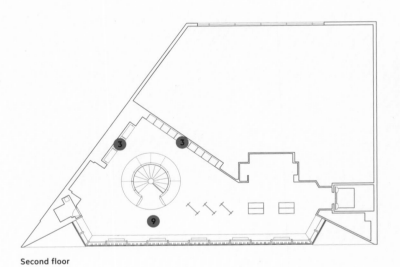

Second floor

1   Cash desk
2   Nike footwear wall
3   Product display
4   Information zone
5   Seating area
6   Runner's studio
7   NikeiD studio
8   NikeiD corner
9   Nike bootroom

View of the storefront.

The imposing glass facade gives visitors an intriguing glimpse into the Nike world

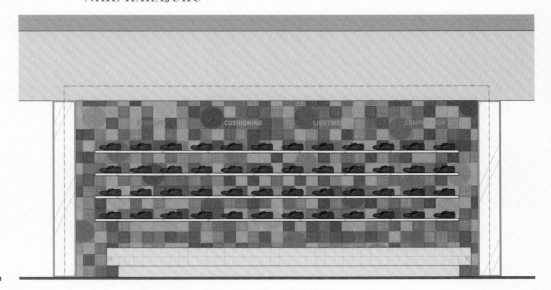

Illustrations of the rubber-soled wall. Fourteen different types of shoe were provided by Nike for the construction of the wall.

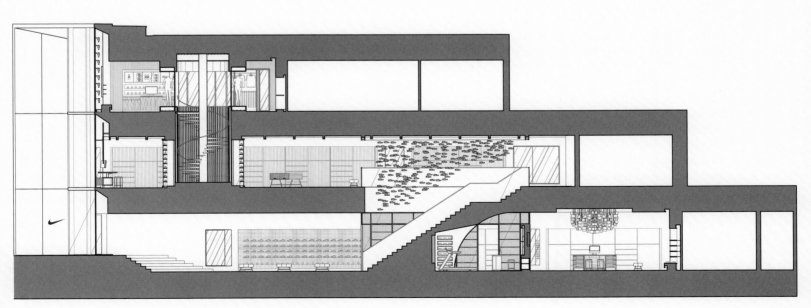

Elevation

QUEEN SHOES

by STUDIO GUILHERME TORRES

1

WHERE Londrina, Brazil **WHEN** March 2009
CLIENT Queen Shoes **DESIGNER** Studio Guilherme Torres (p.686)
TOTAL FLOOR AREA 90 m² **SHOP CONSTRUCTOR** Instaladora Megon
PHOTOGRAPHER Denilson Machado

Brazilian footwear brand Queen Shoes needed a manageable and memorable design for its new outlet in the centre of Londrina, Brazil. The location, in a shopping centre where the policy is for all stores to be renovated every 5 years, led Guilherme Torres to employ wallboards and materials central to the design that facilitated future architectural changes. The inspiration for the all-white concept came from an amalgamation of sci-fi references, from the unblemished white of the imperial soldiers in *Star Wars* to the futuristic voyaging vessel of *2001: A Space Odyssey*. The shop's outer-space expressiveness results from a geometric movement which stems from eighteen 42-cm wide segments which compose the walls and ceiling. The shop facade is the first segment which greets customers and it introduces itself as a solid structure,

sculpted in order to create the entrance. Inside, the subsequent segments obey the same movement pattern to build the shop interior which, when viewed from the storefront, creates a kaleidoscopic effect. The cash desk repeats the angular structure and comes to life as a detached sculpture in the centre of the shop, behind which a panel hides a staircase which leads to a small storage room and mezzanine. Low-energy lighting is used in the store design, with selected segment faces acting as elongated light boxes to create a diffuse, almost shadowless illumination throughout the space.

1 The store is reminiscent of the cave chiselled-out of Arctic snow in Superman's Fortress of Solitude.
2 A pristine white glow emanates from the geometric segments.
3 Angular lines are a repeating theme in the shop design.
4 The patterned panel behind cash desk and the free-standing mirror add a splash of red in an otherwise white environment.
5 Energy-efficient light bulbs were installed behind the polyurethane tensioned screens on some of the segment faces.

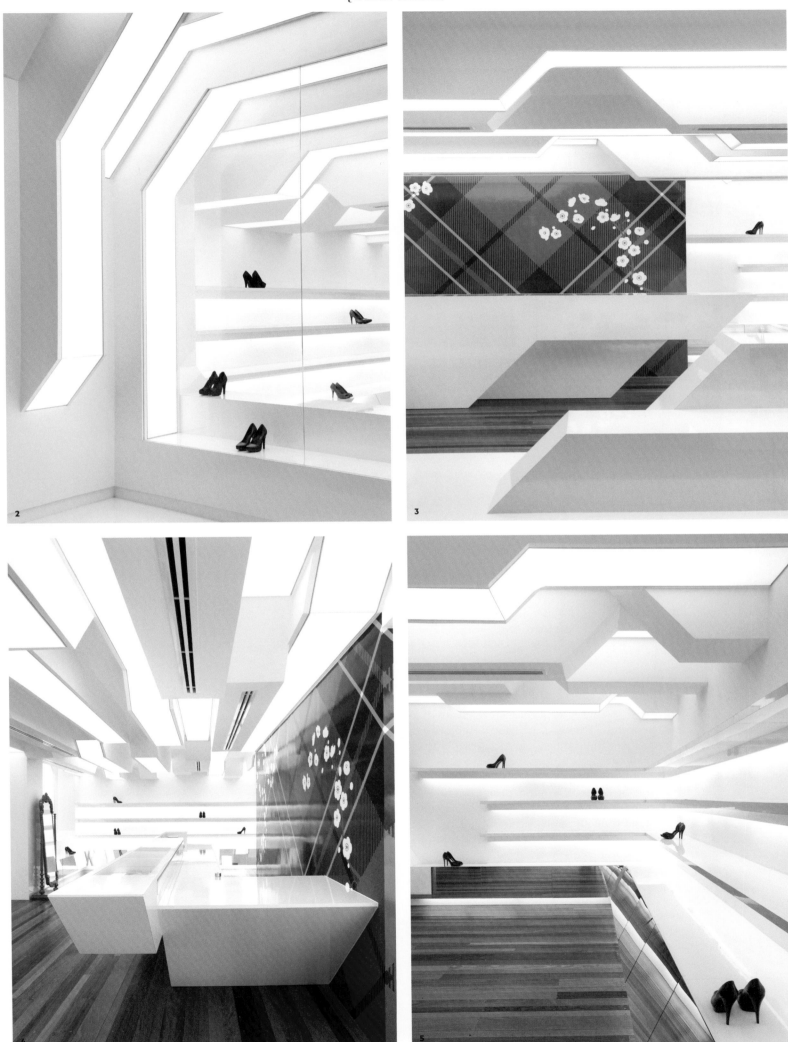

RAGRISE

by JAMO ASSOCIATES

1

WHERE Tokyo, Japan **WHEN** October 2009
CLIENT Abahouse International **DESIGNER** Jamo associates (p.680)
TOTAL FLOOR AREA 325 m² **SHOP CONSTRUCTOR** Sogo Design
PHOTOGRAPHER Kozo Takayama

Ragrise is a men's footwear store located in Tokyo's Jinnan area, a district notable for a profusion of boutiques from high-end brands. In order to create an interior that draws out the beauty of each individual product within a space displaying a large number of items, the Jamo design team paid special attention to the use of fixtures, in particular, pieces that are concertedly non-organic in shape. The overall design direction is governed by the concept of a leather-worker's studio, with tables akin to workbenches arranged in tidy rows. Products are illuminated from a skeleton, stripped-back ceiling by pendant lamps with trailing yellow cables. Wood board, carpet and marble were all used to execute a herringbone pattern running throughout the entire ground floor, with off-white wood panelling covering the walls and also subtly

spelling-out the brand name. Chairs with a refined finish, in differing styles and heights, are interspersed in the space. These not only serve a practical purpose, when customers are trying on shoes, but are also positioned very specifically and act as a display in their own right. The first floor of the shop was given more of an industrial feel, with concrete flooring and white tables displaying a more select collection of products. The orderly theme continues here also with a discrete pattern on the walls – only on closer inspection is it clear that this is due to numerous folded tables being hung in a structured arrangement.

1 The use of simple display fixtures and tables arranged in an orderly set up was an important aspect to emphasize the sense of organisation in the space.
2 On the second floor, which has a more industrial feel, folding tables are stored flat against the wall.
3 The Square Guest Chair and Simple Bench by BDDW can be used by customers when trying on shoes but are also used as displays occasionally.

2

The design is
governed by
the concept
of a leather-
worker's studio

3

1

Subtle illumination creates a floating and ethereal feeling to otherwise heavy, retail objects

RED WING SHOES

by ANOTHER COMPANY AND COMO PARK STUDIO

2

WHERE Amsterdam, the Netherlands WHEN July 2010
CLIENT Tenue de Nîmes DESIGNER Another Company (p.673) and Como Park Studio (p.676)
TOTAL FLOOR AREA 73 m² SHOP CONSTRUCTOR Roeland Interieurbouw
PHOTOGRAPHERS Joachim Baan and Kenneth Jaworski

Red Wing Shoes is a US-brand that has been producing crafted work boots for over 100 years. When it sought to establish its first flagship store in Amsterdam, the footwear company approached Tenue de Nîmes, a boutique which was already a supplier of the brand in the Dutch capital. The Tenue de Nîmes team, together with creative partner Another Company and interior architects Como Park Studio, approached the brief collaboratively to strive to capture the long history and American spirit of Red Wing Shoes. Located in the historic canal district, the building itself was also a willing collaborator in meeting the brief providing an ideal backdrop full of character, with its intricate wooden facade, high ceilings and period details. The challenge was to design an interior that showcased the rich American heritage of the brand without looking like a crowded antique store. The solution was to present the shoes in an orderly and minimalist manner amidst unique detailing, such as the steel-framed display cases made with vintage glass filled with actual lumps of coal. This is a reference to the rich mining heritage of Red Wing shoes, as are the workmen's tools which decorate the dark concrete walls. One wall towards the rear of the shop, which itself is made from materials taken from an authentic Amish water tower, is used to exhibit most of the accessories on offer. Subtle illumination creates a floating and ethereal feeling to otherwise heavy, retail objects.

1 Vintage glass and steel display cases set the mood in-store, with an old shoeshine chair positioned near the entrance adding to the retro feel.
2 Weathered mirror panels line the old chimney breast, serving the function of enlarging the small store whilst also allowing customers to see their shoes.

3

4

Merchandise
is presented in
an orderly and
minimalist manner
amidst unique
detailing

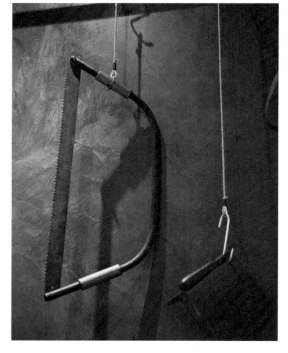

3 Products line the walls to the back of the store where the large back window allows customers to see into the stock room behind the internal garden.
4 Vintage farm tools, sourced in America, complete the historical feel of the store.
5 A stripped metal post-sorting table and vintage display case complement the wall made from wood reclaimed from an Amish water tower.

5

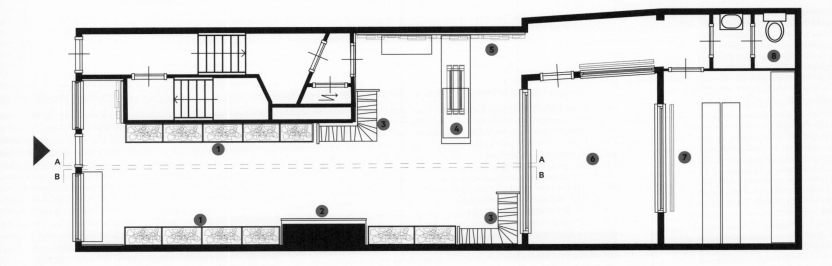

1 Steel-framed display cases
2 Mirror
3 Seating
4 Cash desk
5 Accessories wall
6 Courtyard
7 Storage
8 Lavatory

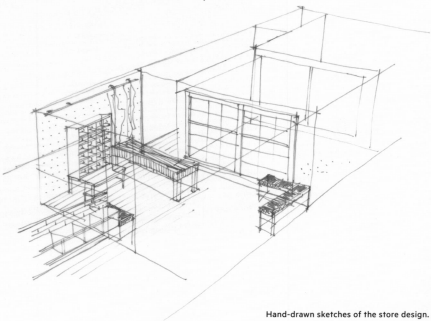

Hand-drawn sketches of the store design.

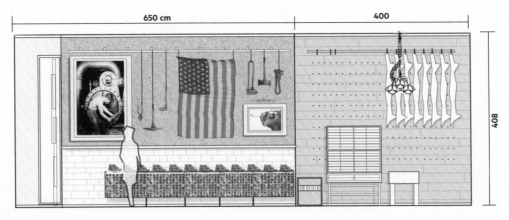

Section AA

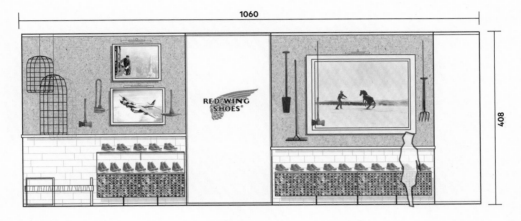

Section BB

One wall is made from materials taken from an authentic Amish water tower

Construction photo showing the steel-framed
display cases being installed on the white tiles
which cover the lower half of the walls.

REEBOK

by CONFETTI

1

WHERE Leusden, the Netherlands WHEN January 2009
CLIENT Reebok Benelux DESIGNER Confetti (p.676)
TOTAL FLOOR AREA 50 m² SHOP CONSTRUCTOR Confetti
PHOTOGRAPHER Confetti

With the expansion of the sports business centre in Leusden, the Netherlands, Reebok required a new showroom to present its seasonal new collections of sports and leisure footwear to customers and industry representatives. Reflecting the energetic, open and informal organisation of the client, the Confetti design team chose to create a space which was also representative of its target market. The concept was based around an urban and freestyle theme, with an innovative club feel. From floor to ceiling, black furnishings and fittings wrap around the space, with wooden panels and cupboards decorated with chalk-like graffiti. Running the entire length of the side walls are black leather bespoke seating elements, above which are ceiling-height box display cases of differing dimensions. The products stand out against the black backdrop with additional illumination coming from the ceiling spotlights. At the far end of the showroom is an expanse of white, with a fluorescing feature display wall glowing like a shining beacon. The client's identity is interwoven throughout the space with the products that are on display. There is no need to spell out the brand name in big or bright letters, although those looking closely enough will spot a single, subtle instance of the Reebok logo.

1 The space is lined with leather seating and stacked high with product display cases.
2 The merchandise adds a vibrant splash of colour to the black and white space.

The concept was based around an urban and freestyle theme

2

REPOSI CALZATURE

by DIEGO BORTOLATO ARCHITETTO

1

WHERE Basaluzzo, Italy **WHEN** March 2010
CLIENT Reposi Calzature **DESIGNER** Diego Bortolato Architetto (p.677)
TOTAL FLOOR AREA 75 m² **SHOP CONSTRUCTOR** F.lli Groppo
PHOTOGRAPHER Daniela Bortolato

In the Piedmont region of northern Italy, near Alessandria, is a historic square with a classic Italian arcade. This is the location of the new store of footwear brand Reposi Calzature, designed by Diego Bortolato Architetto. The interior space is characterised by the use of natural materials for furniture and flooring, in particular light oak strips and panels which have been oil finished. Felt coverings are used on the seating cubes to add texture. The neutral tones of the wood, fabrics and paintwork selected for the walls and architectural columns provide an ideal backdrop for the product displays. Box-like structures have been utilised, for the cash desk and above the seating area, which project into the space adding an abstract three-dimensional quality. An eye-catching feature is included in the two elongated 'sails' overhead running the length of the store, constructed from plasterboard and each having irregular geometry. Suspended beneath these white shapes are the angular light boxes providing diffuse and spot illumination, encased by a black enamel coating. The incorporation of these large reflective surfaces contributes to a propagation of interesting views within the store. Externally, metal cladding has been added to the facade and is designed to blend in with the architecture of the arcade. The windows are underlined by the contrast between the traditional anthracite painted panels and the natural oak boards.

1 The cash desk appears to be cantilevered around the central structural column.
2 Elongated shapes are repeated throughout the store, including the display modules on the wall, the light boxes embedded in the ceiling and the felt-covered seating aspects.
3 The stairway is panelled in the same natural wood used in the store.
4 The redefinition of high-altitude areas is accomplished with the inclusion of two geometric white sails set against an otherwise black ceiling.

2

The interior space is characterised by the use of natural materials

3

4

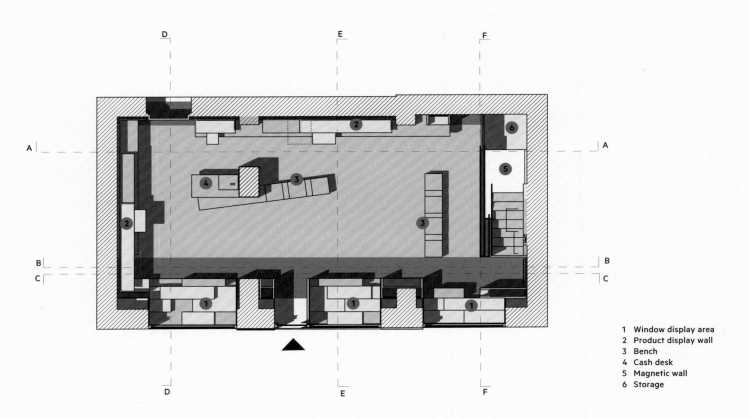

1 Window display area
2 Product display wall
3 Bench
4 Cash desk
5 Magnetic wall
6 Storage

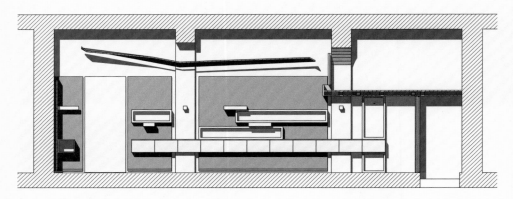

Section AA

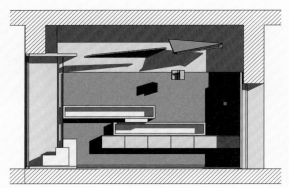

Section DD

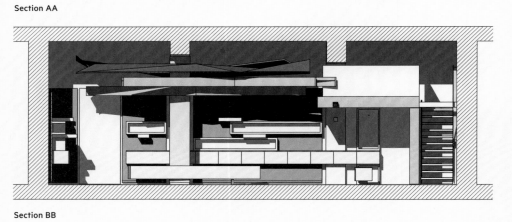

Section BB

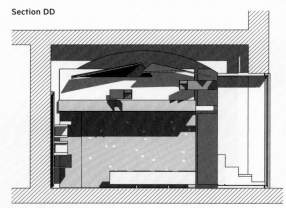

Section EE

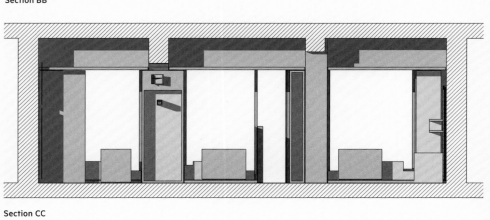

Section CC

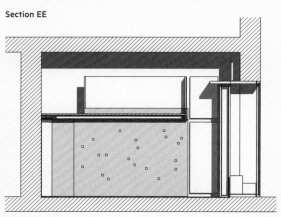

Section FF

Drawing of the shelving modules that make up
the wall display system.

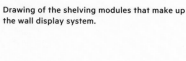

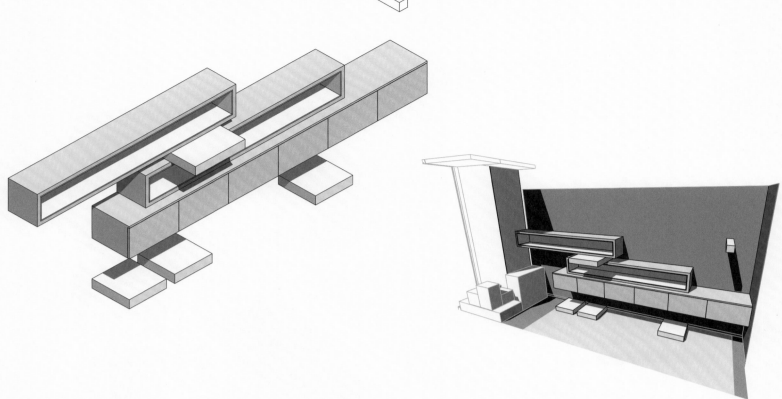

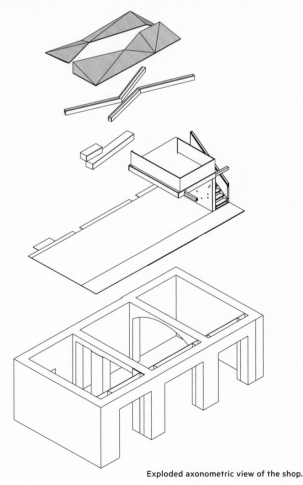

Box-like structures project into the space adding an abstract three-dimensional quality

Exploded axonometric view of the shop.

599

SHOE CLASS

by PINKEYE

1

WHERE Antwerp, Belgium WHEN May 2010
CLIENT Marc Duwyn DESIGNER Pinkeye (p.683)
TOTAL FLOOR AREA 75 m² SHOP CONSTRUCTOR Marc Duwyn
PHOTOGRAPHER Julien Lannoo

Shoe Class, a new sneaker shop, opened its doors on a quiet street close to Antwerp's shopping centre. As it is located slightly off the main shopping route, the interior design had to be such that it made the shop the 'talk of the town' and which would encourage its clientele to go the extra distance to check it out. Pinkeye was asked to make this happen with an extremely tight budget. The team aimed to come up with a clear concept: telling a story, rather than decorating the place focusing on just aesthetics. When the designers first saw the space, they felt it was very suitable for a classroom set-up which would make customers feel at ease and bring to mind their adolescent joy over a pair of new sneakers. After all, the brands that are sold at Shoe Class have been around since most people's adolescent years. A retro-style school shop is the result of their brainstorms. According to the budget, recycled materials from a school that had recently closed were selected to furnish the store. A teacher's desk was placed in the back of the shop, overlooking the entire space and functioning as the cash desk. Classic chairs and desks with teenage tabletop carvings are lined-up in the centre and act as display surfaces. Paying attention to detail, geographical maps adorn the walls and chemistry flasks positioned on the shelves hold the cap collection. Incorporating sports elements, lockers have been placed throughout the shop and one wall is covered with old-school wooden climbing frames.

1 Wherever customers look in the shop, they are reminded of school – although this might be the first time they've seen chemistry flasks adorning cool caps.
2 Sweaters appear to have been casually thrown over the chairs by students.
3 Old-school luggage carriers serve as shelving for skateboard decks on one wall of the stores mezzanine.
4 Next page: One wall of the classroom-style shop is covered by a climbing rack that is transformed to a display system.

2

3

The brands that are sold here have been around since most people's adolescent years

TELE

AN

SERV

604

ECOM
ND
VICES
605

2 OPERA

by ZOEVOX

2

WHERE Paris, France WHEN December 2010
CLIENT BNP Paribas DESIGNER Zoevox (p.687)
TOTAL FLOOR AREA 909 m² SHOP CONSTRUCTOR Talia
PHOTOGRAPHER Veronique Mati

BNP Paribas is a European leader in global banking and financial services. With the opening of its first concept store – in the historical building of 2, Place de l'Opera in Paris – the ultimate objective was to defy the usual aesthetic codes of the banking world. The vision of architect Fabrice Ausset (Zoevox) was to conceive a luxurious experimental space, where innovation and new customs were to be encouraged, breaking the age-old banking set-up where the client and the adviser sit on opposite sides of a desk in a straight-laced atmosphere. A colourful and creative scenography allows customers to discover the banking services on offer in a user-friendly and interactive way, enticing a sense of investigation and discovery with elegance and energy. 'Active waiting' is encouraged in the lounge,

alongside bespoke Zoevox furnishings and numerous designer pieces. A few select historical references and retro features were chosen to provide an elegant link between past and future for the new function of this unique space, such as the sophisticated mirror work and intricate honeycombed ceiling. This tridimensional structure overhead, beneath the building's 11-m-high cupola, also serves a practical purpose to dampen the acoustics and sound vibrations echoing in the atrium. Around the vast central lounge were positioned ten customer interface zones divided by glass walls (by the Ateliers Pictet), striped with fine-featured reflecting lines that create an unexpected kinetic effect. The use of reflective and metallic elements are key aspects to the interior design, enhancing the perception of depth by expanding the feeling of space.

1   Stools by India Mahdavi surround the long
    central table near the entrance which acts
    as the welcome desk. The pattern on the
    rug by Ege is designed by Zoevox.
2   The large honeycombed structures are
    incorporated overhead to break-down
    sound reverberations.

The luxurious experimental space entices a sense of discovery with elegance and energy

3

3   Some lower honeycombed cells are
    lacquered in gold and brown and lined by
    LED lights, providing extra illumination
    above the grand collaborative meeting table
    with its chairs by Bartoli Design.
4   Dividing the zones are 25 inner walls,
    each made of two glass slabs striped with
    fine-featured reflecting lines of digits that
    create an unexpected kinetic effect. This
    wall demarcates the playground zone where
    children can play, draw or watch cartoons.

1

The name '4010' relates to the RAL colour
code of the brand's corporate magenta

4010 TELEKOM SHOP

by PARAT FOR MUTABOR

2

WHERE Cologne, Germany **WHEN** February 2011
CLIENT Deutsche Telekom **DESIGNER** Parat for Mutabor (p.683)
TOTAL FLOOR AREA 180 m² **SHOP CONSTRUCTOR** Dula-Werke Dustmann
PHOTOGRAPHER Mareen Fischinger

Deutsche Telekom opened its first community store designed specifically for a young market in Berlin in 2008. The concept was conceived by Mutabor and was named 4010 Telekom Shop, where the numerical value relates to the RAL colour code for the specific shade of the magenta relating to the brand's identity. The 4010 concept is that of a 'work in progress' and an 'atelier' (artist's workshop) – a place of art, community and exchange. When a store was to be opened in Cologne, Parat was commissioned by Mutabor to successfully transfer the innovative concept to a new city, whilst incorporating a unique personality inspired by its location. The store in Berlin was influenced by street art, whilst the Cologne-based store is inspired by pop art. A vivid, striped design wraps around the walls and floor at the entrance to the shop. The textured lines provide a striking perspective which channels the public to head towards the elongated layout area in the rear, discovering products and services along the way. The narrow storefront and deep floor plan were major challenges for Parat and the design of a strong architectural graphic was vital to attract customers into the shop. Products are displayed in sunken niches in the custom-made furniture and on trestle tables which can be moved to leave space for showcases and workshops. The separate areas are delineated by the use of different materials, such as exposed brick in the service corner and a grey wooden platform in the entertainment zone. A gallery wall towards the back of the shop exhibits work by different artists, which enhances the atmosphere of art, exchange and experimentation.

1 Graphic elements inside the store by Die Krieger Des Lichts create an authentic picture language and a distinctive look.
2 The flexible and convertible nature of the space is the essence of the design concept.

5

The Cologne-based store is inspired by pop art

6

3 The display devices are reminiscent of workspace equipment: trestle tables, stretcher frames and canvas.
4 Customers can relax in the bar area which has Heidi Stools by Established & Sons and Unfold pendant lights by Muuto.
5 The entertainment lounge, with its wall mural, has seating by Martino Gamper (brightly-coloured Arnold Circus stools) and Jens Risom (vintage Vostrum chair).
6 The latest technological gadgets can be tested out in a fun and relaxing atmosphere.

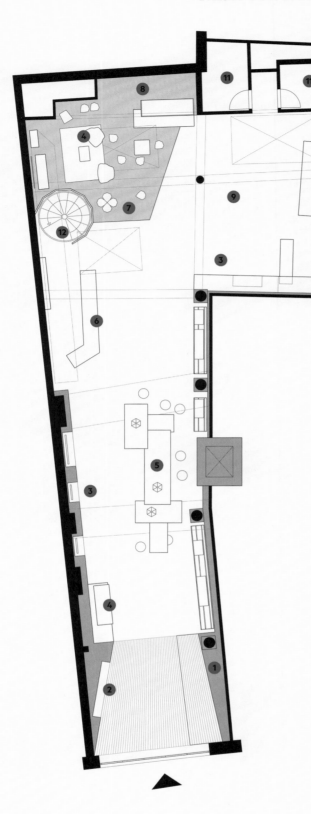

1 Screen wall
2 Highlighted showcase
3 Product display
4 Seating area
5 Cluster tables
6 Cash desk
7 Entertainment lounge
8 Gallery wall
9 Exhibition space
10 Bar/kitchen
11 Lavatories
12 Basement storage
13 Service corner

The space has an atmosphere of exchange and experimentation

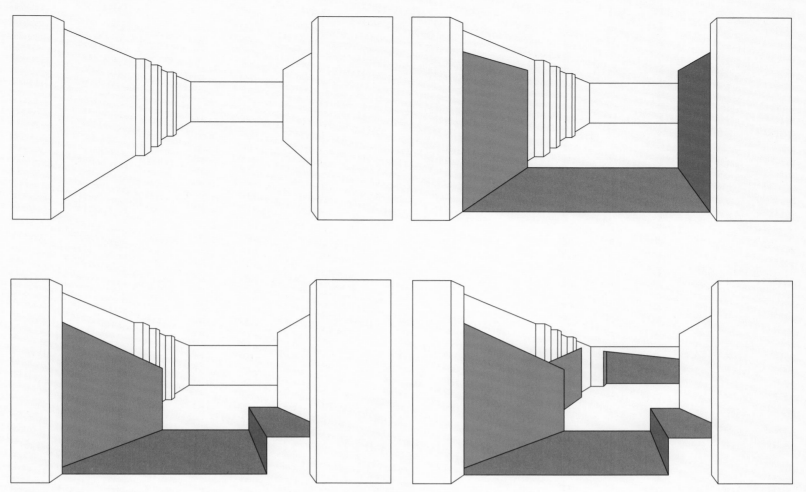

In the concept stages, the graphic gesture
wrapping around the space was developed by first
adding it to the front walls and then extending it
to connect the back of the store with the entrance.

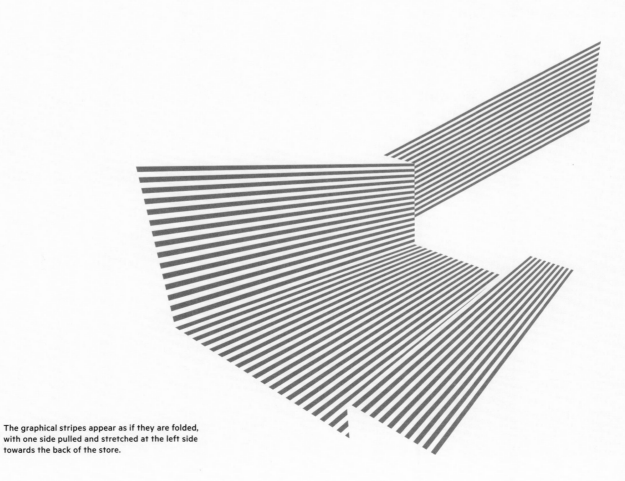

The graphical stripes appear as if they are folded,
with one side pulled and stretched at the left side
towards the back of the store.

BASE

by CRENEAU INTERNATIONAL

◆

2

WHERE Antwerp, Belgium WHEN January 2010
CLIENT KPN Group Belgium DESIGNER Creneau International (p.676)
TOTAL FLOOR AREA 340 m² SHOP CONSTRUCTOR Creneau International
PHOTOGRAPHER Philippe Van Gelooven

The grand architectural landmark of Antwerp's central train station was chosen as the location for the flagship store of Base, Belgian's fast-growing mobile operator and internet services provider. Working with the vast history of the building whilst incorporating the values of the client's brand – user-friendliness, clarity, transparency and emotion – was the challenge facing Creneau International. To merge these two strong identities in one location, the design team played with contrasts; the imposing status of the building with its heavy materials against the light, fresh and clear elements of the Base brand. The monumental structure forms an impressive backdrop for the store, with integrated free-standing elements being effectively positioned in a transparent 'box within a box' in the lofty space. Modern display cases, made from maple wood and white laminate, sit alongside the renovated original features – high ceilings and walls, along with the magnificent windows. Staying true to the historical purpose of the building, the natural marble ticket counter has been transformed into the store's cash desks, which incorporate lamps with illuminated desk numbers. Spherical light motifs are also translated into an impressive bubble-like chandelier hanging over the central hall. Beneath this is a circular module entitled the 'Freedom of Speech' podium, which relates to the client's tagline. Giant block capital letters spell out the brand name, both outside the station – attracting passing customers – and inside the store, where the letters are positioned in a light and playful manner, reflecting the overall design concept.

1 The grand nature of the space, with its original features, is contrasted with modern display elements and fun features like the giant letters.
2 Marble tiles are placed over the original floor in order to protect it.

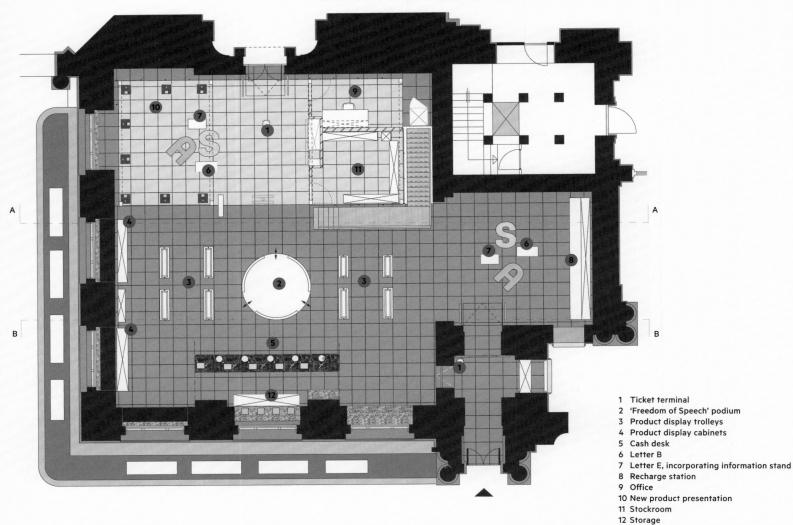

1 Ticket terminal
2 'Freedom of Speech' podium
3 Product display trolleys
4 Product display cabinets
5 Cash desk
6 Letter B
7 Letter E, incorporating information stand
8 Recharge station
9 Office
10 New product presentation
11 Stockroom
12 Storage

A transparent 'box within a box' materialises in the lofty space

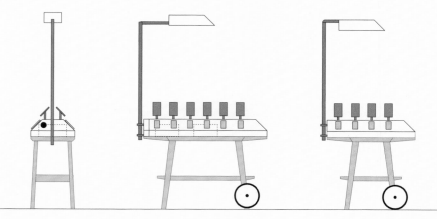

Bespoke display trolleys, with integrated lighting systems, were designed to afford maximum product exposure.

BASE

Front elevation

Section AA

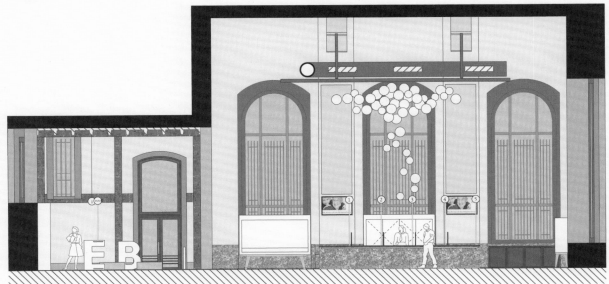

Section BB

DIGITEC

by AEKAE AND SPRINGEN

2

WHERE Zurich, Switzerland **WHEN** December 2009
CLIENT Digitec **DESIGNERS** Aekae (p.673) and springen (p.685)
TOTAL FLOOR AREA 200 m² **SHOP CONSTRUCTOR** Umdasch Shopfitting Group
PHOTOGRAPHER Daniel auf der Mauer

Digitec has grown to become one of the biggest retailers of consumer electronics in Switzerland. Initially an online-only business, the company is now expanding to full showrooms. The Aekae design team was brought on board to create Digitec's flagship retail experience in Zurich, conceiving a new kind of shop with a simple and inviting aesthetic. In collaboration with the interaction designers of springen, an interactive showroom was created, that combines the possibilities and convenience of online shopping with the advantages of a physical shop experience. Arrays of white modular display tables are positioned in clusters, designed by Aekae, to neatly incorporate interactive product presentations with touch screens. This technology works as a digital price-tag, based on real-time data linked directly from Digitec's product database. Visitors approaching the shop can immediately notice – through the glass window facade – the raw concept in the store design with stripped-wood floors and white-washed brick walls. Against the white canvas of the store, black and grey coloured furniture fittings are interspersed with accents of red, seen in the electrical cables trailing from the ceiling and on the tops of display modules. A limited number of physical products are displayed in the shop, with additional items highlighted on numerous large promotional screens and flat-screen TVs. An important visual element of the interior concept, the screens are not only information devices but they are also symbols of fast processes, dynamic data visualisation and automated systems.

1   In the raw and straightforward interior, the bespoke product presentation tables are positioned in playful clusters.
2   The modular store design is immediately obvious to passers-by through the vast windows of the storefront.

3 Special offers are highlighted with red surfaces, which can be interchanged with the regular white tops.
4 The simple and unobtrusive cash desk design complements the sleek and streamlined counters and wall panels.
5 Elongated light boxes hung from the ceiling illuminate the product display modules in their linear arrangements.

Dynamic data visualisation and interactive modules are symbols of the store's high-tech aesthetic

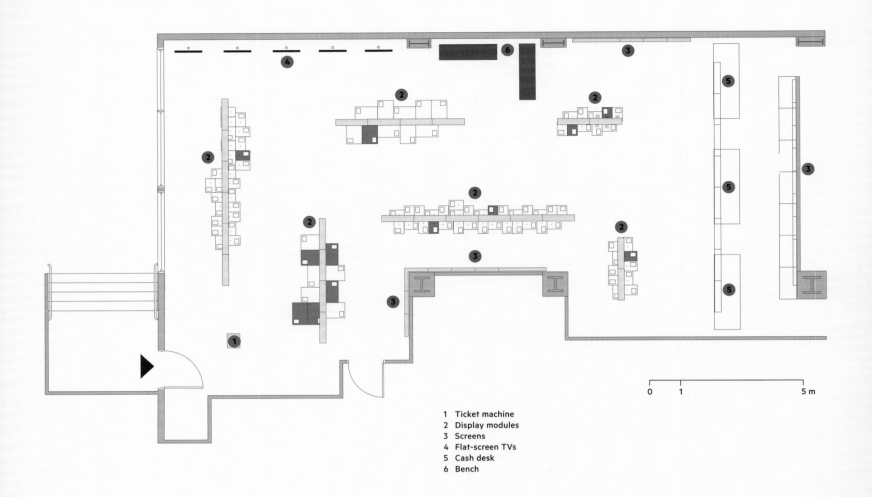

1 Ticket machine
2 Display modules
3 Screens
4 Flat-screen TVs
5 Cash desk
6 Bench

0   1   5 m

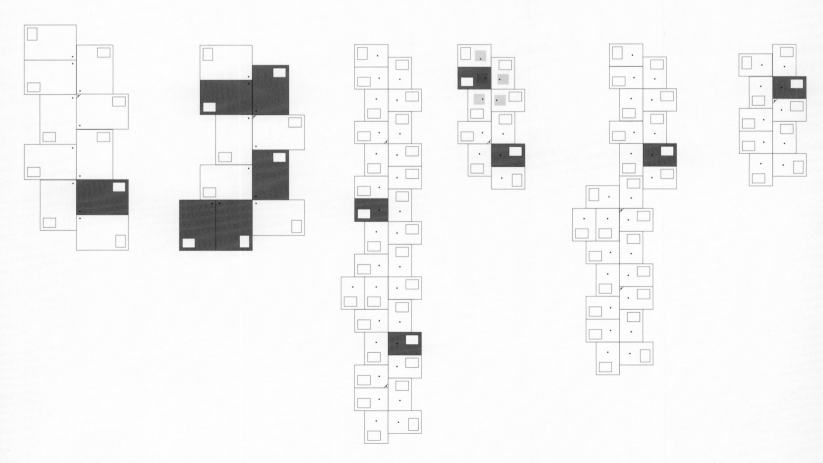

There are six different formations of display
table providing a varied presentation area.

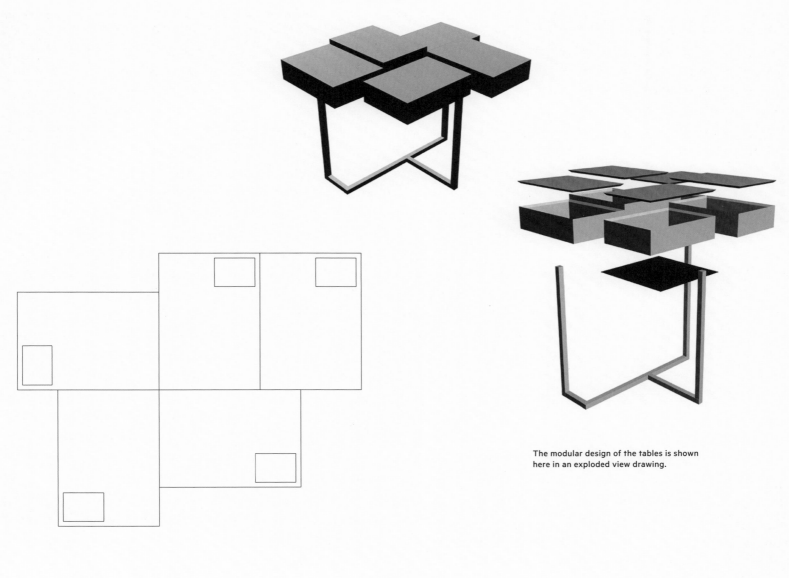

The modular design of the tables is shown here in an exploded view drawing.

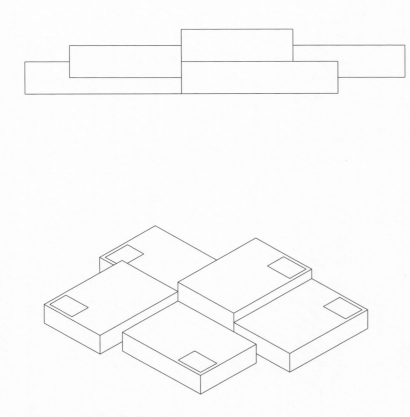

The tables are formed by positioning the sub-units at different heights and different angles.

HP INNOVATION HUB

by STOREAGE

2

WHERE Chongqing, China WHEN January 2010
CLIENT Hewlett-Packard China DESIGNER Storeage (p.685)
TOTAL FLOOR AREA 130 m² SHOP CONSTRUCTOR Kingsmen International
PHOTOGRAPHER Colin Jones

To coincide with the opening of a new production facility in China, Hewlett Packard wanted a regional experience showroom to be created where customers could access first-hand the very latest in computer-related technology. Storeage answered this call by designing an exclusive HP Innovation Hub. The hub is a sleek space that consists of four distinct zones, each of which highlights different aspects of commercial and consumer software solutions, utilising locally-made products. Laptops and desktop computers are available to visitors, displayed alongside presentations of Hewlett Packard's heritage detailing the client's dedication to innovative research and development. The goal for Storeage to balance local relevance with Hewlett Packard's global brand image is achieved through subtle hints of Chinese inspiration seen in the circular doorways and the use of local Szechuan larch wood for the product tables. On gaining access to the new-product zone through the illuminated arched entranceways, visitors can test out future prototypes, in a space that has a futuristic feel with high-gloss surfaces and a monochromatic colour scheme. A relaxed space in the centre of the hub continues to reflect the circular theme of the showroom with the furniture and fittings, such as the overhead lighting feature and the seating area, as well as the corporate logo. Within all the zones, customers have a direct line of sight through all the interconnecting archways to the back wall of the hub where the HP illuminated logo radiates over the space.

1   A spherical concept radiates from the corporate logo on the back wall throughout the showroom and is integrated into the lighting and seating fixtures.
2   From the outside, customers have a direct view through the archways all the way to the back wall. In the gloss floor, circular reflections can be seen; this circular theme continues within the showroom.

3 The innovation area at the back of the
showroom is decorated with black walls.
4 Corporate blue is used as an accent colour
throughout the store.
5 View of the HP Notebook display area.
Customers can test out the products in the
various zones.

5

3

4

The space has a futuristic feel with high-gloss surfaces and a monochromatic colour scheme

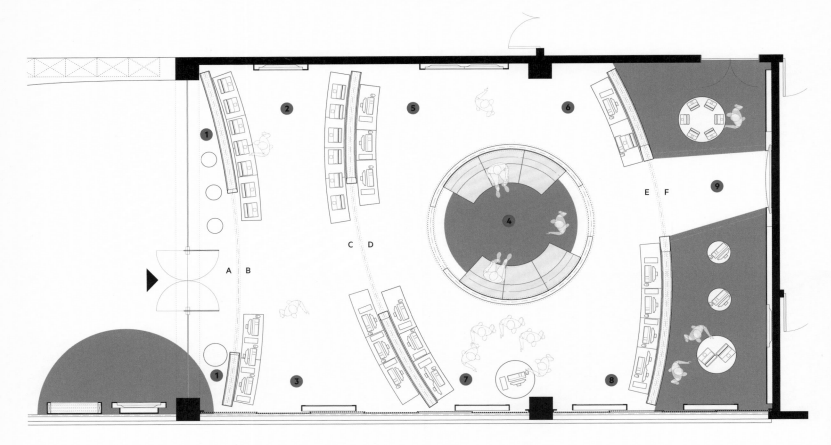

1 Historical window display
2 HP notebook display
3 HP desktop display
4 Seating area
5 HP WS display
6 HP AN display
7 HP DSO display
8 HP BPC display
9 Innovation area

Initial sketches outline the arched corridor concept which
connects the different zones of the showroom.

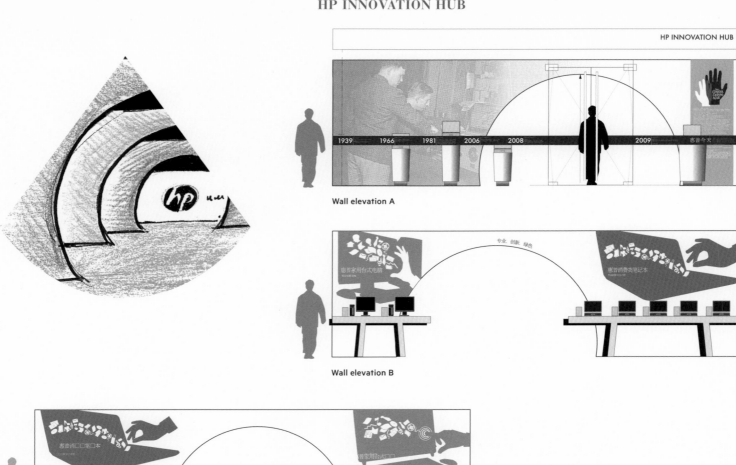

Wall elevation A

Wall elevation B

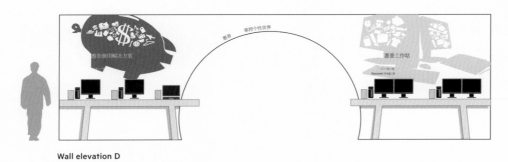

Wall elevation C

The hub is a sleek space that consists of distinct zones

Wall elevation D

The decorated wall elevations document the visitor's journey, starting with HP's heritage and ending with a showcase of newest innovations.

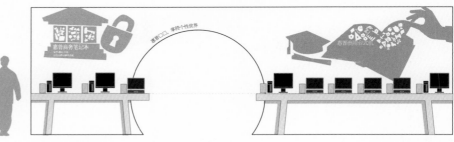

Wall elevation E

Wall elevation F

SNS BANK PLUG & PLAY

by VBAT

2

WHERE Amersfoort, the Netherlands WHEN July 2009
CLIENT SNS Bank DESIGNER VBAT (p.687)
TOTAL FLOOR AREA 112 m² SHOP CONSTRUCTOR Imagebuilders
PHOTOGRAPHER John Lewis Marshall

SNS Bank is the smallest of the big four banks in the Dutch market. Looking to grow its customer base nationally, the client wanted to build on its success in the online banking arena by redesigning 300 high-street branches across the country. The brief to VBAT was to develop a fresh approach to banking and to explore how retail principles could be utilised by SNS Bank. The concept focuses on simplicity and smart thinking. An open and inviting space, which has a strong synergy with the SNS Bank's online interface, gives a central role to staff in helping guide customers through the choice process. A modular approach is key to the commercial success of the new format, allowing for rapid implementation of the roll-out programme. The design features a circular floor plan, based abstractly on the SNS Bank kaleidoscopic logo, comprising a central service point and six colour-coded modules Which form the outer wall. Each segment represents a different product focus, with touch-screen interfaces and information cards offering intangible financial 'products' in a tangible and visual way. The relaxed, central area allows for informal discussions with financial advisors whilst, in a series of meeting rooms hidden from view in a secondary ring of spaces, a more personalised and private consultation experience is offered.

1 Colour is key to the design concept with the display modules around the edge each having a distinct hue in their graphical elements, side panels and built-in dimmed lights with colour filters.
2 The main aspect of the shop's floor plan has a spherical circulation.

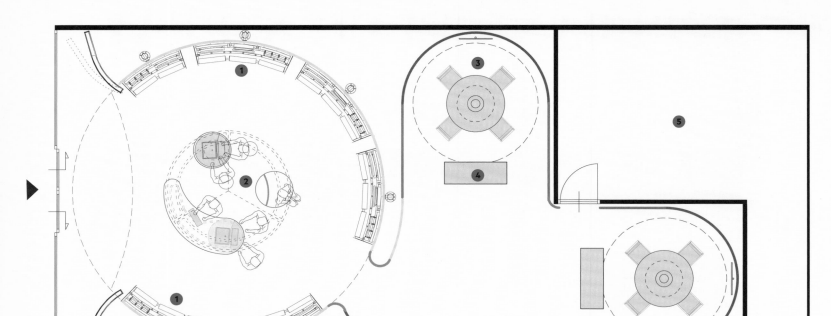

1 Modular display screens
2 Customer service point
3 Meeting room
4 Storage
5 Office

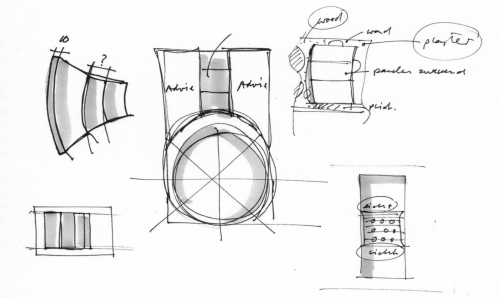

The circular floor plan is inspired by the client's kaleidoscopic logo

Renderings showing the interior design of the series of secluded meetings rooms.

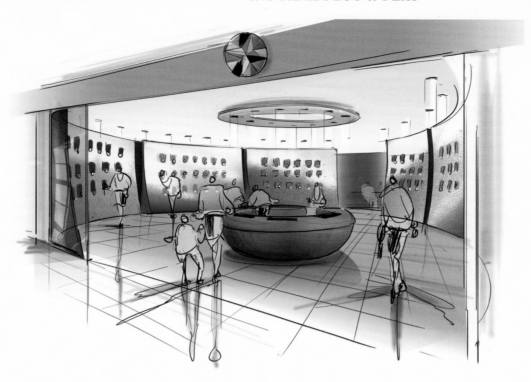

Sketches of the open-plan store with its interactive product panels.

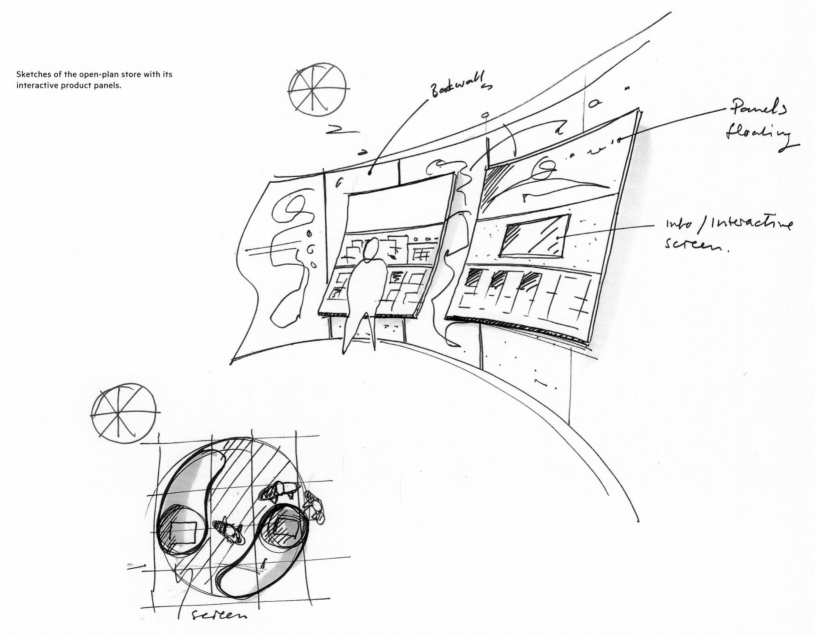

Sketch of the central service point which includes organically-shaped counters.

1

A constellation of leaf motifs in 24 different colours 'grow' on the white branches on the walls

SUGAMO SHINKIN BANK

by EMMANUELLE MOUREAUX ARCHITECTURE + DESIGN

2

WHERE Tokyo, Japan WHEN June 2010
CLIENT Sugamo Shinkin Bank DESIGNER emmanuelle moureaux architecture + design (p.677)
TOTAL FLOOR AREA 734 m² SHOP CONSTRUCTOR Shin-Kogei
PHOTOGRAPHER Nacása & Partners

Sugamo Shinkin Bank is a credit union that strives to provide first-rate hospitality to its customers in accordance with its motto, 'We take pleasure in serving happy customers'. With the relocation of the bank in Tokiwadai, Emmanuelle Moureaux came on board to handle the architectural and interior design of the new branch with a refreshing approach. The concept sought to create a rejuvenating atmosphere for customers and incorporated a white canvas, vibrant leaf motifs and blocks of colour, as well as lots of natural light and pockets of vegetation. Colours are handled as space markers as well as for defining three-dimensionality, for example, on the building frontage. Here, there are an assortment of both large and small windows set into the facade with deep, angled lines defined by different hues arranged in a distinctive, rhythmical pattern. Silhouettes of trees are also immediately obvious on the front elevation, perforated into the white aluminium exterior, and also adorning the doors and windows as adhesive films. Inside, light fills the space thanks to seven glass-encased courtyards, planted with trees and flowering plants. A constellation of leaf motifs in 24 different colours 'grow' on the white branches on the walls and glass windows – alongside the ATMs, bank tellers' counter, meeting rooms and office space – overlapping with the natural foliage of the real trees in the courtyards and creating a relaxing atmosphere of being surrounded by nature.

1 Like glass-encased greenhouses, the internal courtyards rise up through the height of the building, allowing natural light to pour into each floor.
2 The lyrical blocks of colour on the exterior of the building transform the facade itself into signage.

The concept sought to create a rejuvenating atmosphere

3

3   The leaf motifs are immediately obvious to
    customers entering the bank.
4   On the ground floor, an open seating area is
    laid out with chairs in 14 different colours.
5   Adhesive translucent film adorn the glass
    walls, with leaf-shaped coloured film
    positioned along the white branches.

4

5

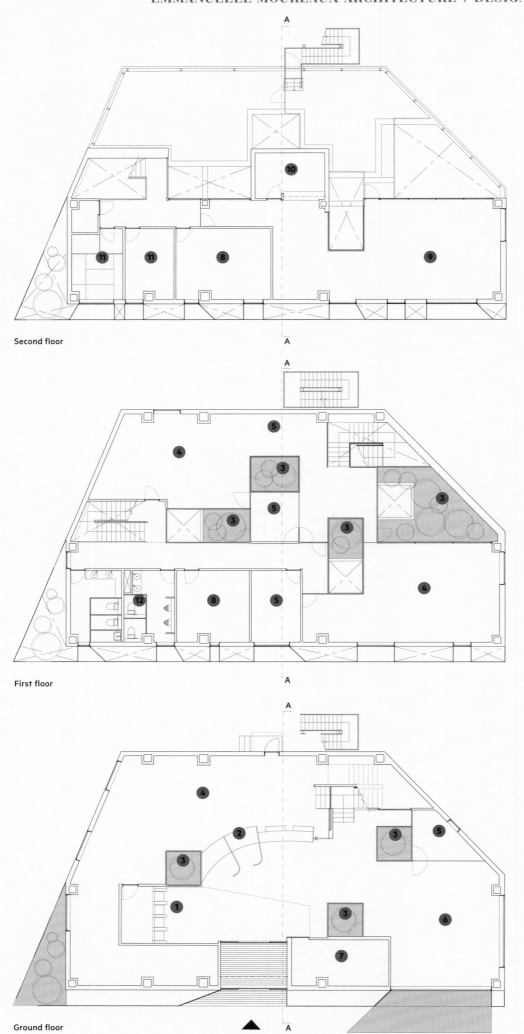

1 ATMs
2 Counter
3 Garden
4 Office space
5 Meeting space
6 Seating area
7 Safe-deposit box
8 Archive
9 Cafeteria
10 Kitchen
11 Locker room
12 Lavatory

Second floor

First floor

Ground floor

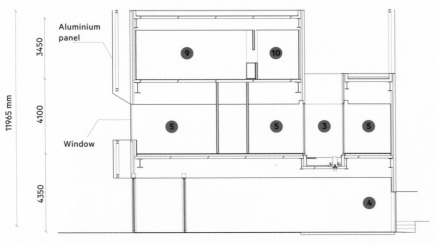

Aluminium panel

11965 mm

3450

4100

4350

Window

9

10

5

5

3

5

4

Section AA

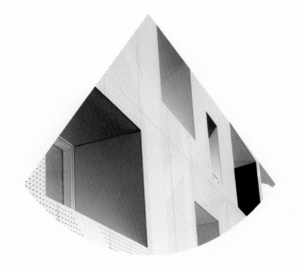

Aluminium perforated panels have been used to build the distinctive exterior, with the surrounds of the deep-set windows having a fluoro-resin paint finish.

Different hues are arranged in a distinctive, rhythmical pattern on the facade

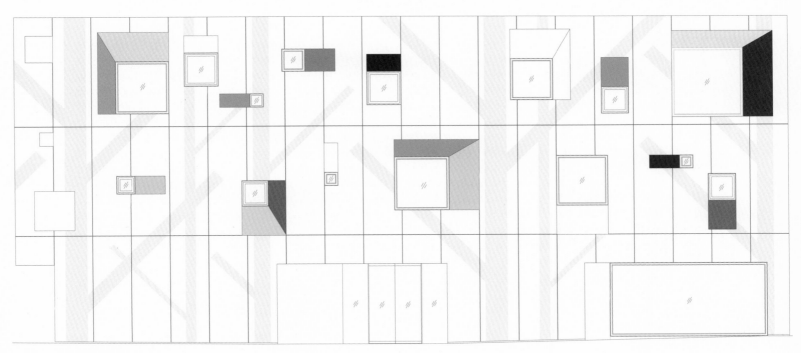

Drawing of the facade on which the tree silhouettes can be distinguished.

TELEKOM AUSTRIA

by BEHF ARCHITECTS

1

WHERE Vienna, Austria WHEN February 2010
CLIENT A1 Telekom Austria DESIGNER BEHF Architects (p.674)
TOTAL FLOOR AREA 102 m² SHOP CONSTRUCTOR BEHF Architects
PHOTOGRAPHER Bruno Klomfar

Telekom Austria aims to provide a reliable service to its customers whilst they live their lives, whether at home or out and about – almost as an inconspicuous part of their daily routine. BEHF Architects answered the brief for a new store in central Vienna with this in mind. The intention was to create a very homely and friendly atmosphere; the open and flexible design is an attempt to communicate to the public that a formerly government-owned company with a monopoly position also has the ability to be empathetic and to engage. The BEHF team decided to focus on one piece of furniture in particular – the table – in order to offer a high degree of recognition of the lifestyle of its customers. The table is a very ordinary object that people encounter every day, the same way in which communication products make a very natural appearance in the people's everyday lives. This stock furniture piece was reinterpreted creatively and given different functions: from the consultants' tables and display elements to cash desks and customer seating zones. The bespoke table designs resulted in a range of circular elements which offer flexibility and a multitude of layout options depending on how they are arranged or morphed into each other. The resulting varied arrangements, in combination with designer chairs and other fittings, create an open and airy shop design. The calming colour palette of white and lime green, with a touch of corporate red, also helps to instigate a relaxed and friendly atmosphere in-store.

1 The conventional counter situation is replaced by an inviting landscape of round tables which act as communication elements for customers, consultants and products.
2 The suspended luminaires combine a cosy and homely atmosphere with a modern, micro-prismatic diffused LED technology.

TICKET

by KONCEPT STOCKHOLM AND BVD

1

WHERE Sollentuna, Sweden WHEN October 2009
CLIENT Ticket Privatresor DESIGNERS Koncept Stockholm (p.680) and BVD (p.675)
TOTAL FLOOR AREA 68 m² SHOP CONSTRUCTOR Decorum
PHOTOGRAPHER Patrik Lindell

Ticket Leisure Travel is a retail chain that sells leisure travel from leading charter and tour operators, cruise lines and airline and hotel companies. In the business arena of private travel, where internet-based sales have taken large market shares in recent years, the competition for customers has increased significantly. Ticket understood that the internet alone would not meet their customers' service requirements and thus decided to invest in a new, modern shop concept. Koncept Stockholm (in charge of the architecture) and BVD (in charge of the graphic design) created a shop based on the idea of enticing emotions; the feeling of excitement that is instilled when you have just bought your ticket, are about to embark on a trip or finally arrive at your destination. The colour palette of red and white has been chosen

to portray a clear and energetic message. The design of the counters, which are positioned so as to reduce the gap between customer and sales staff, increase the feeling of openness and personal contact. Typography and images have received a new tonality, in order to increase the sensation of 'butterflies' and enhance the anticipation of the customer's impending vacation, with the use of dotted line graphics which can be interpreted as all the possible destination routes around the world.

1 The vibrant red colour used in the decor creates an energetic buzz in the shop, instilling a sense of adventure and inspiration to travel.
2 Red furniture, including the Speed chairs by Johansson Design, is positioned in the space decorated with graphics by BVD and phrases by copywriter Mattias Jersild, such as 'The earth has become heaven'.

2

Dotted lines represent all the possible
destination routes around the world

UPC

by STOREAGE

2

WHERE Dordrecht, the Netherlands WHEN October 2010
CLIENT UPC Netherlands DESIGNER Storeage (p.685)
TOTAL FLOOR AREA 125 m² SHOP CONSTRUCTOR Coors Interieurbouw
PHOTOGRAPHER Dim Balsem

UPC is a Dutch cable operator, providing customers with internet broadband, digital TV and telecom services. In an effort to enhance its innovation delivery and improve customer experiences in its stores, a brief was issued to Storeage calling for an attractive new retail experience. In order to meet the client's desire to deliver innovations to a wide audience, an entirely new concept was created for the flagship store. First, a dramatic new layout was incorporated, moving away from having one long service-desk and instead having an open floor-plan divided into separate room areas with multiple customer service points. The store was decorated in a corporate palette, with additional splashes of colour coming from the contemporary-designed sofas (by Nipa Doshi and Jonathan Levien for Moroso).

Furnishings were key to the new design, with carpeting and layered drapes delicately patterned with the client's logo providing a softer edge. This softening of the whole UPC experience – in the hope that this type of male-dominated TV store would become more attractive to the female audience – resulted in there being two distinct areas: the product area, resembling a TV studio behind screens; and the entertainment area 'in front of the screens' allowing customers to enjoy hassle-free entertainment. Connecting these two areas are the service desks that are spread out throughout the store on the divide between the blue product area and light-coloured entertainment area.

1 Home-style cabinets in front of the screens help customers visualise the services UPC can provide in terms of TV and internet.
2 The sofas and drapes in-store, symbolising the softer side of the UPC store, are visible from the exterior.

3

The store's decor targets a female audience in a usually male-dominated TV store

4

3 The upholstery and furnishings are delicately decorated with branded logos.
4 The cash desk and counter in corporate blue has tall glass cabinets positioned alongside displaying accessories and product packages.
5 On entering the store, the division between the 'behind the screens' and 'in front of the screens' areas is clearly visible.

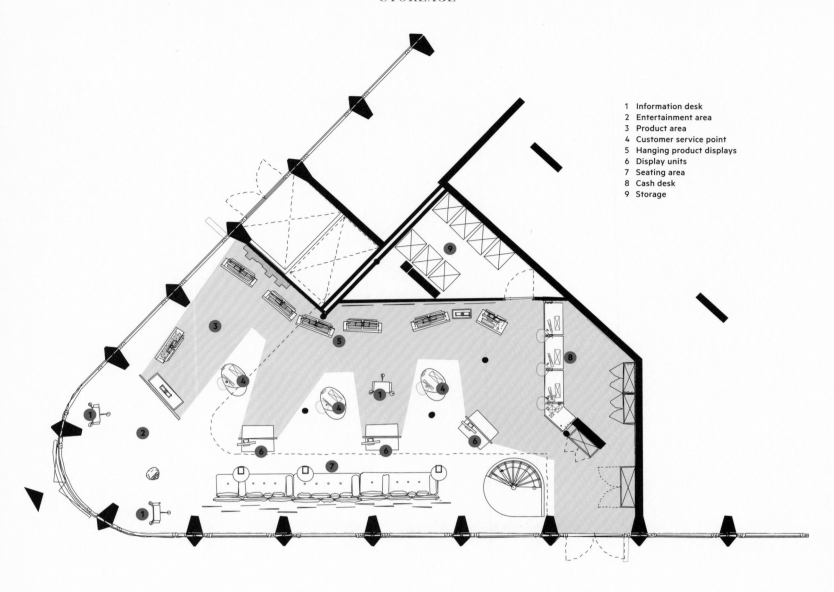

1 Information desk
2 Entertainment area
3 Product area
4 Customer service point
5 Hanging product displays
6 Display units
7 Seating area
8 Cash desk
9 Storage

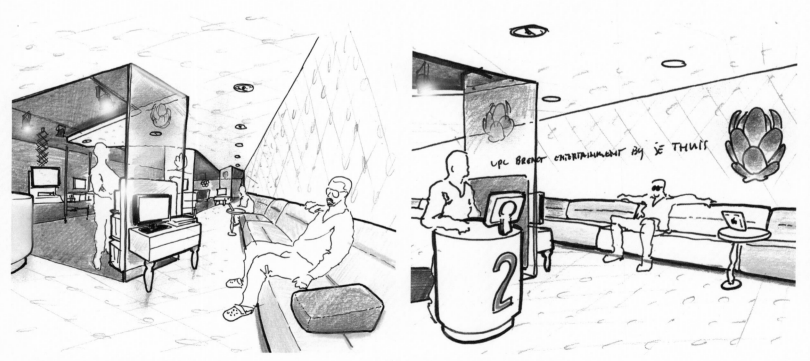

The furnishings act to delineate between the two areas in front and behind the screens.

Near the entrance, two information desks are positioned to welcome customers and direct them through the store emphasising UPC's commitment to friendly service.

A new retail concept was created to improve the customer experience

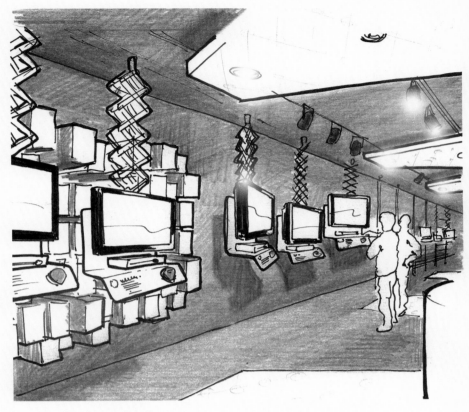

In the rugged product area, large flat-screen TV screens are suspended from the ceiling on chunky accordion-style steel arms.

The store concept delivers a new image for UPC that has kerb appeal and encourages new customers to enter the store.

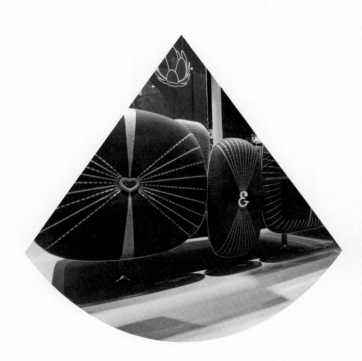

VIDEOTRON

by SID LEE ARCHITECTURE AND RÉGIS CÔTÉ AND ASSOCIATES

2

WHERE Montreal, Canada WHEN November 2010
CLIENT Videotron DESIGNERS Sid Lee Architecture (p.685) and Régis Côté and Associates (p.684)
TOTAL FLOOR AREA 400 m² SHOP CONSTRUCTOR Construction Albert Jean
PHOTOGRAPHER Sid Lee

One of Canada's leading telecommunications companies is Videotron. When seeking to develop a flagship store to showcase its new mobile services and attract potential customers, Sid Lee Architecture was brought on board and essentially given *carte blanche* to devise a project that would instill its unique brand identity. The main objective was to initiate an immersive experience for customers which would allow them to visualise the convergence of Videotron's products and services. With a limited range of physical products to be displayed in the retail space, this was done by offering dynamic platforms and architecture embedded with interactive technologies as a complete experimentation embodying the different services on offer. The illuminated multimedia staircase is the first thing that attracts customers' attention

on entering the store, with every step serving as an animated LED screen streaming promotional videos. The corporate colours of yellow and black are used throughout on reflective and textured materials, such as glass, bricks and porcelain tiles. The entranceway is designed as a glowing yellow cube – Videotron's brand icon – incorporating an intriguing, larger-than-life phone which invites customers to interact and begin to discover the client's expertise even before entering the store. From the street, the entire glass facade of the building is also a showcase of cutting-edge technology with a dynamic lighting grid that is continuously changing throughout the day.

1   The shop's textured glass facade, incorporating a dynamic lighting system, changes appearance over the course of the day and night.
2   The multimedia staircase is visually striking with ever-changing imagery. It is a bright, illuminated feature that captures the attention of customers as soon as they enter the store.

3 The high-tech staircase has LED screens placed behind the glass risers, with steps made of thin structural panels covered in two-colour porcelain tiles.

4 Interactive hub cylinders, suspended over the entrance, introduce customers to showcased Videotron products on touch-screen displays.

5 The client's corporate yellow is used in the glass panel balustrades that connect the lower and upper floors, with a contrasting highly-reflective lacquered black on the stretch fabric ceiling (by Extenzo).

5

3

4

The challenge was to conceptualise a store that provides services rather then products

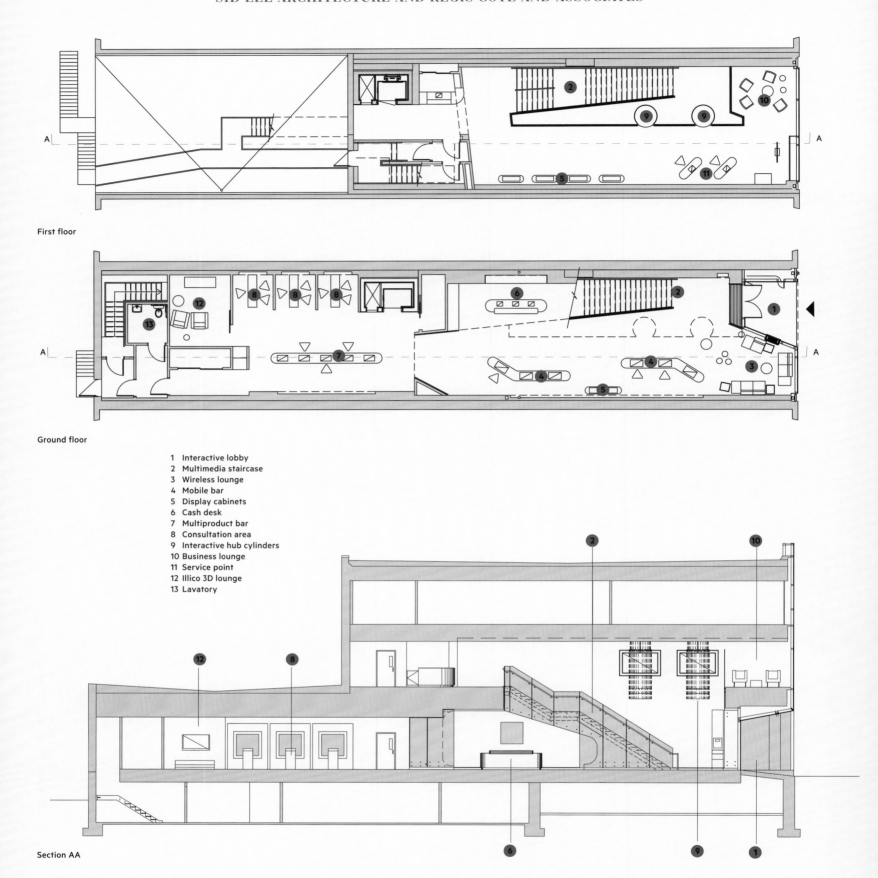

First floor

Ground floor

1   Interactive lobby
2   Multimedia staircase
3   Wireless lounge
4   Mobile bar
5   Display cabinets
6   Cash desk
7   Multiproduct bar
8   Consultation area
9   Interactive hub cylinders
10 Business lounge
11 Service point
12 Illico 3D lounge
13 Lavatory

Section AA

Interactive technologies initiated an immersive experience for customers

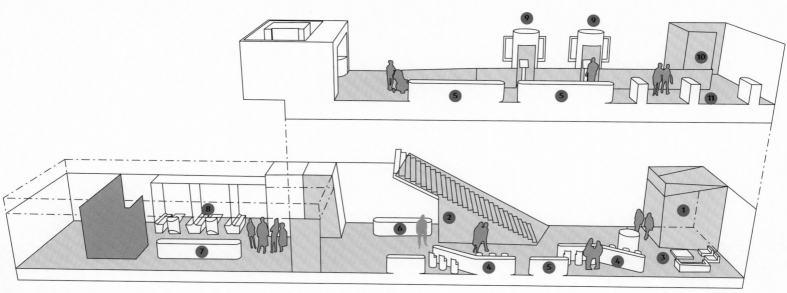

Axonometric drawing of the shop.

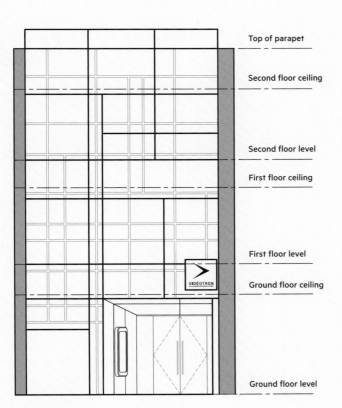

Top of parapet

Second floor ceiling

Second floor level

First floor ceiling

First floor level

Ground floor ceiling

Ground floor level

Front elevation

Stretch canvas ceiling

Stretch canvas ceiling

Curved tempered glass

Interactive console

Light box

Detail drawing of the interactive hub cylinders.

⚡ Novità

PASSA
A
WIND

CON LE OPZIONI
**NOI
TUTTI
NOI
WIND**

E PER UN ANNO
HAI IL
50%
DI SCONTO
SULL'OPZIONE
CHE PREFERISCI

INFORMATI QUI

-1

Offerta wind
Wind Theater
155
Consulenza
Commerciale

WIND

WIND

WIND

by CREA INTERNATIONAL

◆

2

WHERE Milan, Italy WHEN June 2010
CLIENT Wind Infostrada DESIGNER Crea International (p.676)
TOTAL FLOOR AREA 380 m² SHOP CONSTRUCTOR Cassina Contract
PHOTOGRAPHER Daniela Di Rosa

Wind is an integrated telecommunications services operator in Italy. Its flagship store, which opened in Milan in 2010, was designed by Crea International. The team, led by strategy director Marco De Carli and architect Viola Ladjeri, based the concept around the idea of creating a 'biosphere' capable of supporting a new species of retail telecom project. The harmoniously technological environment was to be a habitat sensitive to the balance of the different chromatic and morphological elements, with great emphasis placed on the materials used. Both levels of the shop feature highly-reflective surfaces throughout, with furniture custom-made from Corian. The organic shapes of the product display modules appear beneath the almost mirror-like fluid volumes emerging from the ceiling. These are vividly apparent from the exterior of the store due to the large windows, and the intriguing shapes entice customers to enter. The shop features an all-inclusive lounge and the Wind Theatre, where poplar wood wraps around the space, tinged with warm tones alongside the metallic silver of the back-wall. The incorporation of a scrolling, maxi-pixel screen translates one aspect of the high-tech nature of the concept, along with touch-screen terminals and LCD monitors. Corporate colours of orange and blue are used as visual aids to define specific areas, with vertical orange sections delineating the product display zones. The secondary use of blue has been strategically calibrated to give lightness to the design of the organic shapes. Reflected in the columnar structures, these colours merge creating a chromatic connection across the entire space.

1 An orange-coloured pathway curves from the main shop entrance, directing customers towards the doorway to the lower level.
2 The high-gloss environment is almost entirely devoid of sharp edges.

4

Colours merge to create a chromatic connection across the space

5

3 The storefront has floor-to-ceiling windows which gives maximum visibility of the interior to passers-by.
4 The design features organic shapes and an ensemble of expressions much more related to the hi-tech generation.
5 The scrolling maxi-pixel screen creates dynamic visual and narrative themes in the Wind Theater.

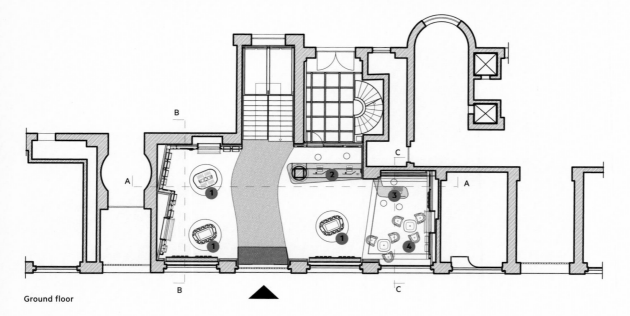

Ground floor

Basement

1 Display modules
2 Cash desk
3 Information desk
4 All-inclusive lounge
5 Wind Theatre
6 Consultation area
7 Locker room
8 Storage
9 Lavatories

The store is designed as a hierarchy-free, open and fluid space

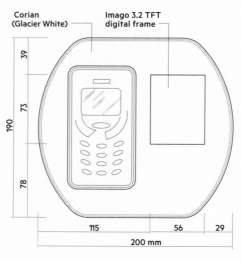

Corian (Glacier White)

Imago 3.2 TFT digital frame

39

73

190

78

115   56   29

200 mm

Front view

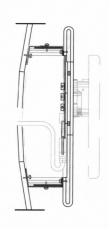

Side view

Innovative mobile holders: the devices are fully operative and secured to the podiums in such a manner so as to let customers handle them in a tangible way; functional and technical information is displayed on the mini-LCD screen alongside.

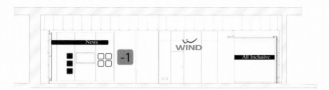

Section AA

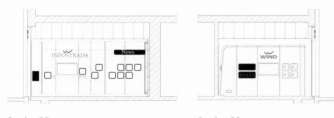

Section BB   Section CC

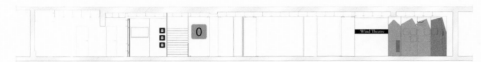

Section DD

Section EE

Section FF

Section GG

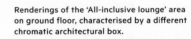

Renderings of the 'All-inclusive lounge' area on ground floor, characterised by a different chromatic architectural box.

Rendering of the organic-shaped display elements and teller stations.

YOU BY DIALECT

by ELECTRIC DREAMS

◆

1

WHERE Stockholm, Sweden WHEN December 2010
CLIENT You by Dialect DESIGNER Electric Dreams (p.677)
TOTAL FLOOR AREA 112 m² SHOP CONSTRUCTOR Expedit/NI
PHOTOGRAPHER Cesar af Reis

You by Dialect is a modern, playful chain of telecommunications stores for the tech-savvy consumer. Electric Dreams was commissioned to design a retail space that should be an appealing place for customers to browse, relax and get a taster for the latest products, whether trying out new apps, listening to music online or blogging directly from the store's computers. The studio's approach resulted in a friendly environment reminiscent of a quirky living room, a far cry from the traditional all-white consumer electronics interior. Dark wood tables in a vintage style were made from clear-lacquered MDF with black edges, on a turned wooden base which reflected the style of the original 1930s staircase. On entering down the stairs, the homely feel of the store – with its oversized, luxurious purple lampshades and glossy black picture frames which housed the product displays – was immediately apparent to customers. Contemporary furniture and an eye-catching chandelier made from laser cut, lacquered mirror lettering and positioned over the interactive display panel, added to the relaxed atmosphere. With staff inviting consumers to settle in with a coffee whilst testing out the high-tech gadgets at their leisure, it seems the concept realised by Electric Dreams certainly created a space where customers could be inspired.

1   The giant purple lampshades, upholstered with double-sided silk fabric on a steel-wire frame, are the biggest the supplier had ever made. The Slab Bar Stools positioned in the store are by Tom Dixon.
2   The chandelier is a typographic cloud and casts beautiful branded shadows. It was built on-site from thousands of lacquered mirror Perspex logo-types, individually hung on fishing tackle hooks from perforated metal panels.

1

The store has a content-centred aesthetic and a studio style

ZIGGO STUDIO

by DAY

2

WHERE Utrecht, the Netherlands WHEN August 2010
CLIENT Ziggo DESIGNER Day (p.677)
TOTAL FLOOR AREA 400 m² SHOP CONSTRUCTOR R2 project
PHOTOGRAPHER Ewout Huibers

Ziggo is a Dutch telecommunication company that recently entered the high-street market, having previously only sold products through selected detailers. For its dedicated retail space, Day was commissioned to develop a concept, design and business model. The brief was clear that Ziggo must set itself apart with fresh ideas and innovation. The solution that the design team came up had a content-centred approach, with the creation of the 'Ziggo Studio'. Here, the client's brand is the focal point having content, service and products on display in a hands-on studio. The interior design of the Utrecht store reflects this style and has a flexibility which makes for an easy environment to develop and update. Live recordings, meet-and-greets and workshops are combined with sales and service. At the entrance to the store, the sales area has a 6-m-high ceiling which gives the shop an open and spacious feeling. Customers can look up to see the mezzanine-type upper level where the stage and workshop areas are located. A bright colour palette is used for direction and way-finding. These fresh colours are also used to coat the metal tubing which is incorporated into the design of the product displays, which feature casters and appear to be on movable trolleys, adding to the flexible atmosphere. Coloured lines on the floor direct customers to the various areas of the shop; down to the lower level 'lab' area, where products can be tested out, or up to the split-level demonstration area or the top level with its stage and workshop areas.

1 The store incorporates creative aspects and is a hands-on experience for customers, with the 'lab area' being the testing ground for new products and installations.
2 From the mezzanine on the first floor, customers can grasp the spacious aspect of the store's entranceway.

5

Live recordings, meet-and-greets and workshops are combined with sales and service

6

3   The display modules can be moved and
    repositioned, giving a flexibility to the store
    design that fits in with the changing pace of
    the telecommunications industry.
4   At the back of the shop, customers can go
    down into the lab or explore upwards to the
    workshop zone. The mid-level is used as a
    pop-up store area.
5   The first floor is where customers can get
    involved in workshops or in any of the
    regular interactive activities. Sometimes
    this area turns into a recording studio.
6   The bespoke displays have metallic
    paintwork on the steel tubing which links in
    with the colours used for way-finding in the
    rest of the store.

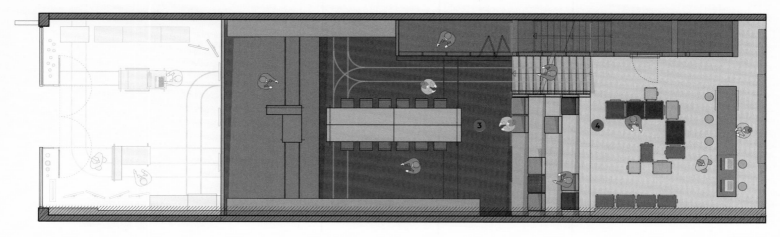

First floor

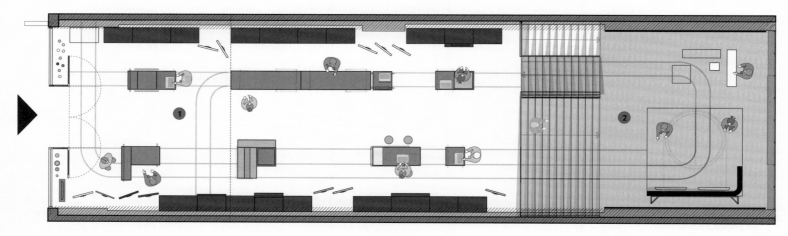

Ground floor

1 Sales and service area
2 Testing lab
3 Workshop area
4 Stage area

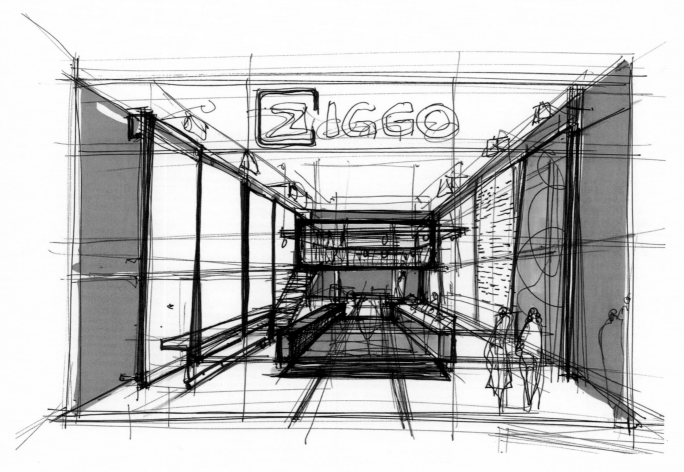

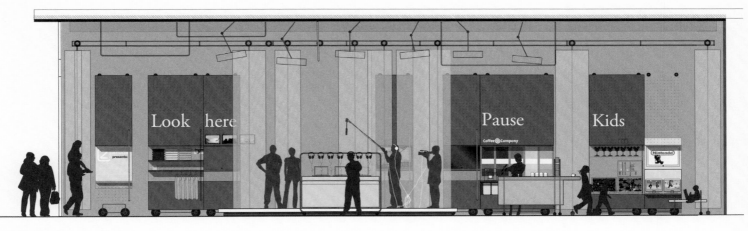

Display wall concept for the ground floor. Due to the modular nature of the design, many arrangements are possible.

Ziggo Studio is the place where consumers literally meet the provider's content

Hand-drawn pencil sketches outlining the store concept.

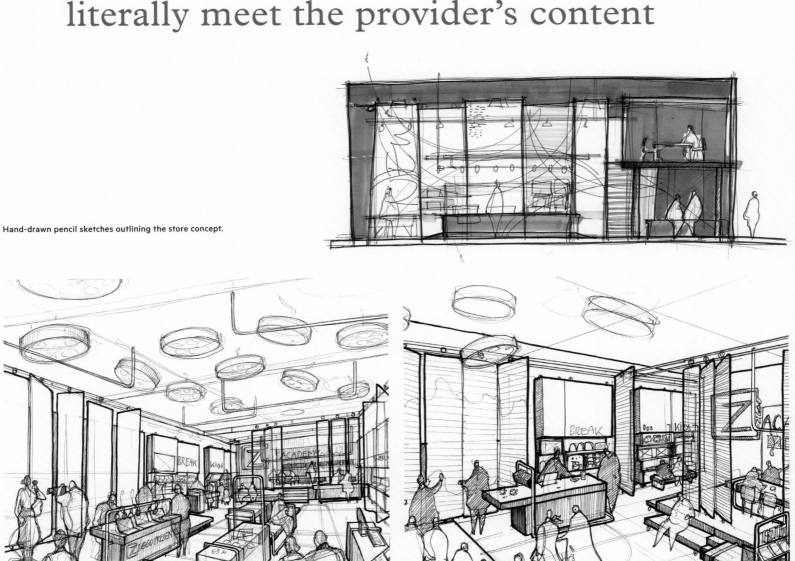

DESIGNER PROFILES

ÆDIFICA
606 Cathcart, Suite 800
H3B 1K9 Montreal
Quebec, Canada
+1 514 844 6611
www.aedifica.com
info@aedifica.com

(p.190, 198, 420)

Ædifica is a unified team of architects, designers, engineers and project managers who share a common desire to create meaningful and long-lasting environments. Operating since 1980, the firm now consists of over 115 professionals and staff providing integrated services with a commitment to sustainable development and a conviction that design is a powerful tool for expressing an identity.

AEKAE
Talwiesenstrasse 17
8045 Zurich
Switzerland
+41 43 960 2061
www.aekae.com
mail@aekae.com

(p.070, 620)

Based in Zurich, Aekae is an internationally-active design studio founded by Fabrice Aeberhard and Christian Kaegi in 2006. With a holistic approach to design, the studio works on a diverse range of projects with international clients across multiple disciplines, including interior, furniture, product, luxury goods, transportation and branding.

AHEADCONCEPT
Fossestrasse 77
30451 Hanover
Germany
+49 511 169 249 31
www.aheadconcept.de
mail@aheadconcept.de

(p.306)

Founded in 2000, AheadConcept is German design studio with offices in Hanover and Hamburg. The office specialises in branding, architecture and interior design by creating communicative spaces from concept to design to realisation. Its portfolio includes private residences, bars, restaurants, event design, retail and exhibition spaces.

ANOTHER COMPANY
Lombokstraat 32
3531 RE Utrecht
the Netherlands
+31 61 506 0581
www.anothercompany.org
info@anothercompany.org

(p.588)

Another Company, founded by Joachim Baan and based in the Netherlands, is a studio that develops and revitalises brands in a creative way. Encompassing communication design in the broadest sense, the company's philosophy on aesthetics goes beyond the boundaries of disciplines and mediums, giving the team the freedom to translate a creative direction through every element of a brand.

ANTONIO GARDONI
Via Ferramola 14
25121 Brescia
Italy
+39 348 259 1730
www.antoniogardoni.com
antonio@antoniogardoni.com

(p.054)

Antonio Gardoni, who spent years in London working with Ron Arad and co-founding Jump Studios, currently operates a design studio in Brescia, Italy and a branch in Beijing. Gardoni and partners Giovanni Pazzaglia and Julie Du believe in the power of combining marketing and design tools, and of using spaces and objects to communicate.

ARCHITECTURE AT LARGE
611 Broadway, Suite 531
New York, NY 10012
United States
+1 212 965 8755
www.architectureatlarge.com
enquiry@architectureatlarge.com

(p.174, 300)

Architecture at Large is the design studio of Rafael de Cárdenas. Based in New York, the company has a portfolio that focuses on residential and commercial interiors, architecture, furniture and integrated objects. The studio favours concept over strategy, the cosmopolitan over the genre- or era-specific, and the atmospheric over the static.
Photo Tim Barber

ARKTEAM
9 Frixou
54627 Thessaloniki
Greece
+30 231 050 0180
www.arkteam.gr
arkteam@arkteam.gr

(p.222)

Arkteam was founded in 1990 by architects Akis Bogdanos and Wassily Karalasos. Based in Greece, the studio has a multidisciplinary team working with an expertise and a core base of common principles to deliver a wide range of projects. Architectural output is driven by inventive ideas and strong concepts, whilst emphasising high quality detailing, atmosphere and materiality.

ART BUREAU 1/1
Leningradsky Propsekt 68/16
125315 Moscow
Russia
+7 495 508 3813
www.oneoverone.ru
studio@1over1.ru

(p.086)

The name of Art Bureau 1/1 reflects their motto: 'all what we do is unique, each design is the only of its kind'. The company's aim is to reflect their own and their clients ideas about art, aesthetics and taste, in both their commercial and private designs. The team of eight is specialised in interior design, architecture and decoration.

AS BUILT ARCHITECTS
Rue des Echevins 22
1050 Brussels
Belgium
+32 2649 9600
info@as-built.be
www.as-built.be

(p.140)

As Built is a Belgium-based architecture firm established by Olivier Hannaert. The company specialises in spaces accessible to the public, focusing on shops and hotels. For each project, the team defines, usually in association with an external designer, a unique theme, which frequently dips out of the architecture and creates a new experience for the user.

ASYLUM
69 Circular Road, #03-01
049423 Singapore
Singapore
+65 6324 2289
www.theasylum.com.sg
info@theasyum.com.sg

(p.124, 432)

Asylum is a creative company based in Singapore made up of a design studio, retail store, workshop and record label. Since its inception in 1999 by founder and creative director Chris Lee, the team has worked on cross-disciplinary projects in the realms of interactive design, product development, environmental design, interior and apparel design, packaging, branding and graphic design.

ATELIER 522
Fitzenweilerstrasse 1
88677 Markdorf
Germany
+49 754 4956 0522
www.atelier522.com
atelier@atelier522.com

(p.202, 226, 362)

Established in 2006 by Philipp Beck, atelier 522 is a creative agency of architects, designers and photographers. Its portfolio includes buildings, retail interiors, products and more. The team engages in new forms of expression through a mixing pot of energy, knowledge, talent and ideas in order to create what they dream.

ATELIER MARKGRAPH
Ludwig Landmann
Strasse 349
60487 Frankfurt
Germany
+49 69 979 930
www.markgraph.de
contact@markgraph.de

(p.528)

Established in 1986, the Frankfurt-based Atelier Markgraph specialises in spatial communication. The scope of the interdisciplinary design office ranges from exhibition and museum design to showrooms, trade-fair presentations and stage productions.

B-ARCHITECTEN
Borgerhoutsestraat 22/01
2018 Antwerp
Belgium
+32 3 231 8228
www.b-architecten.be
info@b-architecten.be

(p.576)

B-architecten is a design studio based in Antwerp which was established in 1997. The three co-founders, Evert Crols, Dirk Engelen and Sven Grooten, met each other through their educational training in Antwerp and Amsterdam where they developed common design interests. The company has an innovative team of 25 architects and designers working on residential, commercial and public projects.

BEHF ARCHITECTS
Kaiserstrasse 41
1070 Vienna
Austria
+43 1 5241 7500
www.behf.at
behf@behf.at

(p.642)

BEHF is an architecture company that was founded in 1995 by Armin Ebner, Susi Hasenauer and Stephan Ferenczy. The Vienna-based company currently has more than 90 employees, and its competencies and experience have established the studio with a network of clients stretching beyond the Austrian borders.

BENSCHOP
THE RETAIL FACTORY
Bleiswijkseweg 39
2712 PB Zoetermeer
the Netherlands
+31 79 330 0123
www.benschop.nl
info@benschop.nl

(p.076, 216, 364)

Dutch design firm Benschop was founded in 1943. With approximately 150 employed professionals, the company focuses on the development and realisation of shops, shopping malls and department stores. Benschop is a full service partner, involved in the whole process from concept development through to final delivery. Operating at an international level, Benschop serves both large and small businesses.

BLEEKER CONCEPTS
Groenmarktstraat 60
3521 AV Utrecht
the Netherlands
+31 30 890 3170
www.bleekerconcepts.nl
info@bleekerconcepts.nl

(p.106)

Interior architect Margareth Bleeker and architectural project manager Theo Franssen bundled their experience and founded Bleeker Concepts in 2006. From its office in Utrecht, the firm takes on projects in the fields of architecture, interior, lighting design, brand design and in-store communication. Although the major focus is on retail design, Bleeker Concepts has also completed hospitality, leisure, public space, office and healthcare projects.

BLOCHER
BLOCHER PARTNERS
Lessingstrasse 13
70174 Stuttgart
Germany
+49 711 22 482 0
www.blocherblocher.com
partners@blocherblocher.com

(p.260, 272)

Blocher Blocher Partners, founded in 1989 by architect Dieter Blocher and interior designer Jutta Blocher, has its core activities based on the competences of architecture and interior architecture. In cooperation with its subsidiaries, Blocher Blocher View and Blocher Blocher Shops, the firm works in brand development, mono brand concepts, corporate, retail and graphic design, as well as in visual merchandising and decoration concepts.
Photo Bernd Kammerer

BOND
Lönnrotinkatu 32 a 28
00180 Helsinki
Finland
+35 8 50 365 7328
www.bond-agency.com
info@bond-agency.com

(p.484)

Bond is a Helsinki-based independent creative agency with a multidisciplinary approach to branding and design. The company was founded and is run by designers with different specialities. The team's skill set covers strategic, graphic, product, digital and retail design. Bond's approach is characterised by attention to detail and a passion for quality.

BONGIANA ARCHITECTURE
Via Fra Giovanni Eremitano 12
35138 Padova
Italy
+39 049 661270
www.bongiana.it
studio@bongiana.it

(p.342)

Architect and designer Pietro Bongiana has worked in Europe and the United States and formed his first company Bong Bong in 1985. He established Bongiana Architecture in 2000 with an aim to pursue new projects collaborating with young architects. Working internationally, the studio focuses in the planning of commercial spaces, interventions and realisations of public and private architecture, interiors, graphics and design.

RONAN & ERWAN
BOUROULLEC
23 rue du Buisson St Louis
75010 Paris
France
+33 1 4200 4033
www.bouroullec.com
info@bouroullec.com

(p.550)

Ronan and Erwan Bouroullec, Breton-born brothers, have worked together as joint partners in their own design firm since 1999. Their collaboration is a permanent dialogue nourished by their distinct personalities. The firm's focus is primarily product design, from small utilitarian objects to furniture. In addition, they design interior spaces, installations and architectural projects.
Photo Ola Rindal

BREIL + PARTNER
INTERIOR DESIGN
Konigstrasse 30
22767 Hamburg
Germany
+49 40 4109 5908
www.breilundpartner.de
info@breilundpartner.de

(p.204)

The Hamburg-based agency Breil + Partner Interior Design was founded by Claudia Breil in 2006. The firm's main focus is overall brand communication within the textile industry and other retail areas. Completed projects include the design and realisation of stand-alone stores, shop-in-shops and department stores, as well as graphic design and brand development.

BRINKWORTH
4–6 Ellsworth Street
London E2 0AX
United Kingdom
+44 207 613 5341
www.brinkworth.co.uk
info@brinkworth.co.uk

(p.568)

Brinkworth is a design-led company working in architecture, interiors and furniture design as well as creative brand strategy and graphics. Formed in 1991 by founder Adam Brinkworth, one of the three directors along with Kevin Brennan and David Hurren, the company is based in London and has active projects around the world.

BUTTERFLY-STROKE
8f Hacchobori
Kitajima Building
1-8-2 Shintomi, Chuo-ku
104-0041 Tokyo
Japan
+81 3 5541 0061
www.butterfly-stroke.com
info@btf.co.jp

(p.448)

The Tokyo-based creative agency butterfly-stroke was established in 1999 by Katsunori Aoki. The company is primarily involved in the creative side of advertising, together with its character licensing division which was launched in 2003. The agency's approach is to find innovation through creation, always offering new insights and content to the world.

BVD
Asögatan 115
116 24 Stockholm
Sweden
+46 (8) 660 00 57
www.bvd.se
info@bvd.se

(p.644)

BVD is a Swedish design and branding agency specialising in every physical aspect of a brand which is related to the retail environment. Founded in 1997, the company has 15 people working on projects using a combination of consumer insights, business focus, ideas and design.

CAMPAIGN
16c Perseverance Works
25–27 Hackney Road
London E2 8DD
United Kingdom
+44 20 3222 0870
www.campaigndesign.co.uk
contact@campaigndesign.co.uk

(p.066, 562)

London-based design studio Campaign was founded by Philip Handford in 2009 to push the boundaries of the consumer experience. The studio is hands-on in exploring different media and methods in order to tell unique and engaging brand stories whilst developing integrated brand experiences through interior architecture and graphic design.

CHECKLAND
KINDLEYSIDES
Charnwood Edge
Cossington
Leicester LE7 4UZ
United Kingdom
+44 116 264 4700
www.checklandkindleysides.com
info@checklandkindleysides.com

(p.280)

The creative firm Checkland Kindleysides was established by Jeff Kindleysides in 1979. The multidisciplinary design studio defines strategy whilst creating brand identities, retail environments, exhibitions, in-store merchandising and graphic communication. The team's creativity is driven by robust customer, design and marketing insight and an ability to make things work aesthetically, physically and commercially.

CHRIS BRIFFA
3c, Old Mint Street
Valetta VLT 1510
Malta
+35 6 2122 1407
www.chrisbriffa.com
info@chrisbriffa.com

(p.476)

Architect Chris Briffa set up his architecture studio in 2004 in Valletta, Malta. The studio's work has become synonymous with skilful design focusing on proportion, materials and detail. Briffa's portfolio includes commercial, residential, public and private projects, from the restoration of historical buildings to the creation of contemporary spaces.
Photo Kris Micallef

COAST
264 Avenue Van Volxem
1190 Brussels
Belgium
+32 2 534 50 08
www.coastdesign.be
info@coastdesign.be

(p.140)

Coast is a Belgian creative studio working in the fields of branding, retail design, creative direction and graphic design. Founded in 1999 by Frédéric Vanhorenbeke, the studio uses research methods and creative processes to develop new ways of communication. Working with architects and designers to develop custom-made solutions for retail brands, the company's portfolio ranges from identity and signage to global rebranding.

COMO PARK STUDIO
Postbox 2032
1000 CA Amsterdam
the Netherlands
+31 20 436 0064
www.comoparkstudio.com
info@comoparkstudio.com

(p.588)

Como Park Studio specialises in interior architecture, from concept and design to execution. Established by Kenneth Jaworski in 2002, the studio has a broad portfolio of projects in the realms of retail, hotels, hospitality, trade fairs and the private sector. The company's mission is to design not only for who its clients are but also for who they'd like to become.

CONFETTI
Sevillaweg 132
3047 AL Rotterdam
the Netherlands
+31 10 476 2726
www.confettireclame.nl
info@confettireclame.nl

(p.594)

Confetti is a Dutch design studio headquartered in Rotterdam. For 25 years, the company has undertaken in-house projects in the realms of interiors, retail and exhibition stands, as well as product, furniture and graphic design. The Confetti team works to provide inspiring solutions with a young, fresh and innovative approach.

CORNEILLE UEDINGSLOHMANN ARCHITECTS
Konrad-Adenauer-Ufer 83
50668 Cologne
Germany
+49 221 355 5370
www.cue-architekten.de
info@cue-architekten.de

(p.240, 302)

The office of Corneille Uedingslohmann Architects seeks to provide comprehensive solutions in the sectors of architecture and shop design. Since its establishment by Yves Corneille and Peter Uedingslohmann in 2002, the office has grown into a mid-size practice with a portfolio that covers residential and commercial constructions and retail concepts for fashion and lifestyle brands.

CREA INTERNATIONAL
Via Voghera 7
20144 Milan
Italy
+39 02 4548 7558
www.creainternational.com
info@creainternational.com

(p.658)

Crea International is an Italian multidisciplinary design company based in Milan. Founded in 2002 by Alberto Pasquini and Massimo Fabbro, the company operates according to its own original design philosophy and methodology called 'Physical Brand Design'. The team delivers architectural brand experiences in retail, hospitality, real estate and corporate-building design.

CRENEAU INTERNATIONAL
Hellebeemden 13
3500 Hasselt
Belgium
+32 11 24 7920
www.creneau.com
info@creneau.com

(p.064, 616)

Creneau International is a global agency that connects brands, interiors and consumers through design concepts. Since it was established in Belgium 1989, the company has established a visionary reputation as an all-round creative consultancy developing concepts for shops, showrooms, hotels, restaurants, bars and nightclubs, as well as offices, exhibition stands and events.

DALZIEL AND POW
5–8 Hardwick Street
London EC1R 4RG
United Kingdom
+44 207 837 7117
www.dalziel-pow.com
info@dalziel-pow.com

(p.352, 356)

Dalziel and Pow is an integrated design consultancy which was established in 1983. The company, with offices in London, Mumbai and Shanghai, develops brand environments across a full range of arenas including retail interiors, graphic design, photographic art direction and website design. The firm uses a four stage process – define, create, realise, review – to harness creativity and deliver effective design solutions.

DAN PEARLMAN
Kiefholzstrasse 1–2
12435 Berlin
Germany
+49 305 300 0560
office@danpearlman.com
www.danpearlman.com

(p.348)

Founded in 1999, dan pearlman is a Berlin-based brand architecture and design agency. The company utilises a multi-dimensional strategy to communicate brands in real spaces and media-generated spaces. A team of 40 people contribute to the development and implementation of holistic solutions, enabling 360-degree communication with its clients working within four independent, specialised units: strategy, retail, exhibition and media.

DASTRO RETAILCONCEPTS
Zwaanshals 50
3035 KS Rotterdam
the Netherlands
+31 10 411 5028
dastro@dastro.nl
www.dastro.nl

(p.046)

In 2007, Rob Hoogendijk founded the design agency Dastro Retailconcepts. With a name that clearly highlights its core business, the firm has gathered experience in various branches of the industry, having designed interiors for fashion, shoe, perfume and jewellery stores, plus pharmacies, opticians and spaces for the automotive and telecom sectors.

DAY
Keizersgracht 121
1915 CJ Amsterdam
the Netherlands
+31 20 771 5077
info@day.nu
www.day.nu

(p.178, 296, 666)

Day was established in Amsterdam in 2006 by Louk de Sévaux, Dennis de Rond and Gesina Roters, and now also has offices in Dubai and New York. Day is a cross between both a management and brand consultancy and an advertising and design agency. The company serves international clients in projects that include consultancy, brand strategy, retail and packaging design, and communications.

DESIGNCULTURE
Sempacherstrasse 15
8032 Zurich
Switzerland
+41 43 960 7080
info@designculture.ch
www.designculture.ch

(p.542)

Established in 2001, Designculture is a creative agency located in Zurich, Switzerland. The company unites comprehensive know-how in the development and design of three-dimensional forms of appearance, developing solutions for spaces, products and furniture. Projects include interior design concepts, guide systems, corporate design, communication design, product development, exhibition styling, trade-fair appearance, retail design and stagings.
Photo L. Eaton

DFROST
Hauptstätterstrasse 59a
70178 Stuttgart
Germany
+49 711 664 8170
info@dfrost.de
www.dfrost.com

(p.096)

Founded in 2008, visual marketing design firm dfrost focuses on the inception and realisation of retail concepts. From interiors and window displays to communication tools and point-of-sale activities, every project is taken on by a multidisciplinary team with a focus on attention to detail. The Stuttgart-based firm is headed by Christoph and Fabian Stelzer and Nadine Frommer.

DIEGO BORTOLATO ARCHITETTO
Via Frontoni 1
15048 Valenza
Italy
+39 0131 482732
info@diegobortolato.it
www.diegobortolato.it

(p.074, 596)

Architect Diego Bortolato began his career in 1998. He has worked in Milan and London and, in 2009, he set up his own architecture firm. Working from his studio in the Italian city of Valenza, Bortolato is specialised in luxury retail spaces and jewellery shops. Currently, he designs private residences.

DITTEL ARCHITEKTEN
Rotenwaldstrasse 100/1
70197 Stuttgart
Germany
+49 711 4690 6550
info@d-arch.de
www.d-arch.de

(p.428)

Dittel Architekten, based in Stuttgart, was founded in 2005 by Frank Dittel. The team manages a wide variety of architectural and interior design projects for retail and corporate clients. A creative approach is at the forefront for Dittel, seeking solutions shaped with the building blocks of contemporary design language and the demands of architecture and design.

D-RAW
23b Goodge Place
London W1T 4SN
United Kingdom
+44 207 636 0016
info@d-raw.com
www.d-raw.com

(p.320, 326)

London-based architectural and interior design collective d-raw has a diverse portfolio of bespoke design which spans every creative niche. Experts in branded environments, retail design and renovation, the team has a passion for unusual commissions and an uncompromising understanding of the dialogue necessary to create great design.

EDGE ARCHITECTURE + DESIGN
3rd Floor, Shand House
14–20 Shand Street
London SE1 2ES
United Kingdom
+44 207 993 9790
www.edge-a-d.com
marketing@edge-a-d.com

(p.454)

Edge Architecture + Design was founded in 2005 by Racheal Cadey and Julia Leckey. Based in London, the design and architectural business offers a holistic mix of design services across the retail, office, leisure, residential and mixed use sectors. Services include workplace and retail strategy, architecture, interior and graphic design, branding and marketing communications.

ELECTRIC DREAMS
Nytorgsgatan 19
116 22 Stockholm
Sweden
+46 736 553 292
www.electricdreams.se
info@electricdreams.se

(p.664)

Electric Dreams is an architecture and design studio based in Stockholm, Sweden. Established in 2006 by Joel Degermark (product designer) and Catharina Frankander (architect), the design team works to create brand environments and products which are based around story-telling and themes, with a fascination for exaggeration, shifting scales and visual effects.

EMMANUELLE MOUREAUX ARCHITECTURE + DESIGN
3f Tounkyo Building, 1-14-14
Uchikanda, Chiyoda-ku
101-0047 Tokyo
Japan
+81 3 3293 0323
www.emmanuelle.jp
contact@emmanuelle.jp

(p.252, 636)

French-born Emmanuelle Moureaux is an architect and designer residing in Tokyo since 1996. Having established her architecture and design firm in 2003, she has been developing her own concept of *shikiri*, which is Japanese for 'dividing (creating) space with colours'. This is evident throughout her portfolio of projects, which includes architecture, interior, furniture and products.

FOUND ASSOCIATES
14–16 Great Pulteney Street
London W1F 9ND
United Kingdom
+44 207 734 8400
www.foundassociates.com
info@foundassociates.com

(p.572)

Found Associates is an architectural and interior design consultancy, based in London, specialising in retail, commercial and residential projects. Established in 1997 by Richard Found, the company has a creative team of interior designers and architects working across a wide variety of sectors from initial concept to complete on-site project management.

FRANCESC RIFÉ STUDIO
Escoles Pies 25
08017 Barcelona
Spain
+34 93 414 1288
www.rife-design.com
f@rife-design.com

(p.410)

Francesc Rifé founded his interior and industrial design studio in 1994. Based in Barcelona with a team of more than ten designers and architects, the studio specialises in commercial and private projects which encompass spatial order and geometric proportion with a portfolio covering interior and industrial landscapes.

FREELANDBUCK
2404 Wilshire Blvd, Suite 9e
Los Angeles, CA 90057
United States
+1 323 540 4346
www.freelandbuck.com
info@freelandbuck.com

(p.374)

FreelandBuck is an architectural design practice based in New York and Los Angeles affiliated to Yale and Woodbury Universities. Founded by David Freeland and Brennan Buck in 2009, the practice focuses on research and design, exploring the overlap between academia and practice in urban and interior architecture.

FREITAG
Binzmühlestrasse 170b
8050 Zurich
Switzerland
+41 43 210 3309
www.freitag.ch
media@freitag.ch

(p.050)

Freitag was formed in 1993 by two graphic designers, brothers Markus and Daniel Freitag, to produce messenger bags made from recycled truck tarpaulins. The original product line, Fundamentals, now has over 40 models, with a second seasonal product line, Reference, introduced in 2010. The company is headquartered in Zurich and has 130+ employees with flagship stores in Austria, Germany, Japan, Switzerland and the United States.

GAD
Tesvikiye Cad. 3b Gunes
Apt, Tesvikiye
Istanbul 34367
Turkey
+90 212 327 5125
www.gadarchitecture.com
gad@gadarchitecture.com

(p.468)

Global Architectural Development (GAD) has offices in Bodrum and Istanbul, Turkey and New York, United States. Founded by Gokhan Avcioglu in 1994, the GAD team performs architectural practice, research and concept design, both independently and with its global collaborators. The company seeks innovative approaches to architecture, creating new spatial experiences with projects and ideas.

GH+A
1100 avenue des Canadiens-de-Montreal, Suite 130
H3B 2S2 Montreal
Quebec, Canada
+1 514 843 5812
www.ghadesign.com
dkalisky@ghadesign.com

(p.416)

Founded in 1985, GH+A has a visionary approach to retail design which focuses on creating dynamic environments. Its portfolio includes specialty store design, shopping centre refurbishments and mixed-use retail programming. With offices in Montreal, Quebec and Detroit, Michigan, the GH+A team designs with an international outlook. Every project is an opportunity to make retail more vital.

GIANLUCA RE ARCHITETTO
C.So Garibaldi 102
15048 Valenza
Italy
+39 013 192 7420
www.unitadiprogetto.it
info@unitadiprogetto.it

(p.074)

With degrees in fashion and architecture, Gianluca Re focuses on retail interiors and exhibition design. Through his renewed and growing interest in energy-efficient architecture and green building technologies, he now specialises in the field of sustainable design.

GIORGIO BORRUSO DESIGN
333 Washington
Boulevard, #352
Marina Del Rey, CA 90292
United States
+1 310 821 9224
www.borrusodesign.com
info@borrusodesign.com

(p.492, 552)

Giorgio Borruso Design is a multidisciplinary design firm, based in Los Angeles, creating innovative works ranging from architecture to interiors and industrial design. Under the leadership of Italian architect Giorgio Borruso, the firm develops projects and unique brand statements for international client brands across the globe.

GLAMOROUS
2f, 2-7-25 Motoazabu
Minato-ku
106-0046 Tokyo
Japan
+81 3 5475 1037
www.glamorous.co.jp
info@glamorous.co.jp

(p.402, 464, 466)

Designer Yasumichi Morita established his own design office in Japan in 2000. The Glamorous office, which relocated to Tokyo at the start of 2011, now has a team of around 30 professionals. The remit of the company lies in various domains, including interior, graphic and product design.
Photo I. Susa

**GLENN SESTIG
ARCHITECTS**
Fortlaan 1
9000 Gent
Belgium
+32 9240 1190
www.glennsestigarchitects.com
contact@glennsestigarchitects.com

(p.332)

Glenn Sestig studied architecture at the Henry Van de Velde Institute in Antwerp and went on to found his own architectural firm in 1999. The focus of the firm is to realise contemporary, chic projects. He aims to evolve cities into better places by applying his signature cosmopolitan and luxurious style to stores, bars, nightclubs, residential buildings, renovations, temporary projects and products.

**GRAYSCALED DESIGN
COLLECTIVE**
1355 48th Ave #3
San Francisco, CA 94122
United States
+1 510 409 8285
www.grayscaled.org
grayscaleddesign@gmail.com

(p.538)

Grayscaled Design Collective is a collaboration between Sarah Hobstetter, Elizabeth Jackson and Jessica Stuenkel, who all met in 2010 whilst studying for their master of architecture degree at the College of the Arts. Based in San Francisco, the studio's work is ongoing alongside the team's individual projects which include a public amenities space and a psychotherapy centre.

HAYON STUDIO
C/ Convento De Santa Clara
10, Puerta 9ª
46002 Valencia
Spain
+34 93 532 1776
www.hayonstudio.com
info@hayonstudio.com

(p.080)

Spanish artist–designer Jaime Hayon started his own studio in 2005. The combination of his industrial design studies and the skateboard and graffiti art culture he submerged himself in as a teenager resulted in the detailed, bold-yet-whimsical imagery so prominent in his work. Starting off with a collection of designer toys, ceramics and furniture, he then began creating interiors and installations.

HEIKAUS INTERIOR
Hessigheimer Strasse 63
74395 Mundelsheim
Germany
+49 7143 969 290
www.heikaus.de
mail@heikhaus.de

(p.246)

Heikaus encompasses more than 30 years of experience in the areas of store design and architecture. The German company, which was originally founded in 1977, has a special focus realising interiors for fashion brands. Following repositioning and expansion over the years, the firm now has two main divisions – Heikaus Interior and Heikaus Concept – with a sister company Heikaus in Switzerland.

HMKM
14–16 Great Pulteney Street
London W1F 9ND
United Kingdom
+44 207 494 4949
www.hmkm.com
info@hmkm.com

(p.248, 346)

Founded in 1990 and based in London's Soho district, design consultancy HMKM consists of specialists in the fields of branding, architecture, interior design, graphic design and art direction. Tailor-made project teams help clients to realise their brand vision, no matter what the scale of the project.

HOUSEHOLD
135 Curtain Road
London EC2A 3BX
United Kingdom
+44 207 739 6537
www.household-design.com
michelle@household-design.com

(p.294, 558)

Household is a design consultancy based in London. Founded in 2004, the company specialises in designing retail brand experiences, communications and identities. An integrated team brings enthusiasm and experience to creatively execute projects in the fashion, food and drink, telecoms, hotel and luxury sectors.

IGLOODGN
2160 de la Montagne,
Suite 200
H3G 2T3 Montreal
Quebec, Canada
+1 514 933 4456
www.igloodesign.ca
hello@igloodesign.ca

(p.228)

Igloodgn is a Montreal-based interior design and branding firm founded by Anna Abbruzzo and Alain Courchesne in 2005. The company utilises an environmental approach to design and strives to create interiors that lift the spirit. Its portfolio includes projects such as poker clubs, hotels, spas, fitness centres, retail boutiques and restaurants.

**INGIBJORG AGNES
JONSDOTTIR**
Marargata 7
101 Reykjavík
Iceland
+354 844 1540
www.ingibjorgagnes.com
info@ingibjorgagnes.com

(p.122)

Ingibjorg Agnes Jonsdottir is an interior and spatial designer based in Reykjavik. After graduating from Chelsea College Of Art And Design in 2001, she worked for architectural firms in London and New York. Since returning to Iceland in the summer of 2006, Jonsdottir has been working independently, creating interiors for residential and commercial design projects.

IPPOLITO FLEITZ GROUP
Augustenstrasse 87
70197 Stuttgart
Germany
+49 7119 9339 2330
www.ifgroup.org
info@ifgroup.org

(p.024, 038)

Ippolito Fleitz Group is a multidisciplinary, internationally-operating design studio based in Stuttgart. The studio is made up of identity architects and aims to develop products, architecture and communication projects that are part of a whole and yet distinctive in their own right. The team conceives and constructs buildings, interiors and landscapes next to products and communication measures.

ITO MASARU DESIGN PROJECT/SEI
101 Daikanyama Tower, 1-35-11
Ebisunishi, Shibuyaku
150-0021 Tokyo
Japan
+81 3 5784 3201
www.itomasaru.com
sei@itomasaru.com

(p.006, 128)

Designer Ito Masaru graduated from Tokyo Zokei University in 1987. He went on to establish his own studio in Tokyo to focus on design projects with a sharp sensibility. The studio's distinct style ensures interior spaces are created from a consumer's perspective. Projects include retail concepts, architecture and exhibition stands.

JAKOB + MACFARLANE
13–15 rue des Petites Ecuries
75010 Paris
France
+33 1 4479 0572
www.jakobmacfarlane.com
info@jakobmacfarlane.com

(p.488)

Jakob + MacFarlane is an architectural firm based in Paris, France. Established in 1992 by Dominique Jakob and Brendan MacFarlane, the studio's work incorporates digital technology both as a conceptual consideration and as a means of fabrication, using new materials as a possibility to create a more flexible, responsive and immediate environment.

JAMO ASSOCIATES
1f Sunflat Iigura Building
1-6-9 Azabudai, Minato-ku
106-0041 Tokyo
Japan
+81 3 5545 3639
www.jamo.jp
info@jamo.jp

(p.044, 350, 586)

Jamo associates is an interior design office based in Tokyo. Established in 2000 by interior designer Norito Takahashi and interior stylist Chinatsu Kambayashi, the office creates concepts that combine the ideas of both designer and stylist from the very beginning of a project, whether shaping retail spaces and interiors or undertaking product design.

JAYME LAGO MESTIERI ARCHITECTURE
Al Casa Branca, 851 Jardins
01408 001 São Paulo
Brazil
+55 11 3062 2885
www.jaymelagomestieri.arq.br
contat@jaymelagomestieri.arq.br

(p.458, 498)

Architect Jayme Lago Mestieri founded his own architecture practice in 1999 in São Paulo, Brazil. Since then, the studio has built up a portfolio which covers retail, commercial and public spaces, as well as food service projects. The team specialises in designing flagships and shopping centres with accompanying brand concepts and graphic design.

K1P3 ARCHITECTS
18 Shmaryahu Levin St Shop
64357 Tel Aviv
Israel
+972 54 300 1213
www.k1p3architects.com
studio@k1p3architects.com

(p.042, 318, 338)

Design studio k1p3 architects was established in 2000 in Tel Aviv by Karina Tollman and Philipp Thomanek. Since its inception, the studio has undertaken a large variety of projects in both the public and private spheres, ranging from private houses to public institutions, commercial spaces, bars and restaurants, as well as art related gallery projects.

KAUFFMANN THEILIG & PARTNER
Zeppelinstrasse 10
73760 Ostfildern
Germany
+49 711 451 220
www.ktp-architekten.de
info@ktp-architekten.de

(p.528)

The architecture office of Dieter Ben Kauffmann, Andreas Theilig and Rainer Lenz – Kauffmann Theilig & Partner – realises projects in the fields of building construction and exhibition design. Founded in 1988, the office cultivates an intensive collaboration with experts and engineers to achieve integrated architectural solutions with an interdisciplinary team.

KEISUKE FUJIWARA
3-20-1-202 Honmachi
Shibuya-ku
151-0071 Tokyo
Japan
+81 3 5333 5791
www.keisukefujiwara.com
design@keisukefujiwara.com

(p.138)

Keisuke Fujiwara is an interior and furniture designer based in Tokyo. After graduating from Musashino Art University, he worked at the Japanese interior design firm Studio 80 from 1992 to 2001. After a brief time in London working for an architectural firm, he then returned home to establish his own design office. The company's portfolio includes commercial and residential interior design, exhibition spaces and product design.

KINNERSLEY KENT DESIGN
5 Fitzroy Square
London W1T 5HH
United Kingdom
+44 207 691 3131
www.kkd.co.uk
hello@kkd.co.uk

(p.218, 258)

Kinnersley Kent Design is an independent retail interior and graphic design consultancy with studios in London and Dubai. Founded by Glenn Kinnersley and Mick Kent in 1990, Paul McElroy became a third partner in 2005. The consultancy's diverse portfolio spans fashion houses to food halls, automotive showrooms to hotels and department stores.

KONCEPT STOCKHOLM
Grev Turegatan 29
114 38 Stockholm
Sweden
+46 8 545 879 00
www.koncept.se
info@koncept.se

(p.144, 644)

Koncept Stockholm is an architecture and design firm based in Sweden. The company has a creative team of 35 employees working in the areas of design, architecture and concept development, with a product portfolio including retail, hotels and offices. Koncept produces unique environments which create value and a competitive advantage for its clients.

KRÄF•TE
301801 Nakatsu, Kita-ku
531-0071 Osaka
Japan
+81 6 6375 8368
www.mdnc-krafte.com
information@mdnc-krafte.com

(p.172)

Designer Yukio Kimura established the kräf•te studio in 2005 in Osaka, Japan. It offers total design solutions for interiors, along with graphic design and product design. The studio's portfolio is primarily split between interior design projects (retail, restaurants and exhibition spaces) and product design (chairs, tables and lampshades).

KUUB
Singel 250
1016 AB Amsterdam
the Netherlands
+31 619210915
www.kuub.nu
info@kuub.nu

(p.310)

Kuub is an Amsterdam-based design studio which was set up by Pascal Hielckert and Jos van Dijk. The studio's portfolio includes architecture and interior projects, as well as furniture design. Architectural identity is at the centre of the studio's working method, which aims for the direct translation of identity to architecture, interior and materials.

LAURENT DEROO ARCHITECTE
5 rue Lesault
93500 Pantin
France
+33 960 085 228
www.laurentderooarchitecte.com
archi.panorama@gmail.com

(p.194, 196)

Architect Laurent Deroo founded his architecture studio near the French capital Paris in 2008. Before that time, his career had a double focus and he worked as both an art director of films and as an independent architect. His studio realises architectural projects including the interior design of various retail, residential, office and hospitality projects, as well as furniture design.

LEONG LEONG
56 Ludlow Street, 35e
New York, NY 10002
United States
+1 917 428 8858
www.leong-leong.com
info@leong-leong.com

(p.184)

Brothers Christopher and Dominic Leong founded the design office Leong Leong in New York in 2008. In constant dialogue, critical conversation, analysis and experimentation, the team uses a concept-based approach to design. The studio practices in the fields of architecture, culture and urbanism, driven by a commitment to ideas and their realisation.

LINE-INC
Kazami Bld-3f, 1-1-6
Higashiyama, Meguro-ku
153-0043 Tokyo
Japan
+81 357 733 536
www.line-inc.co.jp
line@line-inc.co.jp

(p.034, 214, 290)

The design firm Line-Inc was established in Tokyo in 2002 by Katsuta Takao, who had also previously established Exit Metal Work Supply in 1996 with four other designers. Line-Inc consists of a team of eleven professionals, creating interiors for a wide variety of retail projects. The company is also accomplished in product design and in 2004 established the subsidiary Line-Products.

LOGICA:ARCHITETTURA
Via Legnone 4
20158 Milan
Italy
+39 02 4547 4886
www.logica-architettura.it
studio@logica-architettura.it

(p.224)

Based in Milan, the design company Logica:architettura was founded in 1998 by Riccardo Salvi. The studio primarily deals with architecture, interior and furniture design projects from concept to realisation. The studio is dedicated to research, continually looking for new techniques of construction, novel materials and innovative technologies.

LOLA
Joaquin Costa 24-4
08001 Barcelona
Spain
+34 617 297 063
www.lola-architecture.com
info@lola-architecture.com

(p.208)

LOLA, the 'local office for large architecture', was established by Rute Brazão, Sandra Carito Ribeiro and Riccardo Cavaciocchi in 2002 in Barcelona. The studio is a platform for multi-disciplinary architecture and contemporary design. The team's approach utilises critical, positive and pluralist thinking in order to develop projects in various sectors, from the interior design of retail spaces to the full-scale conversion and renovation of buildings.

MADLAB
427 Bloomfield Avenue,
Suite 402
Montclair, NJ 07042
United States
+1 973 233 9296
www.madlabllc.com
info@madlabllc.com

(p.400)

Madlab is an architecture firm based in New Jersey. Founded in 2003 by Petia Morozov and Jose Alcala, the firm has a team of design professionals with a unique vision and a masterful expression of space, materials and systems. Every project is approached with a creative collaborative mindset, from the design of new structures to the renovation of existing buildings.

MAKOTO YAMAGUCHI DESIGN
2-8-17-1f Minami Azabu
Minato-ku
106-0047 Tokyo
Japan
+81 3 6436 0371
www.ymgci.net
mail@ymgci.net

(p.474)

Makoto Yamaguchi Design was established in 2001 in Tokyo. The studio aims to find creative solutions to specific needs and takes an original approach to architectural and interior design. Its portfolio includes private residences and commercial buildings, as well as product design.

MERKX+GIROD ARCHITECTS
Gietersstraat 23
1015 HB Amsterdam
the Netherlands
+31 20 523 0052
www.merkx-girod.nl
arch@merkx-girod.nl

(p.166)

Merkx+Girod Architects offers its clients expertise in both architecture and interior design. Established in 1996, the firm's portfolio includes offices, museums, public buildings, retail spaces and private residences. Based in Amsterdam, a team of over 30 staff employ an analytical approach and a quartet of core values: detail, coherence, elegance and quality.

MICHELGROUP
Binzstrasse 23
8045 Zurich
Switzerland
+41 442 507 474
www.michelgroup.eu
office@michelgroup.eu

(p.216)

For over 40 years, Michelgroup has developed and designed national and international projects with the planning of urban retail projects as the primary focus. Led by Wolfgang Michel and Kevin Roche from its headquarters in Zurich, the firm's core competencies include strategy, architecture, interior design and project management.

MINISTRY OF DESIGN
20 Cross Street #03-01
048422 Singapore
Singapore
+65 6222 5780
www.modonline.com
studio@modonline.com

(p.158)

Ministry of Design was created by architect Colin Seah in Singapore in 2004. An integrated spatial-design practice, MOD's explorations are created amidst a democratic studio-like atmosphere and progress seamlessly between form, site, object and space. The studio's portfolio includes projects in architectural, interior, product and experience design.

MYKITA
Brunnenstrasse 153
10115 Berlin
Germany
+49 30 2045 6633
www.mykita.com
mail@mykita.com

(p.078)

Mykita's in-house workshop in Berlin has been supplying hand-crafted eyewear for the high-end segment since 2003. From the design and production to the marketing; everything is united under one roof at the firm's headquarters. The creative core behind the brand are its four founders, Moritz Krueger, Philipp Haffmans, Daniel Haffmans and Harald Gottschling.

NEZU AYMO ARCHITECTS
Damrak 70, studio 3 58
1012 LM Amsterdam
the Netherlands
+31 20 423 3615
www.nezuaymo.com
info@nezuaymo.com

(p.504)

The studio of Nezu Aymo Architects was founded in April 2009 by Yukiko Nezu and Skafte Aymo-Boot in Amsterdam. The duo has a critical curiosity for the building process and the materials used. Through research and unconventional thinking, the Japanese–Danish design team has developed a portfolio that includes new buildings, urban plans, interiors and spatial concepts.

NINKIPEN!
530-0047 Tomii, Bldg 4f
Nishitenma
1-7-12 Kita-ku, Osaka
Japan
+81 6 6241 0662
www.ninkipen.jp
imazu@ninkipen.jp

(p.404)

In 2005, Yasuo Imazu founded the ninkipen! architecture office in Osaka, Japan. After completing his studies at Osaka University and following a time working for another architecture firm, Imazu decided to establish his own studio in order to concentrate on a broad variety of architectural and interior design, including retail, residential and corporate projects.

NORIYUKI OTSUKA DESIGN OFFICE
6-13-5 Minamiaoyama
Minato-ku
107-0062 Tokyo
Japan
+81 3 3406 6341
www.nodo.jp
nodo@blue.ocn.ne.jp

(p.276)

Noriyuki Otsuka travelled to Europe after graduating from design school in Tokyo. He worked as interior designer at Plastic Studio and Associates after returning to Japan and, in 1990, he founded Noriyuki Otsuka Design Office. The intention to create interiors that 'seem like nothing but are something' is his studio's mission. The company's portfolio includes works for boutiques, restaurants, private residences, furniture and product designs.

NOWOTNY ARCHITECTEN
Vesteplein 106
2611 WG Delft
the Netherlands
+31 15 212 8817
www.nowotny.nl
bureau@nowotny.nl

(p.058)

After completing his architecture study at the Technical University of Berlin, Alexander Nowotny travelled to the United States and New Zealand to gain work experience. In 1999, he established his own architecture studio in the Netherlands that focuses on architecture, urban planning, interior and re-use of buildings. Nowotny Architecten also creates designs for shops and public spaces in banks, cinemas, restaurants and shopping malls.

ONE PLUS PARTNERSHIP
9/f New Wing, 101 King's Road, North Point
Hong Kong
Hong Kong
+852 2591 9308
www.onepluspartnership.com
admin@onepluspartnership.com

(p.156)

One Plus Partnership was formed in 2004 by Ajax Law Ling Kit and Virginia Lung. Based in Hong Kong, the company provides a full range of interior design services from conception to delivery including residential, hospitality, retail, office and cinema projects. The studio is a forum for generating ideas with a design philosophy which selects a theme for each project.

OOBIQ ARCHITECTS
Office 2-3, 10/f Kai Wong
Commercial Building, 222
Queen's Road Central
Hong Kong
Hong Kong
+852 2545 2868
www.oobiq.it
info@oobiq.it

(p.192)

Oobiq Architects is an architectural and design firm based in Hong Kong and Guangzhou. The company's founding partners are Italian architects Giambattista Burdo and Samuele Martelli, who both graduated of the University of Florence. The firm develops projects at differing scales – from master plan to architecture, from interior design to product design – all around Asia.

PARAT
Juliusstrasse 12
22769 Hamburg
Germany
+49 40 4130 4043
www.buero-parat.de
info@buero-parat.de

(p.610)

Parat is a design studio based in Hamburg which focuses on interiors and scenography. Founded in 2010 by Thomas Huth and Matthias Förster, the company approach is to produce unexpected experiences and provide unique benefits. The corporate portfolio includes projects in the fields of retail store design and corporate environments.

PHILIPS DESIGN
Emmasingel 24, P.O. Box 218
5600 MD Eindhoven
the Netherlands
+31 40 275 9000
www.design.philips.com
info.design@philips.com

(p.520)

Philips Design was founded 85 years ago and is a creative force of some 400 professionals working in seven studios across Europe, North America and Asia. The company acts as the international in-house design team for its parent group, Royal Philips Electronics, as well as a design consultancy for third-party companies. It utilises a people-focused and research-based approach.

PINKEYE
Hessenplein 2
2000 Antwerp
Belgium
+32 3 290 6273
www.pinkeye.be
info@pinkeye.be

(p.600)

Pinkeye, founded in 2006, creates total concepts that grasp the consumer's attention from three angles: form, function and feeling. The team members take pride in their geek status mixed with a worldly class. Product designers mingle with software programmers, interior architects, textile designers, artists and trend forecasters. Their speciality: custom-made concepts for interiors, events and brands.

PLAJER & FRANZ STUDIO
Erkelenzdamm 59–61
10999 Berlin
Germany
+49 30 616 5580
www.plajer-franz.de
studio@plajer-franz.de

(p.236, 284, 314)

Based in Berlin, plajer & franz studio is an international and interdisciplinary team of 45 architects, interior architects and graphic designers. All project stages are carried out by the company, from concept to design as well as roll-out supervision. Special project-based teams work on overall interior and building construction projects and on communication and graphic design.

PLAZMA ARCHITECTURE STUDIO
T.Sevčenkos g. 16a
03111 Vilnius
Lithuania
+37 6122 3170
www.plazma.lt
info@plazma.lt

(p.118)

Plazma Architecture Studio is a design office that was established in the Lithuanian capital Vilnius in 1998. The studio primarily works on designing public interiors and building reconstruction projects requiring the ultimate artistic attention. The Plazma team strives to combine architectural formations with visual and applied arts in the projects undertaken, attracted by situations requiring non-traditional solutions.

PORTLAND
63 Gee Street
London EC1V 3RS
United Kingdom
+44 207 017 8780
www.portland-design.com
info@portland-design.com

(p.386)

Portland is a design office based in London. The company has an integrated team of branding specialists, interior, architectural and graphic designers. Creating consumer-facing environments for the retail, leisure and travel sectors, the company's expertise lies in taking the customer on an immersive, multi-sensory journey through brands and experiences.

PROPELLER DESIGN
5-9 Takezono-cho
659-0055 Ashiya
Japan
+81 797 255 144
www.propeller-design.com
info@propeller-design.com

(p.230)

Japanese designer Yoshihiro Kawasaki established his first company Propeller Integraters in 2000. He went on to form the design studio Propeller Design in 2006. The company creates interiors for boutiques, beauty salons, showrooms, exhibition spaces and restaurants, as well as completing projects in the fields of graphic and product design.

PROPERTY OF…
Herenstraat 2
1015 CA Amsterdam
the Netherlands
+31 20 622 5909
www.thepropertyof.com
amsterdam@thepropertyof.com

(p.094)

Property Of… was founded in 2006 by design collaborators Richard Chamberlain and Peter Teo to produce a range of classic men's bags and accessories. The founding retail ideals of the company were shaped by the culture of the cafes which Chamberlain and Teo own and operate in Singapore, with the best of old and new design values being incorporated into the construction and function of the products.

PROTOTYPE DESIGN LAB
22 Enterprise Road
M9W 1C3 Toronto
Ontario, Canada
+1 416 842 0275
www.pdlab.ca
info@pdlab.ca

(p.030)

Toronto-based research and design firm Prototype Design Lab was founded in 2005 and thrives on a philosophy of collaborative innovation and highly personalised detail design. Captivated by all scales of design, the studio is committed to blurring the boundaries between the fields of art, architecture, industrial design, materials research and engineering to create and transform the built environment.

RAËD ABILLAMA ARCHITECTS
Dbaye street 66
2501 0923 Metn
Lebanon
+961 4 541 880
www.raarchitects.com
info@raarchitects.com

(p.102, 264, 268)

A staff of 20 architects, interior designers and graphic designers make up Raëd Abillama Architects. Since its founding in 1997, the Lebanon-based practice has completed many projects including banks, offices, commercial and residential commissions, ranging in scale from complete buildings to interiors and architectural detailing. Several projects involved the rehabilitation, restoration and addition to historical structures.

RÄL 167
Mercedes Formica No.9
Nloqie 4, Portal 12, 3b
28232 Las Rozas
Spain
+34 649 954 147
www.ral167.com
ral167@yahoo.es

(p.150)

Madrid-based Räl 167 is the interior architecture and design studio of Ramses Jimenez and Laura Pol. Working with a strong multidisciplinary emphasis on projects of functionality and structural clarity, the studio's portfolio includes architecture, graphic and product design.

RAW
405-317 Adelaide
Street West
M5V 1P9 Toronto
Ontario, Canada
+1 416 599 9729
www.rawdesign.ca
rrc@rawdesign.ca

(p.534)

Raw, founded in 2007 by Roland Rom Colthoff and Richard Witt, is an architectural and design studio based in Toronto, Canada. Work varies from quirky small-scale urban insertions and unique office environments to large mixed-use projects covering entire city blocks. The Raw team takes a completely open-minded approach to architecture, encouraging a fluid and collaborative design process.

RÉGIS CÔTÉ AND ASSOCIATES
682 William Street
H3C 1N9 Montreal
Quebec, Canada
+1 514 871 8595
www.regiscote.com
info_mtl@regiscote.com

(p.652)

Régis Côté and Associates was founded in 1976 by three architects, Régis Côté, Mario Leblanc and Jocelyn Boilard. The company, with a team of 150 employees based in six offices throughout Canada, seeks innovative solutions using a multidisciplinary focus and integrated design process.

RON VAN LEENT
Peperstraat 130
2801 RH Gouda
the Netherlands
+31 65 460 6772
www.ronvanleent.nl
info@ronvanleent.nl

(p.450)

Ron van Leent established his design studio in the Dutch town of Gouda in the 1990s. With experience extending into both architecture and interiors, he creates communicative spaces within almost every cultural or commercial context. The studio translates marketing themes into the interior design of offices, shops, casinos, private residences and even entire airports.

ROTH TEVET EXPERIENCE DESIGN
26 Ben Avigdor Street
57184 Tel Aviv
Israel
+972 3566 1373
www.roth-tevet.com
info@roth-tevet.com

(p.510)

Roth Tevet Experience Design, based in Tel Aviv, was established 2003. The studio is focused on creating entertainment and retail environments. While combining architecture, design, technology and sound, the duo aims to create projects that enchant, entertain and inspire all the senses.

SCHEMATA ARCHITECTURE OFFICE
2-30-6 Kamimeguro, Meguro
153-0051 Tokyo
Japan
+81 3 5939 6773
www.sschemata.com
info@sschemata.com

(p.110)

Jo Nagasaka was born in Osaka and brought up in the Chiba prefecture. He studied architecture at Tokyo National University of Fine Arts and Music and, after graduating, he established Schemata Architecture Office. Since 2007, the studio has been based in Tokyo from where an ever-expanding portfolio covers projects such as residential and retail interiors, exhibition stands and art installations.

Photo Takashi Kato

SCHWITZKE & PARTNER
Tussmannstrasse 70
40477 Düsseldorf
Germany
+49 211 440 350
www.schwitzke.com
info@schwitzke.com

(p.120, 368)

Schwitzke & Partner, located in Düsseldorf, Germany, was established in 1989 as a specialist in retail design. Today, Schwitzke is a worldwide operating design company with more than 150 employees and a number of subsidiaries and branches, including an office in Dubai since 2006.

SID LEE
75 Queen Street, office 1400
H3C 2N6 Montreal
Quebec, Canada
+1 514 284 6834
www.sidlee.com
info@sidlee.com

(p.190, 420)

The creative agency Sid Lee was first established in Montreal in 1993 and now also has offices in Amsterdam, Austin, Paris and Toronto. The company has a multidisciplinary creative team of 450 professionals who are passionate about embedding brands, products, spaces and services with meaning and resonance.

SID LEE ARCHITECTURE
75 Queen Street, office 1400
H3C 2N6 Montreal
Quebec, Canada
+1 514 284 6834
www.sidleearchitecture.com
info@sidleearchitecture.com

(p.344, 652)

Sid Lee Architecture is a partnership between Montreal-based commercial creative company Sid Lee and architects Jean Pelland and Martin Leblanc. Established in 2009 with a core belief that architecture can shape the identity of organisations, the company has a multidisciplinary approach with architects and artisans from different fields realising retail spaces with immersive brand storytelling.

SLADE ARCHITECTURE
77 Chambers Street,
5th Floor
New York, NY 10007
United States
+1 212 677 6380
www.sladearch.com
info@sladearch.com

(p.548, 566)

Slade Architecture was founded by James and Hayes Slade in 2002, seeking to focus on architecture and design across different scales and programme types. Their design approach is unique for each project with a continued exploration of primary architectural concerns. The studio's portfolio includes commercial, residential and cultural projects as well as furniture.

SOUSASANTOS
Rua Alexandre Oneill No.3, 1d
1300-031 Lisbon
Portugal
+351 210 198 600
www.sousasantos.com
info@sousasantos.com

(p.018)

Jorge Sousa Santos' architecture studio focuses on the connection between the human environment and the cultural and technological context of our time. With a belief that the design process must follow a mutual relationship between architecture, economics, ecology, science, philosophy and technology, the studio tries to reinvent the way things are made with every new design.

SPRINGEN
Talwiesenstrasse 17
8003 Zurich
Switzerland
+41 43 960 9648
www.springen.org
i@springen.org

(p.620)

The communication and interaction design agency springen is based in Zurich. Founded by Flurin Spring in 2009, the company works primarily in the fields of visual communication and interaction design.

SQUIRE AND PARTNERS
77 Wicklow Street
London WC1X 9JY
United Kingdom
+44 207 278 5555
www.squireandpartners.com
info@squireandpartners.com

(p.320)

Squire and Partners is an architectural practice which was established in 1976 by Michael Squire. The firm designs and executes buildings using an approach which assumes that every site has its own history, character and needs. The team works according to underlying themes of materiality, scale and proportion, and is committed to contemporary design and detailing.

STEFAN ZWICKY ARCHITECT
Zweierstrasse 35
8004 Zurich
Switzerland
+41 44 298 3400
www.stefanzwicky.ch
mail@ stefanzwicky.ch

(p.398, 426)

Architect Stefan Zwicky established his own design firm in Zurich in 1983. The studio undertakes a wide range of projects, including interior design, architecture, exhibition stand design and furniture design. In addition to his varied architectural portfolio, Zwicky is also an established author and lecturer of design.

STOREAGE
Overtoom 197-4
1054 HT Amsterdam
the Netherlands
+31 20 422 9520
www.store-age.nl
hello@store-age.nl

(p.626, 646)

Founded in 2000 by Jason Steere and Leendert Tange, Storeage is a design and brand-strategy agency with offices in Amsterdam and Singapore. Incorporating multiple nationalities of retail architects, graphic designers, product designers, marketing and branding professionals, the close-knit team offers a global perspective that allows for out-of-the-box and multicultural thinking.

STUDIO ARTHUR CASAS
Rue Itapolis, 818
01245-000 São Paulo
Brazil
+55 11 2182 7500
www.arthurcasas.com
studio@arthurcasas.com

(p.340)

Arthur Casas graduated in architecture from Mackenzie University São Paulo in 1983. He is the founder of Studio Arthur Casas, with offices in São Paulo and New York. The studio has a varied portfolio covering interior design and architecture projects, including residential and commercial buildings in Rio de Janeiro, São Paulo, Tokyo, Paris and New York.

STUDIO GUILHERME TORRES
Rua Joao Moura 106
05412-000 São Paulo
Brazil
+55 11 2872 8620
www.guilhermetorres.com
info@guilhermetorres.com

(p.584)

Architect and designer Guilherme Torres established his design studio in 2001 in São Paulo, Brazil. His trademarks include slender and marked lines as well as suspended volumes, always investigating the limits of the materials used. With projects ranging from residential and commercial to furniture, the concepts employed are always versatile and free from monotony.

STUDIOPROTOTYPE
48 Aristotelous
582 00 Edessa
Greece
+30 23 8102 8579
www.studioprototype.com
mail@studioprototype.com

(p.380)

Studioprototype is an architectural design practice based in Greece. Established in 2008, it is run by partners Sofia Limpari and Neal Shah. The office has a varied portfolio, including one-off private dwellings, residential housing, commercial and retail environments, and the renovation and conservation of historic and traditional buildings.

SUMA+ESPACIO
Travesia Isla Cabo Verde, 6
28035 Madrid
Spain
+34 91 373 7282
www.sumaespacio.com
info@sumaespacio.com

(p.150)

Suma+Espacio is a Madrid-based architecture and design company with a commitment to design innovation and aesthetics as a luxury available to everyone. The studio realises dynamic interior spaces with unique personalities whilst at the same time integrating contemporary functionalities.

SUPERMACHINE STUDIO
57/7 Soi Chokchairuammit
16/13, Vipawadeerungsit
Road Jompol, Jatujuk
10900 Bangkok
Thailand
+66 2 276 6279
supermachine.wordpress.com
pitupong@gmail.com

(p.514)

Supermachine Studio is a multidisciplinary design studio, founded in Bangkok in 2009, by architect Pitupong Chaowakul. With a team of six designers, the studio's portfolio is diverse and includes architecture, interior, product and exhibition design, as well as art installations.

TONERICO
902 6-18-2, Jingumae
Shibuya-ku
150-0001 Tokyo
Japan
+81 3 5468 0608
www.tonerico-inc.com
tonerico.inc@nifty.com

(p.012, 132, 392)

Tonerico is a Tokyo-based design firm, established in 2002 by Hiroshi Yoneya, Ken Kimizuka and Yumi Masuko. The company specialises in the architecture and interior design of commercial spaces and private residences. The team also works in the areas of exhibition, furniture and product design.

TOOLS OFF.ARCHITECTURE
Arcisstrasse 68
80801 Munich
Germany
+49 8930 66 873
www.tools-off.com
kontakt@tools-off.com

(p.052, 442)

In 1992, Eva Durant and Andreas Notter established tools off.architecture. With offices in Munich and Hamburg, the team works with a premise of 'visions of a future reality as the present'. The office realises projects in the realms of living and working spaces, as well as exhibition stands and public buildings.

TORAFU ARCHITECTS
2f Chikazawa Building, 1-9-2
Koyama, Shinagawa-ku
142-0062 Tokyo
Japan
+81 3 5498 7156
www.torafu.com
torafu@torafu.com

(p.292)

Founded in 2004 by Koichi Suzuno and Shinya Kamuro, Torafu Architects employs a working approach based on architectural thinking. Works by the duo include a diverse range of products, from architectural design to interior design for shops, exhibition space design, product design, spatial installations and film making.
Photo Masanori Ikeda

TRIGUEIROS ARCHITECTURE
Ostgotagatan 67
116 64 Stockholm
Sweden
+46 830 9925
www.trigueiros.net
v@trigueiros.net

(p.480)

Trigueiros Architecture is a contemporary practice that focuses on architecture and design in equal terms. Established in 2003 by Vasco Trigueiros, the company is based in Stockholm. The small team has a diverse range of projects in its portfolio which covers buildings, interiors and furniture development.

UXUS
Keizersgracht 174
1016 DW Amsterdam
the Netherlands
+31 20 623 3114
www.uxusdesign.com
info@uxusdesign.com

(p.090, 162, 388)

Uxus is an international multidisciplinary design consultancy with its headquarters in Amsterdam. Founded in 2003 by George Gottl, Oliver Michell and Erika Gottl, the company provides strategic design solutions across the entire spectrum of disciplines: architecture, retail, hospitality and interior design, identity, graphics and packaging.

VBAT
Pilotenstraat 41a
1059 CH Amsterdam
the Netherlands
+31 20 750 3000
info@vbat.com
www.vbat.com

(p.632)

VBAT is an Amsterdam-based branding and design agency, focused on servicing both consumer and corporate oriented clients in retail formats, products, services and organisations. The company, co-founded by Eugene Bay in 1984, delivers unique brand concepts and benefits from the strong interaction between creatives and brand strategists in the multicultural team.

WE ARCHITECTURE
Havnegade 53A kl
1058 Copenhagen K
Denmark
+45 3537 9335
www.we-a.dk
we@we-a.dk

(p.436)

WE Architecture is based in Copenhagen, Denmark and was founded in 2009 by Marc Jay and Julie Schmidt-Nielsen. The company has a philosophy that architecture is not the result of one person's stroke of genius. Through teamwork and trans-disciplinary networks, the studio's projects span architecture, urban strategies, tangible design and utopian ideas.

WILSON BROTHERS
21 Chippendale Street
London E5 0BB
United Kingdom
+44 7973 667 654
www.wilsonbrothers.co.uk
info@wilsonbrothers.co.uk

(p.568)

The Wilson Brothers, Oscar and Ben, joined forces in 2004 to accomplish creative projects for an international client list. Oscar specialises in 2D image creation and handcrafted typography, and Ben is a 3D industrial designer.

WIT DESIGN
Nieuwe Tijningen 7
5301 DA Zaltbommel
the Netherlands
+31 41 866 7010
www.witdesign.nl
info@witdesign.nl

(p.524)

Wit Design is an interior-design agency based in the Netherlands specialising in brand communication and architectural concepts. Established in 1982 by Hans de Wit, the company has developed a varied portfolio, creating spaces for retail interiors, events, exhibitions and trade fair presentations with a primary focus on branding and achieving commercial objectives.

WITBLAD
Peter Benoitlaan 5
8530 Harelbeke
Belgium
+32 479 443303
www.witblad.com
info@witblad.com

(p.372)

Bob Bulcaen is an interior architect with over 13 years experience in the industry. In 2010, he established his own architecture firm witblad, which specialises in designing for commercial communication needs. The company proffers a full retail package, from corporate identity to interior and website design.

WONDERWALL
3-4-10 Sendagaya, Shibuya-ku
151-0051 Tokyo
Japan
+81 3 6438 1717
www.wonder-wall.com
contact@wonder-wall.com

(p.578)

Founded in 2000 by Masamichi Katayama, the interior design firm Wonderwall is best known for its retail concepts. Katayama's interest in design has always been broad, respecting conventional aspects of architecture, whilst breaking traditional boundaries. The company's portfolio includes projects which are distinctly unique in design and yet attentive to function.

ZEST DESIGN + ARCHITECTURE
55 rue des Anciens Etangs
1190 Brussels
Belgium
+32 2 349 0250
www.zest.be
info@zest.be

(p.114)

Zest Design + Architecture is a creative design agency with a focus on retail and the commercial sector. Architect Paul Buysschaert founded the Brussels-based company 23 years ago, which now also has an office in New York. The firm's philosophy seeks to add value to brands through the development of new service models across all design categories.

ZOEVOX
13 rue de la Montjoie
93217 La Plaine Saint Denis
France
+33 1 4946 0707
www.zoevox.com
zoevox@zoevox.com

(p.606)

Interior design agency Zoevox was founded in 1993 by architects Fabrice Ausset and Eric Bougaud. Specialising in exhibition and retail design, the Paris-based firm has a portfolio of 1500 projects ranging from architecture and interior design, to product and graphic design.

ZOOM INDUSTRIES
Brusselsestraat 55
6211 PB Maastricht
the Netherlands
+31 43 326 0078
www.zoom-industries.nl
info@zoom-industries.nl

(p.288)

Zoom Industries is an architecture and design studio which was founded by René Thijssen in 2000. Operating from two offices located in Amsterdam and Maastricht in the Netherlands, the studio combines multiple disciplines and techniques, developing brand identities and design concepts for projects that include retail concepts and exhibition booths as well as product design.

SHOP ADDRESSES

@BTF (p.448)
by butterfly-stroke
2-8-19 Kachidoki, Chuo-ku
104-0054 Toyko
Japan
www.shopbtf.com

&ROLLS (p.006)
by Ito Masura Design Project/SEI
1f, 10-8 Sarugaku-cho, Shibuya-ku
150-0033 Tokyo
Japan
www.and-rolls.com

2 OPERA (p.606)
by Zoevox
2 place de l'Opera
75002 Paris
France
www.bnpparibas.net

3.1 PHILLIP LIM (p.184)
by Leong Leong
79-16 Cheongdam-Dong, Gangnam-Gu
Seoul, South Korea
www.31philliplim.com

4010 TELEKOM SHOP (p.610)
by Parat for Mutabor
Ehrenstrasse 30–32
50672 Cologne
Germany
www.4010.de

4°C (p.012)
by Tonerico
3-28-13 1f Shinjuku, Shinjuku-ku
160-0022 Tokyo
Japan
www.fdcp.co.jp

A.D.I. SYSTEMS (p.510)
by Roth Tevet Experience Design
Eliahu Eitan 1
5130 Rishon-Lezion
Israel
www.adi-system.co.il

ADIDAS SLVR (p.190)
by Ædifica, Sid Lee and adidas
108 Wooster Street
New York, NY 10012
United States
www.adidas.com

AESOP (p.110)
by Schemata Architecture Office
4-8-2 Jingumae, Shibuya
150-0001 Tokyo
Japan
www.aesop-japan.com

ALLA SCALA (p.192)
by Oobiq Architects
Shop 190, 1/f, Phase 2
Garden City, Nanhai Avenue
Shenzhen
China

ANDRÉ OPTICAS (p.018)
by SousaSantos
Avenue da Liberdade 136a
1250-146 Lisbon
Portugal
www.andreopticas.com

APC ROYALE (p.194)
by Laurent Deroo Architecte
23 rue Royale
75008 Paris
France
www.apc.fr

APC SPECIALS (p.196)
by Laurent Deroo Architecte
92 Perry Street
New York, NY 10014
United States
www.apc.fr

AUDIONOVA (p.114)
by Zest Design + Architecture
Esplanadeplein 6a
9300 Aalst
Belgium
www.audionova.be

AUTOSTELLA (p.514)
by Supermachine Studio
230 Yothinpattana 3 Rd, Klongjun Bangkapi
1024 Bangkok
Thailand

BARLETTI (p.450)
by Ron van Leent
Villa Arena 216
1101 DJ Amsterdam
the Netherlands
www.barletti.com

**BARNEYS NEW YORK
CO-OP BROOKLYN** (p.198)
by Ædifica
194 Atlantic Avenue
New York, NY 11201
United States
www.barneys.com

BASE (p.616)
by Creneau International
Centraal Station, Pelikaanstraat 10
2000 Antwerp
Belgium
www.base.be

BELFRY TASHKENT (p.024)
by Ippolito Fleitz Group
Istikbol Street
Tashkent
Uzbekistan

BERANI JEWELLERY (p.030)
by Prototype Design Lab
Bayview Village Shopping Centre
2901 Bayview Avenue
M2K 1E6 Toronto, Ontario
Canada
www.bayviewvillageshops.com

BOX SHOP (p.454)
by Edge Architecture + Design
229–231 Union Street
London SE1 0LR
United Kingdom
www.rocketvan.co.uk

BREDL BATHHOUSE WOMEN (p.202)
by atelier 522
Bachstrasse 2–4
88214 Ravensburg
Germany
www.bredl.com

BRUNS (p.204)
by Breil + Partner Interior Design
Haarenstrasse 57–60
26122 Oldenburg
Germany
www.bruns-oldenburg.de

BUZZER BEATER (p.548)
by Slade Architecture
254 Greene Street
New York, NY 10003
United States

CA4LA FACTORY (p.034)
by Line-Inc
5-23 Outsuka-chou, Tsumon Nishinomiya
663-8241 Hyogo
Japan
www.ca4la.com

CAMPER (p.550)
by Ronan & Erwan Bouroullec
4 rue Aubry Le Boucher
75004 Paris
France
www.camper.com

CANDIDO1859 (p.208)
by LOLA
Piazza Aldo Moro 9
73024 Maglie
Italy
www.candido1859.com

CARLO PAZOLINI (p.552)
by Giorgio Borruso Design
Piazza Cordusio
20123 Milan
Italy
www.carlopazolini.com

CHRISTIAN LOUBOUTIN (p.558)
by Household
The Shoe Galleries, Selfridges
400 Oxford Street
London W1A 1AB
United Kingdom
www.christianlouboutin.com

COLLECT POINT (p.214)
by Line-Inc
1f, 2f, 3-4-8 Shinjuku-ku
160-0022 Tokyo
Japan
www.collect-point.jp

CONRADT OPTIK (p.038)
by Ippolito Fleitz Group
Hauptstrasse 7
74821 Mosbach
Germany
www.conradtoptik.de

CRÈME DE LA CRÈME (p.118)
by Plazma Architecture Studio
Panorama Shopping Center
Saltoniskiu str. 9
08105 Vilnius
Lithuania
www.cremedelacreme.lt

DANIELLA LEHAVI (p.042)
by k1p3 architects
Rothschild Blvd 21
66882 Tel Aviv
Israel
www.daniellalehavi.com

DE BIJENKORF (p.216)
by Michelgroup
Piazza 1
5611 AE Eindhoven
the Netherlands
www.debijenkorf.nl

DESA (p.218)
by Kinnersley Kent Design
St Martins Courtyard, Covent Garden
London WC2E 9AB
United Kingdom
www.desa.uk.com

DETROIT (p.222)
by Arkteam
6–8 Kiriazi str., Kiffissia
14565 Athens
Greece
www.detroitgreece.com

DIAMANT NOIR HOMME (p.224)
by Logica:architettura
(Riccardo Salvi + Luca Rossire)
10 avenue Paris
20000 Ajaccio
France

DICOKICK (p.044)
by Jamo associates
3-27-4 Jingumae, Shibuya-ku
150-0001 Tokyo
Japan
www.dicokick.jp

DIGITEC (p.620)
by Aekae and springen
Pfinstweidstrasse 60
8005 Zurich
Switzerland
www.digitec.ch

DODENHOF D-STRICT (p.226)
by atelier 522
dodenhof Shopping Center
28869 Posthausen
Germany
www.dodenhof.de

DOM REBEL THREADS (p.228)
by Igloodgn
4030 St-Ambroise
H4C 2C7 Montreal, Quebec
Canada
www.domrebel.com

**DOUBLE STANDARD CLOTHING
BALABUSHKA** (p.230)
by Propeller Design
5-24-2 Sendagaya, Shibuya
Shinjuku, Takashimaya 8f
151-8580 Tokyo
Japan
www.doublestandard.jp

DOUGLAS (p.120)
by Schwitzke & Partner
Tauentzienstrasse 16
10789 Berlin
Germany
www.douglas.de

DR MARTENS (p.562)
(temporary store)
by Campaign
Old Spitalfields Market
London E1 6EW
United Kingdom
www.drmartens.co.uk

DUMON CHOCOLATIER (p.372)
by witblad
Lange Steenstraat 23
8500 Kortrijk
Belgium
www.chocolatierdumon.be

EARL'S GOURMET GRUB (p.374)
by FreelandBuck
12226 Venice Boulevard
Los Angeles, CA 90066
United States
www.earlsgourmetgrub.com

EAU DE PARFUM (p.122)
(temporary store)
by Ingibjorg Agnes Jonsdottir
Klapparstigur 33
101 Reykjavik
Iceland
www.andreamaack.com

ELEKTRA (p.380)
by Studioprototype
22 Dimokratias
58200 Edessa
Greece

EMPORIUM (p.386)
by Portland
Terminal 3
Dubai International Airport
United Arab Emirates

ENGELBERT STRAUSS (p.236)
by plajer & franz studio
Altriper strasse 1
68766 Hockenheim
Germany
www.engelbert-strauss.de

ESCENTIALS (p.124)
by Asylum
290 Orchard Road, #03-02/05
Paragon Shopping Centre
238859 Singapore
Singapore
www.luxasia.com/escentials

ESPAÇO SANTA HELENA (p.458)
by Jayme Lago Mestieri Architecture
Shopping Iguatemi
Av Brigadeira Faria Lima 2232
01489 900 São Paulo
Brazil
www.espacosantahelena.com.br

ESPRIT (p.240)
by Corneille Uedingslohmann Architects
Zeil 121
60313 Frankfurt
Germany
www.esprit.de

FIELL (p.046)
by Dastro Retailconcepts
Shopping Mall Orangerie
7311 WG Apeldoorn
the Netherlands
www.fiell.nl

FLIGHT CLUB (p.566)
by Slade Architecture
812 Broadway
New York, NY 10003
United States
www.flightclubny.com

FOOT PATROL (p.568)
by Brinkworth and Wilson Brothers
80 Berwick Street
London W1F 8TU
United Kingdom
www.footpatrol.co.uk

FRANCFRANC NAGOYA (p.464)
by Glamorous
3-15-36 Sakae, Naka-ku
460-0008 Nagoya City
Japan
www.francfranc.com

FRANCFRANC XINTIANDI (p.466)
by Glamorous
No. 245 Ma Dang Road
Lu Wan District, Shanghai
China
www.francfranc.com

FREITAG REFERENCE EDITORIAL SPACE (p.050)
(temporary store)
by Freitag
Grüngasse 21
8004 Zurich
Switzerland
www.freitag.ch

FREUDENHAUS OPTIK (p.052)
by tools off.architecture
Theatinerstrasse 32
80333 Munich
Germany
www.freudenhaus.com

GOODS (p.054)
(temporary shop)
by Antonio Gardoni
Franciacorta Outlet Village
Piazza Cascina Moie 1/2
Rodengo Saiano
Italy
www.franciacortaoutlet.it

GRACE (p.246)
by Heikaus Interior
Neuhauser Strasse 47
80331 Munich
Germany
www.grace-muenchen.de

HAAZ DESIGN AND ART GALLERY (p.468)
by GAD
Ahmet Fetgari Sokak
No. 62/1 Tesvikiye
34365 Istanbul
Turkey
www.haaz.info

HEINEKEN WORLD OF BEERS (p.388)
by Uxus
Viking Line Ferry
www.vikingline.fi

HOFSTEDE OPTIEK (p.058)
by Nowotny Architecten
Hoogstraat 37
2513 AP The Hague
the Netherlands
www.hofstede-optiek.nl

HP INNOVATION HUB (p.626)
by Storeage
Chongqing, China
www.hp.com

HUNKEMÖLLER (p.064)
by Creneau International
Lijnbaan 71
3012 EL Rotterdam
the Netherlands
www.hunkemoller.com

HYUNDAI DEPARTMENT STORE (p.248)
by HMKM
2602 Daehwa-dong, Ilsanseo-gu
Goyang-si, Gyeonggi-do
413-808 Seoul
South Korea
www.hyundaigroup.com/eng

I FIND EVERYTHING (p.474)
by Makoto Yamaguchi Design
1-14-12-303 Ebisuminami, Shibuya-ku
150-0022 Tokyo
Japan
www.ifindeverythingtokyo.com

ISSEY MIYAKE (p.252)
by emmanuelle moureaux architecture + design
3-18-11 Minami-Aoyama, Minato-ku
107-0062 Tokyo
Japan
www.isseymiyake.com

JAEGER LONDON (p.258)
by Kinnersley Kent Design
St Martins Courtyard, Covent Garden
London WC2E 9AB
United Kingdom
www.jaeger.co.uk

JAGUAR LAND ROVER (p.520)
by Philips Design
45 Leng Kee Road
159103 Singapore
Singapore
www.wearnesauto.com

JAGUAR LOUNGE (p.524)
by Wit Design
Stationsweg 8
4153 RD Beesd
the Netherlands
www.jaguar.com

JELMOLI (p.260)
by Blocher Blocher Partners
Bahnhofstrasse/Seidengasse 1
8001 Zurich
Switzerland
www.jelmoli.ch

JOINWELL (p.476)
by Chris Briffa
Mill Street
QRM 03 Qormi
Malta
www.joinwell.com.mt

JOSEPH AVENUE MONTAIGNE (p.264)
by Raëd Abillama Architects
14 avenue Montaigne
75008 Paris
France
www.joseph.co.uk

JOSEPH WESTBOURNE GROVE (p.268)
by Raëd Abillama Architects
236 Westbourne Grove
London W11 2RH
United Kingdom
www.joseph.co.uk

KASTNER & ÖHLER (p.272)
by Blocher Blocher Partners
Sackstrasse 7–13
8010 Graz
Austria
www.kastner-oehler.at

KIN NO TUBASA (p.392)
by Tonerico
Terminal 2
Haneda Airport, Tokyo
Japan
www.tokyo-airport-bldg.co.jp

KIOSKOOL (p.150)
by Räl 167 and Suma+Espacio
Avenue de Honorio Lozano 11
28400 Collado Villalba
Spain

KIRK ORIGINALS (p.066)
by Campaign
6 Conduit Street
London W1S 1XE
United Kingdom
www.kirkoriginals.com

KLEINER (p.398)
by Stefan Zwicky
Limmatquai 116
8001 Zurich
Switzerland
www.kleiner-konditorei.ch

KOMPLEMENTAIR (p.070)
by Aekae
Im Viadukt 22
Viaduktstrasse 43
8005 Zurich
Switzerland
www.komplementair.ch

KUBRICK BOOKSHOP (p.156)
by One Plus Partnership
Grand Moma, Tower 2
No.1 Xiongheyuan Road, Dongcheng District
100028 Beijing
China
www.kubrick-beijing.com.cn

KURT GEIGER (p.572)
by Found Associates
1 James Street
London WC2E 8BG
United Kingdom
www.kurtgeiger.com

L2 DESIGN GROUP (p.480)
by Trigueiros Architecture
Torsgatan 9a
111 23 Stockholm
Sweden
www.L2.se

LE CIEL BLEU (p.276)
by Noriyuki Otsuka Design Office
3-1-3 Umeda Kita-ku
530-8217 Osaka
Japan
www.lcb.co.jp

LE VIGNE (p.400)
by Madlab
35 Greenwich Avenue
New York, NY 10014
United States
www.levignenyc.com

LEO PIZZO (p.074)
by Diego Bortolato Architetto and
Gianluca Re Architetto
Galleria Vittorio Emanuele II
12123 Milan
Italy
www.leopizzo.com

LEVI STRAUSS (p.280)
by Checkland Kindleysides
174–176 Regent Street
London W1B 5TJ
United Kingdom
www.levi.com

LEVI'S ICON STORE (p.284)
by plajer & franz studio
Neue Schönhauserstrasse 15
10178 Berlin
Germany
www.levi.com

LÓDZ (p.288)
by Zoom Industries
De Lind 7
5061 HS Oisterwijk
the Netherlands
www.lodz.nl

LOGONA & FRIENDS (p.128)
by Ito Masura Design Project/SEI
5-11-11 Ingumae, Shibuya-ku
150-0033 Tokyo
Japan
www.logona-friends.jp

LOOK OPTIEK (p.076)
by Benschop The Retail Factory
Breestraat 133
2311 CX Leiden
the Netherlands
www.lookoptiek.nl

LOVE SWEETS ANTIQUE (p.402)
by Glamorous
1F 5-1-25 Minami-aoyama
107-0062 Tokyo
Japan
www.heart-bread.com

LUNASOL (p.132)
(temporary store)
by Tonerico
5-6-23 Spiral Hall
Minami-aoyama, Minato-ku
107-0062 Tokyo
Japan
www.kanebo-cosmetics.jp/lunasol

MADHECTIC (p.290)
by Line-Inc
6-25-10 Jingumae, Shibuya-ku
150-0001 Tokyo
Japan
www.madhectic.com

MERCEDES-BENZ GALLERY (p.528)
by Kauffmann Theilig & Partner and
Atelier Markgraph
Unter den Linden 14–16
10117 Berlin
Germany
www.berlin.mercedes-benz.de

MINÄ PERHONEN ARKISTOT (p.292)
by Torafu Architects
2f, 5-13-14 Shirokanedai, Minato-ku
108-0071 Tokyo
Japan
www.mina-perhonen.jp

MINATO PHARMACY (p.138)
by Keisuke Fujiwara
3-12-8 Kitazawa, Setagaya-ku
155-0031 Tokyo
Japan

MINI DOWNTOWN (p.534)
by Raw
20 Sunlight Park Road
M4M 1B5 Toronto, Ontario
Canada
www.minidowntown.ca

MISSION BICYCLE (p.538)
by Grayscaled Design Collective
776 Valencia Street
San Francisco, CA 94110
United States
www.missionbicycle.com

MOERNAUT (p.576)
(temporary store)
by B-architecten
Sint-Gillislaan 92–94
9200 Dendermonde
Belgium
www.moernaut.be

MOSS BESPOKE (p.294)
by Household
35 Blomfield Street
London EC2M 7AW
United Kingdom
www.mossbespoke.com

M-WAY (p.542)
by Designculture
Gotthardstrasse 6
8002 Zurich
Switzerland
www.m-way.ch

MYKITA (p.078)
by Mykita
Jose Vasconcelos 150 PB-6D
66257 San Pedro Garza Garcia (NL)
Mexico
www.mykita.com

NIKE (p.296)
by Day
12 rue des Hospitalièrs, St Gervais
75004 Paris
France
www.nike.com

NIKE HARAJUKU (p.578)
by Wonderwall
1-13-12 Jingu-mae, Shibuya-ku
150-0001 Tokyo
Japan
www.nike.jp/nikeharajuku

NIKE STADIUM (p.300)
by Architecture at Large/Rafael de Cárdenas
276 Bowery
New York, NY 10012
United States
www.nike.com

OCTIUM (p.080)
by Hayon Studio
Unit MI-17, 360 Mall
South Surra, Zahra Area
Kuwait
www.octiumjewelry.com

OKINAHA (p.140)
by Coast and As Built Architects
Chaussée de Bruxelles 82, Les Jardins de Diane
1410 Waterloo
Belgium
www.okinaha.com

OLYMP & HADES (p.302)
by Corneille Uedingslohmann Architects
Rathauscenter Essen
Porscheplatz 2
45127 Essen
Germany
www.olympundhades.de

PADDOCK SHOP (p.306)
by AheadConcept
Nürburgring Boulevard 1
53520 Nürburg
Germany
www.paddockshop.de

PANSCAPE (p.404)
by ninkipen!
19-3 Sainokyosyokuji-cho, Nakagyo-ku
604-8801 Kyoto, Japan
www.panscape-kyoto.jp

PLEATS PLEASE ISSEY MIYAKE (p.252)
by emmanuelle moureaux architecture + design
3-17-14 Minami-Aoyama, Minato-ku
107-0062 Tokyo
Japan
www.isseymiyake.com

PINO (p.484)
by Bond
Fredrikinkatu 22
00120 Helsinki
Finland
www.pino.fi

PODIUM (p.086)
by Art Bureau 1/1
334 rue St Honoré
75001 Paris
France
ww.podiumfashion.com

POMME SUCRE (p.410)
by Francesc Rifé Studio
Calle de Covadonga 21
33002 Oviedo
Spain
www.pommesucre.com

PRECINCT 5 (p.310)
by Kuub
Singel 459
1012 WP Amsterdam
the Netherlands
www.precinct-five.com

PRINCESSE TAM TAM (p.090)
by Uxus
4 rue de Sevres
75006 Paris
France
www.princessetamtam.com

PROLOGUE (p.158)
by Ministry of Design
ION Orchard
2 Orchard Turn, #04-16, 05-03
238801 Singapore
Singapore
www.popular.com.sg

PROPERY OF... (p.094)
by Property Of...
Herenstraat 2
1015 CA Amsterdam
the Netherlands
www.thepropertyof.com

PUMA (p.314)
by plajer & franz studio
22 boulevard de Sébastopol
75002 Paris
France
www.puma.com

PUSATERI'S (p.416)
by GH+A
Bayview Village Shopping Centre
2901 Bayview Avenue
M2N 5K3 Toronto, Ontario
Canada
www.pusateris.com

QUEEN SHOES (p.584)
by Studio Guilherme Torres
Shopping Mall Catuaí
Rodovia Celso Garcia Cid, km 377
86050 908 Londrina
Brazil
www.catuaishopping.com.br

RAGRISE (p.586)
By Jamo associates
1-12-14 Jinnan, Shibuya-ku
150-0041 Tokyo
Japan
www.ragrise.com

RAZILI (p.318)
by k1p3 architects
Hatachana, Neve Tzedek
68012 Tel Aviv
Israel
www.razilidesign.com

RBC DESIGN SHOWROOM (p.488)
by Jakob + MacFarlane
45 quai Rambaud
69002 Lyon
France
www.rbcmobilier.com

RED WING SHOES (p.588)
by Another Company and Como Park Studio
Reestraat 15
1016 DM Amsterdam
the Netherlands
www.redwingamsterdam.com

REEBOK (p.594)
by Confetti
Fokkerstraat 2
3833 LD Leusden
the Netherlands
www.reebok.com

REISS (p.326)
by d-raw
145 North Robertson Boulevard
West Hollywood, CA 90048
United States
www.reissonline.com

REISS ONE (p.320)
by d-raw and Squire and Partners
10 Barrett Street
London W1U 1BA
United Kingdom
www.reissonline.com

RENNAISSANCE (p.332)
by Glenn Sestig Architects
Nationalestraat 28–32
2000 Antwerp
Belgium
www.renaissance-antwerp.com

REPOSI CALZATURE (p.596)
by Diego Bortolato Architetto
Piazza Garibaldi
15100 Alessandria
Italy
www.reposicalzature.posterous.com

RHUS OVATA (p.338)
by k1p3 architects
Dizengoff Street 155
68012 Tel Aviv
Israel
www.rhusovata.com

RIJKSMUSEUM SHOP (p.162)
by Uxus
Holland Boulevard
Schiphol Amsterdam Airport
the Netherlands
www.rijksmuseum.nl

ROSA CHA (p.340)
by Studio Arthur Casas
Fashion Mall
Estrada da Gávea 899, shops 318–321
22610 001 Rio de Janeiro
Brazil
www.rosacha.com.br

S.OLIVER ACCESSORIES (p.096)
by dfrost
Zeil 106–110
60313 Frankfurt
Germany
www.soliver.com

SAQ SIGNATURE (p.420)
by Ædifica, Sid Lee and SAQ
2828 Laurier Boulevard
G1V 0B9 Quebec City, Quebec
Canada
www.saq.com

SELEXYZ DEKKER (p.166)
by Merkx+Girod Architects
Jansplein 56
6811 GD Arnhem
the Netherlands
www.selexyz.nl

SHOE CLASS (p.600)
by Pinkeye
Sint-Katelijnevest 44
2000 Antwerp
Belgium
www.shoeclass.be

SISTE'S (p.342)
by Bongiana Architecture
Corso Buenos Aires 7
20124 Milan
Italy
www.sistes.it

SNAIDERO (p.492)
by Giorgio Borruso Design
A&D Building
150 East 58th Street, 8th floor
New York, NY 10155
United States
www.snaidero-usa.com

SNS BANK PLUG & PLAY (p.632)
by VBAT
De Beurs 78
3823 AV Amersfoort
the Netherlands
www.snsbank.nl

SORAYUMEBAKO (p.172)
by kräf•te
3-4-33 Nakatu, Kita-ku
531-0071 Osaka
Japan

SPRÜNGLI (p.426)
by Stefan Zwicky
Gottfried-Keller-Strasse 5
8001 Zurich
Switzerland
www.spruengli.ch

STND/OHWOW (p.174)
by Architecture at Large/Rafael de Cárdenas
The Standard Spa
40 Island Avenue
Miami Beach, FL 33139
United States
www.standardhotels.com

STYLEXCHANGE FAUBOURG (p.344)
by Sid Lee Architecture
1608 Sainte Catherine Ouest
H3H 1L7 Montreal, Quebec
Canada
www.stylexchange.com

SUGAMO SHINKIN BANK (p.636)
by emmanuelle moureaux architecture + design
6-4-14 Maeno-cho, Itabashi-ku
174-0063 Tokyo
Japan

SUSIE STONE (p.346)
by HMKM
60 Bermondsey Street
London SE1 3UD
United Kingdom
www.susiestone.com

SUXXAR (p.498)
by Jayme Lago Mestieri Architecture
Av. Faria Lima 4531
04538 133 São Paulo
Brazil
www.suxxar.com.br

'T JAPANSE WINKELTJE (p.504)
by Nezu Aymo Architects
Nieuwezijds Voorburgwal 177
1012 RK Amsterdam
the Netherlands
www.japansewinkeltje.nl

TALLY WEIJL (p.348)
by dan pearlman
Viaduktstrasse 42
4051 Basel
Switzerland
www.tally-weijl.com

TELEKOM AUSTRIA (p.642)
by BEHF Architects
Lassalle Strasse 9
1020 Vienna
Austria
www.telekom.at

THE CONTEMPORARY FIX (p.350)
by Jamo associates
3-12-14 Kita Aoyama, Minato-ku
107-0061 Tokyo
Japan
www.thecontemporaryfix.com

THE COUNTER (p.102)
by Raëd Abillama Architects
Fakhri Bey Street, Beirut Souks
Beirut, Lebanon
www.thecounter-magrabi.com

THE CUPCAKE BOUTIQUE (p.428)
by Dittel Architekten
Hirschstrasse 16
70173 Stuttgart
Germany
www.thecupcakeboutique.com

THE SALAD SHOP (p.432)
by Asylum
80 Raffles Place, #01-20 UOB Plaza 2
048524 Singapore
Singapore
www.thesaladshop.com.sg

TICKET (p.644)
by Koncept Stockholm and BVD
Sollentunavägen 163
191 47 Sollentuna
Sweden
www.ticket.se

T-MAGI (p.436)
by WE Architecture
Strandvejen 149
2900 Copenhagen
Denmark

TOPMAN (p.352)
by Dalziel and Pow
Oxford Circus
36–38 Great Castle Street
London W1W 8LG
United Kingdom
www.topman.com

TOPSHOP (p.356)
by Dalziel and Pow
Oxford Circus
36–38 Great Castle Street
London W1W 8LG
United Kingdom
www.topshop.com

TRAGBAR.PURE (p.362)
by atelier 522
Unterer Metzgerbach 15
73728 Esslingen
Germany
www.tragbar.de/pure

UPC (p.646)
by Storeage
Achterom 1
3311 KB Dordrecht
the Netherlands
www.upc.nl

VAN GOGH MUSEUM SHOP (p.178)
by Day
Paulus Potterstraat 7
1071 CK Amsterdam
the Netherlands
www.vangoghmuseum.nl

VAN ZUILEN MODE (p.364)
by Benschop The Retail Factory
Arkelstraat 28–38
4201 KD Gorinchem
the Netherlands
www.vanzuilenmode.nl

VIDEOTRON (p.652)
by Sid Lee Architecture and Régis Côté and
Associates
1192 Sainte Catherine Ouest
H3B 1K1 Montreal, Quebec
Canada
www.videotron.com

VILLA OPTICA (p.106)
by Bleeker Concepts
Korenstraat 27
7311 LM Apeldoorn
the Netherlands
www.villaoptica.nl

VOLKHARDTS WEIN (p.442)
by tools off.architecture
Manzingerweg 7
81241 Munich
Germany
www.volkhardts.de

WERDER BREMEN FANWORLD (p.368)
by Schwitzke & Partner
Franz-Böhmert Strasse 5a
28205 Bremen
Germany
www.werder.de

WIND (p.658)
by Crea International
C.so Matteotti 8
20121 Milan
Italy
www.wind.it

YOU (p.144)
by Koncept Stockholm
Birger Jarlsgatan 37
111 45 Stockholm
Sweden
www.youstockholm.se

YOU BY DIALECT (p.664)
by Electric Dreams
Kungsgatan 4a
111 43 Stockholm
Sweden
www.youbydialect.se

ZIGGO STUDIO (p.666)
by Day
Lange Viestraat 2a
3511 BK Utrecht
the Netherlands
www.ziggo.nl

CREDITS

POWERSHOP 3
New Retail Design

PUBLISHER
Frame Publishers

EDITORS
Sarah de Boer-Schultz
Carmel McNamara
Marlous van Rossum-Willems

COPY EDITOR
Carmel McNamara

GRAPHIC DESIGNERS
Barbara Iwanicka
Cathelijn Kruunenberg

PREPRESS
Edward de Nijs

PRINTING
Ofset Yapimevi, Turkey

COVER PHOTOGRAPHY
Nienke Klunder

TRADE DISTRIBUTION USA AND CANADA
Consortium Book Sales & Distribution, LLC.
34 Thirteenth Avenue NE, Suite 101
Minneapolis, MN 55413-1007
United States
T +1 612 746 2600
T +1 800 283 3572 (orders)
F +1 612 746 2606

DISTRIBUTION REST OF WORLD
Frame Publishers
Laan der Hesperiden 68
1076 DX Amsterdam
The Netherlands
www.frameweb.com
distribution@frameweb.com

ISBN: 978-90-77174-46-3

The Koninklijke Bibliotheek lists this publication in the Nederlandse
Bibliografie: detailed bibliographic information is available on the
internet at http://picarta.pica.nl.

Printed on acid-free paper produced from chlorine-free pulp.
TCF ∞ Printed in Turkey. 987654321